Macedonia

THE BRADT TRAVEL GUIDE

Thammy Evans

Bradt Travel Guides Ltd, UK
The Globe Pequot Press Inc, USA

First published 2004
Reprinted with amendments January 2006

Bradt Travel Guides Ltd
23 High Street, Chalfont St Peter, Bucks SL9 9QE, England
www.bradtguides.com
Published in the USA by The Globe Pequot Press Inc, 246 Goose Lane,
PO Box 480, Guilford, Connecticut 06475-0480

The author and publisher have made every effort to ensure the accuracy of the information in this book at the time of going to press. However, they cannot accept any responsibility for any loss, injury or inconvenience resulting from the use of information contained in this guide.

British Library Cataloguing in Publication Data
A catalogue record for this book is available from the British Library

ISBN 1 84162 089 0

Photographs
Front cover Atanas Talevski (Children at Ohrid)
Text Atanas Talevski (AT), Thammy Evans (TE), Laurence Mitchell (LM)

Illustrations Thammy Evans, Carole Vincer
Maps Alan Whitaker

Typeset from the author's disc by Wakewing
Printed and bound in Italy by Legoprint SpA, Trento

Macedonia

THE BRADT TRAVEL GUIDE

PUBLISHER'S FOREWORD

The first Bradt travel guide was written in 1974 by George and Hilary Bradt on a river barge floating down a tributary of the Amazon. In the 1980s and '90s the focus shifted away from hiking to broader-based guides to new destinations – usually the first to be published on these places. In the 21st century Bradt continues to publish these ground-breaking guides, along with others to established holiday destinations, incorporating in-depth information on culture and natural history alongside the nuts and bolts of where to stay and what to see.

Bradt authors support responsible travel, with advice not only on minimum impact but also on how to give something back through local charities. Thus a true synergy is achieved between the traveller and local communities.

*　*　*

Although the name Macedonia has a historical resonance, I knew nothing about the place until Thammy Evans sent us her proposal for a guide. Her enthusiasm and descriptions of the landscape and people of her favourite country convinced us that this was indeed a country just waiting for a Bradt guide and that Thammy was the perfect author for it. I think you'll agree that we made the right decision.

Hilary Bradt

23 High Street, Chalfont St Peter, Bucks SL9 9QE, England
Tel: 01753 893444; fax: 01753 892333
Email: info@bradtguides.com
Web: www.bradtguides.com

Author

Born in London, UK, of Welsh and Malay Chinese parents, **Thammy Evans** has travelled and lived abroad for most of the past 15 years, especially in China and southeast Europe. Professionally, her career lies in the field of Public Information and Political Analysis. Her first overseas trip was to Malaysia at the age of eight, and she has been dabbling in numerous foreign languages ever since. Amongst her many other travels, her most memorable are the Trans-Siberian Railway from Tianjin to Moscow in 1991, and mountaineering in Bolivia in the summer of 1999. Despite many forays to far-off lands, she feels most at home in the southern climes of wider Europe and now resides in Skopje, Macedonia. A volunteer in the Territorial Army, she served in Bosnia-Herzegovina in 1996 and 1997 and in Iraq in 2003. She has a Masters in Political Science from the Graduate Institute of International Studies in Geneva, Switzerland. This is her first travel guidebook.

DEDICATION

To my mother

FEEDBACK REQUEST

At Bradt Travel Guides we're aware that guidebooks start to go out of date on the day they're published – and that you, our readers, are out there in the field doing research of your own. You'll find out before us when a fine new family-run hotel opens or a favourite restaurant changes hands and goes downhill. So why not write to us and tell us about your experiences? We'll include you in the acknowledgements of the next edition of Macedonia if we use your feedback. So write to us – we'll look forward to hearing from you!

Email: bradtmacedonia@yahoo.co.uk

Contents

LIST OF MAPS

Acknowledgements

This book would not have been possible without the help of so many people, not all of whom are mentioned here, but here are a few:

First of all, I must thank Tricia Hayne and Hilary Bradt for having the faith in me to do this, my first guidebook. I would also like to thank the rest of the Bradt team for their help throughout the writing of the book.

A big thank you goes to all the intrepid travellers at the OSCE, who spent unknown hours feeding this author with itineraries, facts and all sorts of other help: Andy Palmer, Andreas Raab, Arbeni Ajrulai, Aytekin Aktas, Danny Renton, Drew Hyslop, Erdogan Halimi, Goran Miševski, Isabelle De Ruyt, Joe Brinker, Jovdat Mammedov, Katie Ryan, Kimberly Reczek, Monika Portillo, Peter Booker, Peter Vos and Ziggy. I would particularly like to thank Ida Nikolovska and Kate Gjorgjevič for their superb coaching in the finer points of Macedonian history – any mistakes in the history section of this book are strictly my own.

I am indebted to all those who work on promoting the tourism sector in Macedonia, in particular: Aleksander Karaev, Anica Palazzo, Margaret Will and Ceca of GTZ; Margareta Lipkovska, Dane Smith and Dori of MCA; Lene Mikkelsen and Gjiorgi Miskovski of SEED; Miguel Misteli of the Brajčino Ecotourism Project; Michael Hegarty of Scanagri; Aleksander Ristovski of Vitis, Anna Burke of the International Women's Association of Macedonia; Gjorgi Balojani of Isidor Tours; Mimi Nuševa and Alex of Tuymada Travel Agency.

I am also grateful to numerous Macedonians who unwittingly dropped all sorts of interesting details into the book as I cornered them in monasteries, hot springs, buses, bars and trains: Baba Tahir of the Tetovo Bektaši Teke, Father Sofrajni of Treskavec Monastery, Pop Dobri of Saint Joakim Osogovski, Vladimir Pivovarov, Ljubčo Mejolovski, Slavčo Hristovski, Nataša Dimitrievska, Stefan Kanevče, Daniela Mavrovska, Branko, Kostaldin, Sisters Nauma, Varvar, Jasmin, Raina, Maria, Eli, Gjufida, Minka and the Janče Lion.

My gratitude goes to other internationals who supported my efforts, including Annemarie Johnson, Nick Robson, Jeffrey Buenger, Nanci Pendulla, John Storey, Jane and David Keating, Mike Rees, Chris Bridge, Dr Nicolaas Biegman, Edwin Baer for his contribution to the section on Katlanovska Banja in *Chapter 6*, Errol Gregory and Henry Bolton for help with maps, my mother for taking care of my affairs and endless list of requests whilst away from London, and Lieutenant Colonel Charles I Watt (retired) for all his advice on reading material and the politics and history of Macedonia.

Finally I would particularly, of course, like to thank my husband, Vic, who let me drag him around Macedonia weekend after weekend to follow up on minutiae and photo opportunities, despite monastery overload and our repeated failure to find a room with a double bed or a hot spring that we could share.

Introduction

This book started when, on moving to Macedonia, I popped into Stanfords in London to get a travel guide on Macedonia, only to find that there wasn't one. There were a few pages here and there in other books on the region, but nothing that would last me at least a year's worth of weekends in an obviously geographically and historically rich country, never mind anything that might include the political reasons why Macedonia has been so volatile.

Having long wanted to get into a bit of serious writing, I did some research and it didn't take long to conclude that Bradt was the publisher to take on such a book. Following on from their recent successful publications of travel guides to Albania, Croatia and Montenegro, they accepted me as the author of the guide to Macedonia.

In an effort to get the book out in time for the 2004 Olympics in Greece, I went through my own marathon of Macedonian politics and places through the ages. There is so much in this small land. It is not a place of extremes, but it is a land of many different layers, each layer a mosaic of different perspectives and perceptions, a kaleidoscope of subtle colours and lights.

As a result, I can only implore you to use this guide for what it is: simply a guide. Geographically and historically there is much more to Macedonia if you veer off the tarred and hardened road, and you will only ever be rewarded for taking that side-road. A 4WD vehicle is very useful for this, for it is a bumpy ride, geographically as well as historically. Talk to the people and you will find them a fount of knowledge on the region, happy to give you their version of events. What is written here is certainly not the last word on the subject.

This guide is just a starter kit, leaving plenty to be discovered, and plenty to be created. It is a snapshot of a country in transition and many things could have changed by the time you buy and use this book. At the time of writing most of the places described are free to visit, you might only gain access if you talk to a local, and there is little of the usual high-end tourist infrastructure. That is what still makes visiting it an adventure, as well as so often frustrating. Macedonia has a wealth to offer the outdoor and historical adventurer, but so little of it is easy to find or well maintained.

A Macedonian friend is invaluable here to help with finding your way around and introducing you to your own adventure, especially once you wander off the edges of this book. And you will pick up many of these friends along the way who will go out of their way to help as if it is really nothing at all, and many of whom will speak excellent English or German or even French.

These frustrations and delights will undoubtedly change as the country becomes a more popular tourist destination. But for the meantime, enjoy its quirks and its freedom from the trappings of tourism. And when all that has changed, then I will look forward to updating the second edition!

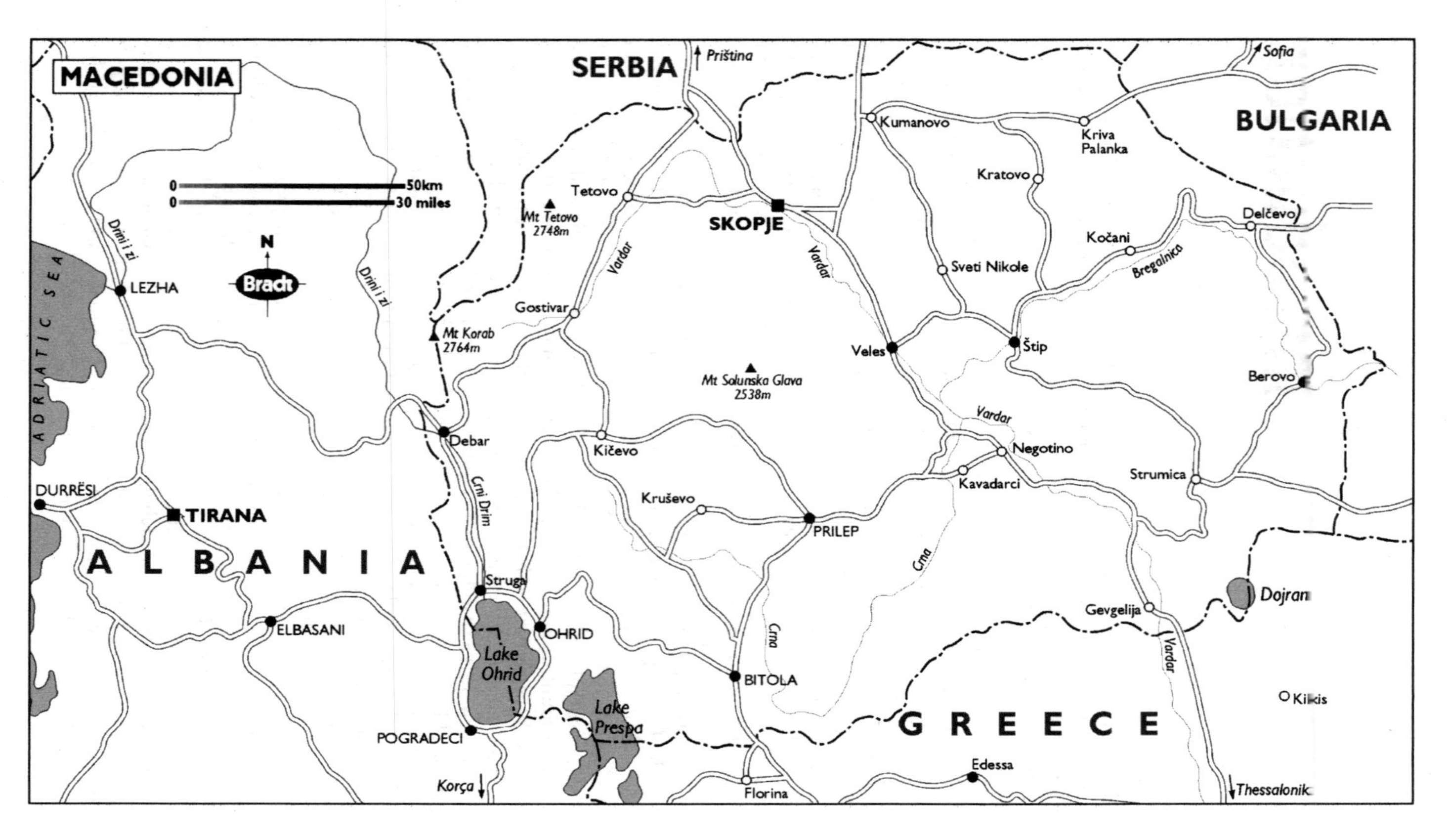

MACEDONIA
SERBIA
Priština
Sofia
BULGARIA
0 50km
0 30 miles
N
Bradt
Drini i zi
ADRIATIC SEA
LEZHA
Drini i zi
Tetovo
Mt Tetovo 2748m
Gostivar
Mt Korab 2764m
SKOPJE
Vardar
Vardar
Kumanovo
Kriva Palanka
Kratovo
Sveti Nikole
Kočani
Bregalnica
Delčevo
Štip
Veles
Berovo
Mt Solunska Glava 2538m
Debar
Kičevo
Vardar
Negotino
Kavadarci
Strumica
DURRËSI
TIRANA
Crni Drim
Kruševo
PRILEP
ALBANIA
Crna
Struga
ELBASANI
OHRID
Lake Ohrid
Dojran
Gevgelija
Crna
Vardar
BITOLA
Kilkis
Lake Prespa
GREECE
POGRADECI
Edessa
Korça
Florina
Thessalonik

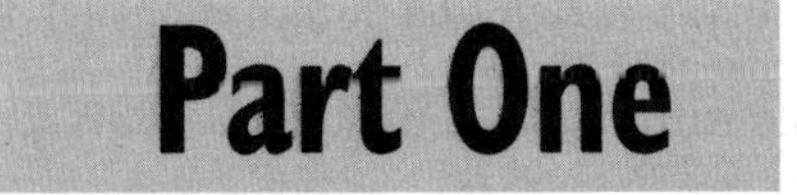

General Information

MACEDONIA FACTS AND FIGURES

Country name (as recognised internationally) former Yugoslav Republic of Macedonia (FYROM)
Macedonian constitutional name Republika Makedonija Република Македонија
Status Independent republic since 1991
Language Macedonian
Alphabet Cyrillic
Population 2,022,547 (2002 census)
Religion Orthodox Christian, Muslim, Roman Catholic
Government Parliamentary democracy
Main political parties Governing coalition: SDSM (Social Democratic Party of Macedonia) and DUI (Democration Union of Integration); in opposition: VMRO-DPMNE (Internal Macedonia Revolutionary Organisation-Democratic Party of Macedonian National Unity)
Next parliamentary elections 2006
President Branko Crvenkovski
Prime minister Vlado Bučkovski
Capital Skopje
Other major towns Bitola, Kumanovo, Ohrid, Prilep, Štip, Strumica, Tetovo
Border countries Albania, Serbia and Montenegro, Bulgaria, Greece
Area 25,713km^2
National parks Three: Mavrovo, Galičica, Pelister
UNESCO protected area Ohrid lake and town
Total length of roads 10,591km
Total surfaced roads 6,000km
Total railway 922km
Airports 16 (international airports are Skopje and Ohrid)
High point Mount Korab 2,753m
Low point River Vardar at Gevgelija border crossing 45m
Time CET (GMT+1)
Currency Denar (MKD)
Exchange rate £1 = MKD90.00; US$1 = MKD 52.00; €1 = MKD61.50
Average annual income US$2,350 (World Bank, 2004)
International telephone code +389
Electricity 220 volts AC. Sockets are round two-pin.
Flag A yellow oval at the centre emanating eight yellow segments against a red background

1 History and Politics

> And she, Deucalion's daughter,
> of Zeus, the thunderer,
> bore two sons:
> Magnet and Macedon – a cavalryman, a warrior…
>
> Hesiod, *Days and Deeds* (7BC)

HISTORY

Geographical Macedonia, covering a large swathe of land from the source of the River Vardar (Axios in Greek) to its estuary at Solun (Thessaloniki in Greek) has a very rich and varied history which is reflected in the present-day political climate and division of the geographical region. Macedonia had its heyday during the build-up of its ancient empire ending with the sudden death of Aleksandar III of Macedon (also known as Alexander the Great), then for a short while again during the reign of Tsar Samoil. The region continued to exert influence afterwards through its status as the Bishopric of Bitola and Ohrid. Then as an independent state, Macedonia did not see the light of day again until the shortlived Kruševo Republic of 1903, and now as the independent (although officially still named 'former Yugoslav') Republic of Macedonia. Today geographical Macedonia is made up of four political entities: Vardar Macedonia which is the Republic of Macedonia; Pirin Macedonia which is in Bulgaria; Aegean Macedonia which is in Greece; and a tiny sliver north and south of Debar which is in Albania.

Chronology

5000–3000BC	First traces of human existence in northern Macedonia date back to the Neolithic period
3000–2200BC	Aneolithic period
2200–500BC	Bronze and iron age of mythical Paeonia
7th century–168BC	Ancient Macedonian royal dynasty
168BC–6th century	Roman period
6th century	Invasion of Goths, Huns and Avars
7th century	Beginning of the Slavic period
976–1014	Reign of Tsar Samoil
1096–97	Crusaders cross Macedonia
1018–1767	Archbishopric of Ohrid
1371–94	King Marko's Kingdom of Macedonia
1394–1912	Ottoman rule
1878	The Treaties of San Stefano and Berlin
August 3–10 1903	The Kruševo Republic
1912–13	First and second Balkan wars between Serbia, Greece, Bulgaria and Turkey

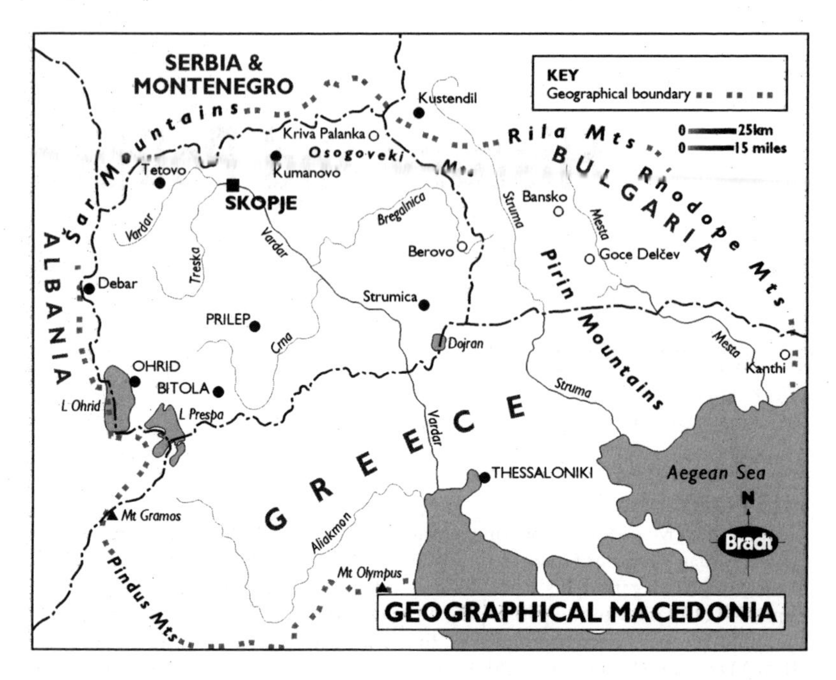

1914–18	Macedonia ruled by Bulgaria
1918–41	Came under the rule of the Kingdom of Serbs, Croats and Slovenes
1920	Ruled for six months by the Yugoslav Communist Party
1941–44	Ruled again by Bulgaria
1944–91	Socialist Republic of Macedonia (within Federal Republic of Yugoslavia)
1991–present	Independent (former Yugoslav) Republic of Macedonia

Mythical Paeonia

According to Homer's rendition of mythical times in the *Iliad,* before Macedonia and the Macedonians came Paeonia and the Paeons. This land stretched from the source of the River Vardar to its estuary at Thessaloniki and across the River Struma to the Rhodope Mountains in the east. The legend goes that the Paeaons themselves were direct descendants of the river god Axios. They were culturally quite close to their Illyrian, Thracian and Greek neighbours, and even took part in the seige of Troy around 1200BC.

Later, other Greek historians such as Herodotus, Livius, Strabo and Thucydides described Paeonia and the Paeons in their writings. There is also mention that in the southwest of the land lay an area called Pelagonia. Named after Pelagon, the son of Axios, this land was located around the River Crni Drim, which runs from Struga at Lake Ohrid through Debar into present-day Albania.

Further descriptions are made of other tribes bordering on, and fighting with, the ancient Macedonians who came to dominate the region. These tribes include the Lyncestis, who used to live in the area around Heraclea (now Bitola); the Brigians who spread out in pockets all over Macedonia, modern-day central Albania and northwest Greece; the Enhelians centred around southeast Macedonia; the Dassaretians settled around Ohrid (then Lichnidos); the Illyrians who moved into present-day Albania and therefore bordered on western Macedonia; and finally the Dardanians who originated from a similar area to the Illyrians, and who some believe may have been related to the Illyrians.

All these tribes are mentioned by Thucydides in his famous *History of the Peloponnesian War*, showing that not only were they more than mythical, but that they often fought side by side against an external enemy, as well as fighting against each other in the absence of an outside aggressor. Traces of their walled towns can still be found around Macedonia, where tumbled piles of limestone blocks tell of the Cyclopean masonry techniques used to build their mighty fortresses. Vajtos, Matka, Mariovo and Demir Kapija are four such sites.

Ancient Macedonia

Legend says that the Macedonians came from Macedon, the grandson of Zeus (the Greek god of thunder) by his first daughter. Hesiod's epic, *Deeds and Days*, goes on to say that Zeus's second daughter also bore two sons: Graecian and Latin. Thus the Greeks and the Romans, according to legend, were brothers, and cousins to the Macedonians. A more superstitious mind might take this rendition of the legend as the origin of the animosity between the Greeks and the Macedonians. Indeed at the time, the Greeks had gone to some lengths to keep their 'barbarian' cousins out of the Delphian Amphyctionic Council and from participating in the Olympic Games. Only in the early 5th century were the Macedonians finally permitted into the Olympics, having been ordained Greek because of their common ancestry and worship of the same Greek gods.

Compared to other tribes in the Balkans, the Macedonians, by virtue of being mountain people, were renowned hunters and fighters, who also took a liking to drink and dance. These traits were equally matched by their desire for political power, which allowed the Macedonian dynasty to expand its empire gradually over the course of almost seven centuries. At the pinnacle of its existence during the reign of Aleksandar III of Macedon (known to Hellenites as Alexander the Great), the Macedonian empire encompassed geographical Macedonia, the Aegean islands, Egypt, Asia Minor, eastern Iran and western India. In 331BC, Babylon (now in modern-day Iraq), was made the capital of Aleksandar's vast Macedonian empire.

Prior to Aleksandar III of Macedon came a distinguished list of 22 Macedonian kings:

808–778BC	Charan, founder of the Macedonian royal dynasty, with the royal seat at Lynk
778–750BC	Koinos, son of Charan
750–707BC	Chyrismasus
707–660BC	Perdiccas I
659–645BC	Argeus
644–640BC	Phillip I
639–574BC	Aeronus, son of Phillip I
573–541BC	Alxatus
540–498BC	Amnitas
498–454BC	Aleksandar I of Macedon, son of Amnitas
451–414BC	Perdiccas II, son of Aleksandar I
431BC	Outbreak of the Peloponnesian War
414–399BC	Archelaus, son of Perdiccas II, moved the capital of Macedonia to Pella from Aegae (modern-day Veryina in Greece) which later became the capital of Greece

399–398BC Orestes, son of Archelaus

397–395BC Aeronus (son of Perdiccas, half brother of Archelaus and formerly Orestes' governor: Aeronus killed Orestes and then proclaimed himself King Archelaus II)

394BC Pausanius, son of Aeronus and killed by Amnitas II, brother of Orestes, who also ruled briefly in that year

394–369BC Amnitas III, whose legitimacy was disputed twice in 393–391BC by Argeus II

369–368BC Aleksandar II, son of Amnitas II and killed by his brother-in-law Ptolomeus

368–365BC Ptolomeus, who married the mother of Aleksandar II in order to gain legitimacy to the throne. Ptolomeus was later killed by Aleksandar II's brother, Perdiccas III

365–359BC Perdiccas III

359–336BC Phillip II, founded Heraclea near present-day Bitola

336–325BC Aleksandar III of Macedon (Alexander the Great)

Aleksandar III of Macedon had squandered the previously good relations with the Greeks won by his father Philip II. His sudden death from fever left behind a weak and unprepared heir, and without the mighty backing of the Greek city states the empire soon crumbled as a result of fighting between the great ruler's generals.

Roman rule

A weakened Macedonian empire made way for Rome to divide and conquer the region. Three Macedonian-Roman wars ensued over the next 150 years: 215–205BC, 200–197BC and 171–168BC. On June 22 168BC, Perseus, the last Macedonian king, was finally defeated at the battle of Pydna. Pondering how to

THE EMPIRE OF ALEKSANDAR III OF MACEDON

Born in Pella (modern-day Greece) in 356BC, Aleksandar III of Macedon was the son of Phillip II, who reigned over Macedonia before him. Aleksandar became famous for continuing his father's dream of an expanded empire. Phillip was assassinated in 336BC before he could realise his plans. But his son, Aleksandar, at the young age of 20, continued to strengthen his father's already expanded empire. A fearless fighter and far-sighted tactician, he spoke both Greek and his native Macedonian, and had been taught in his early years by Aristotle. In his short reign of 12 years his victories are numerous and legendary:

336BC Wiped out all remaining contenders to the Macedonian throne from within Macedonia.

335BC Destroyed the town of Thebes in Greece.

334BC Defeated the Persians in Asia Minor.

333BC Defeated Darius, King of Persia, at Issus.

332BC Conquered Egypt and founded the town of Alexandria.

331BC Defeated Darius again at Babylon, which Aleksandar then made capital of the Macedonian empire.

327BC Defeated King Pora, thereby acquiring the Punjab.

325BC Died on June 10 on his return to Babylon.

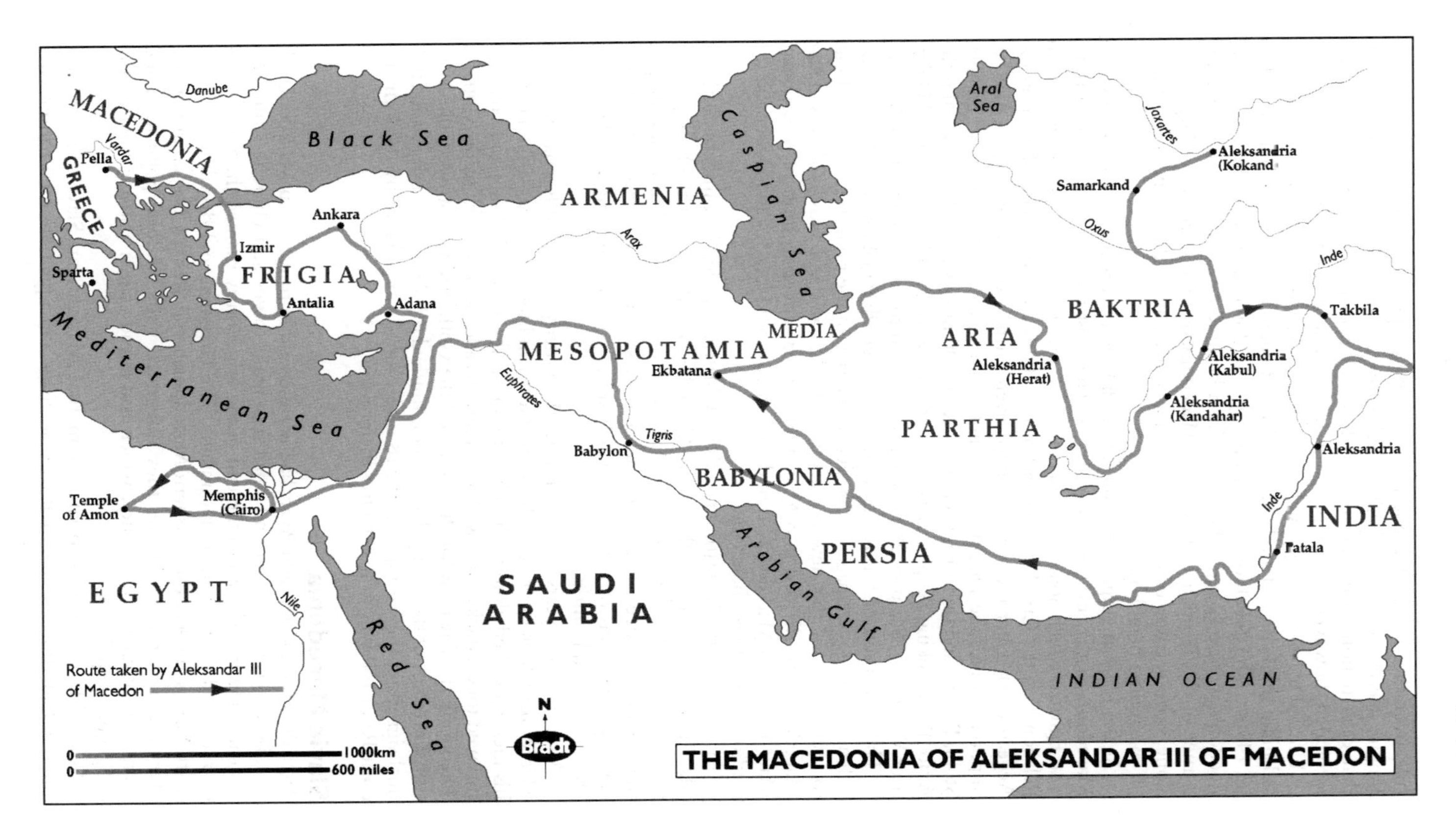

THE MACEDONIA OF ALEKSANDAR III OF MACEDON

rule over the unruly Macedonians, the Amphipolis Council of the Roman Empire declared that Macedonia would be divided into four regions (*meriden*) but that each region would be free to elect its own magistrates and laws. It was forbidden, however, for the regions to co-operate at any level.

Unused to, and unhappy with, these limited freedoms, Andriskos, also known as Phillip the False, led a rebellion of Macedonians against the Roman dictators in 149BC. The rebellion was resolutely put down and Macedonia's former freedoms were revoked. Macedonia then became one province in a far-flung corner of the Roman empire. The Macedonians themselves were largely left alone, but a garrison of soldiers was permanently stationed there in order to fight off marauding neighbours.

As the Roman empire grew bigger, so did the importance of various towns in Macedonia that lay on the trading routes. The most famous trading route was the Via Egnatia which joined the Illyrian port of Durres (now in Albania) with Pelagonia on the Crni Drim, Heraclea near Bitola and on to Thessaloniki on the Aegean coast. Later the road extended even further to Constantinople. Another important route, the Diagonal Way, linked Heraclea with Stibera near Tojkrsti, Stobi, Bargala and on to Pautalija (now Kustendil in Bulgaria). There was also the Axios Road linking Skupi near Skopje with Argos south of Veles, Stobi and Dober near Valandovo. See page 29 for a map of Roman roads and towns in Macedonia.

The expansion of the Roman empire under Illyrian-born Diocletian (who killed St George, see page 187) reduced the size of the prefecture of Macedonia to make way for the new prefectures of Thessalia and Novus Epirus. Later Macedonia was divided into Macedonia Prima, covering most of present-day Macedonia, and Macedonia Secunda which covered Heraclea and Dober and the land to the south of these cities.

After Diocletian's death in AD305, Christianity slowly came to settle in Macedonia. Early in the 4th century Skupi became the seat of the bishopric for the province of Dardania. In the year 325 Stobi also acquired its own bishop at the Council of Nicea. Finally, Heraclea was also appointed a bishop later in the century. The ruins of early Christian basilicas can be found now in Heraclea, Stobi, Skupi and Ohrid.

After over 800 years of Roman rule, the orderly life of the Roman towns in Macedonia fell victim to the Huns, the Goths and the Avars. Attila the Hun and his men ransacked almost a hundred towns in the year 447. Stobi and Heraclea survived these attacks fairly well, but a few decades later they fell to the Goths of Theodorik the Great. What the Huns and the Goths hadn't destroyed, the Avars (tribal brothers of the Mongolian hordes) finished off. And then, as if to add fate's final signature, the earthquake of 518 undermined any attempt by the formerly great Roman towns to re-establish themselves.

Slavic Macedonia

After the Huns, Goths and Avars had left the land in ruins, life in Macedonia fell to subsistence farming around small mountain towns and churches. Into this unguarded territory towards the end of the 6th century roamed the Slavic tribes from beyond the Carpathian mountains. The Draguvite and Brysak tribes of the south Slavs settled in the northern Macedonian and western Bulgarian regions. Over the next three centuries they integrated with the local population and eventually adopted Christianity, which had already taken a strong hold on the indigenous population.

Some Macedonian historians claim that Macedonian Slavs came from a different Slav tribe and had their own language and aspirations for a nation state.

There is little evidence to back this line of thinking, but the development of a Macedonian Church and a language for instruction within the Church are stronger indications of the roots and justification of national aspirations in the future (see page 45).

Shortly after the fall of Tsar Samoil's empire, the Normans came riding into Macedonia under Robert Giscard (1016–85) to plunder and loot. The crusades followed in 1096–97 on their way to pit the strength of Christ against that of Mohammed in the Middle East, levying war taxes on the way. Later on, Giscard's son, Boemund of Tarent (1050–1111), came back like a bad dream in 1107, replaying the plundering and looting of his father.

All the while, the locals tried repeatedly to rise up against their Byzantine rulers who did nothing to help against the Norman invasions, but to no avail.

TSAR SAMOIL OF MACEDONIA

By the end of the 10th century, one family's aspirations for their own state were such that the four sons of the Bryzsak Duke Nikola started to rebel against the Bulgarian authorities ruling over Macedonia. Embroiled in its own fight with Byzantium, Bulgaria had little time for the four brothers, Aron, David, Moses and Samoil. But Bulgaria fell to Byzantium in 971 and with it Macedonia came under Byzantium rule. Five years later in 976, the Byzantium Emperor John I Tzimisces died, and the four sons succeeded in taking Bulgaria and Macedonia back.

When the four brothers became two, after David was killed by Vlach travellers and Moses was killed in the Battle of Serres, Aron and Samoil started to fall out. Soon Samoil had Aron and his family killed, leaving Samoil as the sole ruler of an expanding empire. He brought most of Bulgaria under his rule and most of Macedonia minus Thessaloniki, as well as large parts of Greece, Albania, Dalmatia, Bosnia and Serbia as far as the Danube.

Samoil was crowned king of Macedonia by the Roman Catholic Pope Gregory V at Golem Grad on Lake Prespa. For many Macedonian historians this symbolises the official break with the Bulgarian, quasi-Russian, Orthodox church, and marks the start of a Macedonian branch of the church headed by the archdiocese of Ohrid. Tsar Samoil later moved his capital to Ohrid, where he built the great fortress which is still visible today.

But by 1014, the new Byzantine Emperor Vasilius II had had enough of this young upstart and sent troops to take back the Macedonian empire. At the Battle of Belasica on July 29, 1014, Samoil's troops were resoundingly crushed by the Byzantine troops. Basilius then ordered that the 15,000 troops remaining should be blinded, leaving only one eye per hundred soldiers so that they could make their way back to Samoil (who had escaped during the battle) and he could see their defeat. The battle was at present-day Vodoča near Strumica. Vodoča means 'plucked eye'.

It is believed that when Samoil saw his blinded troops returning to him at Prilep on October 6, he collapsed from a heart attack and died shortly afterwards. Macedonia then fell under Byzantine control and the people had to pay severe reparations to Constantinople for several decades to come.

The Macedonians were being attacked on all sides. And when the Byzantine empire began to fall at the end of the 13th century and beginning of the 14th century, the recently released states of Bulgaria and Serbia followed suit by trying to re-conquer parts of Macedonia.

500 years of Ottoman rule

Like all empires, Byzantium fell, only to be replaced by another empire, this time the Ottomans (for more on the Ottoman rulers, their rules and the ruled see box, page 42). Despite King Marko of Prilep's brave attempts to keep back the Turks (see box, page 121), his defeat at their hands in 1394 signalled the completion of Ottoman victory over Macedonia. Skopje had already been taken in 1392, and although Debar regained some independence under Gjergj Kastriot's Albania from 1444 to 1449, even that, and later all of Albania, fell to Ottoman rule.

With the Ottomans came Islam and the building of mosques, covered markets, balconied houses, an increase in trade and eventually clock towers and railways. Like when the Romans arrived all those centuries earlier, Macedonians did not take kindly to these new foreign rulers and many fled the country. Whilst the Ottomans encouraged the rule of the Orthodox élite over its millet (see box, page 44) and even went to some lengths to help preserve and protect some churches, such as Lešok and Joakim Osogovski, other churches of particular significance, such as Sveti Sofia and Sveti Pantelejmon in Ohrid, were converted into mosques.

In the wake of emmigrating Macedonians, the Turks themselves moved in to fertile Macedonia in droves to build new villages and towns. This built up ethnic tensions and despite the superficial improvement in trade and town life, Macedonians rose up again and again against their new masters. Macedonian bandits did all they could to oust the Turks and many were outlawed and hunted down by Ottoman *janissaries* (the military élite, see below) and their *arnauts* (special forces largely recruited from Albanian communities).

The Ottoman rulers adhered to the Sunni school of Islam, and therein to the Hanafi legal code. They also, however, tolerated and legitimised the Sufi side of Islam, which heralded from the more folklorish beliefs of Islam and emphasised the mystic communion of its disciples with Allah. Many Macedonians converted to Islam during the Ottoman period, either as Sunnis, or to a Sufi order. The Sufi orders, being less strict and more tolerant of individual expression, were more open to converts from other faiths. This was particularly true of the *Bekteši* order (see box, page 180) who were appointed the priests of the *janissaries*.

The treaties of San Stefano and Berlin

By the second half of the 19th century, the Ottomans' iron-like grip over their empire was beginning to loosen. The Habsburg Empire had won back Serbia and Bosnia, and Greece was also independent again. The newly freed states in turn wanted their share of Macedonia. This played itself out first of all in the sphere of the Church. In 1870 Russia ordained the independence of the Bulgarian Orthodox Church, with rights of influence over Macedonia as a means of extending Russia's influence into the area. The Greek Orthodox Church took umbrage with this turn of events, and pushed Turkey into taking the issue up with Russia. Among many other issues this prompted war between the two nations.

The Treaty of San Stefano was the result of Turkey's defeat by Russia in the Russo-Turkish war ending March 1878. The treaty allowed Romania, Montenegro and Serbia to extend their borders to include much of the land

KING OF KUMANOVO

In 1689, Austrian Emperor Leopold I of the Habsburg empire sent General Piccolomini towards Macedonia to beat off the Ottoman army which had been encroaching upon Habsburg lands. Karpoš, chief of a band of outlaws based in the mining village of Kratovo, was quick to respond to the General's call for war and decided to rebel against the Ottoman overlords. The outlaws first rose up against the Ottoman stronghold of Kriva Palanka, and this started what came to be known as the Karpoš Uprising. More bandits joined Karpoš and the rebellion next took Kumanovo, then spread east towards Kustendil (now in Bulgaria) and west towards Skopje.

When Leopold heard that Karpoš had taken Kumanovo, the Emperor promoted him and named him King of Kumanovo. But Leopold's further assistance to the new king, after Piccolomini had to beat a hasty retreat later that year, came too late. Six weeks after taking Kriva Palanka, Karpoš and two hundred of his men were brutally killed and then impaled on the Stone Bridge in Skopje. Leopold's letter of encouragement to the Macedonian people a year later in 1690 fell on deaf ears.

which they now have. Bulgaria, however, was made an autonomous new state, whose new borders extended as far as Niš and Vranje in present-day Serbia, Mount Korab and Ohrid in today's Macedonia, and to the far side of Prespa and Mount Gramos in Greece.

The great European powers of Austro-Hungary, France and Great Britain were not happy, however, with Russia's new extended spheres of influence through Bulgaria, and they managed to convince Russia to redraw the map. The new treaty, put together in Berlin in June and July 1878 essentially gave Macedonia back to the Ottoman Empire for its fate to be decided upon later. Bulgaria was duly annoyed and cries for a greater Bulgaria hark back to these three months when northern Macedonia was part of the newly autonomous Bulgaria created by the San Stefano Treaty.

Some have interpreted the Berlin Treaty as laying the foundation for an autonomous Macedonia, which in turn fed Macedonian nationalism. At the same time, Bulgarian forces worked to annex Macedonia to Bulgaria. In either case an autonomous Macedonia did not materialise under Ottoman rule despite repeated protests and armed clashes by Macedonians throughout the three Macedonian *vilayets* (administrative regions) of Skopje (now lacking Kosovo and Metohia which had gone to Serbia), Bitola and Thessaloniki.

The Ilinden uprising

The various uprisings against the Ottoman rulers led eventually to the formation of a group of intellectuals under the name of the Internal Macedonian Revolutionary Organisation (VMRO). The founding members, Dame Gruev, Petar Pop Arsov, Anton Dimitrov, Ivan Haži Nikolov, Hristo Tatarčev and Hristo Batanžiev founded the organisation on October 23 1893 in Thessaloniki, with the goal of creating an independent Macedonia according to its historical and geographical bounderies. Other Macedonian heroes joined up, such as Pitu Guli and Goce Delčev.

It took another ten years of internal and external disputing for VMRO to engineer the uprising which would hopefully secure Macedonia's independence.

THE DEVŠIRME TAX AND THE JANISSARIES

When the Ottomans started to expand their empire over the Balkans they also started to run out of the manpower needed to run the ever-expanding empire, keep order and conquer new lands. As a result the Ottomans started a tax system in the 1380s which was levied on non-Muslim families within the new territories. This tax, called *devširme*, required between 2.5 and 10 percent of boys within the ages of seven to fourteen (not usually the first born) to be taken for education and training to run the Ottoman Empire. The boys were encouraged to convert to the Islam faith and could be enrolled in either a civilian or a military capacity.

For many non-Muslim families this tax was understandably extremely unpopular, and certainly did not help to ingratiate the new rulers with their new subjects, no matter what other 'freedoms', donations and perks may have been given in return. But as time went on, non-Muslim families found that the *devširme* was also a means of advancement within the Ottoman system, and soon selection criteria were attached to the *devširme* in order to keep down the number of applicants.

On the military side these boys went into the élite troops of the *janissary* (meaning literally 'new troops' from the Turkish *yeni čeri*). Their training was harsh; once in the *janissary* it was forever; and they were forbidden to marry. But these elite troops soon realised their own importance and in 1449 they rebelled, demanding higher pay, pensions and other rights. It took another century before, in 1566, they won the right to marry. By the middle of the 17th century the demand to enter the *janissary*, particularly from Albanian, Bosnian and Bulgarian families, was so high that the *devširme* could be abolished.

Although these troops were formed, supposedly as a more loyal section of the army, in order to serve as the Sultan's personal household troops and bodyguards, they proved in the end to be no more loyal than the rest of the Ottoman army which was also made up of conscripted soldiers and tribal warriors. By the 18th century the *janissary* practically held the Sultan hostage against his own imperial affairs and even his daily household. The *Bekteši* order of dervishes, the appointed priests of the *janissary*, supported them in their efforts.

The empire was already beginning to shrink due to the ineffectiveness of combat troops and many of the *janissary* weren't even serving soldiers. By 1826 the *janissaries* were so out of control that Sultan Mahmoud II finally abolished them, after several years of wresting back power from them and creating a totally new army. Their end, in a bloody revolt of the old 'new troops' against the new 'new army', was a sign of things to come over the next century; the demise of the Ottoman Empire.

At the Congress of Smilevo (20km northwest of Bitola) the Bitola Revolutionary District set the ball rolling for an uprising in their district. This was later expanded to a general uprising throughout all of Macedonia set for the auspicious date of St Elijas Day (literally *Ilij den* in Macedonian), August 2 1903.

In the end it was the Kruševo Revolutionary District led by Nikola Karev who gained the upper hand over the ruling Ottomans, and on August 3 they announced the formation of the Republic of Kruševo. Unfortunately, it was only to last ten days before a detachment of the Ottoman army, outnumbering the

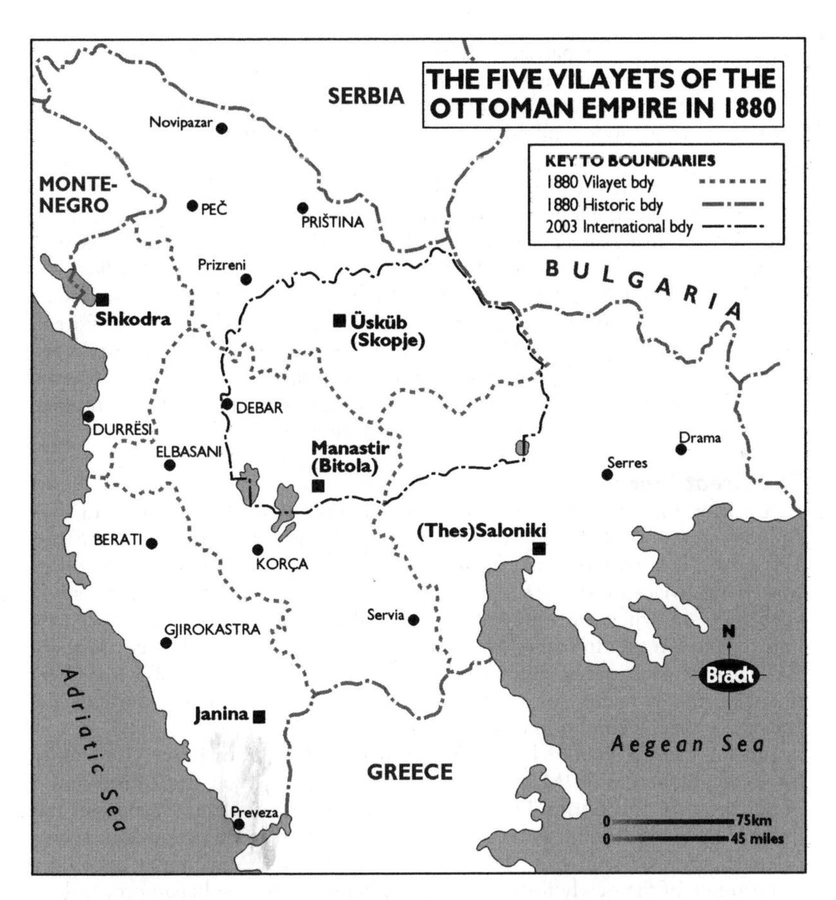

1,200 rebels sixteen to one, surrounded Kruševo and brought it to heel. Pitu Guli and Goce Delčev among many others died in the fighting.

The terror wrought on the local population thereafter was without precedent and much of it was recorded in the photography of the Manaki brothers (see box, page 148). But this repression only succeeded in indelibly marking in the minds of the Macedonian consciousness that freedom and independence from foreign rule was the only way out.

20th-century Macedonia

The first and second Balkan wars

Ottoman rule could not last forever and, weakened at last by economic fraud, political in-fighting and a costly war with the Italians in 1911, the Ottoman Empire fell prey to the territorial ambitions of its remaining Balkan neighbours. Serbia, Montenegro, Bulgaria and Greece declared war on Turkey on October 18 1912, and signed up the help of the Macedonian people by declaring that their anti-Ottoman league was for the liberation of the Macedonians. No such thing was to transpire, but instead the four nations divided Macedonia up amongst themselves as soon as the devastated Ottoman Empire finally retreated to Turkey.

Bulgaria, with ambitions of a greater Bulgaria, took the lion's share of Macedonia, to the annoyance of the remaining nations of the anti-Ottoman league. Macedonian expatriate communities appealed to the Great Powers in London, and the Macedonian refugees in St Petersburg, Russia, even sent ahead a map made by Dimitrija Čupovski proposing the ethnic and geographical boundaries of an independent Macedonia in order to bolster their case. The neighbouring Balkan states, however, would have none of it. Serbia was vying for an outlet to the Aegean Sea, and Greece wanted control of Thessaloniki. Thus they decided the following year to challenge Bulgaria militarily for the land.

Unlike the first Balkan war the year before, which had the strategic goal of ousting the Ottomans in order to divide the land up later, this second Balkan war was all about painstakingly gaining land and advancing the front line. Macedonian villages were razed to the ground and their inhabitants massacred in an effort to make sure that insurgents could not rise up as the battle moved ahead. And even after the Bulgarians were put back in their box, the suppression did not stop as the new masters of Macedonia, now divided between Greece and Serbia, continued to put down any hint of independence by Macedonians for their own state.

The Great War

A year later, the Great War broke out following the assassination of the Austrian Archduke Ferdinand in Sarajevo. The Central Powers of Germany and Austro-Hungary sided with Bulgaria against Serbia and Greece over the division of Macedonia. Macedonia, for the most part, chose the lesser of two evils by siding with only one of its former oppressors (Bulgaria) against Serbia (backed by France) and Greece. In reality Macedonians were drafted into all three armies to fight against each other. But Germany also enlisted the help of VMRO by financing the formation of a 'Macedonian' army, which fought alongside the Bulgarians on the condition of independence for Macedonia.

But the Central Powers lost the Great War, and the Paris Peace Conference set to negotiating the 'Macedonian Question', already an institution and a headache since the Berlin Treaty 40 years earlier. Of the three proposals put forward by Great Britain, France and Italy, it was the French proposal in favour of the Serbs that won out. The British proposal that Macedonia become a protectorate of the newly formed League of Nations, and the Italian proposal for autonomy were rejected as too risky. So without heed of what the Macedonians wanted, Macedonia was returned to the 1913 borders of the Treaty of Bucharest. Vardar Macedonia belonged once again to the enlarged Kingdom of Serbs, Croats and Slovenes (later Royal Yugoslavia) and a repressive colonisation of Macedonia by the Serbs began.

VMRO, however, would not be silenced and continued to fight for freedom from the Serbs, leading in 1934 to the assassination of the Yugoslav King Aleksandar I. The fighting continued and when in early 1941 Yugoslavia refused to side with the Germans, Germany declared war on Yugoslavia, bringing Vardar Macedonia into the fray with it.

The communist struggle for Vardar Macedonia

Inviting its allies to re-divide Macedonia yet again, the Germans, Italians and Bulgarians surrounded and then moved into Vardar Macedonia in April 1941. Soon British officers of the Special Operations Executive (SOE), a secret British military organisation established to bring down the Axis forces through sabotage and subversion, were parachuted into Macedonia in order to help fight the fascist forces. Working initially with IMRO they later switched to the partisan forces of the Communist Party of Macedonia (CPM), set up in October 1941, when it became clear that the communist forces were the more coherent and successful.

Promising national liberty, the CPM managed to recruit many Macedonians to swell their ranks, despite the fact that it was formerly a sub-group of the Communist Party of Yugoslavia under Tito. Most Macedonians feared returning to rule under anything relating to Royalist Yugoslavia and fought with the CPM, therefore, for the liberation of their nation rather than for any communist ideals. Under the auspices of the CPM, the Macedonians even set up their own government, the Anti-fascist Assembly of the National Liberation of Macedonia (ASNOM), on August 2 1944, exactly 41 years after the Ilinden uprising of 1903. The government was headed up by the pro-independence politician Metodija Andonov, more commonly known as Cento.

One month later, in September, the Bulgarians withdrew from Vardar Macedonia, suffering heavy losses to partisan forces. The Germans followed in their wake, beating a hasty retreat towards Greece, and ordering the deaths of hundreds of Macedonians after the failed attempt to bring a puppet government into Macedonia through the right-wing faction of IMRO. As it turned out, less than 300 Macedonians were actually killed under German Captain Egbert's orders, as many German soldiers let the Macedonians escape.

With the end of World War II, the CPM, with a decidedly pro-Yugoslav leadership, reneged on its promises of independence for Macedonia. The new borders around Vardar Macedonia enclosed the new People's Republic of Macedonia (later the Socialist Republic of Macedonia) firmly within communist Yugoslavia. Cento and his supporters were removed from office and replaced by the pro-Yugoslav Lazar Kolievski, who remained in power until the fall of Yugoslavia 55 years later.

As the capital of the SRM, Skopje, formerly a political backwater, was firmly oriented towards Serbia for leadership, and its pro-Serb partisan leaders were not well versed in government. Meanwhile, Bitola, traditionally the powerhouse of the region, languished in the shadows. Cut off from its usual orientation towards the southern regions of geographical Macedonia, Bitola's previous political and intellectual capacity was lost on the partisan government of the SRM. Any hint of dissension by Macedonia's pro-independence intellectuals was firmly put down.

Under Tito's communist Yugoslavia, although the SRM was nominally given the status of a federal republic, thereby giving it the right to decentralised government of its own people, this was not the case in reality. Limited autonomy was a move by Tito to divide up Serbian ambitions to take over Yugslavia as a whole. Interdependence was brought to the Federation, however, by dividing up its economic capabilities among the republics.

The SRM became the centre of electricity production and produced a quarter of Yugoslavia's electricity through its many hydro-electric dams, such as at Debar and Crni Drim, as well as through the more traditional polluting method of coal. Fortunately, Yugoslavia never acquired aspirations of nuclear power production. Then, as again in recent years, SRM exported much of its electricity to neighbouring Greece. Socialist-style tourism was also developed, as well as mining and tobacco production.

For the first time in the region's history, ethnic Macedonian arts and literature were encouraged, for which a distinct Macedonian language was recognised and strengthened. The man commissioned to do this was Blaže Krctežanec, a distinctly pro-Serb man, who essentially 'serbified' Macedonian in order to further differentiate it from the Bulgarian influence on the language.

Despite efforts to revitalise SRM's economy, Macedonia remained the poorhouse of Yugoslavia. This was not helped by the isolation of SRM from three of its neighbours: Albania became deeply introverted, Bulgaria shunned the pro-Serb authorities, and civil war raged in northern Greece until 1949. At the end of the civil war the border with Greece was closed as Greek authorities tried to stamp out any further spread of communism or sessionist claims by Aegean Macedonians for an independent Aegean Macedonia.

Life in communist Macedonia followed a similar path to that of many other communist countries, although to much lesser extremes. The fifties saw experimentation with collective production farms and state ownership of land and property. Many officials used these measures to line their own pockets, and although collective production had to be abandoned and a limited private business model was re-introduced in 1965, state ownership remains a problem today even after ten years of independence.

Yugoslavia's break from Soviet tutelage allowed Macedonia to benefit from Yugoslavia's greater freedom of movement and other civil liberties. Nevertheless, one-party rule remained and any talk of an independent Macedonia or a reunification with the other parts of Macedonia was not entertained.

After Tito's death in 1980 and the decline of the Yugoslav economy throughout the eighties, the Yugoslav republics and its many nationalities started to vie for greater degrees of autonomy and power in the Federation or even out of it. As Serbia's president, Slobodan Milošević, became more belligerent at the end of the eighties, the end of Yugoslavia became increasingly inevitable. Despite Lazar Koliševski's attempts to keep the Federation together, the decision to move to a multi-party democracy in 1990 essentially spelled the end of communist ideals in Macedonia.

In January 1991, Kiro Gligorov was appointed president of the SRM by the new multi-party parliament of Macedonia, and on September 8 1991 the people of Macedonia voted in a referendum for the independence of the Republic of Macedonia and bloodlessly left the Federation of Yugoslavia. The Yugoslav army, needed elsewhere in dying Yugoslavia to fight Croatians and Bosnians, left Macedonia in April the next year.

Despite the fact that 74% of the population of Macedonia voted on the referendum for independence, of which 95% voted for independence, the Albanian community claims that most of the remaining 26% of the non-voting citizenry were ethnic Albanians who do not want to live under the alternatives being offered, ie: as a minority within an independent Macedonia, or as a minority within Yugoslavia. Even if their vote *against* independence had been included in the referendum, this would have made no difference to the two-thirds majority needed for a constitutional change, but it is significant that this hefty percentage of Macedonia's citizens feel so disenfranchised from the political developments of the country.

The Former Yugoslav Republic of Macedonia

Troubled first years

With the additional difficulties of a disenfranschised Albanian community, the infant years of the Republic of Macedonia have been fraught with the usual post-communist problems and entrenched thinking. In Macedonia's case this was compounded by its formerly strong dependence on Belgrade. From the beginning, a citizenry used to monopolistic centralisation and hand-outs was faced with a plethora of 17 political parties and 43 independents in the first multi-party elections of 1991 without any historical backing, corroboratory information or experience to select them with. Candidates were divided along political as well as ethnic lines, with no real pan-ethnic party to choose from.

The result of the election gave Macedonia neither a clear winner, nor a clear opposition, so a governing coalition of three parties from the old communist leaders was formed with the leading Albanian party, while the VMRO-DPMNE (Internal Macedonian Revolutionary Organisation-Democratic Party of Macedonian National Unity) took up parliamentary seats in opposition along with several other parties. As head of the leading party in the coalition, Branko Crvenkovski, at the young age of 27, became prime minister.

Two and a half years of political back-biting, in-fighting and head-clashing ensued until October 1994 when new elections were finally held. But the bickering continued over the cast of the votes and it was not long before the main party in opposition, VMRO-DPMNE, and others withdrew from the election altogether. As a result, the existing governing parties, presenting themselves for one vote together, won three quarters of the vote. Forming a government in coalition with the Albanian majority vote, the new government took 112 of the 120 seats in parliament, leaving any form of opposition essentially untenable.

The Albanian community had long been unhappy with their representation in the new Macedonia, which many had not voted on in the first place. In November 1993, Macedonia's police force, strongly linked to the SDSM, arrested 12 people in Tetovo, allegedly for attempting to form an Albanian paramilitary organisation. The police claimed to have found hideouts, weapons caches and other incriminating evidence. Nine of the 12 were jailed for conspiracy and other related charges.

This did not deter the Albanian community, however, who continued to demand greater representation and started to set up their own university in Tetovo in 1995. Considering this a breach of the constitution, in which Macedonian was the only officially recognised language of the new Republic, the authorities declared the university illegal and tried to close it down. In the ensuing public demonstrations, three Albanians were killed and ten policemen injured. Shortly thereafter an assassination attempt on President Kiro Gligorov was carried out. He lost one eye in the incident and his driver was killed outright. Almost a decade later the assassin has still not been apprehended and in 1999 the government offered US$530,000 for information leading to his arrest.

Despite the Liberal Party leaving the governing coalition in early 1996 in order to join the non-parliamentary opposition of VMRO-DMPNE and the attempt by the opposition to call for new parliamentary elections, the governing coalition continued to hold on to power. But international observers were at last allowed to monitor the local elections held that year which resulted in an even greater division between the ruling coalition in parliament and the opposition, who had won most of the main local elections. Tensions increased and in 1997 the mayors of Tetovo and Gostivar were jailed for raising the double-headed eagle flag of Albania over government buildings in their respective towns.

During the course of 1998 the National Liberation Army (NLA), a newly formed rebel group fighting for the liberation of Albanians, made its first public announcement by claiming responsibility for the bombings of several police stations and judicial courts in the lead-up to the internationally observed parliamentary elections of autumn 1998. Their tactics did not succeed in bringing greater autonomy to the Albanian community, but the ineffectiveness of the ruling coalition to alleviate tensions with the Albanian community and to curb the economic difficulties of the transition to a post-communist system brought the electorate to vote in a new government. The winners, VMRO-DMPNE and the DPA (Democratic Party of Albanians), are both right-wing nationalist parties.

Ljubčo Georgievski, leader of VMRO-DMPNE, became prime minister.

The new government was not helped to an easy start by the crisis raging in neighbouring Kosovo, and by the time NATO bombing of Serbia had secured Kosovo later in 1999, 360,000 Kosovar Albanians had fled into northwestern Macedonia. Although the great majority of these refugees eventually returned to Kosovo or went on to other countries, the Macedonian authorities still feared a rise in the number of Albanians claiming citizenship in Macedonia and forcibly bussed tens of thousands of refugees into neighbouring Albania in April of that year. This fear was aggravated by the Albanian community claiming to make up over one third of the population in Macedonia (as opposed to less than 20% in the last census of 1994), and by the unclear status of a number of ethnic Albanians who had never applied for the change from a Yugoslav passport to a Macedonian passport in the window allowed for them to do so back in the early nineties, but were still claiming citizenship. Fraudulent local elections in northwestern Macedonia in 2000 only made matters worse, and some people in Macedonia started to believe that the prolific birthrate in Albanian families was becoming a threat to Macedonian life as they knew it.

Throughout the year 2000, attacks on the police continued in ever greater numbers until, on February 26 2001, the Macedonian authorities retaliated against suspected armed rebels in the village of Tanuševci, north of Skopje on the border with Kosovo, for an attack by the NLA on the police station there. Armed conflict between the authorities and the NLA raged for the next six months, both sides taking casualities and alleging war crimes for the deaths of civilians and the desecration of churches and mosques.

A peace deal and amnesty

After President Trajkovski (elected after Gligorov stepped down in 1999) requested help from NATO on June 20 2001, the international community managed to broker a ceasefire and a peace agreement. The Ohrid Framework Agreement was signed on August 13 2001 by a new unity government, comprising VMRO-DMPNE, the SDSM, DPA and PDP, and NLA leaders. The agreement essentially gave the Albanian community much greater representation in government and society as well as recognition of their language and culture (see box, opposite).

At the end of August, Operation Essential Harvest was launched by NATO troops on invitation by the government to collect arms from rebel forces. Almost 3,500 weapons were collected in the month-long operation, which was half the number that the government had claimed were out there, but twice what the rebels had claimed they had. Another 7,571 were collected in 2003. Essential Harvest was replaced by Operation Amber Fox in September 2001 to oversee the security of the implementation of the Agreement and particularly to ensure the security of EU and OSCE (Organisation for Security and Co-operation in Europe) personnel working in Macedonia.

In addition to the Framework Agreement, the government agreed an amnesty for all former rebel fighters except for those who had committed war crimes. The Albanians read this, as was clear in their negotiations with NATO, to mean an amnesty on all except those cases taken up by the International Criminal Tribunal of Yugoslavia (ICTY) in The Hague. The Macedonian authorities interpret the amnesty clause to mean that they can prosecute those cases not taken up by ICTY. Of the one hundred plus alleged cases, most have been thrown out of court for lack of evidence.

THE OHRID FRAMEWORK AGREEMENT

In the relative calm and cool of the breezes off Lake Ohrid the international community brought the government and rebel leaders together to thrash out their differences around a table and a piece of paper. The result brought greater rights for the Albanian community and hopes of guaranteed peace for all Macedonians.

Constitutional changes

The preamble of the new constitution of November 2002 deleted references to Macedonia as the 'national state of the Macedonian people' whereby Albanians and other minorities were singled out as only having rights as equal citizens, without being acknowledged as actual Macedonian people. The new constitution refers to all Macedonia's population as 'citizens of the Republic of Macedonia', equal before the law.

Official recognition of the Albanian language

In areas with at least a 20% population of ethnic Albanians, Albanian will be used in official institutions alongside Macedonian. Albanian can also be used in the national parliament but not in government proceedings or international communiqués. Ethnic Albanians are also entitled to bi-lingual identity papers and other official documents if they so wish.

Devolution of authority

In line with the wishes of the Albanian community for more say over their own affairs and also, as it happens, in line with decentralisation from one-party communist rule to a multi-party democracy, limited powers of authority are being devolved to the local administrative level throughout the country.

Ethnically mixed policing

The police force will increase their number of ethnic Albanians from 5% to 25%. But these will be spread throughout Macedonia and not just concentrated in the northwest. Neither will the police be answerable to local leaders as the Albanian community had originally wanted in the devolution of power, but the police will remain under the watchful eye of the national government, or possibly a regional governor (yet to be finalised at time of writing). Over a thousand ethnic Albanians have been recruited since the Agreement in order to fulfill this measure.

Only five war crimes cases have been considered serious enough to be taken up by ICTY. These include the massacre at Ljuboten, north of Skopje, where at least six men of Albanian ethnicity were found shot in suspicious circumstances, and the mass grave found in Neprošteno containing four Macedonian bodies. The ICTY completed indictments at the end of 2004. In the Macedonian cases, only one indictment was made against the former Minister of Interior, Ljube Boskovski, for his involvement in the massacre at Ljuboten.

To put some of these war crimes into perspective, it is worth taking a look at some of the atrocities committed in Bosnia during the early nineties. There are over 40 indictments at The Hague for these attrocities including that of the massacre at Srebrenica, where thousands are alleged to be buried. Many hundreds of bodies have been found, but up to 20,000 remain missing from the whole war. There are 22 people missing from the Macedonian conflict, six ethnic Albanians and one Bulgarian national. Eight bodies have been found to date.

Despite the ceasefire agreement and the Ohrid Framework for peace, incidents between the Albanian community and the Macedonian authorities continued throughout 2002. The global war on terror made the authorities bolder in using harsher measures against suspected terrorists and this resulted in the deaths of seven Pakistanis and one Indian in spring 2002 when Macedonian authorities bungled an attempt to stop and search their car. The families claim that they were economic migrants on their way to take up construction work in Greece, but Macedonian authorities may be covering up a duff tip-off by counter-claiming that these men were mujaheddin who had come to join remnant Muslim Albanian rebels to bomb embassies in Skopje. Whatever the true story, the difficulty of carrying out a thorough investigation has frustrated the families and the international community, and shows how far Macedonia has to go before a transparent civil service with appropriate checks and balances is really in effect in this infant pluralist democracy.

Attempts to hold early parliamentary elections failed, and the number of armed incidents in the lead-up to the scheduled elections in September 2002 increased. By the time the elections came around, the electorate, disillusioned by the nationalist rhetoric of the VMRO-DPMNE coalition with the DPA and by the ineffectiveness of the unity government to move forward on the Ohrid Agreement, brought back the SDSM government of Branko Crvenkovski.

The SDSM rode to victory on the electoral promises of a speedy return to normality, the elimination of fraud and nepotism, and the claim that they had learnt from their previous mistakes and were now a more mature and experienced party, having been in opposition. However, not winning outright this time, the SDSM formed their government with the new party on the block, the Democratic Union for Integration, lead by the former rebel leader Ali Ahmeti, who had won the majority of votes from the Albanian community.

Moving forward

Since the formation of the new government, incidents between the Albanian community and the Macedonian authorities have decreased in severity and number, although tensions still exist over issues like war crimes allegations and the arrest of individuals connected with these. The international community is working hard to bring about serious reform of how the government effectively runs the country and in rooting out endemic problems of corruption and nepotism. On a global scale these are minor fry compared to Western Africa or South America, but if Macedonia wishes to join the EU and NATO, there is a long way to go. To this end the international community has pledged and is implementing over €500 million in aid to Macedonia since the end of the conflict.

As the country's situation improves (the economy improved 1.5% over inflation in June 2003) post-conflict agencies are moving out, or at least scaling down. NATOs forces under Operation Amber Fox, for instance, became Operation Allied Harmony from January to March 2003, whilst EU military forces prepared for their very first mission ever, Operation Concordia, which was deployed on March 31 2003. The security situation in Macedonia has now improved so much that on December 15 2003, Concordia was replaced by an EU police mission, Proxima, comprising only 200 mostly unarmed EU police. (Concordia had some 350 soldiers.) Since 15 December 2005, only a small 30-man police advisory team remains.

On the one hand these are good signs for Macedonia, but there are also fears that too early a withdrawal of or scale down by the international community could leave a vacuum for unresolved tensions to re-emerge. A number of events on the horizon could give rise to further tensions and community reaction to them will be indicators of how well rifts are healing and people are moving on.

One such indicator is the results of the 2002 census, that came out in December 2003. The Albanian community came to 25.17% according to the census, but there are some who believe their total should be no less than 29%. Although this discrepancy has yet to bring renewed conflict, the full effect of these figures has yet to be played out.

For example, the census results have been an important factor in determining the downsizing of Macedonia's unwieldy 123 municipalities to a more manageable system of 84. After local elections in March 2005, the government has been moving slowly towards decentralising power. So far this seems to be having the desired effect of some rejuvenation of local economy and may therefore bode well for the government in the 2006 parliamentary elections. Some fear that decentralisation will increase the opportunities for institutional corruption, which is already high at the central level. Some also fear that greater autonomy is in fact polarising the ethnicities rather than bringing them together.

The transition from one-party rule to a multi-party democracy has brought its usual share of problems to Macedonia, compounded by inter-ethnic problems and a lack of support from neighbouring countries. Some of the problems which Macedonia is still tackling range from the lack of a fully participating civil society, the lack of independence of state institutions and with that the lack of public faith in those institutions, the problems of transition from state to private ownership and an antiquated education system. Finally, the continued lack of an independent civil service able to keep the country running effectively whilst parties argue out their differences deprives the country of the continuity needed to keep moving forward, as if with each newly elected government the country's institutions have to start again from scratch.

Not to be confused with Greece

Before you picked up this book, how many of you knew about the independent (former Yugoslav) Republic of Macedonia? Probably not many, and if you ask your friends you'll find the same answer. At best, most people have heard of Macedonia connected with Greece, and I usually have to explain to friends and relatives that Macedonia is north of Greece. People get a fairly good idea then, but if I say south of Serbia many are still flummoxed.

Greece and Macedonia have had tenuous and delicate relations since time immemorial. Up to and including the time of Aleksandar of Macedon (the first, not the third), Macedonians were viewed by the Greeks as barbarians from the north, and they were not allowed to take part in the Olympics in Athens. Then his namesake, Aleksandar III of Macedon, conquered all of Greece along with Asia Minor, Iraq, Egypt, Persia and parts of India, and the Greeks have since claimed him as Alexander the Great. True he was born in Pella, now in northern Greece, but he moved his capital to Babylon, now in Iraq. He spoke Macedonian and learnt Greek. It is not for me to assert whether Macedonia is part of Greek history or whether it has a history of its own, or how much of that history belongs to the (former Yugoslav) Republic of Macedonia, independent since 1991, but I bet if we could conjure up old Alex now and ask him his nationality, I am sure he would not deny his Macedonian roots.

Not that most Greek historians would dispute that. What is in dispute is the use of the word 'Macedonia' in naming the country. When Yugoslavia named Vardar Macedonia the 'Socialist Republic of Macedonia' after World War II, Greece had enough to do fighting its own civil war and keeping out communism to worry too much about the name of a neighbouring country. But internally Greece continued its policy since the end of World War I of moving ethnic Greeks and Greek speakers into Aegean Macedonia and moving Macedonians out whilst surpressing the use of their language and traditions. In this way Greece could at least control from its side any irredentist wishes that the SRM might have for Aegean Macedonia.

However, when the Republic of Macedonia claimed itself as the independent 'nation state of the Macedonian people' writ large in its new constitution of 1991, this was too much for the Greeks, who feared an uprising in Aegean Macedonia and a desire by the two sides to rekindle long-lost dreams of the ancient royal dynasty of the Macedons. Newly independent Macedonia did not help matters by adopting the star of Vergina, formerly the flag of the ancient Macedonian kingdom, as their flag and stamping the star on their coins. Greece slammed a unilateral economic boycott on the fledgling state.

Fearing more troubles in the Balkans the international community worked hard for an interim solution, whereby the country's title as 'former Yugoslav Republic of Macedonia', or fYROM for short, would be used officially until a better name could be found. The flag was also changed to its present amended form and the coins were reissued without the star of Vergina. Although the boycott was lifted, relations remained sour, and many in Greece still refer to the state as simply Skopje.

In 2003, relations between the two states have started to improve. For the first time since World War II, visas have been granted to Macedonians who previously lived or had family on the Greek side of the border. Tearful reunions have abounded and in 2004 Greece opened a consular office in Bitola.

The dispute over the name had quietly fallen by the wayside in everyday relations until in 2004 a leaked document from the Council of Europe brought the issue back into the spotlight. Encouraged by new members of the EU and NATO, Macedonia is working away to have countries recognise it under its constitutional name, or even simply as Macedonia. Macedonia's 2003 bilateral agreement with the USA that Macedonia will not indict Americans in the newly established International Criminal Court is signed simply referring to Macedonia as 'Macedonia'.

Certainly in recent years, and with the European Union light at the end of the tunnel looming ever brighter, Macedonia has made no hint of irredentist claims towards Aegean Macedonia. And anyway, once in the EU, Macedonians on both sides of the border will have the opportunity to live together happily ever after. Of course, they will speak slightly different Macedonian, and the many inter-ethnic marriages which have taken place in the past century or so will have brought about an even less pure 'ethnic' Macedonian. But that will not have changed since inter-ethnic marriages in Aleksandar's time.

Macedonia and the European Union

On November 24 2000, at the Zagreb Summit, the EU extended the possibility of invitation into the EU to all the remaining states of the Federation of Yugoslavia (Slovenia had already been extended the invitation under the Europe Agreement early in the 1990s) and Albania. In order to be extended an invitation, each country must go through the Stabilisation and Association process (SAp) which has two stages.

The first stage occurs when the EU takes a look at the prospective member country to see what is needed to bring the country into line with EU standards of democracy and free trade. Once the country has shown its ability and willingness to reform key political, economic, military and legal institutions to integrate successfully into the EU, then the second stage Stability and Association Agreement (SAA) can be signed, which is the second stage of the process.

Macedonia was the first to achieve the second stage of the SAp with an SAA extended to it in April 2004. The country also sent its application to join the EU at that time. On 9 November 2005, Macedonia received a positive Opinion from the European Commission recommending that the country be given candidacy status. The European Council is likely to respond in agreement on 15 December 2005. The country will probably not get a start date for negotiations until almost 2007 as there are still a lot of conditions for the country to fulfil with regards to reforms in the judiciary, police, economy, decentralisation and combatting organised crime and corruption. In addition, the mood in Europe is not favourable towards enlargement, as illustrated by the French and Dutch 'no' votes to the proposed European constitution in 2005. The European Agency for Reconstruction, which has been in the country since June 2001, has poured significant funds into Macedonia to help bring its institutions towards European standards.

GOVERNMENT

The government system in Macedonia is a parliamentary democracy. Due to the infancy of Macedonia's democracy, political parties, electoral practices and the parliamentary system are in a fairly regular state of flux. The Ohrid Framework Agreement brought about some wide-reaching changes to the electoral system, which seem to have been successful in ensuring fairer and more transparent elections, but there are still many problems especially regarding appeals, establishing the results and the rights of non-resident citizens to vote.

The 1998 parliamentary elections saw a consolidation of the main contestants to eight political parties, but the conflict of 2001 brought about a more fractious political arena and doubled the number of main contenders. Political parties, and therefore government, are still very green to the political, economic and legal intricacies of successfully governing the country. As a result, and as a remnant from communist times, government institutions are not very open and transparent, and therefore engender little public faith. Macedonia's fledgling civil society has a long way to go to achieve full participation in local and national governance, and a paucity of dialogue between government and civil society does not help.

The current head of state, President Branko Crvenkovski, was elected in early presidential elections in April 2004 after the previous president, Boris Trajkovski, died tragically in a plane crash in February of that year. Turnout for the elections only narrowly achieved the 50% requirement, and a second-round run-off between the top two candidates still saw some voting irregularities, showing that many recommendations made to the country by international observers after the 2002 parliamentary elections have still not been executed. As Macedonia is a parliamentary democracy, the president holds little real power and is largely ceremonial. In Macedonia's volatile ethnic environment, however, the president can, and does, play an important role in inter-ethnic and inter-party negotiations.

Parliamentary elections are held every four years based on multi-district proportional representation. Registered parties or coalitions put forward closed candidate lists in six electoral districts in one round of votes. The six districts are a new innovation as a result of the Ohrid Framework Agreement in an attempt to more fairly represent minority numbers. In addition, the elimination of a second round of voting has helped to reduce political intimidation against election officials and the electorate. In former years, heavy-handed political parties would forcibly influence voters and those counting the vote to vote or count in their favour.

Parliament is a unicameral assembly (*sobranje* in Macedonian), which consists of 120 seats. Eighty-five of these seats are elected by popular vote, and the remaining 35 come from party lists divided among the parties according to the overall percentage of votes gained during the election. Since 2001 there is no threshold for winning a seat in parliament. As of 2002 the number of Assembly seats by party are as follows:

Together for Macedonia coalition (consisting of the Socialist Democratic Party of Macedonia (SDSM in Macedonian), Social Democratic Party and Liberal Democratic Party) 57
VMRO-DPMNE 11
VMRO-NARODNA 12
Democratic Union of Integration (DUI) 16
Democratic Party of Albanians 7
Party for Democratic Prosperity 2
National Democratic Party 1
Socialist Party of Macedonia 1
Independent Parliamentarians 4

The ruling coalition, comprising predominantly the SDSM and DUI, has the majority in Parliament and so can usually pass most legislation. Constitutional changes require a two-thirds majority, which means that the Government must compromise with the Opposition to pass such laws.

The head of government is currently Prime Minister Vlado Bučkovski, who is elected by majority vote by the Assembly, as is his cabinet, the Council of Ministers. Of the 17 cabinet posts, five are held by Albanians: Local Self-Government Minister, Economy Minister, Transport and Communications Minister, Agriculture Minister and Education Minister. One of the four Deputy PM posts is held by Musa Xhaferi, also an ethnic Albanian. Ethnic Albanians also hold a number of deputy minister posts, but these hold little real authority, as it is the state secretary of each ministry who actually holds the most authority after the minister.

All court judges are appointed by the Assembly. Although the court system in Macedonia is designed to be independent of politics, there is in fact still much overlap and little self-regulation. This is not helped by the fact that there is no independent protection for judges who do want to go against the political line. Serious reform is required not only amongst judges, but also to the court administration system and the legal system. The lack of outlets for alternative resolution means that the basic courts are so overwhelmed with minor traffic offences that serious murder and fraud cases can wait months for trial. There is also no enforcement system to deliver summons or to ensure that those summoned turn up to trial. As a result many cases are perpetually delayed because either the defendant or the prosecution, or even their lawyers, simply don't turn up to the hearing.

ECONOMY

Macedonia's economy is not in great shape. Already the poorhouse of Yugoslavia, Macedonia's economy deteriorated even further in the early nineties through the sanctions imposed on Serbia, a unilateral economic boycott levied against Macedonia by Greece, inimical relations with Bulgaria and minuscule trade relations with even poorer Albania. Although all these areas of trade relations have improved, the conflict of 2001 has not helped to alleviate the situation and like many post-communist countries, Macedonia is experiencing the brain drain so familiar when the country's young and educated, needed to revitalise the economy, leave for more prosperous jobs abroad.

In 2003 the number of unemployed registered in Macedonia was 32% of the working population, although surveys show that half of these do have part-time work of some nature, or work on the black market. Over 20% of the population lives in poverty (UNDP, 2004). Macedonia's currency, the denar, has remained fairly stable as it has been pegged to the Deutschemark and now the Euro since 1998. Inflation in 2004 was 0.5%, in part helped by depressed food prices.

Macedonia exports a number of raw materials such as iron and zinc, but it has very few exports from skilled labour or light industry, never mind anything high tech. Textile manufacturing had been developed during the 20th century but, although Macedonia continues to export some clothing, it has proved difficult to compete against the likes of China and India. Macedonia imports almost twice as much in dollar value than it exports.

Macedonia's natural metallic resources have included copper, gold, iron-ore, manganese, nickel, tungsten lead, silver, and zinc, but these are rapidly running out. Abundant for the building industry it also has granite, gypsum, lignite, siliceous and quartz sands, as well as marble for which there is a large quarry and factory near Prilep.

Being located so far south in Europe but with ample rivers and water resources Macedonia also grows large quantities of corn, grapes, peppers, rice, tobacco, tomatoes and wheat. Unfortunately, without suitable cooling houses to store this produce out of season, Macedonia's agricultural industry remains tied to the seasons. It has to sell far too cheap in the summer and has nothing to sell in the winter. In order to join the EU Macedonia will also have to start regulating produce size and quality, which will require expensive changes to agricultural practices and probably put small farms out of business.

Tobacco has been one of Macedonia's main exports, and you can see it drying almost everywhere, but especially in Prilep where Macedonia's main tobacco factory is located. In recent years though, with the trend towards producing less harmful cigarettes, Macedonia's heavy tar tobacco has become less popular.

Grapes on the other hand are on the rise as Macedonia's wines and liquors become more popular. The wine industry is poised to take off, and so now is a good time to get in if you want to try Macedonian wines whilst they are still inexpensive and unadulterated. For more information on Macedonia's wines including wine tours see page 216.

Much of Macedonia's farming is still done by hand, and although the industry is slowly becoming more mechanised, you will also see donkeys used for ploughing the fields and hauling crops. Land is terraced in many of the mountain areas and families and neighbours will resource labour during intensive planting and harvesting times. Macedonia is full of contrasts like that – one week you will see snow on the mountain tops, and the next week families are planting rice in the paddy fields.

Golden eagle

2 Geography and Climate

TOPOGRAPHY

Geographical Macedonia is bounded by the Šar and Osogovska Mountains to the north, Lake Ohrid and the Pindus Mountains to the west, the Rhodope Mountains to the east, and by Mount Olympus and the Aegean Sea to the south. This area was divided into four parts after the Berlin Treaty of 1878, and although Vardar Macedonia in particular may have changed hands several times since then, the division of the four parts has largely stayed the same. The four parts are now Vardar Macedonia in the northwest, Pirin Macedonia encompassing the Pirin Mountains in the northeast (now part of Bulgaria), Aegean Macedonia to the south as part of Greece, and a tiny sliver of land north and south of Debar and part of Lake Ohrid which now belong to Albania.

Vardar Macedonia, which is the land around the upper reaches of the River Vardar, is divided from Pirin Macedonia in the east by the peak of Mount Ruen and the Vlaina Mountains above the River Struma in Bulgaria. The mountain ranges of Kožuf and Nidže divide the northern Vardar region from the southern plains. This area is completely landlocked and is divided almost in half by the River Vardar which runs south to the Aegean Sea. Only the River Crni Drim, which starts in Lake Ohrid and ends in the Adriatic, and the Strumica, which drains into the Struma in Bulgaria, also lead to a sea port.

As is already evident, there are numerous small mountain ranges in Vardar Macedonia, and in fact 80% of the country is considered mountainous. This is due to the fact that three tectonic plates, African, Asian and European, meet in this region. It is mostly the work of the African plate sliding beneath the Eurasian plates under Greece that causes the geographic formation of Macedonia which we see today, and it is also the reason why there are frequent earthquakes in the region and many hot springs.

The friction between the plates has brought about a number of fault lines which run across Macedonia approximately along the course of river beds. The one under Kočani along the River Bregalnica contributed to the 1904 earthquake, and the Skopje faultline along the Vardar contributed to the 1963 earthquake which destroyed most of the city. The earliest well-recorded earthquake of the region was in AD518 when Heraclea was destroyed, and it is likely that earthquakes will continue for many more centuries to come. Scientists claim that these earthquakes are moving eastward in intensity, but with the recent earthquake of 2002 in Italy, this doesn't necessarily bode well for Macedonia.

There are eight well-developed hot springs in Vardar Macedonia and dozens more that are undeveloped. They have all been developed for medicinal purposes, although moves are afoot to open them up for recreational use. The medicinal qualities of the water depend on the mineral deposits beneath the spring which the water has been forced through in order to reach the surface. Yugoslavia put a lot of research into understanding the medicinal properties of these hot springs and Macedonian doctors will frequently prescribe a sojourn in a particular hot spring for its healing qualities.

The border of Vardar Macedonia shares three tectonic lakes, Ohrid, Prespa and Dojran, with it neighbours Albania and Greece. As their name implies, these lakes were formed millenia ago from movements in the tectonic plates. Lake Ohrid in particular is so old and the lifeforms in the lake so unique that it is comparable to Lake Baikal in Russia and Lake Titicaca in Peru/Bolivia, and it is under UNESCO protection. There are also ten manmade lakes, which were formed to create a hydro-electric production capability under Yugoslav Macedonia, and a number of glacial lakes high up in the mountains of the Baba, Jablanica and Šar ranges.

The longest river in Macedonia is the Vardar, which starts in the mountains above Gostivar and drains out at Thessaloniki in Greece. The Vardar collects 80% of the water run-out of Macedonia. The next longest rivers are the Bregalnica, and Crna, both of which empty into the Vardar.

The highest peak in Macedonia at 2,753m, Mount Korab, is on the border with Albania. The highest peak wholly within Macedonia is Titov Vrv at 2,748m in the Šar Planina range, which is surpassed in the former Yugoslav states only by Mount Triglav in Slovenia. The lowest point in Macedonia is where the River Vardar exits into Greece at 45m above sea level.

Years of communist neglect and a poor economy have done little to improve transportation lines within the country. The only railway line which presently runs through Macedonia is from Ljubljana to Thessaloniki. The line to Priština has been out of action since hostilities in the nineties, and the line to Greece via Bitola does not run trains beyond Bitola. The original line to Ohrid was not updated with the wider gauge rails beyond Kičevo and so stops there. The line from Kumanovo, planned to go to Bulgaria, stops 40km short of the border. A working passenger line runs from Veles to Kočani via Štip, but the side line from Prilep to Sopotnica is no longer working.

In line with preparation for EU entry, the European Agency for Reconstruction is pouring money into the main highways through Macedonia, so Motorway 1 (E75) along the Vardar, Motorway 2 from Kumanovo into Bulgaria and the E65 from Skopje through Tetovo, Gostivar and Kičevo to Ohrid and Bitola are in good condition, with dual carriageways on portions of those roads leading out of Skopje. Other roads are being improved such as the road to Prilep and Bitola, but most are in a bad state of repair and many fairly well-used roads are still mostly cobbled, such as from Strumica to Radoviš, the roads around Lake Prespa, and the roads on either side of Kočani. A great many villages in Macedonia are still only accessible by dirt track or goat path, although these tend to be way up in the mountains where village life is dying out (partially because of lack of accessibility).

ANCIENT ROADS IN MACEDONIA

The ancient Roman road of the Via Egnatia, Via Axios and the Diagonal Way, as well as numerous other smaller roads, all pass through the present-day Republic of Macedonia. The most famous, the Via Egnatia, connected Italy via the port of Durres in Albania to Elbasan and Ohrid, mostly along the River Shkumbin on the Albanian side. The Via Egnatia entered Macedonia near the village of Radožda on the western side of Lake Ohrid, then went around the north side of the lake to Ohrid and around the north side of the Galičica and Baba mountains to Heraclea near present-day Bitola. The road exited Vardar Macedonia via the ancient city of Lynk on the River Crna and then went on

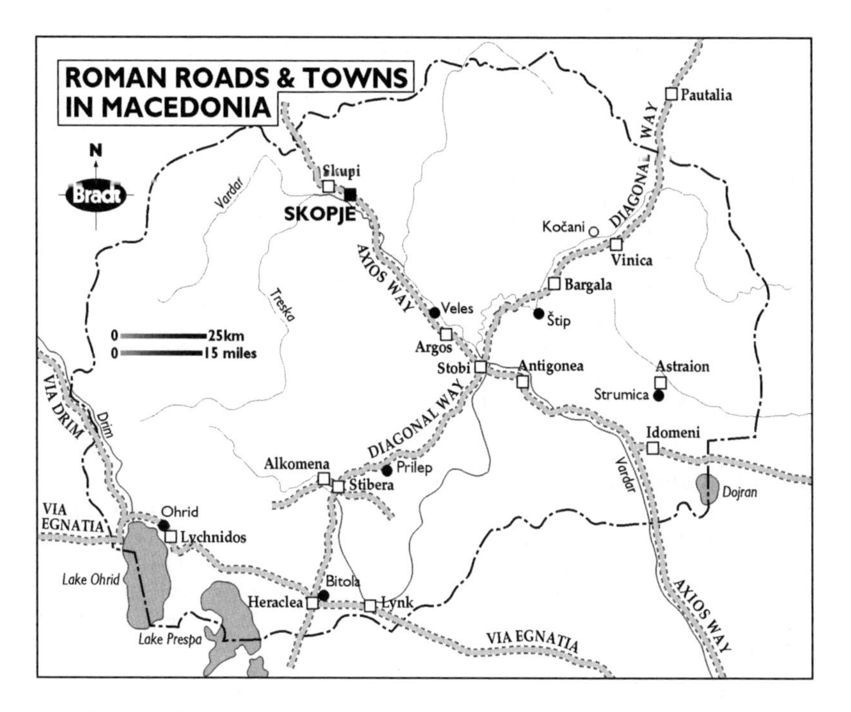

to Edessa, Pella and Thessaloniki, and eventually to Constantinople (today's Istanbul, *Carigrad* or Tsar's Town in Macedonian).

If any of the Roman surfaces still exist in Macedonia, they either remain buried or have been resurfaced. The most well-known section of the road in Macedonia is the cobbled section between Magarevo and Turnovo to the west of Bitola. This road was cobbled by French troops during World War I offensives. Some of this can still be seen but the remainder has since been tarmacked.

There are claims that sections of the Via Egnatia are visible between Oktiši and Gorna Belica at a stopping point called Vajtos, which is believed to be the eighth stopping point on the road. But this location would be a complete dogleg off the Radožda to Ohrid route and it is more likely that this section of ancient Roman road belonged to the road which followed the River Crni Drim from Enchelon (now Struga) via Debar to the mouth of the Crni Drim in present-day Albania.

The Diagonal Way linked Heraclea with Stibera, which lies halfway between Bitola and Prilep, with Stobi, Bargala near Štip and Pautalija (now Kustendil) in present-day Bulgaria. It was an important road linking the Vardar Valley with the Struma Valley (now in Bulgaria) and crossed other important roads along the way. At Stibera it met the road from the mining town of Demir Hisar which followed the River Crna. At Stobi it crossed the Via Axios (the ancient Greek name for the Vardar River) which ran along the Vardar, and at Bargala it crossed the road from Strumica to the Ovče Polje plains around Sveti Nikola.

OUTDOOR PURSUITS

Macedonia is a haven for the outdoor sports enthusiast. Its mountains and waterways and lack of paved roads make it a pleasure to hike and bike in, and offer countless opportunities for paragliding, climbing, caving and kayaking. The Macedonians themselves are keen outdoors people too, and so although there is little in the way of ready-made package outdoor holidays or even just a bit of information in English, there are plenty of clubs who welcome outside interest and some are even opening up courses and guided tours.

Hiking and mountaineering

This is by far the most popular outdoor sport in Macedonia and there are over 70 clubs to choose from, some of which are more active than others. You'll find somebody who speaks English at most of these clubs. A few of the clubs are listed here, and are mentioned in relevant sections throughout the guide. For a complete list of all the clubs contact Anela Stavrevska of Matka Climbing Club (see below).

Korab Mountaineering Club Tel: 070 712 573; email: contact@korab.org.mk, for club president Kotevski Ljubomir.
Pelister Mountaineering Club Ttel: 047 262 100 for club secretary Blagojče Lazarevski, based in Bitola.

Mountain hut system

Serving the needs of the clubs and individuals there is an extensive system of over 30 mountain huts in Macedonia. Most of these rarely require you to book ahead, offer clean sheets in a dormitory bed space, and cost around 300MKD for the night. This does not include food and most huts only offer small snacks and drinks, so bring your own food. Here is a list of most of the huts (called *planinarski dom* in Macedonian):

Outside Skopje

Karadžica (50 beds) Tel: 02 3112 199 ext 630; hut wardens: Atanas Ovnarski or Blagoja Petrusevska; location: 1,450m on Karadžica Mountain near the village of Aldinci, south of Dračevo.
Kitka (60 beds) Tel: 070 246 419, or 02 3117 100; hut warden: Sašo Popovski; location: 1,560m on Kitka Mountain near the village of Crvena Voda south of Dračevo.
Dare Džambaz (50 beds) Tel: 02 3234 365 or 02 3143 236; hut warden: Živko Temelkoski; location: 1,066m, peak of Mount Vodno, south of Skopje.
Matka (30 beds) Tel: 02 3052 655 or 02 3022 922; hut warden: Borče Danilovski; location: edge of Lake Matka, next to the church of St Andreja. Bus 60 goes hourly from anywhere on Boulevard Partizanska in Skopje to within 1km of the hut. 400MKD per person per night excluding breakfast.

Veles area

Breza (44 beds) Tel: 043 228 622; hut warden: Vasko Gjorjievski; location: on Mount Golešnica.
Čeples (60 beds) Tel: same contact details as Breza above; location: at 1,445m near the village of Nežilovo on Jakupica Mountain.
Maslodajna (30 beds) Tel: 043 221 110; hut warden: Mičo Kirov; location: near the village of Oreov Dol on Babuna Mountain.
Šeškovo (50 beds) Tel: 043 411 964 for Ljubčo Binor, the president of Mountaineering Club Orle who run the hut; hut warden: Momčilo Gjorgjevik; location: near the village of Šeškovo, southwest of Lake Tikveš and Kavadarci.

Strumica area

Ezero (20 beds) Tel: 034 325 282 for hut warden Krume, or 043 343 122 for Ilija or Lenče Končaliev of Mountaineering Club Ezero who run the hut; location: on Lake Vodoča near the village of Popčevo, southwest of Strumica.

Dedo Koljo Murtinski (8 beds) Tel: 034 347 409; hut warden: Gjorgje Krmzov; location: 1,160m on Belasica Mountain near Strumica.
Šarena Češma (16 beds) Contact details as for Dedo Koljo Murtinski above; location: 1,300m near Šarena springs on Belasica Mountain near Strumica.
Gorna (30 beds) Tel: 034 178 150; hut warden Slave Spasov; location: 1,420m on Pljačkovica Mountain near Radoviš.
Vrteška (64 beds) Tel: 032 393 044 or 032 384 788/299; hut warden: Marjan Ljubotenski; location: on Plačkovica Mountain.

Popova Šapka

Jelak (55 beds) Tel: 044 361 101 or contact Zoran Kostadinov on 02 308 6235; hut warden: Dragica Gjekikj; location: 1,750m north of Popova Šapka ski resort east of Tetovo.
Smreka (100 beds) Tel: 02 322 5958; hut warden: Duško Boskovski; location: ski resort of Popova Šapka.
Tri Vodi (60 beds) Tel: 044 397 680; hut warden: Stojce Krstevski; location: near the village of Tearce north of Tetovo.

Northeast

Kozjak (15 beds) Tel: 031 430 990; hut warden: Momšilo Jakimovski; location: near the village of Malotino, northeast of Kumanovo, towards Prohor Pčjinski.
Divlje (20 beds) Tel: 02 2781 686; hut warden: Mijalčo Nikolov; location: near the village of Divlje, east of Katlanovo.
Pojak Kalman (20 beds) Tel: 031 373 216; hut warden: Ljubisa Ivanovski; location: near the village of Dejlovce, northeast of Kumanovo, south of Mount Peren.
Toranica (15 beds) Tel: as above; hut warden: Stojko Velkovski; location: near the village of Kostur, east of Kriva Palanka.

Baba Mountain

Golemo Ezero (45 beds) Lies 600m below Pelister peak at 2,000m. To arrange an overnight stay contact Sterjov Zlatko, tel: 047 221 605 (afternoons only).
Kopanki (110 beds) 1,600m Mount Baba, tel: 047 222 384. 200MKD per person per night without breakfast, so bring your own food.

Gostivar-Kičevo

Tajmište (35 beds) Tel: 045 323 102; hut warden: Bosko Talevski; location: near the village of Tajmište, northwest of Zajas, Kičevo.
Treška (30 beds) Tel: 042 214 505; hut warden: Marjan Kuzmanovski; location: between the villages of Izvor and Drugovo, near Kičevo.
Sarski Vodi (8 beds) Tel: as above; hut warden: Gojko Gegovski; location: near the village of Gorno Jelovce, west of Gostivar.

Climbing

This is also a growing sport in Macedonia, and there are some truly excellent climbs to be had at Lake Matka and Demir Kapija amongst other places. Active clubs include:

Matka Climbing Club Tel: 02 2533 877, or 070 528 237 for club secretary Anela Stavrevska based in Skopje (for more information on the club see page 117).
Extreme Sport Climbing Club Tel: 02 2432 503 or 070 242 028 for club secretary Martin Trajkovski or 02 3111 460, 070 333 517 for club president Vladimir Trpovski both based in Skopje; email: shara@mpt.com.mk, or extremeclub@hotmail.com. The

club has an indoor climbing wall in Skopje in the basement of Kibo restaurant, and have put together the first Macedonian climbing guide to Lake Matka.

Issak Ruso Climbing Club Tel: 02 3123 026 or 070 617 821 for club secretary Dario, based in Skopje.

Everest Climbing Club Tel: 034 213 743 or 070 218 811 for club secretary Živko Murdžev based in Gevgelija.

Caving

Of all the outdoor sports, Macedonia is probably most well known outside Macedonia for its speleology or caving. Some of the underground caves are quite spectacular and very big, such as Alilica, Bela Voda, Dolna Duka, Krštelna, Ubavica and Slatinksi Izvor (page 161). For more information contact Ivan Žežovski of **Speleology Club Peoni**, tel: 02 2041 206 (answering machine) in Skopje, or Divna Žežovska on 070 265 677.

Paragliding

Paragliding is very popular in Macedonia, which is crammed with great sites to take off from, such as Mount Vodno outside Skopje, Popova Šapka above Tetovo, Kruševo, Strumica and Prilep. It is also relatively cheap to learn to fly here compared to clubs in western Europe. **Vertigo Club** will charge a mere €300 including loaning out equipment for you to learn to fly. Here are some clubs to choose from:

Vertigo Tel: 02 2778 319; email: vertigo@mt.net.mk for club president Sašo Smilevska based in Skopje. The club meets every Thursday evening at London Cafébar in Skopje. They can also sell you equipment.

Heli Club Narodna Tehnika, 1000 Skopje; tel: 02 2425 841

Extrema Naroden Front 21/4/5, 1000 Skopje; tel: 02 3126 202

Bufekal Struska 36, 1000 Skopje; tel: 02 3243 642

Diving

If you fancy exploring the tectonic edges of Lake Ohrid then get in contact with Ivan Mirkovski at **Korali Dive Club** (email: korali@mt.net.mk; web: www.korali.xmkd.com). The club also arranges dives along the rest of the Balkan Adriatic and in Greece. Lake Ohrid has a dramatic drop-off at its tectonic shelf, which is worth exploring, and there is also a sunken village, which can be accessed with special permission. Try also **Amfora Dive Centre** at the Hotel Granit in Ohrid; tel: 070 700 865; www.amfora.com.mk.

Kayaking

Once a big sport in Macedonia, this appears to be on the decline, perhaps due to the expense of equipment and the need to upkeep courses. Nevertheless, Macedonia offers numerous fantastic white water rapids and a number of competition courses including on the River Vardar in Skopje itself and at Lake Matka just outside Skopje. For more information contact the **Association of Kayak on Wild Waters Fans of Macedonia** (Rabotnički Sport Hall, 1000 Skopje; tel: 02 322 5234). The Rabotnički Sports Hall also houses the **Swimming Association of Macedonia** (tel: 02 3236 223) and the **Bicycling and Mountain Bike Association of Macedonia** (tel: 02 3236 305, also the number for the **Chess Association of Macedonia**). Mountain biking is also a growing sport in Macedonia, where there are literally thousands of off-road and dirt tracks. The best mountain bike shop in Macedonia if you need parts, service or a whole bike is Bikestop owned by Ljubče Kondev on Michael Sokov 6, tel: 02 3231 772; open 12.00–20.00 every day except Sunday.

CLIMATE

Macedonia has the full array of four seasons, although spring can be quite short, and each season is tempered by the altitude. So in the Vardar Valley, Ovče Polje and the lower Pelagonia plains, temperatures tend to be roasting hot in the summer and relatively mild in the winter. Skopjites tend to empty out of the capital during the hottest months of July and August, when temperatures can reach into the mid thirties. Further south on the Vardar, the small town of Demir Kapija regularly hits the record high of 40° Celcius. These summer highs are infrequently punctuated by summer storms, but they do occur especially above the mountains. On the whole, however, Macedonia has a relatively dry Mediterranean climate, so bring the lipsalve and plenty of moisturiser.

Although the winters are mild in these low areas of Macedonia, rarely getting below freezing, there are occasionally freak winters, such as in 2001–2 which saw Skopje come to a standstill when snow and ice blocked the roads and pavements. The mountains are, of course, much colder, and regularly see 70–100cm of snow. This makes for good skiing, limited only by the standard of facilities or a skier's own abilities to go off-piste. Regions above 2,000m will often see snow as late as June, and the peaks are certainly dusted with a light coat of snow by early November.

In the summer these mountainous regions are much cooler than the Vardar Valley floor, especially at night, and so many Macedonians escape to the mountains for the weekend where they might have a house. Favourite summer mountain retreats are Pelister National Park, Popova Šapka, Kriva Palanka, Berovo and Kruševo. Bitola, a mere 380m above Skopje, is usually a good 10–12° lower in temperature year round than Skopje.

Macedonia is generally dry and sunny, although September and April may see longer spells of cloud and rain. In general though, the weather is warm and sunny from March through to November and perfect for outdoor sports. October and November is when the mountain trees turn colour before they shed their leaves and this is the time to take a drive through the ravines of Mavrovo, the Radika, Treška, Babuna and Maleševo.

FLORA AND FAUNA

Due to Macedonia's location between the Mediterranean and Euro-Siberian regions, the variety of flora and fauna is extensive. During the seventies and eighties extensive research and records were made of all the animals and plants in the Yugoslav Federation. Since then, however, Macedonia has had few resources to spend on maintaining these records and so even approximate figures on how many of each type of animal there is in Macedonia are few and far between. Macedonia has worked jointly with other countries, such as Greece, to try to establish approximate numbers of wolves for instance, but more research needs to be done in order to confirm these figures.

There are eight protected species in Macedonia, among which is the brown bear. The last study done in 1997 assessed their figures at somewhere between 160–200, of which there were around 70 in Mavrovo National Park, 30 in Pelister, and only three or four in Galičica. Since brown-bear hunting became illegal in 1996, it is believed that the bear population is slowly increasing. Other

Brown bear

protected species include the lynx (depicted on the back of the five *denari* coin) of which there are around 120, and the jackal for which there are no available numbers.

Wolves on the other hand are not protected as they are considered a pest, preying on sheep and other farm livestock. Some 350 are killed every year, but their population remains stable at around 700. Because the government has decreased the amount paid for a wolf skin in recent years from 100DM to 10DM, it is assumed that the wolf population will increase.

The national parks and Jasen Forestry Reserve are home to many of the hunted species in Macedonia such as wolves, marten, wildboar, chamois, deer, and roebuck where their numbers are meant to be regulated through the use of an hunting licence system. Despite this, however, many of these animals are in decline. According to the Open Society Institute (www.soros.org.mk) most of the hunted animals' stocks have been reduced to less than 25% of their former numbers, and sightings are definitely not as common as they used to be. The deer population in some gaming areas is less than 7% of their former numbers.

Macedonia does have some poisonous insects and reptiles, including the *poskog* jumping snake and a few species of spiders. Like most wild creatures, these will run in the opposite direction of a human being if given enough chance to do so. Many types of lizards will be seen scurrying from footpaths as you walk through the mountains, and frogs are abundant at Lake Prespa. Mosquitoes are common in marshy areas in the lowlands, but these areas are few and far between. Watch out also for tortoises crossing the roads – these are as much of a hazard here as hedgehogs are in Great Britain. Fortunately, there are fewer cars here.

There are over 3,500 different plants in Macedonia. The variety in types of plants here is represented by Alpine flowers such as gentian and furry Alpine bluebell, all the way through to imported stocks of kiwi, pomegranates and rice, usually the preserve of more tropical climates. The great variety of flowers here also attracts an incredible number of different butterflies and moths. Look out particularly for the humming-bird hawk-moth, *Macroglossum stellatarum*, which is not commonly found in northern Europe.

Over 35% of the country is forested, the grand majority of which is deciduous. Less than 10% of Macedonia's forests are evergreen, but amongst that 10% is the Molika pine, which is unique to the greater Macedonia region, Bulgaria and Albania. In Macedonia the Molika pine is mostly found in Pelister National Park.

Macedonia's freshwater fish include carp, bream, catfish, barbell and perch. Dojran bleak, Strumica bleak, and Macedonian dace are some which are peculiar to Macedonia, as is the Dojran roach, *Ratilus ratilus dojrovensis*, and Ohrid trout, *Salma trutto letnica*. The latter are in decline and the increasing urbanisation of Lake Ohrid is endangering a number of different flora and fauna from the lake. Another type of Ohrid trout, *belvitsa*, is also served in restaurants. A July 2003 article from *The Guardian* highlights the declining numbers of Ohrid's trout, www.guardian.co.uk/international/story/0,3604,1007062,00.html. Fishing for Ohrid trout is now illegal.

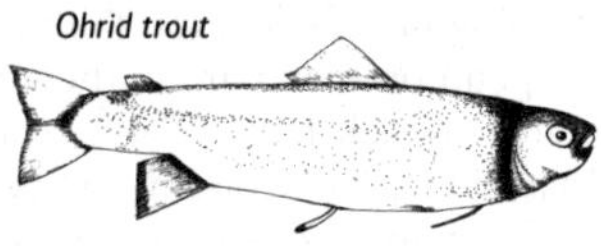
Ohrid trout

Eel is common in Macedonia and a favourite dish of the locals. The eel from Lake Ohrid used to spawn in the Sargasso Sea until dams were built along the Crni Drim River. It is not yet clear how this is affecting their population, but they still seem very abundant. Of the many small fish in Lake Ohrid, the *plašica* is the most famous, for its scales are used to make Ohrid pearls, using a painstakingly intricate technique fiercely guarded by the the artisans of Ohrid.

There are over 330 kinds of birds in Macedonia, and almost 100 migratory bird species which spend some of the year in Macedonia. Fifty-six of Macedonia's native birds are protected. Amongst those protected are vultures and eagles. Vultures were undergoing study during 2003, when there was estimated to be between 35–40 pairs of Griffin vultures, 40–60 pairs of Egyptian vultures, and only one solitary male bearded vulture and one male black vulture. Both these last birds lost their mates well over a decade ago, and as they are monogamous creatures it is extremely unlikely that they will find new mates. There are plans afoot to introduce new pairs of bearded and black vultures into the country, but once again resources to fund such initiatives are limited.

Although eagles used to be abundant in Macedonia, only a dozen or so pairs can be found now around Mount Korab and the Šar mountain range. Storks, both white and black, are also on the decline, but you will still see them nesting in a number of villages and towns. Macedonian folklore believes they bring luck especially with regard to childbearing.

Pelicans and cormorants are quite common and fishermen still use cormorants to catch fish on Lake Prespa. A wetland reserve at Ezerani is home to many of Macedonia's birds. Imported birds include peacocks, to be found at the monastery of Sveti Naum and at New Age Teahouse in Skopje, swans, introduced to Lake Ohrid in the early seventies, black turkeys at the Monastery of Zrze, and an ostrich farm near Strumica.

A number of hotels and travel agencies, such as Hotel Bistra in Mavrovo, Gorsko Oko Mountain Lodge in Pelister and Isidor Travels in Bitola can arrange hunting and wildlife observation trips by jeep if you are interested. Lake Dojran and Golem Grad Island in Prespa Lake are havens of water wildlife, insects and birds, and if you take a guided tour in one of the national parks, such as from the village of Brajčino, your guide will be able to show you the tracks and beds of many of the local animals. Bats can often be seen in the evening around many of Macedonia's caves such as at Leskoec, Matka and Treskavec.

If you just want a quick overview of Macedonia's wildlife then the Natural History Museum in Skopje houses everything (stuffed) in one convenient location. Although the museum is in desperate need of attention and a good English brochure, it is quite interesting and also houses the skeletons of prehistoric animals that used to roam through Macedonia. For the most current information on Macedonia's wildlife contact the Macedonian Ecology Society, email: mes@iunona.pmf.ukim.edu.mk.

ENVIRONMENTAL EFFORTS

For all its faults, the communist period of Macedonia's history had gone a long way, both deliberately and inadvertently, towards helping preserve Macedonia's rich wildlife and unspoilt natural environment. All three national parks, Pelister (1948), Galičica (1949) and Mavrovo (1958), were set up in this time, as well as Jasen Forestry Reserve (1958), and 48 natural monuments were designated for protection. Inadvertently, Macedonia's poor economy, low levels of tourism and lack of urbanisation has helped to preserve many areas of natural beauty.

Industrial pollution has been, and still is, a problem, as is the Macedonian disregard for litter, especially the non-biodegradeable kind. The Macedonians may try to blame the government for a lack of litter bins and nobody to take the litter away (which is true) but Macedonians don't help themselves. As every responsible hiker knows, if you pack it in with you, then pack it out with you, and get rid of your rubbish through the waste disposal service rather than leave it as an eyesore and health hazard. There are efforts underway by NGOs to move the government towards a policy of solid waste management, but it may be a few years before the effects of this is seen.

Macedonia does have some environmental groups which go back to the communist era of social awareness, and even more are springing up now in the wake of international money earmarked for building civil society and civil participation. Although these groups do good work, and go some way towards educating local communities about environmental concerns in their area, a nationwide effort really needs to be led by the government. At present, this is not particularly high on the government's agenda.

Believe it or not, recycling does exist in Macedonia, although it certainly doesn't come to the door, and won't even be in a nearby street. Newspaper and magazine recycling is the most ubiquitous, with large bell-like green drums in main streets in which you can slot papers and mags. These are picked up by Skopje's paper recycling company, Komuna (tel: 02 551 088) on Goce Delčev behind the Skopje Fair, open 08.00–14.00 every day. They also collect office paper and will supply special cardboard cartons for offices to do so. Cardboard is also recycled there, and when you see it being collected by people on the streets, you'll be glad to know that it is not for the homeless to build a cardboard house under a bridge, but to be sold to Komuna for recycling.

Whether you are living in or just visiting Macedonia, don't add to the garbage which is already here, but follow these simple ten points:

- Keep Macedonia Tidy.
- Reduce the amount you have to throw away, such as packaging.
- Re-use disposable items, such as bags, paper and containers.
- Recycle what you have to throw away.
- Keep Macedonia Tidy.
- If you pack it in, then pack it out.
- Take a bag (preferably cloth) with you to the shops, so that you don't have to keep taking new ones.
- Keep Macedonia Tidy.
- Buy recycled and biodegradable products.
- Keep Macedonia Tidy!

3 People and Culture

THE MACEDONIAN PEOPLE

La salade macedoine

The French rightly call a 'mixed salad' *une salade macedoine*. In fact anything mixed up is *macedoine*. A quick look at Macedonia's history will show you why (if you got this far without reading the first chapter then just take a look at the chronology on page 3 for a gallop through Macedonian history). Macedonia has been anything but a homogenous nation. Aside from various settlers in the Neolithic, Bronze and Iron ages, Macedonia has been invaded starting with the Romans by over a dozen tribes, races, empires and probably the odd Unidentified Flying Object. And those are just the ones that didn't stay. Then there are those who made a home in Macedonia and added spice to the salad.

This has largely to do with the fact that Macedonia lies on the crossroads of important trading routes across Europe. The Via Egnatia linking the Romans via the sea port of Durres in Albania to Constantinople in Byzantium brought Romans, Albanians, Gauls, Crusaders, Byzantines, Turks, Bulgarians, Roma and Greek tribes. The crossroads linking northern Europe with Greece brought Vlachs, numerous Slav tribes, Goths, Huns, Avars, more Serbs and more Greeks.

The question of Macedonian identity then is one that numerous PhD students have written about, and there are a plethora of books on the subject too. If you want a lively discussion in Macedonia, then ask about this topic, and you'll find that your interlocutor will furnish you with a complicated family tree as long as your arm, and each person's background will be different.

If Macedonians cannot agree on who they are then I could not possibly hope to write an accurate account of such a topic. Nevertheless, from a lay perspective, which is often at least simple, I shall give an overview of some of the aspects which have contributed to Macedonian identity, and some of the arguments which are out there at the beginning of the 21st century, some 7,000 years after mankind is believed to have first settled in Macedonia.

Neolithic settlers into Macedonia from 5000 to 2500BC are believed not to have spoken an Indo-European language, but by 2000BC Greek speakers were settling in the area. According to Herodotus, the Dorian tribe moved up into southwest Macedonia some time before the Trojan War, around 1200BC. There they became known as *Makedoni*. These may have moved on, but some remained to become and rule the kingdom of Macedonia.

The royal house of Macedon, which ruled in the millenium before Christ, has legendary origins from the Greek god of thunder, Zeus. In reality, they are likely to have been a tribe who migrated up from beyond the Greek islands, and became known as the ancient Paeons in legend. Descriptions of these people from the classics of Thucydides, Herodotus and Tacitus show that the Paeons were mostly mountain people, strong and quick, who when they were finally allowed into the Greek Olympics in 5BC, were apt to win.

When the Romans invaded in the 2nd century BC, they most certainly left their seed in Macedonia. The invaders from the north, however, Goths, Huns and Avars, seem to have left nothing behind, not even a village or a crop, but razed everything in their way.

The next most influential invasion was by the Slavic tribes from beyond the Carpathian Mountains. There are many of these tribes, tall and hardy, but those thought to have settled in northern Macedonian were the Bryzaks. They came believing in fairies and the moon and were gradually Christianised by the indigenous folk of Macedonia. They are allegedly also quite different Slavs from the Slavic tribes of Serbia and those of Bulgaria, although they all spoke a commonly rooted language.

The creation in AD862 by the monks Cyril and Methodius of a script for the Slavic language (Glagolithic, which was later superseded by Cyrillic) helped them to convert many Slavs to Christianity, and helped to formalise the language of numerous Slav tribes. Bulgarian and Macedonian tribes spoke a very similar language due to the influence of the Bulgarian Empire over Macedonia, and the influence of the Byzantine Empire over both Bulgaria and Macedonia.

Slav origins remain the base of the Macedonians today, despite Ottoman rule over Macedonia from 1392 to 1912. Although many Slavs converted to Islam they continued to speak Macedonian. It wasn't until the Serb annexation of northern Macedonia to the Kingdom of Serbs, Croats and Slovenes at the end of the Second Balkan War of 1913 that the Serb people and language started to gain a serious foothold in northern Macedonia. This was continued during communist Yugoslavia with the Serbification of the Macedonian language under Blažo Krstenovski, and the prominent influx of pro-Serb Yugoslav partisans into positions of power in the government.

A growing number of Macedonians prefer to see themselves and their country as a heterogenous mix of the rich tapestry that makes up this crossroads in the Balkans. As a result some prefer not to be called 'Slav' Macedonian as they are no longer purely Slav. Foreigners have always come their way, some bringing products and prosperity, others bringing domination and destruction. New Macedonia wants peace, prosperity and freedom from persecution in a civic-based society rather than to get hung up on ethnic terminology.

Today's Republic of Macedonia, although truncated from Aegean and Pirin (Bulgarian) Macedonia, has been independent for the longest period in Macedonia's history since Tsar Samoil ruled his Macedonian Empire for the 38 years from 976 to 1014. With the Hellenisation of Aegean Macedonia and the Serbification of Vardar Macedonia, these two parts along with Pirin Macedonia seem to have little in common to be worth fighting about, but plenty in common to be worth working together towards the goal of a common Europe. The only sliver of Macedonian life which is still a significant bone of contention is that of Albanian Macedonia.

Ethnic minorities in Macedonia today

Albanians

Believed to be descendents of the Illyrian tribes, Albanians have bordered on the northwest of Macedonia for millennia. They have a unique language which, although it has adopted many words over the centuries from Greek, Latin, Turkish and Italian, remains for the most part grammatically distinct and one of the oldest branches of the Indo-European linguistic tree.

Albanians only started to make serious inroads into northwest Macedonia and Kosovo, however, in the 17th century when Ottoman persecution of the native

Slav population emptied these areas of their inhabitants. During the Ottoman Empire, Albanians, once they were subjugated after the fall of the empire of Gjergj Skenderbey (see box, page 186), were largely loyal to the Ottoman *beys*. Most converted to Islam and were rewarded with new lands bordering Albania. Many also learnt the Ottoman élite language and schooled in Anatolia, later becoming *beys* in their own right.

However, when the Turkish nationalism of the Young Turks started to rise up at the beginning of the 20th century, Albanians in Macedonia, fearing repression from the encroaching Serbs, started to assemble themselves for their own cause. In 1912 at the end of the First Balkan War, Albania became an independent state and with it went a small slice of Macedonia which lay south and north of Debar.

Much of Macedonia's Albanian question is linked with the rise of nationalism in neighbouring Kosovo in the face of Serbian persecution, rather than with any significant desire to join Albania. Communist Macedonia did not help this perception and Albanians were almost as badly persecuted in Macedonia as they were in Kosovo. Fortunately, Serbian/Yugoslav persecution of ethnic Albanians in Macedonia does not go back the centuries that it does in Kosovo, and so there is hope yet that a civic-based state (rather than an attempt at a nation state, where minorities were supposedly equal with the dominant nationality of Macedonians), might work out for the Albanians in Macedonia.

Unfortunately, however, new Macedonia has inherited the discriminatory leftovers of the SRM, which have been compounded by the sudden curb on movement instigated by the erection of borders between the formerly borderless communist republics. So whereas ethnic Albanians used to be able to go to university in Priština in Kosovo to receive teaching in Albanian, suddenly they had no access to teaching in their own language. The number of schools where children could receive instruction in Albanian was also heavily reduced. Less than 5% of the police force were Albanian in a country where Albanians claimed they made up more than a third of the population, yet over 80% of prison inmates were from the Albanian community. Moreover, the 1991 constitution stressed the nationality of the Macedonians, with Albanians as equals, rather than that the new Macedonia was a home for a mix of ethnicities as it had been for many centuries.

Furthermore, disenfranchised from the emerging political process in the new pluralist republic, ethnic Albanians refused to take part in the referendum on independence, and in the census of 1991 which would have established their numbers, fearing that the manipulation of the figures by the government would be used against them. Instead the Albanian community carried out their own census of their population in 1992, and it is starting from this time that other Muslim groups in Macedonia, such as the Turks and the Torbeši (see below) have alleged that the Albanian community has pressured them to count themselves among the Albanian community in order to swell the numbers for their census.

The Ohrid Framework Agreement of August 2001 (see box, page 19) has made significant adjustments in these areas and has brought many more civic rights to the Albanian community. The Albanian community itself is now split as to whether they have won enough rights through the conflict or whether they should keep on fighting. Further battles have stuck so far to political turf and the census of 2002, which numbers the Albanian community at 25%, appears to have settled any disagreements about population numbers. Undoubtedly, however, the lure of EU membership in the years to come will prove to be a stabilising factor in relations among the communities.

Roma

The Roma are a numerous group of people who, along with their Sinti cousins, total almost nine million throughout Europe. They migrated from northwestern India between the 11th and 14th centuries as gypsy labourers, and although most have settled, many still live transient lives. In Macedonia the biggest settlement of Roma in the world, some 23,000 out of 54,000 in the country, have their home in Šuto Orizari, Skopje (see page 118). Along with other Roma communities throughout Macedonia the total Roma population is about 2.7% according to the 2002 census.

The Roma's origins from northwestern India are very obvious from their facial features and elaborate traditional dress. They are dark skinned, speak their own language originating from Sanskrit and have their own distinctive customs and traditions. They mix very little with the remainder of the Macedonian community and inter-ethnic marriages are extremely rare.

Part of the reason that they have not mixed with their host communities has traditionally been because of their transient lifestyles. In Macedonia in recent decades, however, this has not been the main attributive cause as many Roma have settled in the country. Rather, it is because of discrimination and a significant difference in lifestyle and outlook that the Roma have continued to keep to themselves.

Traditionally, the Roma have been skilled labourers in carpentry, copper and goldsmithing, leather upholstery, basket weaving, the repair of all these things and more. They are also skilled musicians and dancers. Their transient lifestyle has not led them to put much emphasis on formal education, and so as the 20th century has moved away from a product-based economy towards a service and technologically based economy, the Roma and their skills have been left behind. The move towards a throwaway society has not helped either, and so the Roma are largely left to manual labour and menial jobs or have taken to begging.

In Skopje you will see many of the Roma hawking clothes, hats and alarm clocks on the Stone Bridge, or plying the street with their boxes of cigarettes, tissues and chewing gum. They are also at traffic lights cleaning windscreens, or simply begging outright. There is an allegation that the Roma women drug their babies so that they appear ill and lethargic and then pinch the baby's ear in order to make it cry on demand. This strategy is designed to appeal to the sympathy of the potential donor. Roma will beg from Macedonians and foreigners alike.

Often you can also see a matriarchal figure order children to beg from potential clients as they come along the street. Suddenly a happy, laughing, playing child will turn on a sad face and start to beg. Occasionally, if they receive no alms they will get abusive and angry, not exactly a good sales technique, but understandable when they are likely to receive a clip around the ear from Mum for not returning with any money. Then they will return to playing a game of tag or jumping in the water fountain. It is questionable how much of the money they receive from begging ends up in their pockets or is taxed from a cartel which 'runs' the area.

The spiral of poverty that the Roma have found themselves in has lead to international efforts to try to bring them back up above the bread-line. The OSCE's High Commissioner for National Minorities, based in the Hague, does significant work in this regard throughout Europe, and a number of non-governmental international Roma networks have started up as the Roma themselves try to lift themsleves out of poverty. In Macedonia there are also a whole host of charities – for more information see *Giving Something Back* on page 85.

Donating to a charity which has long-term goals for the community as a whole has proved to be far more successful than putting money directly into a bottomless pit. Unfortunately, like most of those living on the bread-line of poverty or below, the Roma see little use for training in computers and sewing when what they really want is food and housing. Trying, therefore, to get past the initial stumbling block of teaching a man to fish rather than giving him the fish is still proving difficult.

Aromanians/Vlachs

The Aromanians (known as *Vlach* in Macedonian) arrived in Macedonia in Roman times from the 2nd century BC onwards. They are not related to the Romanians of Romania in language or ethnicity, although many did emigrate there over time. They have always spoken a Latin-based language and refer to themselves as Armãnji. There are a number of names for them, however: the word *vlach* comes from the Greek and, along with other derivatives, has a mostly derogatory meaning centred around 'idiot' or 'bleat'. The Greeks in fact call them *Koutzovlachs*, *koutzos* meaning 'lame' – connected to a story that the Aromanians refused to participate in the Greek wars by claiming to be lame in one leg! They are called *Ulah* in Turkish, *Tschobani* in Albanian and *Cincari* by the Serbs. *Cincari* denotes 'stingy' and is often confused with the Aromanian and Romanian word for 'five'.

The Vlachs have always been in the business of trade. Many did well out of sheep farming, and it is not difficult to suppose that they may have followed the Roman legions providing valuable trading in needed supplies. Certainly the main Vlach settlements in Macedonia are along the Via Egnatia, and their traditional villages, such as Maloviŝte, show a wealthy standard of living.

Although the Vlachs today are well integrated into Macedonia society, and now mostly live in the towns rather than in their old villages, many Vlachs can still be found at the fore of prosperous local businesses and hotels. They remain well educated, often speaking a number of languages and have a knack for figuring out good market niches.

Due to their relatively recent assimilation into Macedonian life it is difficult to assess the exact numbers of Vlachs, not least because many Vlach descendents may no longer consider themselves Vlach, but prefer in these times of possible ethnic segregation to call themselves simply 'Macedonian'. The 2002 census numbered Vlachs at less than 0.5% of the population.

Turks

After the demise of the Ottoman Empire and the withdrawal of the Ottoman élite, many Turks fled back to Turkey in the wake of widespread retaliation by the Serbs who replaced the Ottoman leaders. This policy of encouraging what can only be described as 'ethnic cleansing' was continued under communist Yugoslavia in the fifties and sixties through handshake deals with Turkey whereby anywhere between 80,000 and 150,000 'Turks' left Yugoslavia via Macedonia and Bulgaria for Turkey. Many were not in fact Turks at all nor did they speak Turkish, but were Albanians or Macedonian Muslims who took advantage of the offer to escape further persecution in Yugoslavia.

Ethnic minorities in Yugoslavia continually claimed different nationalities in order to avoid such persecution. So the number of Turks, Albanians or any other ethnic or religious group fell or rose according to whom was most in or out of favour with the authorities in the year of the census. Sadly this phenomenon has continued in the years since the independence of Macedonia (see above). At the last census of 2002, less than 4% of Macedonians declared themselves to be of Turkish descent.

OTTOMAN VERSUS TURKISH

It is important to note that the rulers of the Ottoman Empire were not necessarily Turkish. They were a ruling élite made up first and foremost of Muslims, and secondly of those who spoke Ottoman Turkish. As a result, Albanians such as Skenderbey (see box, page 187), and the Christian boys taken by the dervish orders of Islam under the devširme tax (see page 12) would become a part of the Ottoman élite who ruled the empire on learning Ottoman Turkish and converting to Islam.

Turks on the other hand were considered by the élite to be the uneducated masses of peasant Anatolia. It is from these masses that Ataturk rose up from within Anatolia against the Ottoman sultans and pashas to bring about modern Turkey. The masses spoke a different Turkish from that of the Ottomans of the *Osmanli* élite, which acted as a class barrier in everyday life.

Ottoman Turkish, however, was a language of convoluted court phrases, with words and grammar borrowed from Persian and Arabic for which the Arabic script was used. Arabic words stress the order of consonants as their distinguishing framework, and have little representation for short vowels. This does not suit other languages very well, such as the Turkish of the masses, Macedonian or Albanian. As a result, towns like Debar could be transliterated back out of Arabic script as any variety of spellings such as Diber, Dibrah or Debar, so long as d, b and r were in the same order. The Arabic script seen today above many mosque doorways and windows is therefore the script of Ottoman Turkish, and not related to the modern Latin-script based Turkish of today.

Other minorities

There are lots of other very small ethnic groups in Macedonia due to the nature of its geographical location. The next most significant group are the Serbs who were encouraged to settle in Macedonia when Vardar Macedonia became a part of the Kingdom of Serbs, Croats and Slovenes after World War I. Serbs made up 1.8% of the population in the 2002 census, but they do not form a particularly homogenous group as they are scattered throughout the country and are completely assimilated into Macedonian life.

Another minority sometimes singled out are the Muslims of Macedonian descent as opposed to Albanian or Turkish. These Muslim Macedonians are sometimes called *Torbeši*, although this is often seen as a derogatory term, and applies to Muslim Macedonians in Macedonia as well as those in Albania. The Albanians sometimes refer to Muslim Macedonians as *Pomaks* even though Macedonians might argue that this is a term reserved for Muslim Bulgarians who come from the Rhodope mountain region. Albanians have historically often seen the Bulgarians and Macedonians as one and the same.

LANGUAGE

There are two official languages in Macedonia, the Slavic-rooted Macedonian spoken by the majority of the country, and Albanian, which has equal status alongside Macedonian in municipal and government affairs where Albanian-speaking citizens make up 20% or more of the citizens in a particular municipality.

The Macedonian language is firmly based in the Slavic family of languages. Traditionally written in Cyrillic, it is occasionally found in Latin script especially in advertising. In past centuries it was closely related to Bulgarian and remains very similar in certain aspects of grammar and some vocabulary. Macedonians and Bulgarians can usually understand each other even if they can't speak the other's language. During World Wars I and II Bulgaria's short rule over Macedonia attempted to sway the Macedonian language back towards Bulgarian. When communist Yugoslavia won Macedonia, it set about reversing this and Serbifying the language. Today Macedonian is more similar to Serbian but has 31 letters instead of Serbian's 30 and four differing letters. Serbia is also now increasingly using the Latin script rather than Cyrillic.

The Macedonian brother-saints Kiril and Metodi, followed by saints Clement and Naum, invented and spread Cyrillic throughout Slavic-speaking countries (see *Religion*) from the 9th century onwards. Old church Slavonic is still the language and script used in sermon books today in Macedonia.

Albanian belongs to the Indo-European family of languages, but its roots, going back to the ancient language of the Illyrians, are some of the oldest and as a result its basic grammar and vocabulary resembles no other in the same family. Since its evolution in Albania, however, it has come under the influence particularly of Greek, Latin, and Italian, therefore you will find a lot of words which are similar to these neighbouring languages. There are also some Slav and Turkish words.

There are two main dialects in the Albanian language, *Gheg*, spoken in the north of Albania, Kosovo and northwestern Macedonia, and *Tosk*, spoken in southern Albania. Up to the 19th century, Albanian could still be written in five different alphabets. This made communication and learning difficult, and in 1908 at the Conference of Manastir (Bitola) the decision was made to try to unify the language under one alphabet and literary standard. The Latin alphabet was chosen to provide 36 letters.

It was not until the sixties and seventies that a standard literary form of Albanian was finally formalised. This standard form, which is taught throughout the Albanian-speaking world, consists mostly of the Tosk dialect and grammar, with some Gheg additions. The Albanian given here is the standard literary form. Because of these recent developments in the Albanian language, make sure you don't take your grandfather's World War II dictionary with you, as you'll find it more unhelpful than helpful!

Most young Macedonians below the age of 40 will speak at least a smattering of English and some are very fluent. Among older Macedonians and especially in the Albanian communities German is more likely to be the second language of choice. On the odd occasion when you will find explanatory literature at a historic site or church, it will probably be in French rather than English.

RELIGION

Today, most of Macedonia is either Orthodox Christian, or Sunni Muslim. There are some Roman Catholics, Evangelists, Jehovah Witnesses, *Bektaši* and a good smattering of agnostics and atheists. Despite Yugoslavia's efforts to keep the states secular and to discourage religious life, the downfall of communism has brought about a revival in religion which is now proving to be both a unifier within a community, and a separator of those communities within the state.

Many Macedonians have rallied around the Orthodox Church as a means of expressing their hard-won nationality, a trend that was inadvertently encouraged through the Ottoman millet system (see box, page 44). The rise of

THE MILLET SYSTEM OF GOVERNANCE AND ITS AFTERMATH

The Ottoman millet system, whereby people were classed according to religion rather than race, allowed Christianity to live effectively alongside Islam. For the Ottomans an élite ruling class was important, and so the Church's influence over its subjects was just as much an integral part of their rule over the empire as the Islamic faith was over its respective followers. Within each millet system, the Ottomans were just as likely to inflict havoc on the lower echelons of the Christian millet as they were on the Muslim millet or the Jewish millet. The corollary of this millet system was that several religion-based 'nation states' grew up alongside each other. In addition, political in-fighting within each millet system caused even further rivalry in the power vacuum left by the Ottomans following their demise, as played out in the desire of various factions of the Orthodox Church and their national leaders to 'rule' over Macedonia in the Balkan wars of 1912 and 1913.

Whereas the Jews were deported en masse during World War II to gas chambers such as those in Treblinka in Poland, many Muslims remained, and some believe even today that they should still be allowed free rein over their followers as in the millet days. The Orthodox Church, already disunited by national factions within the Church, more easily made the transition to the Westphalian nation state system, which upholds sovereignty and non-interference in internal affairs as the key pillars of government and international relations. Unfortunately, the Westphalian nation state system does not sit alongside the millet system so well, as a nation state must have complete jurisdiction over a geographical area, whereas the millet system allows for several separate jurisdictions to apply to different people within the same geographical area.

the Orthodox Church is most obvious by the increasing number of huge metal crosses lit up across the country, and the number of new churches being built despite the terrible state of the economy (a lot of this money comes from the Macedonian diaspora). Monasticism has also been injected with a new lease of life as of 1995, with the revivival and refurbishment of a great many monasteries in Macedonia.

Muslim Albanians have expressed their distress at the use of the Orthodox Church as a symbol of the Macedonian nation, and whilst this has fuelled the conflict between the Albanian community and the Macedonian authorities, Muslim Albanians have also retaliated with the construction of many new mosques. This has not helped matters, especially as non-Albanian Muslim numbers have been used to justify the need for new mosques, yet services are often only held in Albanian.

Both sides in the conflict of 2001 desecrated churches and mosques, which of course is a war crime under the Geneva Conventions.

At the end of the day, Christianity has had a longer foothold in Macedonia than Islam, which only came with the Ottomans at the end of the 14th century, and the fervour of the Orthodox Christians in those early years brought about the plethora of churches and monasteries to be found in Macedonia today. Although many churches were destroyed or built over by the Ottomans, even more mosques were destroyed by the Macedonians when the Ottomans finally left.

Due to the greater accessibility of Orthodox churches to the layman and traveller and due to the extensive history of the Orthodox Church in the region, I shall look more closely here at Orthodox Christian life in Macedonia.

History of the Orthodox Church in Macedonia

As written in Acts 16:9 of the New Testament of the Bible, Jesus' disciple Paul was called upon by the vision of the 'man of Macedonia' to spread the word of God along the River Vardar. His journey in the middle of the 1st century is detailed in Acts 16:10–17:15, but does not seem to refer to him making it as far as northern Macedonia. Timothy and Silas stayed on in Macedonia after Paul left, and they may have made greater inroads into the wilds of the upper Vardar. But by the 4th century, Macedonia had an established Christian Church under the Metropolitan of Skopje. Aside from written records elsewhere, early evidence of Christianity in northern Macedonia can be seen by the remains of the Christian basilica in the ancient town of Skupi outside Skopje.

When the Slav tribes came in the 7th century, they too were converted to Christianity. These newcomers brought with them the problem of how to teach the scriptures through a foreign language such as Greek or Latin. To alleviate this problem the Byzantine Emperor Michael III summoned the monks Cyril and Methodius (Kiril and Metodi in Macedonian), who were natives of Macedonia, to go forth and teach the scriptures to the Macedonians in their native language. This they did in the year 862 and to do so they created the Glagolitic and Cyrillic scripts, variations of which we are familiar with today.

Thus Byzantium increased its influence over Macedonia by using the Macedonian language to win over the Macedonians. Shortly afterwards, as Byzantium began to fall and Bulgaria was first made a state, Bulgaria continued this practice of exerting influence through the Church, but instead used the Macedonian language as a means to establish a new Church, the Bulgarian Patriarchate, with its sphere of influence away from the Greek Orthodox Church and the influence of Byzantium.

The Bulgarian Prince Boris ordained Clement in 893 as the first Macedonian Slav Bishop of the Bishopric of Velika (believed to be around the River Treška). Clement had been a disciple of Kiril and Metodi during their travels in Macedonia, and so had much influence in the land. His seat was at Ohrid, and he brought his fellow disciple from those travelling days, Father Naum, with him to Ohrid. There they set up the first Slavic monastery and school.

Later in 976, Tsar Samoil (see box, page 9), who had rebelled against Bulgarian authority and founded his own Macedonian empire, also founded his own Church, the autocephalous Ohrid Archdiocese, in order to bolster his own empire. But with the fall of Samoil in 1014, the Byzantine Emperor Basilius reduced the new archdiocese to a mere archbishopric.

Thus the Archbishopric of Ohrid remained for the next seven and a half centuries until in 1767 the Turkish Sultan Mustapha III gave in to Greek pressure and allowed the archbishopric of Ohrid to be dissolved, and even the eparchy of Ohrid was reshuffled to have its seat at Durres in present-day Albania, thereafter known as the Eparchy of Albania.

Thus after many centuries of a Macedonian Church centred around Ohrid, Greek influence suddenly came back into upper Macedonia. New churches built in upper Macedonia during this period of the late 18th century and 19th century show a lot of Greek influence and engravings, as do older churches which were renovated or refurbished during this time, and many of them were refurbished purely in order to secure the influence of the Greek Church.

During the Russo-Turkish wars of the late 19th and early 20th centuries, Russia granted Bulgaria its wish for orthodox influence over northern Macedonia. Bulgaria then lost out to the Serbs at the end of the Second Balkan War of 1913 and northern Macedonia fell under the influence of the Serbian Orthodox Church, long since separate from the Greek Orthodox Church.

It was not until March 1945 that the Archdiocese of Ohrid put forward a resolution to create an autonomous Macedonian Orthodox Church. The Serbian Orthodox Church, of course, refused. Thirteen more years of discussions ensued until finally, in 1958, the Serbian Orthodox Church gave in and the following year the Macedonian Orthodox Church gained its autonomy, although still under the Patriarch and canonical unity of the Serbian Church.

The Macedonian Church was still not happy, however, and after more heated debate, the Holy Synod of the Macedonian Orthodox Church proclaimed itself autocephalous and completely independent of the Serbian Orthodox Church on July 19, 1967, exactly two centuries after the Archbishopric of Ohrid had been dissolved by the Ottomans. The legality of this move under the respective constitutions of both the Macedonian and Serbian Orthodox churches is still a bone of contention between the two churches, and the Serbian Orthodox Church still doesn't recognise the independence of the Macedonian Orthodox Church.

ARTS AND LITERATURE

The arts in Macedonia, like its nationhood and politics, are extremely fractured and certainly during Ottoman times appear to have had as little chance to flourish as possible. Pre-20th-century art mostly took the form of church **frescos**, icons and woodcarvings of which there are a great many in Macedonia that are literally priceless and uninsurable.

Makarije Frckovski and the brothers Filipovski were famous in the early 19th century for their **iconstasis carvings**, such as the one in St Spas Church in Skopje, and the one in the Monastery of St Jovan Bigorski. Recently a tourist is alleged to have given the head priest there a blank cheque for the iconstasis. Aside from the fact that dedications to God cannot be bought at any price, the piece is irreplaceable and so it remains there today and hopefully forever.

Icons up until the 10th century were made of terracotta, such as those found in Vinica (see page 197) and many are now on view at the National Museum of Macedonia in Skopje. Thereafter they were generally paintings inlaid with silver and sometimes gold from the gold mine outside Radoviš. Most of these are still in their original churches, but some of the most important icons and frescos, rescued from centuries of neglect during the Ottoman Empire, have been saved and put on display in Skopje and Ohrid's galleries.

Modern art has taken hold of Macedonian artists in a big way, as if trying to catch up with centuries of artistic deprivation. The Museum of Contemporary Art, which was set up in 1964 after the disastrous earthquake in Skopje the year before, houses a permanent collection of modern art as well as frequent travelling exhibitions. The Museum of the City of Skopje (the old railway station) and the national galleries of Chifte Amam and Daut Pasha Amam, both former Turkish baths, also hold travelling exhibitions. Those living in Skopje will not have failed to notice the amount of modern art, alongside the compulsory icon or two, that adorns the walls of modern Skopje apartments. Today the works of Macedonians such as Iskra Dimitrova, Omer Kaleši and Ibrahim Bedi are beginning to travel the world.

Since Yugoslav times, and especially since independence, Macedonia has encouraged **art colonies** to grow and flourish. Ohrid is home to many

Macedonian artists and you will frequently see budding artists in Ohrid trying their hand at their representation of Ohrid life. The monasteries have also encouraged art, where the tranquility of monastic life is often conducive to artistic development. The Monastery of St Joakim Osogovski has a big art colony in August, as does the Monastery of St Petka in Velgošti near Ohrid.

Photography and photojournalism have strong pioneering roots in Macedonia going back to the early 19th-century days of the Manaki brothers (see page 148). Today exhibitions of the works of Alexander Kondev or Atanas Talevski can be found around Macedonia, and the works of Rumen Kamilov and Marko Georgievski can be seen in numerous magazines and articles about Macedonia.

The Manaki brothers also experimented in **film** back in the early 1900s, and Macedonia had a vibrant film-making industry during Yugoslav times. Unfortunately, the break-up of Yugoslavia put a dampener on the film industry for a while, when access to equipment shared with other republics in the Yugoslav Federation was cut off with the rise of borders and national agendas. In a recent turn of events, however, Milčo Mančevski's 1995 release of *Before the Rain* has brought life back into Macedonian film-making, which is continuing its revival with *Dust* (Mančevski, 2001), *The Great Water* (Ivo Trajkov, 2004, based on the book of the same name by Živko Cingo), *Soul Hunter* (Oliver Romevski, 2004), *Secret Book* (Vlado Cvetanovski, 2004), *How I Killed a Saint* (Teona Mitevski, 2004) and *Bal-Can-Can* (Darko Mitrevski, 2004).

For an interesting and thought-provoking insight into life in Macedonia, *Before the Rain* (available from Amazon.com) is an excellent introduction to modern Macedonia. *Dust* gives a view of early 20th-century Macedonia under the Ottoman Empire, and *The Great Water* and *Bal-Can-Can* promise to fill in the periods around World War II up to the present. *The Peacemaker*, featuring George Clooney, is designed to be a Hollywood blockbuster using the recent difficulties and porous nature of Macedonia's borders as an excuse for excessive violence beyond anything ever seen here in reality. Fortunately for English speakers visiting Macedonia, foreign films are usually given Macedonian subtitles rather than dubbed, so going to the cinema needn't be hard work if you don't speak Macedonian, and it is one of the reasons why so many young Macedonians speak such good English.

The soundtrack for these films has also injected life into Macedonian musical compositions by bands who combine traditional music with modern sounds such as Anastasia (*Before the Rain*) and DNO (*How I Killed a Saint*). Other popular new artists on the scene are Kiril Dzajkovski (*Dust, The Great Water*), Trifun Kostovski (Macedonian soul) and Toše Proeski (modern pop). Many of these new beats can be enjoyed in the summer at Skopje's outdoor nightclubs, such as the Coloseum, Element and Cabrio, where UK and US disc jockeys also regularly perform.

Unless you look out for these new sounds, however, you will find an overwhelming amount of **traditional Macedonian music** in restaurants and family gatherings all over Macedonia. This is an acquired taste and a must for traditional ceremonies where Macedonia's national dance, the *kola*, is compulsory for all participants. The *kola*, a circle of dancers holding hands, proceeds in an anticlockwise circle using a fairly basic set of steps. The *kola* appears to be quite a serious affair as I have yet to see anybody actually smile during the dance, although allegedly they are having fun.

Many of the bands hired for traditional functions and festivities are **Roma** bands (see page 40), and one of the songs almost invariably played is *Mjesečina*, meaning 'moonlight' by Goran Bregovič, made famous in the Yugoslav film *Underground* (Emir Kusturica, 1993). The Roma have a strong history of music making, immortalised in the songs of Esma Redzepova-Teodosievska, the queen of Roma music.

Skopje at least, and some of the other larger towns in Macedonia, has a small but thriving classical arts scene in music, ballet, opera, and drama, as well as modern drama in Macedonian and minority cultures. (See *Chapter 5* for more on when and where to see these attractions.) Often, venues and playlists are announced only a few days before the event, so you need to keep your eyes peeled for the information or log on to www.culture.in.mk regularly. Festivals and saints' days also have a big following in Macedonia. A list with approximate dates is covered in *Chapter 4*.

Macedonian **literary history** is also split into two sections. The spread of the Cyrillic and Slavic languages is very much connected to the saints Kiril, Metodi, Clement and Naum (see page 127) and the development of the Archbishopric of Ohrid. Ohrid's Museum of Slavonic Literacy is dedicated to the historiography of its development.

Whilst much of the rest of Europe underwent a great literary phase during the Renaissance, Macedonia was firmly under Ottoman and Greek repression. The 19th-century Miladinov brothers (see page 140) went a long way to cast off this dark period in Macedonian song, poetry, literature and literacy. A whole slew of authors and poets have appeared since then, most recently Živko Cingo, Radovan Pavlovski and Petre M Andreevski. The works of Božin Pavlovski, now living in Australia, are also available in English (see *Appendix 2* for titles).

Macedonian **architecture** goes back a long way, the earliest discoveries of which date back to the Bronze and Iron ages. During this era the ancient Paeons built fortresses out of huge limestone blocks, using a technique called Cyclopean masonry. No mortar was used, but the precise joints of the rocks and their huge size kept these contructions together for thousands of years. Very little of this architecture is visible today, although some remains can be found at Mariovo and Vajtos (see page 143).

Thereafter, Macedonian architecture is centred largely around the development of the Church, until the arrival of the Ottomans at the end of the 14th century when Turkish inns, baths, mosques and clock towers influenced the skylines of towns like Skopje and Bitola. During the 18th century the development of what has become known as the 'old style of Ohrid, with extended eaves, spacious and splendid, with two entrances' (Pavlovski, *The Red Hypocrite*) became common among the rich and influential, such as the Ottoman lords, monastery inns and wealthy traders. One of the finest examples of this type of house is the Robev residence, now the National Museum of Ohrid, but they can be seen all over Macedonia in various states of disrepair, desperate for renovation.

Sadly, the renovation is costly, and it is much easier for Macedonians to apply for 'reconstruction' money for new houses. To add to this disaster in town planning, many of the beautiful 19th-century buildings of the grand European style, which used to adorn most of central Skopje, collapsed during the earthquake of 1963. In the aftermath, the money donated by hundreds of international donors to rebuild Skopje was used to bring in the latest competitive craze in concrete creations, both communist and international, which are still to be seen today. A fine example of this is the main post office in Skopje next to the Stone Bridge.

CUISINE

Macedonian cuisine is a far cry from anything you might find in France, Malaysia, or even the nouveau English style of Jamie Oliver. Dishes here tend to be fairly simple, heavy on the palate and doused in oil, and if you don't like grilled meat then you'll have some difficulty making your way through Macedonia eating from the local restaurants.

Taking a break from Macedonian, or at best Italian cuisine, is even more difficult, if not impossible outside Skopje, and finding foreign ingredients like raisins, lemon grass, creamed coconut and Chinese five spice is almost impossible. Even ingredients that can be grown here, such as basil, are not easy to find nor available in forms like pesto. The lack of its own coastline and the difficulties with importing produce mean that good-quality fresh seafood is not easy to find in any large quantity in Macedonia, with the exception of a few restaurants in Skopje.

Nevertheless, Macedonia does have many dishes peculiar to the country and depending on your taste, these are of course all very tasty. Unfortunately, many of the better home-style dishes are difficult to find in restaurants.

The main fare of any Macedonian meal is either meat or freshwater fish. **Lamb** is the most expensive and therefore not often served in cheaper restaurants. It usually comes roasted either in the oven or on a spit, and served in a big chunk on your plate. You'll need to order a side dish to go with it unless you really do just want to eat a plateful of meat, and don't even think of mint being served with it. You might get some rosemary if you are lucky.

Otherwise the staple meat dish for most Macedonians is ***skara***. This is plain grilled pork or chicken, usually salted and basted, although rarely succulent, which has nothing to do with the cooking, but is probably due to the pureness of the meat without the additives, preservatives and e-numbers injected into most meat in the West. *Skara* is so popular that you can buy it from street stalls by the kilo!

Freshwater fish, either trout or carp (*krap* in Macedonian), is abundant in Macedonia. Ohrid is most famous for its *letnica* and *belvica* trout, and Dojran for its native carp. These particular fish varieties are peculiar to the lakes and cannot be found outside Maceodonia, and for this reason (among others) Ohrid is protected under UNESCO. Nevertheless, there are rumours that Ohrid trout up to 16kg in weight is being overfished (see www.guardian.co.uk/international/story/0,3604,1007062,00.html) and this is not helped on the Albanian side of the border by lakeside boys selling trout by the bucketful. You may, therefore, want to think twice before partaking too often of this famous and increasingly rare Ohrid dish. It is now illegal to fish for Ohrid trout, although you can still find it in some restaurants.

Veal, beef, eel, cordon bleu, stroganoff, liver, schnitzel and skewered kebabs are also prolific on the menu. *Kebapci* are also an extremely popular form of *skara*. They are a Balkan speciality of small sausage-shaped burger meat, well seasoned and very tasty with a beer and some good bread. Other popular traditional meat dishes are stuffed peppers, pork knee joint and *selsko meso* (village meat) which is a stew of different meats and sausages in an earthenware pot. With the influence of Italy, pizza is very common. I once saw an advertisement for a Macedonian pizzeria which said 'Italians invented them, Macedonians perfected them!' For those of you who have ever eaten a pizza in Naples, I'll let you decide that one. All I can say is, beware the tinned mushrooms.

If you are ever invited into a family home you will often be offered syruped and candied fruits and a glass of home-made ***liker*** or ***rakija*** (see box page 169) made from grapes. Macedonia's particular speciality is ***žolta*** (meaning literally 'yellow') which is *rakija* yellowed by the addition of extra wheat at a secondary fermenting stage. It is usually very strong, but often sipped rather than thrown back in one as *rakija* is in many other Balkan countries. *Mastika* is another Macedonian speciality liquor, which is remarkably similar to *ouzo*. If you stay to eat, the meal will start with salad, followed by a hearty soup, the main course and then a dessert.

Fresh salads in Macedonia, especially outside Skopje, are not very inventive. Your four main choices are: a green salad consisting of lettuce; a mixed salad consisting of cucumber, tomato, grated cabbage and carrot; a Šopska salad of cucumber, tomato and grated white goat's cheese; and Greek salad with more cucumber and tomato but with cubes of feta and maybe some olives. Vinaigrettes and salad dressings are almost unheard of, so don't expect a choice of thousand island dressing, blue cheese or ranch, or even salad cream. There might be olive oil and vinegar served alongside if you are lucky! Argula/roquette arrived in Skopje in the summer of 2003 and some of the Italian-style restaurants there are more adventurous with their salads and even serve balsamic vinegar.

On the plus side Macedonian cold cooked starters are fantastic. The most common are sweet grilled red peppers doused in garlic and oil (when they can be found in late summer), and Macedonian ***ordever*** (literally 'hors d'oeuvres', also known by the Turkish word *meze*), a tasty starter which can often make up a whole meal. The Macedonian *ordever* consists of a variety of cold 'creamed' vegetables, initially cooked till soft and then hand blended with herbs and spices, onions and garlic, and doused with not too much oil. Eaten with pizza bread, sarma (stuffed vine leaves), local cured ham, parmesan and a beer, it is a real delicacy.

The most famous of these *ordever* is ***ajvar***. This is made every autumn when red peppers are at their most abundant and the best, of course, is home-made. To be invited into a Macedonian home to make *ajvar* is quite a privilege, and will give you an idea of the meticulous preparation that must go into preparing this Macedonian speciality. Some say that to be invited to make *ajvar* is like being offered the possibility of citizenship. Once you have mastered its preparation, then you have the qualifications to become a Macedonian.

Without giving away the secret recipe, in essence the peppers must be softened so as to have their skins removed and then simmered for hours, whilst stirred constantly, in order that the peppers plus other added ingredients become a rough paste. The prepared *ajvar* is then sealed in jars for use throughout the coming year till the next pepper harvest. Macedonians will make *ajvar* by the vat-load, and family members will often come home from distant lands in order to partake in the occasion.

Other Macedonian specialities include: ***tavče gravče***, butter beans stewed in an earthenware pot; ***selsko meso***, a mixture of meats and sausage also braised in an earthenware pot; ***pastrmajlija***, a famous bread dough, pork and egg dish from Strumica; ***turlitava***, a vegetarian baked mix of local vegetables; and '**pies**'. These are not pies in the English sense with a shortcrust top and bottom and fruit or stewed meat in the middle, but a *burek* type affair consisting of layers of pastry or pancake interlaced with egg and cheese, or sometimes meat and the odd spring onion. Usually pretty stodgy.

There are also plenty of other Macedonian dishes that are usually cooked at home rather than served in restaurants as they are more labour intensive. These include: ***juvki***, a semolina-based pancake which is allowed to dry crisp before being broken and re-cooked with milk and water for breakfast or lunch; ***sirden***, which as near as I can tell is the Macedonian equivalent of haggis; and ***pača*** (brawn), made from the boiled meat of a pig's head or knuckles, fried with onions and herbs, and served cold in slices.

Macedonian **desserts**, if you still have room by the time you have eaten your hearty soup, *skara* by the kilo served with fried chips and several glasses of Macedonian wine, are few and mostly borrowed from other cultures, such as pancakes, *baklava*, fresh fruit and ice cream. *Ravanija* and *gurabii* are two types of cake which you may get served in a Macedonian house, but rarely in a restaurant. A *seksi salad* under the dessert menu for those of you wanting to be spared the embarrassment on delivery, is a peeled banana, uncut, stuck upright next to a couple of balls of ice-cream and sprinkled with nuts! For more on Macedonian wines see page 216.

The art of **breakfast** has not really arrived in Macedonia yet, although Tivoli's in Tetovo does serve omelettes and Mečo's, next to Zlaten Pat Chinese restaurant on Leninova in Skopje, has three cooked-breakfast choices before midday everyday. Breakfast for Macedonians consists of a strong coffee before work possibly with bread and cheese or jam, and at the weekends *juvki* or *tarama* (a cereal-based baked dish), then a break at around ten for a sesame bread ring and plain drinking yogurt before settling down for a long lunch around 14.00. Kelloggs or Nestlé cereals do exist in the supermarkets, but are rarely served in hotels. It is wise to make sure you have breakfast included in your hotel bill, or buy something in, as you'll find few places on the streets that will serve you anything to eat. And beware the hot chocolate – it is often a warm chocolate mousse served in a cup!

Otherwise the preferred **drink** in Macedonia is coffee. Either the strong Turkish variety which is a challenge to drink without sugar, served in espresso-size cups, or the usual cappucinos, machiattos and espressos. Turkish tea, served in small glasses, is popular in the Albanian parts of town, and you'll sometimes see servers on bicycles or rollerblades carrying trays of them through the streets to customers. Fruit tea is usually considered a drink for the sick, but don't be deterred! Macedonia has lots of fruit teas (*ovočen čaj*) and mint tea (*čaj od nane*), and their mountain tea (*planinski čaj*) is a refreshing drink served in all the mountain huts and many restaurants. *Majčina dušica* (mother's little soul) tea is also a very popular mountain herbal tea. *Salep*, a drink made of ground wild orchid root and hot milk, is of Turkish origin and usually served with a sprinkling of ground cinnamon. You won't find it everywhere, but it's very tasty and warming on a cold winter's day.

Macedonian sheepdog, šarplaninec

Practical Information

4

WHEN TO VISIT

Located so far south in Europe, Macedonia is great to visit most of the year round. It is particularly welcoming during spring and autumn outside the high tourist seasons and when the weather is at its most pleasant. Here are the main highlights of Macedonia month by month:

January

Macedonia is at its coldest this month, and the snow is at its freshest. Skiing in Macedonia is very cheap, as little as 700MKD per day, and facilities are improving every year. This is also the month that Orthodox Christians celebrate Christmas, and Muslims celebrate Eid-al-Adha. Vevčani has its big Twelfthtide carnival on January 13 and 14, and of course there is New Year's Day itself.

February

The snow is still great for skiing at this time of year and the weather is also beginning to warm up. February 14 is the Day of St Triphun, the patron saint of wines and vineyards, and is increasingly celebrated with Macedonia's excellent wines.

March

By this time of year Macedonia is sunny and warm during the day and still cool in the evening. There is still some skiing to be had, but hiking and other outdoor pursuits are beginning to come into their own.

April

Spring is taking full effect by April and everything is green again. Surprisingly hot spells of weather make a welcome change from winter, but there are extended periods of showers. April 1 is celebrated in fancy dress.

May

A truly magnificent month in Macedonia filled with fields of bright red poppies and trays of fresh strawberries sold along the roadside. It can get into the high 20sC during the day, but the evenings are often still cool enough for a light jacket, especially in the mountains. Another great month for all the outdoor pursuits.

June

A month for cherries and wild flowers and the first dips in Macedonia's many lakes. Paragliding takes off on all the mountain outcrops at Vodno, Ohrid, Prilep, Kruševo, Bitola and Štip, as the warm currents really start to swirl up from the valley floors.

July

This is when Macedonia hits its hottest time of the year, and it is also when Macedonians themselves will be crowding the lakes and other tourist spots. Hotel spaces are therefore at a premium and it is advisable to book several weeks ahead. Get to Galičnik to see the national wedding festival if you can.

August

Festival month in Ohrid, Bitola, Strumica and Kruševo. August 2 is a national holiday celebrating the Ilinden uprising of 1903 when the Macedonians rebelled against Ottoman rule. Government goes on holiday during the second week of August, as do a lot of other Macedonians, so Skopje is practically empty, but Ohrid is bursting its seams.

September

A month of grapes by the vine-load and the very youngest wines. You'll see all and sundry from the roadside collecting car-loads of grapes, from the wizened old farmer with his donkey and cart to the young policeman in his Lada policewagon. From here on in is the time to visit the vineyards of Bovin, Čekorov, Fonko, Ezemit, Skovin and Tikveš to name a few, and discover the best of Macedonia's little known wines. By this time of year the local tourists are thinning out, although weekends can still be busy. The weather is no longer the scorching sun of July and August, but definitely still T-shirt weather. This time of year is once again very pleasant for outdoor pursuits.

October

This is one of the finest months of the year for visiting Macedonia, especially for touring round the country. The weather is still warm during the day, and as autumn takes hold of the trees the woods burst alive with startling reds, yellows and oranges. This is a fantastic month for hiking, wine-tasting and taking dramatic photos of Macedonia's mountainous scenery. October also sees the Jazz Festival in Skopje, where you can see the likes of Manu Chao, Omara Portuondo, and Natalie Imbruglia for as little as €20.

November

Still a very pleasant month to visit Macedonia. The sun is bright and brings warmth to the skin, but atop the mountains fresh snow glistens, beckoning hikers to their first winter walk and exciting skiers for the months to come.

December

Winter has definitely settled in by December. The trees are bare and snow is on all the mountains and sometimes a metre deep in the towns. Despite the shortening hours of daylight, the local Christmas market brightens most towns, and so this is a good time to buy local crafts and handiwork. Steaming cups of mulled wine at local stalls keep the cold at bay and bring a rosy tint to any cheek.

HIGHLIGHTS/SUGGESTED ITINERARIES

Scenic

The lake and town of Ohrid (see page 125) are seen as the jewel of Macedonia's scenic crown. And it is not without reason that Ohrid's medieval architecture and pristine natural setting are preserved by UNESCO as a place of historic, cultural and scenic significance. Outside the height of the summer season it remains a wonderful little getaway spot, and should not be missed on any trip to

Macedonia. The back route from Skopje through Debar to Struga and on to Ohrid is worth the extra time.

All three of **Macedonia's national parks**, Pellister, Mavrovo and Galičica, offer a plethora of hiking trails and beautiful scenic drives. The one hike not to miss though is the 10km hike from Mount Vodno just outside Skopje down to Lake Matka (see page 116), which also offers rock climbing, caving, camping, kayaking and yet more scenic hikes to local monasteries and beyond. A shorter but equally stunning hike is the 5km hike from Janče to the cliffside village of Galičnik (see page 183).

Architecture and historical culture

Other spots though, which are equally stunning and unique to Macedonia and which are much less well-known, are the 16th-century villages of the Macedonian minorities. **Galičnik** village hangs on the edge of a deep ravine and by car/public transport can only be accessed from the Mavrovo Lake side over the plateau of Galičnik National Park. Every July, as in days of old, the local men who have gone away to work, return to Galičnik to marry their beloved. The ritual continues today and is a festive occasion open to all.

Malovište village, located in Pellister National Park, is an old Vlach village, formerly housing rich Vlach traders. It is now being renovated to preserve its heritage and is a beautiful example of the rich variety of Macedonian culture. There are hundreds of other fine old villages off the beaten track which have yet to be fully discovered and you'll find that taking a trip away from your main route will always reap an enlightening reward.

Macedonia's **Turkish history** is well worth looking into, and is best preserved in Skopje's old town, *Čaršija*. See *Chapter 5* for details of the old trading inns of Suli An, Kapan An and Kuršumli An, the bath houses of Chifte Amam and Daut Pasha Amam, and the mosques of Mustafa Pasha and Sultan Murat.

Spiritual inns

A trip to Macedonia would not be complete without at least visiting one monastery for its intricate woodwork and magnificent architecture and for some of their remote but beautiful locations. The country boasted over a thousand churches and monasteries at the zenith of Orthodox ministry in the region during the 14th to 16th centuries. Ohrid was the centre of the Orthodox Church at the time and still has over 200 churches and monasteries overlooking its shores. Some of the most spectacular working monasteries to visit are St Joachim Osogovski (page 205) near Kriva Palanki; St Jovan Bigorski (page 205), near Debar; Treskavec Monastery (page 157) near Prilep; St Gavril Lesnovski near Kratovo (page 207), Kališta Monastery (page 144) for its nearby cave churches looking over Lake Ohrid; and Zrze Monastery (page 160) set high on a cliff.

All these spiritual inns are covered in greater detail in the relevant chapters of this guidebook. For those who want to make churches and monasteries the theme of their visit, here are some further suggestions: the Monastery of St Naum (page 136) on Lake Ohrid, the women's monastery of Jankovec (page 166) near Resen, the Monastery of St Leonthius (page 214) near Vodoča village, the women's Monastery of Eleusa (page 214) in Veljusa village, the Monastery of the Archangel Michael (page 157) in Varoš, Prilep, the women's Monastery of St George (page 187) in Debar, the church of St Spas (page 108) in Skopje, the Church of St George (page 139) in Struga, the cave Church of Archangel Michael (page 144) in Radožda on Lake Ohrid, the Christian basilicas in

Heraclea (page 153), Oktisi (page 143) and Plaošnik (page 133) for its early Christian mosaics, and of course all the churches listed in the chapter on Ohrid (page 133).

An additional score of must-sees and must-dos

Aside from the outdoors, architecture and monasteries, here is a more eclectic list of Macedonian highlights.

- Ascend to the towers of King Marko in Prilep for a 360° view of the Pelagonia plains (page 156).
- Hike and climb (both traditional and bolted routes) around the stunning Lake Matka, then eat in the tiny cave restaurant of Manastirska Pestera (page 116).
- Bath in the original Turkish baths at Bansko near Strumica, and see the progress of the restoration of the neighbouring Roman baths (page 215).
- Visit Kruševo (page 161), the capital of the ten-day Republic of Kruševo in 1903 where one of the most successful Macedonian revolutions against the Ottoman Empire took place, to see some of the best-preserved architecture from the 18th and 19th centuries.
- Eat traditional Macedonian *ordever*, a selection of prepared creamed vegetable and cheese hors d'oeuvres, with tasty pizza bread and the local beer, Skopsko.
- With over 30 mountain huts (page 30) and over a hundred peaks of 2,000m and higher to choose from, both low-level hiking and more challenging mountaineering is available for a range of abilities.
- Taste a variety of trout unique to Macedonia, such as *letnica* and *belvica*, or eat some of the most smooth-tasting carp in the world from Lake Doijran.
- Visit the old Turkish trading inns, mosques and Bit Pazar market in Skopje's old town (page 111).
- Marvel at the Motley Mosque in Tetovo, beautifully painted on the outside resembling a house of cards (page 179).
- Cast yourself back to Roman times in the barely uncovered ruins of Heraclea and Stobi, and stop at the local vineyards on the way.
- Ski at Popova Šapka, Mavrovo, Kruševo or Pellister, and relax afterwards with a massage and a choice of local grills.
- Ride Lipizaner horses, famous for their dressage at the Spanish riding school in Vienna, at the El Kabon stables, and eat in their famous Cherry Orchard restaurant featured in the Macedonian film *Dust* (page 103).
- Eat at the Monastery of St Pantelejmon with stunning views overlooking the Vardar Valley (page 118).
- Learn to paraglide for a mere €300 with Club Vertigo, Bufekal or Extrema over the mountains of Vodno and Kruševo, or the lakes of Ohrid and Matka (page 32).
- Visit the Dervish Baba Arabati Teke spiritual inn in Tetovo (page 179).
- Hike from Demir Kapija Iron Gate ravine along the stream bed to the mountain villages of Čelevec, Iberlija and Košarka (page 219).
- Stay at the Monastery of St Petka in the old trading village of Brajčino, centre of eco-tourism in Pellister National Park (page 170).
- Visit the market of the largest Roma settlement in the world, a settlement of gypsies heralding several hundred years ago from northwestern India (page 118).
- Go caving in over 200 underground caves, such as Slatinksi Izvor, Bela Voda, Ubavica and Alilica (page 32).

- Visit the village of Kratovo, situated around an old volcanic crater (page 207).

And much more: summer festivals, kayaking, local art galleries, fishing, hunting, Christmas fairs, village saint's days, glacial lakes, mountain biking, spit roast lamb…

TOUR OPERATORS

There are very few tour operators outside Macedonia who can book your ticket and hotel and make up an itinerary for you, so you really are pretty much on your own. In the UK, **Regent Holidays** (15 John Street, Bristol BS1 2HR; tel: 0117 9211 711; fax: 0117 925 4866; web: www.regent-holidays.co.uk) has recently started to book accommodation in Macedonia. **Explore**, based in Aldershot (tel: 01252 760 200; fax: 01252 760 201; web: www.explore.co.uk) have just started adventure package tours. Macedonia's tourist industry is at a very adolescent stage in its development. There is international expertise at hand, but for the time being there are almost a dozen tourist associations in Macedonia, without a single one that covers the whole country, never mind one that presents a united front to prospective visitors.

There are plenty of travel agents once you are in Macedonia, although they are sometimes limited in what they can do, as they are not used to holidaymakers who go off the beaten track. They will happily book accommodation for you, sometimes even into a monastery, and they'll manage to sort out travel arrangements and tour guides. Most travel agents will go out of their way if they are dealing with groups, but they are less likely to go out on a limb for individuals. The **Association of Tourist Guides**, tel: 02 3118 498; fax: 02 3230 803; address: Dame Gruev, Block 3, Skopje, can also help with guides. To arrange outdoor sports activities get in touch with the clubs themselves as listed in *Chapter 2*.

Marco Polo Tours Trgovski Centar, First Floor, Skopje; tel: 02 3133 233; email: info@markopolo.com; web: www.markopolo.com. Marco Polo pride themselves on providing more for foreign tourists than any other agency in Macedonia. They are also expanding into wine tours.

Savana 27th Mart 7, Skopje; tel: 02 3115 825; fax: 02 3114 206; email: savana@savana.com.mk; web: www.savana.com.mk. Savana has a good website on Macedonia in English and will even book your accommodation in a monastery.

Atlantis Mito Hadži Vaslilev 22, kula 10, Skopje; tel: 02 322 9922; email: atlantis@mt.net.mk or info@atlantismk.com; web: www.atlantismk.com. This chain travel agency also has branches in Strumica, Radoviš and Delčevo, and provides FedEx services.

Tuymada Dame Gruev 16-2/14, DC Paloma Bjanka, Skopje (in the same building as Kibo Restaurant); tel: 02 312 0255 or 02 3211 3755; fax: 02 3213 8382; email: tujmada@yahoo.com. Offers monastery tours but overnight stays are in nearby hotels. Has good rental car rates.

Isidor Travel Solunska 111-d, 7000 Bitola; tel: 047 220 204; email: isidor@mt.net.mk. Run by a friendly Vlach family (see page 152) this agency has expanded links into Greece and eco-tourism. Within Pelagonia Isidor Tours can set up your travel, accommodation, outdoor pursuits, monastery tours, and wine tours in the Tikveš region. They will also organise visas to other countries as well as international travel.

RED TAPE

Members of the European Union, Switzerland, New Zealand and the USA do not need visas at present for stays of less than three months, and it is so easy to get over the border to get a new stamp in your passport that it is not worth applying for an extension if you want to stay longer. For an up-to-date check on which countries do require visas, visit the website of the Ministry of Foreign Affairs www.mnr.gov.mk/consular/vizaEN.htm. In 2003, for instance, Macedonia revoked the 90-day visa waiver for Australians, much to the annoyance of Australians in the country who suddenly found themselves without the correct legal papers to stay in the country. Canadians have had to apply for visas since Canada also revoked visa waivers for Macedonians in 2001.

Macedonian embassies abroad

For a full and up-to-date list of Macedonian embassies abroad see www.faq.macedonia.org/travel/mac.dipl.missions.abroad.html.

Austria Botschaftskanzlei, Kaiserstrasse 84/Stg. 1/top 5, A-1070 Wien, Austria; tel: +43 1 524 8757/8756; fax: +43 1 524 8753. Visa section: Konsularabteilung, Walfischgasse 8/20 , A-1010 Wien, Austria; tel: +43 1 512 8510; fax: +43 1 512 8512
Australia Perpetual Building, Suite 2:05,10 Rudd Street, Canberra ACT 2600, Australia; tel: +61 2 6249 8000; fax: +61 2 6249 8088
Canada 130 Albert St, Ottawa, ON K1P 5G4, Canada; tel: +1 613 234 3882; fax: +1 613 233 1852; email: emb.macedonia.ottawa@sympatico.ca
France 21 rue Sébastien Mercier, 75015 Paris, France; tel: +33 1 4577 1050; fax: +33 1 4577 1484
Germany Hubertusalee 5, 14193 Berlin; tel: +49 30 893 8730; fax: +49 30 8909 4141
UK 10 Harcourt House, 19a Cavendish Square, London, W1M 9AD; tel: +44 20 7499 5152; fax: +44 20 7499 2864; email: mkuk@btinternet.com
USA 3050 K St, NW, Suite 210, Washington DC 20007, USA; tel: +1 202 337 3063; fax: + 1 202 337 3093; email: rmacedonia@aol.com

Foreign embassies and consulates in Macedonia

Albania Hristijan Todorovski Karpoš 94/A, Skopje; tel: 02 2614 636; fax: 02 2614 200
Austria Vasil Stefanovski 7, Skopje; tel: 02 3109 550; fax: 02 3110 336
Bulgaria Zlatko Šnaider 3, Skopje; tel: 02 3116 320; fax: 02 3116 139
Bosnia and **Herzegovina** Mile Pop Jordanov 56b, Skopje; tel: 02 3086 216; fax: 02 3086 221
China, People's Republic of 474 St, no 20, Skopje: tel: 02 3213 163; fax: 02 3212 500
Croatia Mitroplit Teodosij Gologanov 59/II-IV, Skopje; tel: 02 3127 350; fax: 02 3127 421; email: velhrskp@mpt.com.mk
France Salvador Aljende 73, Skopje; tel: 02 3118 749; fax: 02 3117 713; email: france@france-mk.net; web: www.ambafrance-mk.org
Germany Lerinska 59/1, Skopje; tel: 02 3083 182; email: dtboskop@unet.com.mk
Greece Borka Talevski 6, Skopje; tel: 02 3130 198; fax: 02 3115 718
Hungary Mirka Ginova 27, Skopje; tel: 02 3063 423; fax: 02 3063 070
Iran Georgi Peskov 6, Skopje; tel: 02 3118 020; fax: 02 3118 502
Italy 8-ma Udarna Brigada 22, Skopje; tel: 02 3117 430; fax: 02 3117 087; email: segretaria@ambasciata.org.mk; web: www.ambasciata.org.mk
Malta Blvd Aleksandar Makedonski bb, Skopje; tel: 02 3118 348; fax: 02 3230 975
Netherlands Leninova 69-71, Skopje; tel: 02 3129 319; fax: 02 3129 309; email: nethemb@mt.com.mk; web: www.nlembassy.org.mk
Norway Mitroplit Teodosij Gologanov 59-2A, Skopje; tel: 02 3129 165; fax: 02 3111 138
Poland Djuro Djakovic 50, Skopje; tel: 02 3112 647; fax: 02 3119 744

Romania Londonska 11a, Skopje; tel: 02 3070 144; fax: 02 3061 130; email: romanamb@unet.com.mk
Russian Federation Pirinska 44, Skopje; tel: 02 3117 160; fax: 02 3117 808; email: rusembas@mol.mk
Serbia and **Montenegro** Pitu Guli 8, Skopje; tel: 02 3129 298; fax: 02 3129 427
Slovenia Vodnjanska 42, Skopje; tel: 02 3178 734; fax: 02 3176 631
Sweden Nikola Vapcarov 2.11-4, Skopje; tel: 02 3112 828; fax: 02 3112 065; email: gkskopje@mt.net.mk
Switzerland Maksim Gorki 19, Skopje; tel: 02 3128 300; fax: 02 3116 205
Turkey Slavej Planina bb St, Skopje; tel: 02 3113 270; fax: 02 3117 024; email: turkish@mol.com.mk
Ukraine Helsinki 25, Skopje; tel: 02 3090 399; fax: 02 3090 400
UK Dimitri Čupovski 26, Skopje; tel: 02 3299 299; fax: 02 3117 555; email: consulate@britishembassy.org.mk; web: www.britishembassy.org.mk. Passport renewal only available in Belgrade.
USA Blvd Ilinden bb, Skopje; tel: 02 3116 180; fax: 02 3117 103; email: irc@usembassy.mpt.com.mk; web: usembassy.mpt.com.mk

Consulates

Austria Blvd Sveti Kliment Ohridski bb, Skopje; tel: 02 3126 200; fax: 02 3214 502
Australia Londonska 11b, Skopje; tel: 02 3061 114; fax: 02 3061 834
Belgium Koruška 9, Skopje; tel: 02 2043 314; fax: 02 2043 314
Denmark Aleksandar Makedonski 12, Skopje; tel: 02 2614 332; fax: 02 2612 291
Hungary Mile Pop Jordanov 12, Skopje; tel: 02 3090 858; fax: 02 3090 849
Japan Blvd Ilinden 9, Skopje; tel: 02 3117 440; fax: 02 3118 731
Slovak Republic Skopska Crvena Opstina bb St, Skopje; tel: 02 3137 095; fax: 02 3122 105
Spain Dame Gruev 3/8-2, Skopje; tel: 02 3227 751; fax: 02 3220 205

Police registration

By law, you must register with the police within three days of arriving in Macedonia. If you are staying in a hotel, the hotel will do this for you automatically, however, if you are staying in private accommodation or a monastery then you must do this yourself. Ask at your place of stay for a registration card (which Macedonians must also fill out) and ask for the nearest police station to hand it in.

Some of the monasteries will insist that you go through this process, but most private rooms do not even have the cards. I spent a year going backwards and forwards to Macedonia before I realised I had to register, so it is perfectly possible to travel around without the police picking you up for not being registered. However, if you do get picked up and have been wandering off the beaten track for some time the police have every right to deport you, even if you do plead the innocent tourist.

Customs

You can bring in as much personal luggage as you like, although expensive items such as laptops, cameras, musical instruments, sporting equipment, radios and jewellery should be declared on entry if you want to leave with them without any hassles. Having said that, I have never been given a customs declaration form to fill out, but if you want to be on the safe side then ask for one.

You can pretty much leave with what you like too, providing you can prove that it was bought with legally exchanged money! Antiques and icons require a certificate of approval from the Ministry of the Interior before they can be exported.

Duty free allowances are 1l of spirits; 200 cigarettes, or 50 cigars, or 250g of tobacco; perfume for personal use.

The maximum amount of currency you can bring into the country without having to declare it is €10,000.

GETTING THERE AND AWAY

Sadly, Macedonia is very badly served by good and cheap transport in and out of the country. Flights are usually expensive, buses are few and bad quality, and the train is slow. There's always the option of the car, and if you are thinking of walking in, make sure it is at a designated border crossing (see *Safety* below).

By air

For daily flight times in and out of Macedonia see www.airports.com.mk. Airlines that fly into Skopje are: Austrian Airlines, Cirrus Airlines (from Frankfurt), Malev (Hungarian), Croatian Airlines, JAT (former Yugoslav airlines based in Serbia), Olympic Airways and Slovenian Airlines. The latter also does flights to Ohrid from Ljubljana. In the summer Croatian Airlines does a once-a-week flight between Dubrovnik and Skopje. MAT (Macedonian airlines) does limited flights within Europe and in summer 2003 started a weekend flight in and out of Amsterdam for €199. Otherwise a flight from the UK to Skopje will cost in the region of £200–500 plus tax.

The alternative to expensive flights into Skopje is to look at neighbouring aiports for cheap deals and then take the bus or the train. There are often cheap flights to be had to Thessaloniki in Greece, and then the train (twice a day) costs a mere €10. British Airways does a direct flight to Priština in Kosovo, and the bus from there only costs €4. There are also direct bus services from Sofia, but not Tirana.

You may find it difficult to book flights to Macedonia on the internet as there are so few flights and so many variations. You might try the following agents for cheap flights: **Dial-a-flight** in London, tel: 020 7464 1018; **Travelbag**, web: www.travelbag.co.uk, tel: 0870 890 1456; **Trailfinders**, of which there are many branches worldwide, web: www.trailfinders.com; and **STA Travel**, which also has many offices around the world, web: www.statravel.com.

MAT offices are at Vasil Glavinov 3, Skopje; tel: 02 3292 333; web: www.mat.com.mk.

By rail

If you love rail travel, and hanker after those old eastern European trains, then of the four international trains which enter Macedonia direct every day (two from Thessaloniki, and two via Belgrade) you'll be glad to know that one is a 20-hour overnight train from Ljubljana. The scenery isn't all that exciting, and from further afield you'll have to make connections at other international cities. An excellent website giving all the domestic train times as well as international connections can be found at www.geocities.com/CapeCanaveral/3976/macedonia.html. The domestic timetable can also be found at www.mz.com.mk/patnichki/timetable.htm.

By bus

At time of writing, luxury coaches coming in or out of Macedonia are extremely few and far between, but they are on the increase. The many passing through to Greece do not stop. As with flights and trains, you could get a coach to another former Yugoslav city, such as Ljubljana, Zagreb or Belgrade, or to Sofia and then get a connecting local coach. There are several coaches a day serving Belgrade. The following website gives a fair idea of coaches travelling out of Skopje, but does not give incoming information, and the information given is not always up to date, so check again at the station when you go to buy your ticket: www.skopje.com.mk/angliski/megju.asp.

By car

The easiest and most convenient way to get around Macedonia is by car, preferably 4WD if you plan to go anywhere off the beaten track (which is quite a lot of the country). But driving to Macedonia from the further reaches of Europe, especially places like Great Britain and Finland, is an extremely long journey, at least three days, unless you don't intend to sleep (not advisable).

If you do intend to drive from Great Britain, for instance, a recommended route would be to cross at Calais for a cheap short ferry journey, drive through the roads of France, which are usually fairly empty although there are road tolls to pay (German roads are toll-free, but packed, and speed restrictions are becoming more widespread), cross the Alps at the Simplon pass and head for Venice. From here take the overnight car ferry to Durres in Albania, or Igoumenitsa in Greece. Either journey from these ports to Skopje is arduous mountain driving (six hours from Durres via Ohrid, or ten hours via Bitola from Igoumenitsa), but the scenery is fantastic. The drive down through Italy, whilst making the ferry journey shorter, is packed with other drivers, especially in the summer, and therefore not necessarily very fast. For times and prices of ferries between Italy and the Balkans see www.cemar.it/ferries/1_ferries.html.

MAPS AND TOURIST INFORMATION

This is where the adventure starts! Macedonia has very unco-ordinated tourist representation both outside and inside Macedonia. There is a tourist office in Skopje on the old town side of the bridge, but it has very little information, and often isn't even open, especially in the winter. You will be much better off going to a travel agency for information, especially in towns outside Skopje.

Macedonian maps are even more disorienting. If you come from a country like the UK, France, Germany or the US, where maps are blissfully accurate and well laid out, then be prepared to be massively frustrated with Macedonian maps. Aside from the 1:250,000 country maps which are widely available all over Macedonia, and good map stores internationally, there are very few town maps, and only one (bad) hiking map for the Šar Planina (1:60,000, 1cm = 0.6km, available from Tabernakul bookstore in Skopje). Good indexed maps of Skopje are readily available from most bookstores and big supermarkets, such as Vero or Tinex. Town maps of Ohrid, Struga and Kruševo have recently become available. A map of Bitola can be purchased for €3 from Hotel Šumski Feneri outside Bitola.

Outside Macedonia, the best available country map is the 1:260,000 map (1cm = 2.6km) by Gizi Publishers, Hungary, 1999, ISBN 963 02 9667 5. It is available from most good travel stores or from www.themapshop.co.uk/Macedonia.htm for £5.95, www.maps2anywhere.com/Maps/maps_-_macedonia.htm in the USA for US$7.95, or www.abera.de/index.htm?europa_suedosteuropa_mazedonien_landkarten_stadtplaene.htm in Germany for €10.95. Take care not to get the 1995 Maplink map as this information is out of date and many of the roads were wrongly labelled even at the time of publication.

Within Macedonia the Trimaks map of Macedonia, published 2001, still does not have all the roads marked correctly. For instance, you cannot drive through Dabnica to Treskavec Monastery (there isn't even a footpath), but must go via Varoš on the other side of Prilep; Stobi is marked down on the wrong side of the highway; and the wide asphalt road to Berovo Lake is not marked at all. In addition, the scale is wrong – not that it makes much difference for most people, but it is in fact a 1:280,000 map and not as stated a 1:250,000 map.

As if the maps aren't bad enough, the **street naming** is even worse. Many streets in Macedonia don't have a name, but simply a number. Even worse, some street names have changed since independence and the name given on the map may not correspond to the name actually signposted on the street and used by the locals. Maršal Tito Street in Skopje, the main pedestrian street, is a case in point. On the Trimaks map of the city it is named Makedonija. On the street itself it retains its old name and that is still what people call it.

In this guide I have followed Macedonian common usage as much as possible and street names are in their Macedonian spelling followed by the house number. If it is a numbered street then it is given as 000 Street, followed by the house number. Many streets are named after dates in history, so house number sixty on the street of First of May is written here as '1st Maj 60'. As if all this is not confusing enough, some houses, especially large factories or institutions, do not have numbers at all, in which case the street name is followed by *b b*, indicating *bez broj* meaning 'without number'.

Note that some streets have been renumbered several times due to new building work, so some streets may have several buildings with the same number or with their old number still showing!

HEALTH

Important numbers: 94 for an ambulance, 93 for the fire service, and 92 for police.

Make sure you get health insurance that is valid for Macedonia before getting into the country, unless you are prepared to pay for any mishaps yourself. Macedonian doctors and hospitals expect to be paid in cash on the spot from foreigners seeking treatment, and once furnished with your receipt, appropriately translated, then you can reclaim your money back from your insurer. Most travel agents abroad will be able to sort you out with the appropriate health insurance, and some give a good deal combining health and travel insurance with insurance against theft.

It is also a good idea to get any treatment that you need before you go travelling. It is not necessarily any cheaper to get things done in Macedonia and standards may not be as high as your home country. Common illnesses can be treated in Macedonia by the pharmacists in any local drugstore (*farmacija*), many of whom have English-speaking staff (seems to come with the medical territory), and they can also advise you of the nearest family practitioner if you are in need of a doctor. If you need hospitalisation, this is best left till you get home, unless it is an emergency, in which case either call 94, or it may be quicker to get a taxi to take you to the nearest hospital (*bolnica*). In Skopje, City Hospital (*Gradska Bolnica*), the newish looking red brick building on 11th Oktomvri opposite the parliament, deals with all emergencies requiring anaesthesia. The emergency outpatients' entrance is around the back.

Vaccinations are not legally required to enter Macedonia, but doctors will advise the following to be on the safe side: tetanus, diphtheria, hepatitis A and typhoid. It is wise to visit your doctor or a travel health clinic about 4–6 weeks before travel. If you are going to be in the country for a long time (four weeks or more) or are dealing with refugees or children or working in a medical setting then immunisation against hepatitis B is worth having. Ideally three doses of vaccine should be taken before travel. These can be given at 0, 1, and 6 months,

0, 1 and 2 months or if time is short at 0, 7 and 21–28 days. Only Engerix B is currently licensed for the last schedule. Polio may also be advised for longer trips, especially for areas where sanitation is poor.

Tick-borne encephalitis (TBE) – a potentially fatal disease – is spread by bites from infected ticks. Vaccination would be recommended if you are intending to walk through forests, or are a long-term resident in rural areas. Three doses of vaccine are ideal and can be given over a three-week period if time is short. At the time of writing only Encepur is licensed to be used in this way. TBE vaccine can only be obtained on a named-patient basis in the UK, which means that you have to pre-order the vaccine from either your GP or a travel clinic.

Lastly, BCG vaccine for tuberculosis may be recommended (if not received previously) if you are likely to be mixing closely with the local population. This is more important for longer stay trips. Tuberculosis is spread through close respiratory contact and occasionally through infected milk or milk products.

Travel clinics and health information

A full list of travel clinic websites worldwide is available on www.istm.org. For other journey preparation information, consult www.tripprep.com. Information about various medications may be found on www.emedicine.com/wild/topiclist.htm.

Common problems

Without stating the absolutely obvious, it is a good idea to be fit and healthy before going on holiday! Many of us though have usually just raced through a work or college deadline before going on holiday and the time to unwind and relax is just when the common cold or stomach flu takes hold. Food **hygiene standards** and tap drinking water in Macedonia are safe for the average traveller. If you are one of those fussy types, who has never allowed your stomach to harden to foreign bacteria, then drink the ubiquitous bottled water, and avoid drinking from mountain streams and water fountains. Water fountains in towns are usually from the same source as tap water.

Unless you are a seasoned world traveller and have a stomach like cast iron, you may get a small bout of the trots on coming into contact with new foods, water and cooking. This is why it is a good idea to be fit and healthy before you leave home. If you are, you'll be able to weather those loose stools for a few days and soon toilet visits will return to normal levels. In Macedonia, a small bout of the trots is unlikely to turn into full-blown **diarrhoea** requiring antibiotics to clear it up. If it does, the pharmacy can sort you out, or bring some suitable medication with you from home, if you are prone to a bit of delhi belly.

There are many old wives' tales which are alleged to help you avoid this phenomenon. In Macedonia they believe that if you eat the onions of the new country within 24 hours of getting there, then your stomach will settle into the new environment. A good remedy I have found for the trots which just keep trotting is to constrict yourself to a diet of well-boiled salted carrots and salted white rice for a day or two. This will bung you up in no time at all, and although a somewhat bland diet, you may be glad to know that purification of the bowels is helped by a glass of wine or beer! Keep off dairy products, eggs and fresh fruit or juice for a few more days and things should return to normal. I have administered this remedy to several travelling partners of mine, for whom it has worked wonders. I must confess to never having had to undergo these rigours myself, because I do have a stomach of cast iron. Always drink plenty of water if you have diarrhoea, and take in plenty of salt. The locals will recommend tea, others recommend flat Coca-Cola.

As with any travels away from your medicine cabinet at home, it is a good idea to have a small **first-aid pack** with you. You can buy these ready made from any good drugstore at home, such as Boots in the UK, or Walgreens in the US, or you can just make up a small kit yourself from the following items: plasters/band aid; painkillers such as aspirin, paracetemol or tylenol; lipsalve; sunscreen; antiseptic cream and mosquito bite cream (diluted tea-tree oil does well for both); spare contact lenses if you are a contact lens wearer; and I usually throw in a small sewing kit for when I've eaten too much of the local food and need to re-sew on a button, or my trousers have ripped on a hike in the forest.

Mosquitoes are not prevelant in most of Macedonia as the country is so mountainous, but in the low-lying areas around Skopje and south along the Vardar, you might find one or two. You'll find many more to the north and south of Macedonia in Serbia and Greece. Luckily there is no malaria in Macedonia so it is not necessary to take antimalarial tablets.

Leishmaniasis is spread through the bite of an infected sandfly. The cutaneous form of the disease causes a slow growing skin lump or ulcer. However, there is a more serious life-threatening form (Kala-azar), of which the symptoms are fever, anaemia and weight loss. Sandfly bites should be avoided wherever possible so it is wise to take a good insect repellent.

Health and safety in the mountains

In the mountains, anywhere in the world, health and safety go hand in hand. Although Macedonia's mountains are not very big, they are sufficiently remote, and trails sufficiently obscure, that without a good hiking map (preferably 1:25,000, 1cm = 0.25km, and these do not yet exist in Macedonia) it is very easy to get lost. Make sure you are a proficient hiker before venturing for long hikes into the mountains here, otherwise a two-hour walk in the park could turn into an eight-hour mountaineering ordeal. Alternatively, and preferably, go with a guide (the travel agents above, or the clubs in *Chapter 2* will be able to find a guide for you).

Know the potential dangers of mountaineering and how to deal with them before you venture out on a hike, and preferably be first-aid proficient. If you've no idea what you are getting into and have come to Macedonia for the mountains, then there are safer playing grounds than these for an introduction to mountaineering, but the list of health and safety considerations below will give you an idea of what you are up against. If you get into trouble, call 92 for the police who will be able to get the mountain rescue service out.

Your medical pack for any extended hiking trip (more than two hours) needs to be more than basic, and should contain at least the following: large plasters/band aid and surgical gauze; antiseptic cream and wipes; pain killers; crêpe bandages x 2; surgical tape and zinc-oxide tape; *Compeed* for blisters; iodine-based water purification tablets (available from any good mountaineering shop, and hard to find in Macedonia); emergency blanket and inflatable splint if you are going on a long trip.

Dehydration

In these untamed mountainous regions, the going can get tough, and like all mountains, water can sometimes be hard to find when you need it. Bring plenty of water with you, at least a litre per hour of uphill in the summer, and especially if you don't know where your next water source will be. It is very arid here and the lack of overhead cover can cause excess sweating. Dehydration will make you tired and prone to injury, and makes some people's vision blur. If you find yourself short of water, try to conserve what you have left, and take small sips every now and again. Don't over-exert yourself, and breath through your nose rather than your mouth to stop excess moisture escaping. Keep covered to prevent excess moisture being lost in sweat.

Injury

Injuries are usually caused when you are tired and/or hiking beyond your limit. It is, therefore, important to know what your limit is, and those of your travelling partners, and to recognise when it is time for a rest. Come properly equipped for the task at hand, with good hiking boots and an appropriate overcoat as a minimum. Many Macedonians wander around in flimsy, trendy sports shoes, or even worse open-heeled clogs or slip-ons. This may suffice for a hike to a popular monument, but will get you in trouble further afield. If you do sustain an injury that would normally require stitching, then bind the wound with a large plaster or surgical tape and then secure it laterally with zinc-oxide tape.

Sunburn

Do wear a hat, sunglasses and plenty of sunscreen (available in the pharmacies). The sun here is stronger than in northern Europe and it is easy to forget that point until it is too late. If you do get badly burnt, apply an after-sun cream (not so easily available here) or calamine lotion, cover up and don't go back out in the sun without a total sunblock. A cold wet teabag also works for sunburn if you can't get anything else.

Sunstroke

After the onset of dehydration and sunburn you are heading for heat exhaustion and then sun/heatstroke. While heatstroke can be fatal, if you recognise the early stage symptoms soon enough you should never get that far. It is usually more difficult to tell in oneself than in others, so watch your hiking partner carefully. The easiest signs to look for are muscle cramps, dim or blurred vision, weakness, irritability, dizziness and confusion. If any of your hiking partners are talking utter drivel (more than normal anyway), are not able to have a logical conversation with you, and particularly if they say they don't need water or to get out of the sun, then sit them down in the shade immediately, loosen any tight clothing, sprinkle water on them and fan them to cool them down. They should take regular sips of water, but not drink a pint down flat. If your hiking partner shows the above signs, and feels sick, and particularly if their skin feels hot and dry, then the body has gone into shutdown mode. They may soon fall unconscious and medical attention is required quickly. Phone 94 for help.

Altitude sickness

You are unlikely to suffer from altitutude sickness in Macedonia, as it is difficult to gain enough height to be able to do so. Nevertheless, altitude sickeness is indiscriminatory, and should you decide to climb Mount Korab or Titov Vrv in one day from Skopje, no matter how young you are, nor how much mountaineering you have done sometime in the past, it may still hit you here. The best way to avoid altitude sickness is to acclimatise over time. If you don't have that option open to you, and you start to feel dizzy, sick and overly short of breath, then the next best thing to do is to stop and rest. If this doesn't help then descend slowly to a lower level (500m is usually enough), and consider doing something else for the day. Sadly, there is no coca tea in Macedonia to help with altitude sickness.

Hypothermia

Hypothermia occurs when the body loses heat quicker than it can make it. This is most likely to happen when the body is wet and cold, inactive, hungry and tired. Uncontrollable shivering, drowsiness and confusion are tell-tale first signs. If the person has stopped shivering, is physically stiff, and indifferent to their surroundings, then the body is already in shutdown mode. The person's body temperature must be warmed up immediately with plenty of warm, dry clothing, shelter and warm sweet drinks to increase the blood sugar level. Exercise will not help. At severe levels, skin contact with another warm body, preferably in a sleeping bag, might be required. At this point the medical services should be brought in. Do not heat the person with anything hotter than body temperature, nor immerse the person in hot water as this might simply cook outer extremities. Do not rub or massage the person, but warm the core of the body first.

Wild and deadly nasties

Some poisonous snakes and spiders do exist in Macedonia, such as black and brown widow spiders, and some adders and vipers. They do not seek out humans, so you are extremely unlikely to come across one. If you do get bitten, then the best thing to do is not to panic, to move as little as possible, and lower the bitten area below the level of the heart. This is contrary to your instincts and any John Wayne movies showing him sucking out the venom and spitting it on the ground. It is the best thing you can do though, along with getting to hospital as fast as possible.

SECURITY AND SAFETY

The security situation in Macedonia

The security situation in Macedonia has calmed down significantly since the end of the hostilities of 2001 (see page 20) and, even during hostilities, foreigners were not the target. Nevertheless, sporadic occurances of inter-ethnic hatred continue several years on. These have so far been restricted to former conflict areas in the northwest and sometimes in Skopje. Although these incidents are not aimed at foreigners, foreigners can of course get caught in the crossfire, as happened in July 2003 when a small petrol bomb exploded in Skopje's Čair district.

To put this in perspective, the likelihood of being caught in such an incident is probably no more than in a big city at home. The trick is to avoid areas known to be unsafe, and to avoid large public demonstrations which may get heated. The website of your embassy in Macedonia will usually carry the most up-to-date information on the security situation, and the US embassy site also has comprehensive security and safety advice: travel.state.gov/macedonia.html. Many embassies advise their citizens to register at the embassy if they intend to stay in the country for any length of time, and to phone for the latest security advice on a particular area if you are going off the beaten track.

It is likely that hostile acts will decrease over time as the country is being helped by the international community to bring its government and law enforcement gradually in line with EU standards. Allegations of police abuse and government discrimination have been the basic cause of the violence and, while some of these allegations may be misplaced, it will be a while before the civil service here works with the transparency and appropriate checks and balances of equivalent systems in western Europe and northern America.

A time of possible unrest may be the municipal elections at the end of 2004, when the boundaries of the present 123 municipalities will be redrawn to create anywhere between 33 and 60 larger municipalities. The new municipalities will have greater decentralised powers. The use of these new powers from 2005 onwards might give fresh cause for friction.

Minefields

In theory, all the minefields from the conflict of 2001 were de-mined by explosives and ordnance engineers in 2002. Those who were confident of this skied at Popova Šapka the following winter (including myself), but those who still fear Albanian nationalism in the northwest border areas will tell you that it is not safe. There was a land mine incident which killed two Polish soldiers on a side-road near the Tabanovce border crossing in March 2003, but this was from a land mine recently laid by locals who were pissed off with patrols into their area.

If you are unsure of the safety of an area from landmines, then stick to tarmacked roads. Dirt-tracks are always more risky than asphalt and generally it is advisable not to travel off-road close to any borders, especially in the north and northwest where the exact border is still disputed between Macedonia and its neighbours. There have been no reports of land mines outside the northwest border areas.

International trafficking of weapons, drugs and people

While national crime levels are relatively low (see *Personal safety*), international trafficking of humans more than makes up for the deficit. The borders of Macedonia, especially in the northwest on neighbouring Albania and Kosovo, have become difficult to police since independence and so its porous borders are easy to traffic humans across.

Policing the border had not been such a big problem prior to independence, in part because Albania was so paranoid about foreign invasion that there was little worry about illegal international trade, and in part because there were no customs restrictions between Macedonia and its other Yugoslav neighbours. Macedonia's borders are high up in the mountains, especially in the northwest, and covered in acres of dense forestry which obscures the many mountain tracks and any illegal trade which takes place over them. Now, locals, who harbour and profit from a lot of cross-border trade, are resisting the need to patrol the border and put in customs controls. Enforcing border controls in the north and northwest is not helped by the dispute over the exact border line in this area nor by local ethnic tension. The Albanian community believe that the Macedonian authorities are using this issue to discriminate against the them.

Aside from designated crossings, the border areas are **restricted military zones**, and it is forbidden to enter them without first seeking permission and having an appointed military guide. This applies to Macedonians as well as foreigners.

Illegal trade in weapons and cigarettes has decreased since the end of hostilities and the lifting of sanctions against Serbia, but trafficking in women is on the increase. Macedonia is both a transit country and an end user of trafficked women. Very few Macedonian women end up being trafficked, but it is not without precedent. Most of the women come from countries even poorer than Macedonia and, tempted by the lure of easy money abroad waitressing or as domestic helps, they are often beaten, raped and forced into prostitution. Victims include minors who believe they are going for better schooling. In January 2003, MSNBC carried a very good article on this very issue in Macedonia, which can be found at www.msnbc.com/news/sexslaves_front.asp.

Because of the difficulty of policing this issue, foreign visitors who bring their children with them are advised to bring the appropriate documents proving the legal relationship of parent and child. A passport may suffice, especially if the child is on your passport, but if you have separate passports with different names then you may want to bring additional proof. Although traffickers don't usually take children so blatantly over an established border crossing, border police may suspect the worst. The same goes for young couples entering Macedonia. I've been asked my relationship to my husband more than a few times, and I'm not even that young! If you would like to help against the anti-trafficking effort here in Macedonia see the *Giving something back* section at the end of this chapter.

Personal safety

In many respects crime is lower in Macedonia than in many countries in western Europe or in America. Nevertheless, you should take the usual precautions: this is not a country where you can leave your car and house unlocked when you are out, and you should keep your valuables close if you are going through a crowded place or travelling by public transport.

If you come to live in Macedonia as part of the international community then, as with a move into any new flat, you may want to make sure the locks are changed in case old tenants have a key that falls into the wrong hands. Although car theft is not a big problem in Macedonia, you are still better off putting your flashy foreign-registered car in safe guarded parking or a garage.

If you get stopped or detained by the **police**, for any reason whatsoever, remember to stay calm and polite. In any nation, smart alec wisecracks, sarcasm, anger and lack of co-operation are seen as suspicious behaviour. You do have the right to ask why you have been stopped or detained, however, and, of course, the right to legal representation once you have been charged. You can be detained for up to 24 hours without being charged, by which time your embassy or consulate should have been informed of your detention. You also have the right to be spoken to in a language which you understand, so you might be better off waiting for an interpreter or a policeman who speaks your language rather than digging yourself into a bigger hole. The interpreter may take a while in getting to you!

Driving and road safety

Speed restrictions are enforced here, and it is illegal not to wear a seat belt in the front seats of your car. You will find, however, that few Macedonians heed these rules or any form of lane discipline and driving etiquette. Some drivers here don't have licences and some cars wouldn't pass a road test either. If you are a Brit and have never driven on the right-hand side of the road, I would not advise Macedonia as a good place to start learning. If you are going to drive here, then don't be surprised to find vehicles without headlights at night, extremely little use of indicators, lorries backing down the road when they have missed their exit, parking on the pavement and two cars stopped in the middle of the road to have a chat.

As a pedestrian, you'll also have to keep your wits about you when crossing the road, as drivers often don't heed traffic lights, and certainly pay no attention to zebra crossings.

Sexual harassment

This is not usually a problem in Macedonia, and many women here dress as skimpily as in the West. The locals think it is a bit strange, however, to travel on your own, especially as a woman; and keeping in mind the high level of trafficking in women which goes on in Macedonia, you'd better have your wits about you if you travel alone as a women in strange places after dark. There are no obvious red-light districts in Macedonia, as prostitution is illegal, but there are bars and hotels that service this trade.

Personal harrassment

Don't expect to always be left alone as you wander around Macedonia looking at antique treasures and antiquated institutions. You will almost definitely come across two situations where you will wish that you could be left in peace. The first form of harassment will come from begging Roma (see page 18) who may follow you around for up to 15 minutes quietly begging for money, and may even get angry, though rarely if at all physically violent, if you don't give them money. Macedonians get this treatment too, and the best thing to do is not to give them any, which only encourages the phenomenon, but do what most Macedonians do which is to say sternly *begaj, odmah*, meaning 'scram, immediately' to make your intentions clear, and if this does not succeed then dive into a café where the waiter will take care of the little beggar for you, or see how long he (it's very rarely a girl) will carry on begging until they find more promising prey.

The second form is really just an uncomfortable invasion of personal space, usually from teenage boys who are bewildered and defensive about what on earth you think you are doing on their turf. Trying to engage them in friendly conversation with a winning smile (which usually works, see below) may only raise their defences as a battle of hormones, pride and stubbornness ensues. This is how fights start, and no matter how much you might want to push him away or punch him in the face for getting too close to you, your belongings or your car, you are at the end of the day a guest in his home town or street, so back off confidently, and remember that locals at home probably aren't too friendly either; the difference is that you don't usually wander into that part of town at home.

Dogs

There are a lot of stray dogs in Macedonia, and while they don't tend to be savage, or even a nuisance, some of them do carry disease and infections, so don't approach them, or take them in. Rabies is not common here, but leishmaniasis is more prevalent. Leishmaniasis is transferred by sandflies from host to new prey, and can be deadly if left untreated. Dogs with mangy appearance and losing clumps of hair could have leishmaniasis.

If you do take in a stray dog, take it to the vet immediately for a check-up and all the necessary injections. There is no animal home here in Macedonia, and most dogs are not treated too well, so you probably have more to fear from a kept dog than a stray dog. The big shepherding dogs here, the *šarplaninec*, are well trained to guard their flock, so don't approach them or the flock, no matter how docile they may appear from several metres away. You may not return with your hand, and the dog won't be put down. The only approachable docile *šarplaninec* I have seen is the two-year-old puppy at the Monastery of Treskavec. See also page 64.

WHAT TO TAKE

Clothing

Unless you know you are only staying in Skopje and Ohrid in the summer, then bring an overcoat or jacket, and it is cold enough for a fleece in the mountains no matter what time of year. Casual dress is the norm on the streets, although you'll see a lot of young women in Skopje in skin-tight clothes, make up and high heels no matter what time of day, year or occasion. Businessmen tend to wear short-sleeved shirts in the summer, and you may wish to pack such a shirt or polo shirt if you intend to go to one of the nicer restaurants in Skopje. Nightclubs here don't have a dress code, but some churches and mosques do. Bring a pair of long trousers, shoulder covering, and for women, a scarf, in case these are needed. In spring and autumn it may be very warm during the day, but in the evening it can also get quite cold, and some hotels may have not yet turned on or already turned off the central heating, so bring warm enough clothes.

Plugs, adaptors and converters

Macedonia's electricity is 220 volts and uses two types of plugs both with the same two round pins commonly used in northern Europe. Plug casings come in the round case variant as well as the six sided flat case variant.

There are a number of great travel adaptors available now which take a multiple choice of plugs and give multiple options in pins. If you are coming from northern America and wish to bring American electrical appliances with you, then you can also purchase a power voltage converter which will convert the 220 volts of European electricity into 110 volts before it gets to your appliance.

Toiletries and medicines

You can buy all the basics in Macedonia, although if you are coming here to live for a while you may wish to bring your favourite face cream or aftershave lotion. Contact lens solutions are expensive here, and contacts can take a while to order, so bring plenty with you. Always bring spare glasses if you wear them, it is a nightmare anywhere in the world if you break your only pair.

Bring a universal plug, especially if you will be staying in lower-end accommodation, and clothes washing powder (unless you want to buy a large tub in the supermarket here) as launderettes are almost impossible to find, although there are dry cleaners. The western four- and five-star hotels have a laundry service. A basic first-aid pack as mentioned above under *Safety* is also useful.

Documents

Obviously, passport with visa if required, ticket and money (see below) are essential. If you are travelling with children, then some sort of proof that you are their legal guardian is advisable to stop a potentially harrowing ordeal at the border when police might think you are trafficking children. If you are bringing your own car, then make sure you have the right insurance. The international blue or green card insurance, which does not have Macedonia (MK) or any other countries you want to visit or travel through struck off, is valid here. Photo ID driver's licence is required here, both to drive and to hire a car.

Gifts

It is always a good idea to bring family photos and postcards of your hometown with you on holiday. They make good talking points and you can give the postcards out as a small gift. If you are invited into a Macedonian home, you may be given sweet syruped preserved fruits as a welcome. It is also a good idea to give something in return, and sweets from your home country are a good gift. Note that Macedonians can get all the German chocolates and some of the Swiss ones here, and anyway chocolate is not a good thing to bring in the summer as it will almost definitely melt. More permanent small souvenirs are ideal.

Outdoor sports

Light sports shoes or open-toed hiking sandals like Teva's are fine for walking around or a short hike to a popular monument, but anything more arduous requires suitable hiking boots. You may also find a long pair of hiking trousers useful as the paths here are often overgrown and prickly, thorny or full of nettles and sadly, unlike in the UK, dock leaves as a remedy for nettle stings do not seem to grow here.

Bring a good day pack and your favourite water container: wide-mouthed Nalgene bottles are far easier to fill than re-used plastic water bottles, but my favourite has to be the Camelbak (www.camelbak.com), especially in this arid climate.

You'll need to bring your own climbing boots if you intend to do any rock climbing, but the rest you can hire here from one of the clubs. You may also wish to bring your own skis in the winter, as skis here have yet to get to the carving stage, and some of the equipment is so old that it's unreliable and at worst unsafe.

Camping

There are no dedicated basecamp stores here, so you'll need to bring pretty much everything with you. There is only one type of bottled stove fuel here, and it is not the butane/propane self-sealing screw-on Coleman type, so you'll either need to bring plenty of canisters (and most airlines won't let you bring them any more) or buy one of the local stoves which you can find in any outdoor market here. Alternatively, bring an all-purpose fuel stove and buy petrol from the petrol stations.

It does get very hot in the summer, so bring enough changes of clothing so that you can swap out of your sweaty T-shirt when you get to the top of your hike. This helps to prevent you from getting a chill, which can be easily done when you reach the colder climes of the summit.

MONEY

The Macedonian *denar* has been pegged to the euro since 1998, and is therefore very stable. There is no smaller division of the denar, as 100 *denar* already equals about one British pound sterling (£1 = 92MKD, US$1 = 53MKD), so one penny per denar. MKD is the international three-letter code, which is also used when Latin rather than Cyrillic script is used.

The denar comes in 10, 50, 100, 500, 1,000 and 5,000 notes, although you'll often find the 1,000 denar note hard to change, even if it is the only note to come out of the cash machine. I've only ever seen the 5,000MKD note on the cashier's side of the bank counter. Macedonian shops never seem to have much change, so hoard your small notes, and change large notes whenever you can. Coins come in 1, 2 and 5 denari.

There are no money changers on the street here, so money is either changed in banks or in the many legal money-changing booths in the main towns. Travellers' cheques are good for backup funds, but if you have a direct debit or credit card then you'll find lots of cash machines available in Skopje and Ohrid, although still very few outside these two main towns. Stopanska Bank (pink signage) is the most ubiquitous bank to offer cash machines. One can be found on the ground floor of the Trgovski Centar in Skopje. You can change money at the airport both before you exit the arrivals lounge and in the departure hall.

Euros are the foreign currency of choice here. All the main hotels, restaurants and even a lot of the bed and breakfasts, especially in Skopje and Ohrid, will accept euros, although they may not always be able to give you all the right change in euros.

On the meagrest of budgets, staying at monasteries and campsites, buying from the market or *kebapci* stalls, and using public transport, you could manage on around €10 a day, excluding your ticket to Macedonia. €20 a day would bring you into the bed and breakfast bracket and at the other end of the scale you would be hard pressed to spend €300 a day here even if you were staying at the Aleksandar Palace Hotel in Skopje for your entire trip and hiring a 4WD vehicle.

GETTING AROUND

There are no internal flights within Macedonia, so your options are train, bus, car or walk. The locals do hitch around, although usually only locally, so you can get a ride. Biking tours would be a great way to get around Macedonia for the fit, but they haven't arrived yet. Maybe later.

Train

There are fairly limited options available for travel by train. There is a line from Skopje to Kičevo through the northwest of the country, which will take you to Tetovo and Gostivar, but not to Mavrovo and Debar. The line to Bitola via Veles and Prilep is a pretty ride, and certainly a recommended route to Prilep. The line to Gevegelia and Thessaloniki is also a pretty ride although there is not much to stop for on that route unless you want to get out at Demir Kapija for some hiking in the area. The lines to Kumanovo and Kočani also don't hold much attraction and you would be better off taking buses direct to places further afield like Kriva Palanka or Berovo. The maximum you could pay for a train ride anywhere in Macedonia at time of writing was 370MKD for a return ticket to Bitola. The domestic timetable can be found at www.mz.com.mk/patnichki/timetable.htm.

Bus

The bus service is the prefered mode of transport for Macedonians because it is frequent and cheap. That said, there is only one bus a day to Brajčino and Kruševo from Skopje, although towns are also served by buses from other towns. Buses are not airconditioned and do sometimes break down; few of them have on-board toilet facilities either, so you may have to wait for the toilet break along the road. A return ticket to Ohrid costs 360MKD.

Car

This is definitely the best way to get around Macedonia, especially 4WD if you want to go and do a bit of exploring and are not so keen on the hiking option. See the section on *Driving and road safety* above before considering this option though, especially if you are not used to driving on the right-hand side of the road. There are many places to hire clean, reliable, modern cars in Skopje and other big cities, as well as at the airport. **Tuymada**, tel: 02 311 3755, in the Kibo Restaurant building in Skopje rents out a Ford Focus for as little as €45 per day for a long weekend or week. **Marco Polo**, tel: 02 3133 233 rents out a Nissan Patrol 4WD for €140 per day going down to €115 per day for 14 days or more. It's best to book a few days in advance especially in the summer, and if you prefer to book online before getting to Macedonia, then worldwide agencies like **Avis**, tel: 02 3222 046; web: www.avis.com.mk; and **Budget**, tel: 02 3290 222; web: www.budget.com.mk, are also available although these are a lot more expensive. You'll pay about 50MKD per litre for unleaded petrol in Macedonia, and about 40MKD per litre for diesel.

Taxi

Taxis are often a quick and cheap way to get around town, but also to places further afield. Taxis in Skopje have a minimum fare of 50MKD which will get you most places in town. Outside Skopje the minimum fare is usually 10MKD. All official taxis should be metered and carry a taxi sign on the roof of the car. A taxi ride from Ohrid to Brajčino, which is a one-hour journey, is €40. Make sure you agree the price before taking a longer journey as the driver will probably turn the meter off and pocket the money himself.

If you are going to a remote part of town, there's quite a high chance that the taxi driver taking you there will not know where it is, so you may wish to ask a few drivers until you get one who knows, or make him phone into his radio centre so that they can give him directions (there are extremely few female taxi drivers). Otherwise they may drive around for a while and charge you the extra time.

ACCOMMODATION

Accommodation in Macedonia is generally on the cheap side, with a few exceptions in Skopje such as the Holiday Inn, Best Western and Aleksandar Palace, but the standard you receive for the price you pay can be a bit of a lottery.

Hotels

Generally speaking, state-run hotels built before the 1990s are in pretty bad shape and not worth the money even if you do get the added live or dead cockroach. Often, however, there is no other choice. Hopefully, international financial initiatives to boost the tourist industry will help to upgrade some of these. In late spring and early autumn between April 15 and October 15, state-run hotels may get a bit cold as the heating is turned off during this period.

Family-run hotels, such as the **Šumski Feneri** or **Gorsko Oko** near Bitola, are excellent value for money but few and far between. Many petrol stations have small motels on the side and as most of them have been built fairly recently they are usually clean and tidy if basic, but reasonably priced. Hotel prices usually include breakfast, although only the top notch hotels will manage to serve a buffet breakfast or provide room service.

In this guide, unless otherwise stated, all rooms have an en-suite bathroom, and all prices are per room. If you ask for a room for two people you will usually get a twin room with two single beds in. To get a room with a double bed in, you must ask for *soba co eden krevet za dvojica*, 'a room with one bed for two people', sometimes called a *francuski krevet* meaning French bed. Even if you ask for this, don't be surprised if you end up with a twin room in which the hotel staff expect you to simply push the beds together. Or they may give you the *apartmen* which is the Macedonian equivalent of the honeymoon suite and usually much more expensive. Rooms with three single beds are also quite common.

Bed and breakfast

In days gone by there was a whole bed and breakfast world in Macedonia. The collapse of the Yugoslav economy and the recent conflict in Macedonia have all but killed off this industry and as a result they are difficult to find. Travel agents will say they'll try to find bed and breakfast options for you, but will probably cajole you into a hotel as they don't make much money off the bed and breakfast industry. Once again, however, the nascent tourist industry in Macedonia is trying to encourage this sector. For rooms in the Ohrid area see www.magiclakes.com/indexEn.asp, or www.lakes-travel.com. Sometimes the bed comes without breakfast, so make sure you ask what your options are. Bed and breakfast usually starts out at about €10–15 per night.

Monasteries

The monasteries are usually excellent value for money, even if you are not on a shoestring budget. As most of the monasteries were only revived less than ten years ago, accommodation in their new inns is generally better than in most state-run hotels and half the price. Prices range from about 250MKD for a bed in the old quarters with bathroom on the corridor, to 500MKD for a bed in an en-suite room in the new quarters. Treskavec Monastery doesn't charge anything at all, although a donation is kindly received. The monasteries don't usually have a restaurant attached, but as they are remote, they usually have cooking facilities available to guests, which is a wonderful option if you have got a bit bored of Macedonian fare and fancy doing your own cooking.

The catch with staying in the monasteries is that they are not always very convenient to book into and as they are popular with Macedonians they are often booked up quite early. Very few of the staff/monks/nuns in them speak any English so you may need to get a Macedonian friend to help you, or a travel agency. If you can't get a travel agency to help you book in (Marco Polo will for a fee) or opt to do so yourself, try to phone during normal working hours as the staff who run the inns usually go home in the evening. If you want to try to turn up without a booking, then at least try to get there before 17.00 otherwise the inn staff may have gone home already, as they usually only stay around until all the pre-booked guests have arrived. Finally, soon after you arrive, you will need to get a registration card from the inn staff and go and register yourself at the local police station. Unlike in hotels, the inn staff will not do this for you.

Camping

Yugoslav style camping is not always public transport friendly. People usually come in their car, hence they are called *avtocamp*, and they are not, therefore, necessarily close to public transport. They are often large, full of people's old caravans, and not always scrupulously clean. They are cheap, however, and 500MKD will usually get you a tent space for four plus your car. Tax is an additional 20MKD per person.

Strictly speaking freelance camping is illegal, but many Macedonians do it, especially at a local festival or event. If you are going to camp wild, then please take away all your rubbish and leave the place in a good condition.

Mountain huts

Most of the 30 mountain huts in Macedonia are listed in *Chapter 2*. They cost about 300MKD for a bed with bedding, and you do not need to book in advance as they are usually open all year round. As there are no detailed hiking maps, however, you will either need to phone for directions (Macedonian usually required) or go with one of the many hiking and mountaineering clubs. The huts rarely provide food, so you will need to bring all your provisions, but there is always plenty of hot water there.

Youth hostel

There is one youth hostel in Macedonia in Skopje. It is no cheaper than some of the bed and breakfasts, but if you are a YHA member then it is the cheapest accommodation in Skopje. It is popular in the summer so book ahead.

PUBLIC HOLIDAYS AND FESTIVALS

National holidays

Macedonian national holidays are as follows:

January 1 and 2	New Year's Day
January 7	Orthodox Christmas
Easter	
May 1 and 2	Labour Day, when everybody goes picnicking
August 2	Ilinden (see page 11)
September 8	Referendum Day
October 11	National Day

Saints' days

Every saint has his or her festival day and these are celebrated by the locals at the church dedicated to the named saint. Usually, the villagers gather at the church or monastery with pot luck food dishes, drink and music, and make merry. Some of the bigger monasteries such as Sveti Joakim Osogovski attract thousands of visitors on these days, and donations to the church funds are usually generous.

As the Macedonian Orthodox Church runs on the amended Gregorian calendar first adopted by the Eastern Orthodox Church in 1923, some of the saints and holy days that western Europeans might know are celebrated in Macedonia 13 days later. Some have a completely different celebration day. Here are a few of the Orthodox saints' days with their western Gregorian dates:

February 14	St Trifun and St Kiril
March 22	St Leonti
April 6	St Metodi
June 14-15	St Erasmus of Ohrid
July 2-3	St Naum of Ohrid
August 2	St Elija
August 7-8	St Petka (Peter, or Paraškjevija in Vlach)
August 9	St Clement of Ohrid and St Pantelejmon
August 14	St Stefan (celebrated on December 26 in the UK)
August 28	St Bogorodica (the Virgin Mary)
August 29	the 15 martyrs of Tiberiopolis (Strumica)
September 10	St Jovan Krstitel (John the Baptist)
November 8	St Dimitri
November 21	St Archangel Michael
December 19	St Nikola (known to many of us as Father Christmas)

Festivals

There are a number of festivals throughout the year, but the majority take place in the summer especially around Ohrid and Skopje. The year kicks in with an

Orthodox New Year festival, also known as the Twelfthtide carnival, in the village of Vevčani (see page 143) on January 13 and 14. It is a colourful two-day event attracting several thousand visitors who dress up in fancy dress and masks. Later in the month, on January 19, is the celebration of Epiphany, when Bishop Naum throws a golden cross into Lake Ohrid in honour of John the Baptist and thereby blesses the lake. The practice is repeated all over Macedonia at local lakes and rivers, where men dive in after the cross purely for the honour of retrieving it. In 2003 the cross thrown into Lake Ohrid (which is a very deep lake) was not found, and has still not been found by divers at time of writing.

February 14 is St Trifun's day, the patron saint of wines, which is increasingly celebrated throughout Macedonia. April 1 sees much fancy dress.

After Easter the festivals start up again in July, when Skopje and Ohrid both hold summer evening concerts, plays, ballet and opera in historical venues and open-air theatres. In Skopje these finish in August when the government goes on holiday, but they continue in Ohrid, which also holds a Folklore Festival early in July. Ohrid finishes its summer of festivities on the last weekend of August with the International Swimming Marathon, a 30km course from Sveti Naum to the town of Ohrid.

The second weekend in July is the very popular Galičnik wedding festival (see page 183) which attracts many thousands of visitors and it is well worth the visit up to this pretty mountain village. For Macedonians, one of the most important events of the year is Ilinden on August 2 (see page 11), when the people of Macedonia stood up against the Ottoman Empire and brought in the ten-day Kruševo Republic.

Other summer festivals and events include the International Pottery Workshop in Resen in early August, the Traditional Costumes Exhibition on the first weekend after August 2 in Struga, and at the end of August the Struga Poetry Evenings (see page 139). The Monastery of Sveti Joakim Osagovski holds a Young Artists Convention in the last week of August which is also when its very popular saint's day falls.

Štip holds its international film festival in July, and its popular Macfest of international music in October. In September Bitola holds the International Film Camera Festival in honour of the Manaki brothers. Skopje holds its international film festival in October along with the Skopje Jazz Festival which usually puts on some excellent artists. September and October are also very good months for wine tours (see page 216).

December finishes up the year with Christmas markets selling local crafts and hot mulled wine.

SHOPPING

There is not much to shop for in Macedonia, although it does have its share of hand-embroidered linen, fur, leather goods, woodwork, art, filigree and manmade pearls. Most of these items are best bought in Ohrid which has lots of little craft shops along its meandering old town. Skopje's old town also has some linen, fur and leather shops. Skopje's Roma market (see page 118) is the best place to find their hand-embroidered costumes, but traditional Macedonian costumes, like you might see at Galičnik or Ilinden, are harder to find. See also www.aidtoartisans.org/macedonia for more on local crafts to buy.

For those living and working in Skopje, *Chapter 5* covers more of the items which you may be looking for whilst living away from home. Some English books can be found at Ikona, Matica and the English Learning Centre, but bring a good supply with you if you're going to stay here a while.

If you get hooked on the Macedonian starter *ajvar*, a delicious dish consisting of stewed red pepper and herbs, you can buy this in jars in the supermarket. However, the best *ajvar* would be home-made so try to buy it locally in places like Brajčino, where you can also buy local *rakija*, *liker*, jams, wild mushrooms and excellent home-made *baklava* if you eat in a local home (see page 169).

ARTS AND ENTERTAINMENT

Skopje is the best place for most arts and entertainment in Macedonia. With a population of only 500,000 it is not, of course, on a par with London, Paris or New York, but it does have a few drama theatres, its own philharmonic orchestra and a number of art galleries. For more information on all of these see *Chapter 5*.

Summer festivals are plenty (see above) and most towns do something. For cinema-goers, you won't find the latest blockbusters in the cinemas, but they also won't be dubbed, so you will be able to hear them in their original language.

Macedonia's football team, Vardar, plays in Skopje throughout the football season, and the popular match of the year is usually the match against England. In 2003 the England–Macedonia match was held in Skopje, but tickets for Brits were very hard to get hold of due to the fear of football hooliganism.

PHOTOGRAPHY

It is forbidden to take photos in churches, restricted military areas, and of military installations. Most people do not mind if you take their photo, but you should always ask first, and if they say no, do not insist. In the more remote villages farmers may also not agree with you taking photos of their animals. They believe that if you take a photo even of only one animal it will affect the whole flock.

Negative film is easy to get here, and development costs around 350MKD. Slide film is more difficult to get and can cost up to 500MKD just for the development. A good photolab which also has a good supply of Fuji Sensia, Provia and Velvia slide is Digital Studio Profoto Zdravko, tel: 02 322 7080, opposite the British Embassy on Dimitri Čupovski in Skopje. On the whole, however, you may be better off waiting till you get home in order to ensure high-quality film development and printing.

For more top tips on photography see box on pages 78–9.

MEDIA AND COMMUNICATIONS

News outlets

For such a small country, Macedonia has a lot of news outlets, TV and radio stations. On the one hand this could be a healthy indication of freedom of speech and freedom of the media, but quantity doesn't make quality. Many of the TV and radio stations have strong links to political parties and so their coverage of daily issues can be biased towards that party. At time of writing, the most reputable TV station which gives relatively balanced news coverage is A1 Television.

The daily papers produced in Cyrillic are *Dnevnik*, *Večer*, *Nova Makedonija*, *Makedonija Denes*, *Vest*, *Vreme*, and *Utrinski Vesnik*, which is the most serious of them all. There are five weekly Macedonian-language news magazines: *Denes*, *Aktuel*, *Start*, *Focus* and *ZUM*. *Forum* is a bi-weekly politics and life magazine which caters to a politically more analytical sector of Macedonians, and which critiques without necessarily being critical. *Forum* also has an interesting quarterly magazine.

The two main Macedonian language news agencies are MIA and Makfaks, and there are six main Macedonian-language TV stations: A1, Kanal 5, MTV (not Music TV!), Sitel, Skynet and Telma. Macedonian Radio and Channel 77 are

MAKING THE BEST OF YOUR TRAVEL PHOTOGRAPHS

Subject, composition and lighting

If it doesn't look good through the viewfinder, it will never look good as a picture. Don't take photographs for the sake of taking them; film is far too expensive. Be patient and wait until the image looks right.

Never take photographs in sensitive areas and always check with your guide that photography will be acceptable.

People

Photographing people is never easy and more often than not it requires a fair share of luck plus sharp instinct, a conditioned photographic eye and the ability to handle light both aesthetically and technically.

- If you want to take a portrait shot, always ask first. Often the offer to send a copy of the photograph to the subject will break the ice – but do remember to send it!
- Focus on the eyes of your subject.
- The best portraits are obtained in early morning and late evening light. In harsh light, photograph without flash in the shadows.
- Respect people's wishes and customs. Remember that infringement can lead to serious trouble.
- Never photograph military subjects.
- Be prepared for the unexpected.

Wildlife

There is no mystique to good wildlife photography. The secret is getting into the right place at the right time and then knowing what to do when you are there. Look for striking poses, aspects of behaviour and distinctive features. Try to illustrate the species within the context of its environment. Alternatively, focus in close on a characteristic which can be emphasised.

- The eyes are all-important. Make sure they are sharp and try to ensure they contain a highlight.
- Get the surroundings right – there is nothing worse than a distracting twig or highlighted leaf lurking in the background.
- A powerful flashgun can transform a dreary picture by lifting the subject out of its surroundings and putting the all-important highlights into the eyes. Artificial light is no substitute for natural light, so use judiciously.
- Getting close to the subject correspondingly reduces the depth of field; for distances of less than a metre, apertures between f16 and f32 are necessary. This means using flash to provide enough light – build your own bracket and use one or two small flashguns to illuminate the subject from the side.

Landscapes

Landscapes are forever changing; good landscape photography is all about light and mood. Generally the first and last two hours of daylight are best, or when peculiar climatic conditions add drama or emphasise distinctive features.

- Never place the horizon in the centre – in your mind's eye divide the frame into thirds and exaggerate either the land or the sky.

Cameras

Light, reliable and simple cameras will reduce hassle.

- For keen photographers, a single-lens reflex (SLR) camera should be at the heart of your outfit. Look for a model with the option of a range of different lenses and other accessories.
- Totally mechanical cameras which do not rely on batteries work even under extreme conditions. Combined with an exposure meter which doesn't require batteries, you have the perfect match. One of the best and most indestructible cameras available is the FM2 Nikon.
- Compact cameras are generally excellent, but because of restricted focal ranges they have severe limitations for wildlife.

- Automatic cameras are often noisy when winding on, and loading film.
- Flashy camera bags can draw unwelcome attention to your kit.

Lenses

The lens is the most important part of the camera, with the greatest influence on the final result. Choose the best you can afford – the type will be dictated by the subject and type of photograph you wish to take.

For people

- The lens should ideally have a focal length of 90 or 105mm.
- If you are not intimidated by getting in close, buy one with a macro facility, which will allow close focusing. For candid photographs, a 70–210 zoom lens is ideal.
- A fast lens (with a maximum aperture of around f2.8) will allow faster shutter speeds, which will mean sharper photographs. Distracting backgrounds will be thrown out of focus, improving the images' aesthetic appeal.

For wildlife

- Choose a lens of at least 300mm for a reasonable image size.
- For birds, lenses of 400mm or 500mm may be needed. They should be held on a tripod, or a beanbag if shooting from a vehicle.
- Macro lenses of 55mm and 105mm cover most subjects, creating images up to half life size. To enlarge further, extension tubes are required.
- In low light, lenses with very fast apertures help.

For landscapes

- Wide-angle lenses (35mm or less) are ideal for tight habitat shots (eg: forests) and are an excellent alternative for close ups, as you can shoot the subject within the context of its environment.
- For other landscapes, use a medium telephoto lens (100–300mm) to pick out interesting aspects of a vista and compress the perspective.

Film

Two types of film are available: prints (negatives) and transparencies (colour reversal). Prints are instantly accessible, ideal for showing to friends and putting into albums. However, if you want to share your experiences with a wider audience, through lectures or in publication, then the extra quality offered by transparency film is necessary.

Film speed (ISO number) indicates the sensitivity of the film to light. The lower the number, the less sensitive the film, but the better quality the final image. For general print film and if you are using transparencies just for lectures, ISO 100 or 200 are ideal. However, if you want to get your work published, the superior quality of ISO 25 to 100 film is best.

- Film bought in developing countries may be outdated or badly stored.
- Try to keep your film cool. Never leave it in direct sunlight.
- Do not allow fast film (ISO 800 or more) to pass through X-ray machines.
- Under weak light conditions use a faster film (ISO 200 or 400).
- For accurate people shots use Kodachrome 64 for its warmth, mellowness and gentle gradation of contrast. Reliable skin tones can also be recorded with Fuji Astia 100.
- To jazz up your portraits, use Fuji Velvia (50 ISO) or Provia (100 ISO).
- If cost is your priority, use process-paid Fuji films such as Sensia 11.
- For black-and-white people shots take Kodax T Max or Fuji Neopan.
- For natural subjects, where greens are a feature, use Fujicolour Reala (prints) and Fujichrome Velvia and Provia (transparencies).

Nick Garbutt is a professional photographer, writer, artist and expedition leader, specialising in natural history. He is co-author of 'Madagascar Wildlife' (Bradt Travel Guides), and a winner in the BBC Wildlife Photographer of the Year competition. John R Jones is a professional travel photographer specialising in minority people, and author of the Bradt guides to 'Vietnam' and 'Laos and Cambodia'.

the two main news-heavy radio stations broadcast in the Macedonian language, but there are dozens of local radio stations. Some of the most popular radio stations which a lot of the restaurants tune in to are Antenna 5 (95.5), City Radio (94.7), and Radio Uno (103.3).

On the Albanian side the news agencies include Balkanweb, Kosova Press, Kosova Live, Kosovo Information Centre and Albanews. There are two main newspapers, *Fakti* and *Lajm*, one weekly, *Lobi*, and one major national TV station, MTV3.

There are also Roma and Turkish media stations and papers produced in-country, as well as most of the major international newspapers and magazines available in Skopje after 19.00 every evening.

Post

The post in Macedonia is relatively reliable for low-value items, although not very fast. Most packages are opened on arrival in the country and items of value will often be stolen. I have yet to receive a package of books sent to me by normal post, the only exception being a particularly boring (but useful to me) book which I had bought in Macedonia, left in London and had to have sent back to me. The package arrived having been opened, sealed again with string and soldered with the Macedonian Post Office seal. Privacy, as guaranteed in international postal agreements, is obviously not observed in Macedonia.

As a result, high-value items, and even books, should be sent by FedEx or DHL. FedEx services in Skopje can be found at Blvd Partizanski Odredi 17, tel: 02 3137 233; DHL can be found at City Travel on the ground floor of the Kibo Restaurant building, tel: 02 3212 203 204. It usually takes between one and two weeks for letters to be delivered between Europe or America and Macedonia by standard post.

If you want post sent to you whilst travelling, have it addressed to you at Poste Restante, Pošta, Town Name. You will be able to pick it up at the town's main post office. Make sure that your surname is printed clearly in capitals and underlined, and bring some identification with you when you go to pick it up.

Stamps can only be bought at the post office, although there is a philatelic bureau at the *Ploštad* end of the Trgovski Centar in Skopje if you are looking for commemorative stamps.

Telephone

Phone numbers are constantly undergoing change in Macedonia, which does not make writing a guidebook very easy! All telephone numbers now have either six numbers outside Skopje, or seven numbers in Skopje, after the prefix. The prefixes were only changed in October 2001 and if you find really old numbers with the old prefixes, the guide below should help you to redial the new number. If there aren't enough digits then you will need to phone 988 for the new number. You can also phone the local telephone directory by dialling the new prefix below followed by 988. Two useful telephone directory websites, which you can use to find any new telephone number, are 988.mt.com.mk and www.yellowpages.com.mk. Both have an English interface, but the answers will appear in Cyrillic. For instructions on how to input Cyrillic on a Latin keyboard see the 'help' option.

Skopje's numbers also changed in June 2003 to add an extra digit to each number. Once again if you get given an old number with only six digits then the following guide will help you convert the number to the new seven-digit number:

Replace the first digit of these telephone numbers with:

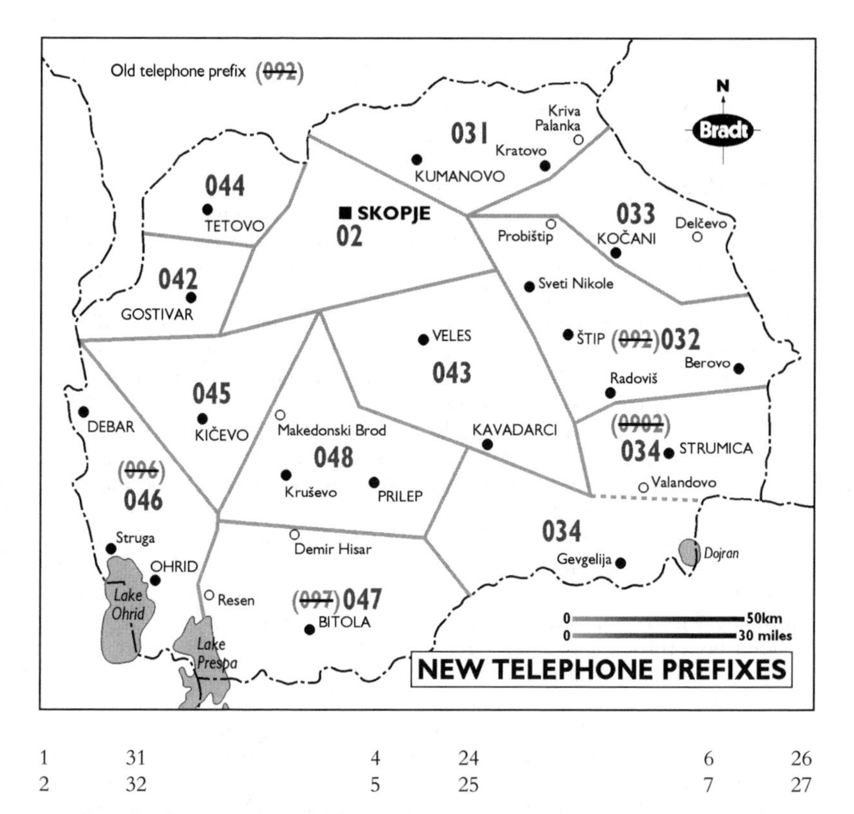

1	31	4	24	6	26
2	32	5	25	7	27

Replace the first two digits of these telephone numbers with:

33	203	36	306	39	309
34	204	37	307		
35	205	38	308		

Mobile phones are all the rage in Macedonia, although picture messaging hasn't caught on here any more than anywhere else. A new mobile phone company, Cosmoton, started up in 2003 which finally brought some competition into the market and prices have dropped slightly. Using internet telephony, eg: Skype (www.skype.com) is a cheap way to phone home.

Internet

Internet is king here. Everyone and their dog likes to have their own free internet site, but they are rarely updated, and are often inaccurate. Most towns will have an internet café or two, although they are usually slow, and may not have the latest internet browsers and software. The Contact internet café on the top floor of the Trgovski Centar in Skopje is at least on ISDN and has the latest software, so Mac users like me can access their account. They do charge 120MKD per hour though, whereas most other internet cafés will charge half that amount.

More and more of the new or refurbished hotels, such as Dal Met Fu in Skopje, and Millennium in Ohrid, also have internet hook-ups in every room. For those moving into Skopje to live, ADSL at 8mbps can be installed into your flat and is available for Apple Macs (see www.mt.net.mk).

As with writing to any person in anything other than their mother tongue, Macedonians are unlikely to answer an email that is not in Macedonian. So don't expect a reply too quickly, or at all, unless you have already established contact with them by phone or in person (see *Business* below).

BUSINESS

Business hours in Macedonia are sometimes quite difficult to pin down. Opening times vary from 06.30 (post offices), 07.00 (banks) 08.00 (supermarkets and green markets), 09.00 (some shops) to 10.00 (other shops, unless the proprietor is going out for breakfast coffee). Some places shut for lunch, especially in the summer when the day is hot, and some travel agents outside Skopje for instance will close from 11.00 to 17.00 and then open again till 20.00. Closing times also vary from 15:00 (some museums and repair stores, even if their stated closing time is in fact 16.00), 16.00 (government and media offices) to anything between 17.00 and 22.00. Bars, restaurants and nightclubs are required by law to be closed from midnight on weekdays and from 01.00 at the weekends. If you are trying to get hold of government officials it is best to do so between 10.00 to 12.00 and 14.00 to 15.00. Most shops are shut on Sunday.

If you have not done business in the Balkans before, and especially if you come from a time-driven and impersonal business culture like the US, UK, Germany or Switzerland, you'll probably find doing business in Macedonia utterly frustrating. First of all, Macedonians do not see time as a product, ie: as money, so don't be surprised if you don't get your delivery on time, people are late for meetings, or cancel with little or no notice, and don't meet deadlines. In that sense, Macedonia is very Mediterranean.

Secondly, while they may openly condemn nepotism especially in the government, they rarely carry out any business transaction that does not involve a friend or relative. This is not difficult in a country of only two million people. On the contrary, Macedonians think it mighty odd not to use their friend's service, even if this means receiving an inadequate, delayed and substandard product. Moreover, of course, because the transaction has been done through a friend, you can't exactly complain when things don't work properly without sacrificing a friendship. Beware, therefore, of the business associate who becomes too friendly – he (sadly, there are still few women in the upper echelons of business here) is almost definitely going to call you for a favour later, and if you refuse he may cut the 'favours' in return.

Thirdly, few Macedonians see service as a product that can earn money. This is a leftover from the communist days, when state-owned shops were the only ones you could shop in and so, because there was no competition, it didn't matter how badly the customer was treated; they didn't have anywhere else to purchase products from anyway. You'll find bolshy service and a complete lack of customer appreciation particularly apparent in so-called 'civil' services such as the post office, the police and almost any state-run business.

Finally, as another leftover from a centralised communist economy and government and probably from several hundred years of Ottoman overlordship, many Macedonians have simply got too used to state handouts and to not having to think laterally or for themselves, never mind in terms of a market economy and what makes business tick. What may seem like a blatantly obvious moneymaker and business opportunity to you will be shot dead in the water after an initially positive greeting. Follow-up and follow-through are not strong points in Macedonian business culture. Most

Macedonians would rather wait for a financial initiative from the international community than put their own sweat and savings into a new idea. And even then don't expect the internationally financed idea to roll on once the funding has dried up.

In defence of this lack of initiative, it is admittedly difficult to be proactive in an unstable and insecure economic environment. Theft and fraud are currently endemic in the system, making it difficult to guarantee the arrival of a part from overseas or the secure delivery of an order to an outside buyer. This book may never make it on to the shelves of Skopje's bookstores without government intervention and personal assurances from those on high.

Of course, there are some successful business people. Macedonia has a thriving black market, so somebody must know how to make money. The Vlach people have always been good at trade and you'll find them behind many of the successful, small, family-run businesses. The wine industry is also growing and many of the Albanian community who have worked abroad and come back, bring good earnings with them which they turn into cafés, bars and new homes, although rarely much beyond that.

On the whole though, business is done through personal contact. Don't expect a Macedonian business to answer your email or call (especially if it was in English) nor to follow up on a contact if you did not personally introduce them. This may be time consuming, but time isn't money here anyway. Fortunately, unlike in most of the rest of former Yugoslavia, you won't usually have to start the meeting or seal the deal with a shot of local *rakija*.

CULTURAL DOS AND DON'TS

Dress

Macedonia is a modern country where for the most part modesty is not an issue. That said, you'll find many Muslim ladies here of all ages dressed from head to foot in a long overcoat and headscarf no matter what time of day or year, and as a woman you may find it uncomfortable to wander around strongly Muslim areas in a crop top and low-cut shorts. Nudism is unheard of on the lake beaches.

Religious etiquette

You should certainly be modestly dressed to enter a mosque and its grounds, and while most churches don't seem to mind what you wear, there are a few which require decent dress, such as Treskavec, Lesnovo and Marko's Monastery. Decent dress means covered shoulders, torso and legs. It is forbidden to take photographs inside churches.

Although many Macedonians are atheist as a leftover from communist days, many have retaken to the Macedonian Orthodox Church with renewed vigour. These are the Macedonians whom you'll usually find at the churches and, outside Ohrid, they will find it odd if you don't cross yourself three times before entering the church and light a candle immediately on entering it. Practising Macedonians believe that you will not enter through the gates of heaven if you do not bring oil or wax with which to burn the light of God.

Drugs

As everywhere in the world, there is a drugs scene in Macedonia, although it is small. It is also illegal, even marijuana, so don't do it unless you want to risk ending up in a Macedonian jail. Dealing in drugs carries a hefty penalty, doubly so if you are caught taking it over an illegal border crossing. Finally, make sure you keep an eye on your bags at all times while travelling into Macedonia so that no-one can stuff anything illegal in there without you knowing.

Tipping

Tipping is not a necessity here, where most Macedonians can hardly afford more than a coffee in a bar. However, it is greatly appreciated by waiting staff, and as a foreigner if you can afford it, it's certainly a small boost to the economy, morale and attitudes towards tourists. An extra 10 or 20 denar is suitable on smaller sums of money up to 500MKD, usually rounded up to the nearest 50 or 100, and on larger sums, up to 10% is appropriate.

Gays/lesbians

The gay and lesbian scene here is very underground, and it would be considered most strange if not offensive for same-sex couples to walk hand in hand down the street, never mind kiss in public. Booking into a hotel would not be considered so strange unless you insisted on a *francuski krevet* (double bed), as double rooms normally come with twin beds.

Since being gay was decriminalised in 1996, the gay community in Macedonia is cautiously taking steps to promote greater acceptance. The first openly gay bar, the Baron, opened behind Bunjakovič market in 2003, and the first conference promoting the rights of sexual minorities took place in November 2003.

INTERACTING WITH LOCAL PEOPLE

Macedonian hospitality

Macedonian hospitality is extensive and often overpowering. Especially outside Skopje and Ohrid, where people are not used to contact with foreigners, Macedonians whom you meet will go out of their way to show you a site or monument and then insist on giving you a cup of thick black sweet Turkish coffee and a gift from their garden or some other memento. They will do this, even if you speak no Macedonian at all and they do not speak your language, which can make the conversation somewhat one-sided! They are not looking for a passport to your home country or even any other favour, and if you exchange addresses they will not usually follow up on it unless you do.

Macedonians would simply consider it too rude not to follow up on your request to the fullest extent, and then offer you a coffee in their home, and of course they are inquisitive to know who you are, where you come from and how you live at home. Trying to say no is extremely difficult without being rude, unless you have some handy pressing excuse, like 'I will turn into a pumpkin at midnight if I don't leave right now' or 'We left my mother in the car and she needs to go to the hospital for brain surgery'. In other words, no excuse will be satisfactory and especially the lame excuse that you do not have enough time, for the one thing that Macedonians do have a lot of is time, and they know that if there is five minutes' leeway in the schedule somewhere then you can fit in a half-hour coffee, and if there isn't five minutes in the schedule then you wouldn't be visiting their remote village anyway.

My advice is to make the most of this laid back way of life. It probably won't be around for much longer, as the fast pace and impersonal attitudes of modern-day life catch up with Macedonia. You may have to reschedule your cramped itinerary and knock something else off the list in order to fit in that coffee, but an invitation into the tenth house is still a privilege and will give you a momentary snapshot of how Macedonians live today.

A smile

As you travel around Macedonia, especially off the beaten track, you may be greeted at first with a cold, hard stare. Some communities are not often visited by outsiders and so the locals will be suspicious and inquisitive if not bewildered by your intentions to sightsee around their home. Even other Macedonians from a far-away town get this treatment. A smile, a wave and a greeting like *Zdravo*, or *Tungjatjeta* in Albanian regions, will miraculously make your intentions to the locals clear, and their hostile glare will instantly dissolve into a winning smile and a greeting in reply. Initiate a conversation and the obligatory coffee is bound to follow along with a personal tour of their home and town.

Cultural quirks

Every society has its little idioms and beliefs – here are a few from Macedonia.

Promaja is the Macedonian word for 'draught', not as in beer, but as in the wind/breeze which blows in through an open door or window. Many (particularly older) Macedonians, like many people in the Balkans, believe that *promaja* is the root of all illness, so don't be surprised if you are asked to close a window or door even on a blistering hot day.

Le le is an exclamation which Macedonians say all the time to add emphasis to a sentence. It's not directly translatable into anything in English, but other languages use similar expressions, like *ahh yoaaaa* in some Chinese dialects. *Ajde* is another exclamation which means 'let's go' or 'come on' or 'you're kidding'. You'll hear these two exclamations in the Macedonian language all over the place.

Politics and history

Macedonians are painfully aware of their history and politics, and are extremely interested in the slightest rumour of political intrigue. Macedonians will happily talk politics and history with you, but beware that you may not get them off the topic once started, no matter how many times you've heard the same tale of oppression and inequality. As a foreigner, you'll also never be right, and whatever you read in *Chapters 1* and *3* of this book is bound to offend someone, be they Macedonian, Albanian, Turk, Orthodox or Muslim. So take what you hear with a small pinch of salt and debate politics with great caution, even if you are a top scorer in the debating society at college.

There is a Macedonian proverb which goes 'If my cow dies, may my neighbour's cow die too.' This, sadly, does sum up a lot of the attitude of the people here. But, as Mahatma Gandhi said, 'An eye for an eye makes the whole world blind.'

GIVING SOMETHING BACK

The interaction of the outside world with Macedonia can have a variety of effects. Hopefully, your visit to Macedonia will have a positive impact on the tourist industry and, indirectly, on the economy and the people. If you would like to get more personally involved with charities and institutions in the country then here are a few to start you off. The website directory.macedonia.org/organizations lists hundreds more.

Roma

To read more about the Roma see page 40. There are a number of organisations which are trying to serve their needs and bring the very poor back out of poverty and into education and jobs. **ARKA** in Kumanovo has been instrumental in this regard. Contact the president Feat Kamberovski: 11 Oktomvri 17/1-1, 1300 Kumanovo; tel: 031 421 362 or 070 629 105; email: arka@arka.org.mk or arka_ku@yahoo.com; web: www.arka.org.mk.

For a Roma organisation based in the Roma settlement of Šuto Orizari contact Ahmed Naser of **CDRIM**, Viničaka 10, Šuto Orizari, 1000 Skopje; tel: 02 2654 839 or 070 544 266; email: nasersept@yahoo.com.

Anti-trafficking

The trafficking of women through and into Macedonia is a particularly entrenched problem (see above), not helped on the Macedonian side by a weak police and judicial system, and on the international side by the difficulty that the international community has in classing it as a crime separate from slavery, abduction, rape, torture, theft and prostitution. The whole issue is driven by huge financial profits and made easy for traffickers by the lack of public awareness.

TEMIS (Macedonian Women Jurist Association), who provide legal protection for trafficked women's rights and campaign to raise public awareness of the issue, and **Open Gate**, who are also campaigning and setting up a safe house and helpline for trafficked women in Macedonia, are two organisations who are helping to eradicate the trafficking of women. TEMIS can be contacted at Vasil Gorgov 34, 1000 Skopje; tel/fax: 02 3082 932/933, email: info@temis.com.mk; web: www.temis.com.mk and Open Gate at Otvorena Porta-La Strada Macedonia, PO Box 110, 1000 Skopje; tel: 02 2700 107; fax: 02 2700 367; email: lastrada@on.net.mk.

Churches, mosques and monasteries

Whether you are a believer or not, the churches, mosques and monasteries in Macedonia are amazing treasures which deserve to be kept for posterity. Although monastic life and the church have received a new boost since the independence of Macedonia, many of the churches and monasteries do not receive much funding. It is obvious which ones receive fewer donations by the state of disrepair that the churches and inns are in. The more remote and less well-known monasteries are particularly badly off. Consider giving generously to at least one or two of the churches and if you would like to make a larger donation by banker's draft or international money order, the residing father or sister will be able to furnish you with suitable details.

Environment

Macedonia's environment is at a critical point in its development (see pages 35–6) and so now is the time to ensure that it gets saved for the likes of you and I to enjoy when we come to visit another day. **Proaktiva** is a young enthusiastic group which has worked hard to increase public awareness of the importance of Macedonia's environment. Contact Slavjanka Miladinova at Dame Gruev 1-4/7, PO Box 695, 1000 Skopje; tel/fax: 02 321 5881; email: info@proaktiva.org.mk; web: www.proaktiva.org.mk.

Above Baba in local dress with Šarplaninec sheepdog (AT)
Below Chilli peppers and tobacco drying (AT)
Below right Cow in doorway (AT)

Above Skiing at Popova Šapka, Tetovo (TE)
Below View of Prilep from King Marko's Towers (TE)

Part Two

The Guide

Dojran roach

5 Skopje

The up-and-coming town of Skopje is divided by the River Vardar into the predominantly Muslim half to the north of the river, and the predominantly Orthodox Christian half to the south. Most government offices, main shopping centres, the main railway station and modern hotels are found on the southern side of town, although the old Turkish side of town, known as Čaršija, remains the main tourist attraction, with a large daily bazaar, an abundance of interesting old buildings and cafés, and the remnants of the Kale fortress.

Although life in the city has benefited in many ways from the influx of internationals since the Kosovo crisis, the conflict of 2001 almost killed off tourism from further afield. The long-term nature of the UN interim government in Kosovo means that Skopje will continue to see large numbers of foreigners in the city and the city will continue to cater to their needs, but Skopje's own international community is seeing a steady decline since the signing of the Ohrid Framework Agreement on Peace in August 2001. This in itself is an indicator of prevailing stability in the country, especially as emergency aid, such as medical care, housing reconstruction and mine clearing, is no longer needed or has been taken over by indigenous services. The United Nations Development Programme (UNDP), the European Agency for Reconstruction (EAR) and the Organisation for Security and Co-operation in Europe (OSCE) continue to work on long-term stability within the country, however, and will probably be in the country for a few more years yet. There are plans afoot to spruce up the city, and although these will no doubt take a while to come to fruition, the city is seeing a slow and steady increase in amenities, shops and entertainment.

Skopje makes an excellent base from which to see the rest of the country and is worth at least a couple of days in itself.

HISTORY

Nestled in the valley of the Vardar River, Skopje has been a welcome respite from the surrounding mountains since Neolithic times. It first became a major settlement around 500BC when it formed part of the outer reaches of the Illyrian nation now known as Albania. As Rome moved its empire eastward, the settlement became known as Skupi, and later came under Byzantine rule upon the division of the Roman Empire. At the crossroads of two major trading routes, one between Constantinople and Rome, and the other between Thessaloniki and northern Europe, the area has constantly changed hands between nations vying for control of this geopolitically strategic area. Byzantines, Slavs, Greeks, Bulgarians, Austro-Hungarians, Serbs and Turks have all ruled the city. 1392 began 520 years of Ottoman rule when the city became known as Üsküb and

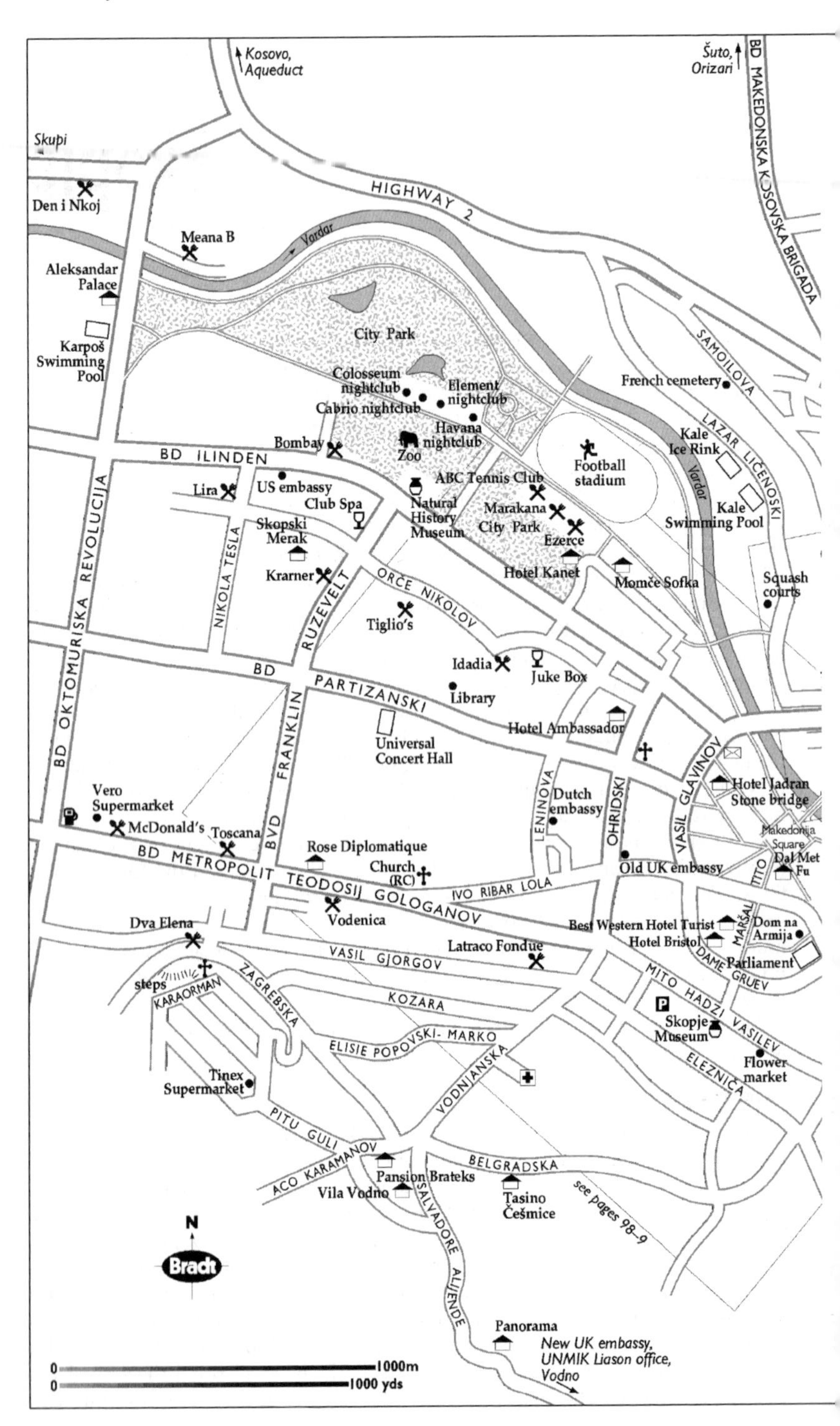

Kosovo, Aqueduct
Šuto, Orizari
Skupi
Den i Nkoj
Meana B
Aleksandar Palace
Karpoš Swimming Pool
HIGHWAY 2
Vardar
BD MAKEDONSKA KOSOVSKA BRIGADA
City Park
Colosseum nightclub
Element nightclub
Cabrio nightclub
Havana nightclub
Bombay
Zoo
BD ILINDEN
Lira
US embassy
Club Spa
Natural History Museum
ABC Tennis Club
Marakana
City Park
Ezerce
Hotel Kanet
Momče Sofka
Football stadium
SAMOILOVA
French cemetery
LAZAR LIČENOSKI
Kale Ice Rink
Kale Swimming Pool
Squash courts
Skopski Merak
Krarner
NIKOLA TESLA
BD OKTOMURISKA REVOLUCIJA
RUZEVELT
ORČE NIKOLOV
Tiglio's
Idadia
Juke Box
BD PARTIZANSKI
Library
Hotel Ambassador
Universal Concert Hall
BVD FRANKLIN
LENINOVA
Dutch embassy
OHRIDSKI
VASIL GLAVINOV
Hotel Jadran
Stone bridge
Makedonija Square
TITO
Dal Met Fu
Vero Supermarket
McDonald's
Toscana
BD METROPOLIT TEODOSIJ GOLOGANOV
Rose Diplomatique
Church (RC)
IVO RIBAR LOLA
Old UK embassy
Vodenica
Dva Elena
Best Western Hotel Turist
Hotel Bristol
MARŠAL
Dom na Armija
DAME GRUEV
Parliament
Latraco Fondue
VASIL GJORGOV
steps
KARAORMAN
ZAGREBSKA
KOZARA
MITO HADZI VASILEV
Skopje Museum
ELISIE POPOVSKI- MARKO
VODNIANSKA
ELEZNIČA
Flower market
Tinex Supermarket
PITU GULI
ACO KARAMANOV
Pansion Brateks
Vila Vodno
SALVADORE ALIJENDE
BELGRADSKA
Tasino Češmice
see pages 98–9
N
Bradt
Panorama
New UK embassy, UNMIK Liason office, Vodno
0
1000m
0
1000 yds

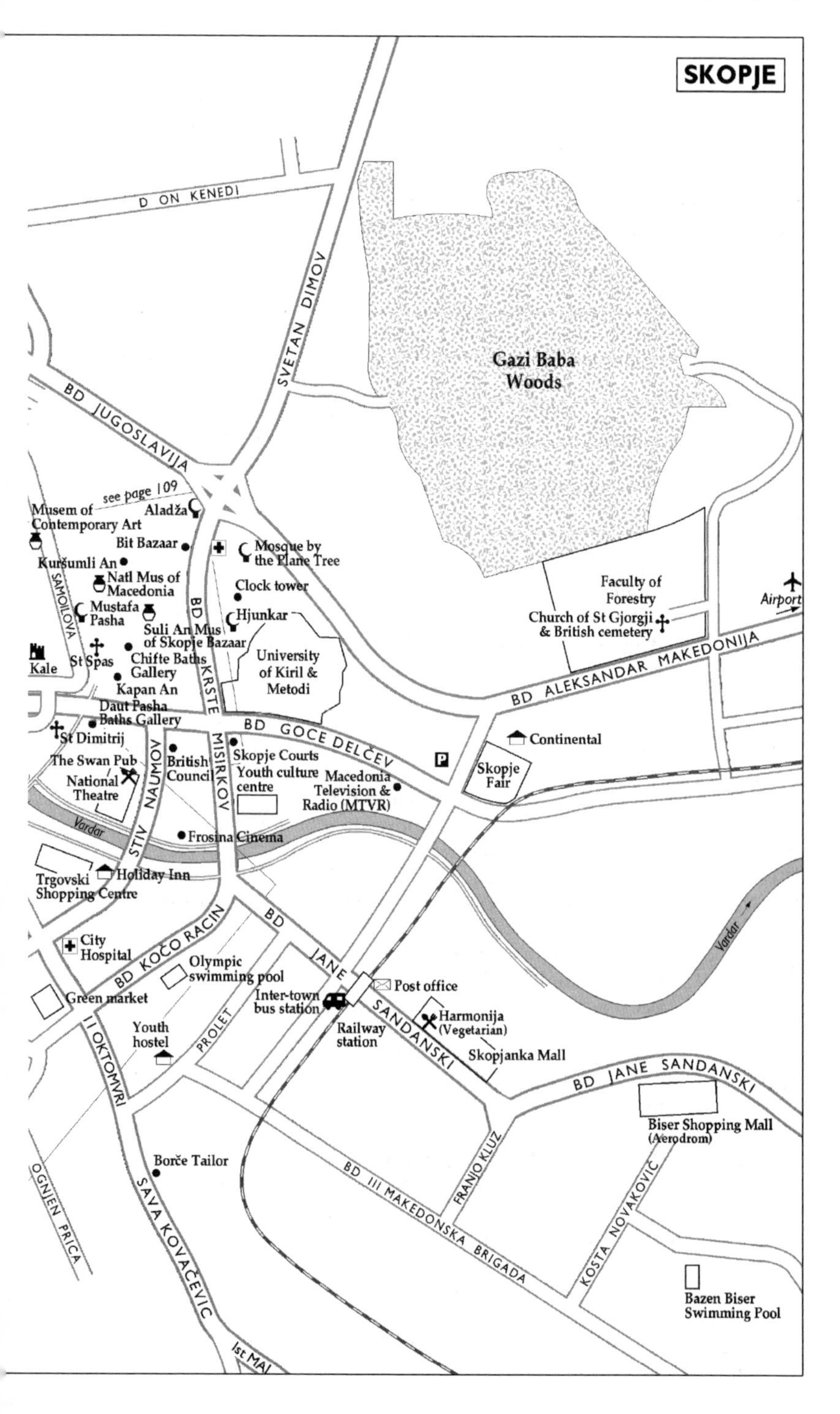
SKOPJE
D ON KENEDI
SVETAN DIMOV
Gazi Baba Woods
BD JUGOSLAVIJA
see page 109
Musem of Contemporary Art
Aladža
Bit Bazaar
Mosque by the Plane Tree
Kuršumli An
Natl Mus of Macedonia
Clock tower
Faculty of Forestry
Airport
SAMOILOVA
Mustafa Pasha
Suli An Mus of Skopje Bazaar
Hjunkar
Church of St Gjorgji & British cemetery
Kale
St Spas
Chifte Baths Gallery
Kapan An
University of Kiril & Metodi
BD KRSTE MISIRKOV
BD ALEKSANDAR MAKEDONIJA
Daut Pasha Baths Gallery
BD GOCE DELČEV
St Dimitrij
Continental
The Swan Pub
National Theatre
British Council
Skopje Courts
Youth culture centre
Macedonia Television & Radio (MTVR)
Skopje Fair
STIV NAUMOV
Vardar
Frosina Cinema
Trgovski Shopping Centre
Holiday Inn
BD KOČO RACIN
BD JANE SANDANSKI
City Hospital
Olympic swimming pool
Post office
Green market
Inter-town bus station
Harmonija (Vegetarian)
Railway station
Youth hostel
PROLET
11 OKTOMVRI
Skopjanka Mall
BD JANE SANDANSKI
Biser Shopping Mall (Aerodrom)
Borče Tailor
FRANJO KLUZ
KOSTA NOVAKOVIC
OGNJEN PRICA
SAVA KOVAČEVIC
BD III MAKEDONSKA BRIGADA
Bazen Biser Swimming Pool
1st MAJ

after further swaps in sovereignty during and between both World Wars, it was finally incorporated in 1944 into Federal Yugoslavia as the capital of the autonomous republic of Macedonia. Since 1991 Skopje has been the capital of the independent Republic of Macedonia when it broke free from the Federation during the breakup of Yugoslavia

Chronology

3500BC	Neolithic tribes inhabited the Skopje region.
700–500BC	Illyrians of the ancient Greek Empire founded a settlement at present-day Zlokučani and a fort at Kale.
148BC	Skupi made the seat of the Roman district government of Dardania as part of the larger province of Moesia superior.
AD395	Under the division of the Roman Empire Skupi became part of the Byzantine Empire ruled from Constantinople.
518	Skupi almost completely destroyed by earthquake. Emperor Justinian rebuilt the town a few kilometres further south.
695	Skupi taken over by Slavs.
10th century	Known as Skoplje under the Macedonian-Bulgarian Empire.
1189	Became part of the Serbian Empire before reverting to Byzantine rule.
1282	Conquered by the Serbian King Milutin II.
1346	Milutin's grandson, Stefan Dušan, claimed Skopje as his capital and proclaimed himself Tsar.
1392	Beginning of Ottoman rule over the Balkans for the next 520 years. Town known to the Turks as Üsküb.
15th century	Many Jews fled to Üsküb from Spain.
1555	Earthquake destroyed much of the centre of Üsküb.
1689	Occupied by the Austrian General Piccolomini. Plague infested the city, and on leaving Piccolomini burned it down.
1873	Üsküb to Saloniki railway line built.
1889	Mother Teresa – Gondza Bojadziu – born in Skopje.
1912–13	First and second Balkan wars.
1914	Skopje ruled by Bulgaria.
1918	Came under the rule of the Kingdom of Serbs, Croats and Slovenes.
1920	Ruled for six months by the Yugoslav Communist Party.
1941	Ruled again by Bulgaria.
1944	Became the capital of the Federal Yugoslav Republic of Macedonia.
1963	Earthquake razed much of Skopje.
1991	Skopje became the capital of the independent Republic of Macedonia.

The ancient sites of Skupi and Kale

Kale, the Ottoman fortress that overlooks Skopje and the Vardar Valley, houses human settlements from as early as Neolithic times c3500BC. Geographic evidence shows that such prehistoric settlements would have been on the edge of a marsh, but later mountains surrounding Skopje turned the area into the fertile plains of the River Vardar. It became a natural route of passage between greater cities further east and west, and between the Aegean Sea in the south at Thessaloniki (earlier known as Saloniki and today still called Solun in Macedonian) and any travels further north into central Europe.

In the 7th and 6th centuries BC many Greeks, tempted by trade and lands elsewhere, travelled and settled further north. The Illyrians settled in what is now known as Albania, and the outer reaches of their nation covered the source of the River Vardar all the way down to the foothills of the Vodno and the Skopska Black Mountains. They built the first fort at Kale, and others on Gradište above the present- day district of Dolno Nerezi, and later founded the town of Skupi in the area of present-day Zlokučani village to the northwest of the town centre.

While other ancient cities of today's Macedonia, such as Hereaclea near Bitola and Stobi near Gradsko, came under the rule of the Macedonian Empire of Aleksandar III of Macedon, Skupi remained part of the Thracian earldom of Dardania until the 2nd century BC. Roman expansion east brought Skupi under Roman rule in 148BC when it became the seat of local government for the district of Dardania as part of the province of Moesia superior.

A part of the Byzantine Empire

When the Roman Empire was divided into eastern and western halves in AD395, Skupi came under Byzantine rule from Constantinople (today's Istanbul) and became an important trading and garrison town for the region. The Byzantine Emperor Justinian (AD527–65) was born in Tauresium (about 20km southeast of present-day Skopje) in AD483, and after Skupi was almost completely destroyed by an earthquake in 518, Justinian rebuilt a new town at the fertile entry point of the River Lepenec into the Vardar. The town became known as *Justiniana Prima* during his reign.

Towards the end of the 6th century, Skupi itself had declined in prestige, although newer settlements were emerging on the southern slopes of the Vardar Valley below Mount Vodno. These were destroyed, however, by invading Slav troops in AD695, who fortified Kale and the northern side of the Vardar for some years to come.

The region soon came back under Byzantine rule. The town prospered and expanded, whilst many churches and monasteries were established in the tranquility and remoteness of the surrounding hills.

In the 10th century the town was known as Skoplje under the Macedonian-Bulgarian Empire, and in AD996 it fell within the independent state of free Macedonia, having been liberated from the Bulgarians by Tsar Samoil (see box, page 9). Although Skoplje was not made capital of the new Macedonian state, the town retained its strategic trading importance until Tsar Samoil's death in 1014, when Skoplje withered again into decline, aided by another earthquake hitting the town at the end of the 11th century.

The Byzantine Empire took advantage of the decline in Skoplje to regain influence in the area, but lost control of it once again in 1282 to Serbian King Milutin II. Milutin's grandson, Stefan Dušan, then made Skopje his capital, from which he proclaimed himself Tsar in 1346.

Five hundred years of Ottoman rule

Rolling back Byzantine rule across much of the Balkans, the Ottoman Turks finally took Skopje under their rule in 1392 beginning 520 years of Ottoman rule in the town, called Üsküb by the Turks. At first the Ottomans divided the greater Macedonian region into four *vilayets*, or districts – Üsküb, Kjustendil, Manastir and Saloniki – and as the northernmost of these, Üsküb was strategically important for further forays into northern Europe. (Later Kjustendil was given back to Serbia and Bulgaria, but Janina and Shkodra were gained on the Albanian and Greek side.)

Under Ottoman rule the town moved further towards the entry point of the River Serava into the Vardar. It also became predominantly Muslim and the architecture of the town changed accordingly. During the 15th century, many travellers' inns were established in the town, such as Kapan An and Suli An, which still exist today. The city's famous Stone Bridge – *Kameni Most* – was also reconstructed during this period and the famous Daud Pasha baths (now a modern art gallery) was built at the end of the 15th century. At this time numerous Jews driven out of Spain settled in Üsküb, adding to the cultural mix of the town and aiding the town's trading reputation.

At the beginning of Ottoman rule, several mosques quickly sprang up in the city, and church lands were often seized and given to ex-soldiers, while many churches themselves were converted over time into mosques. The most impressive mosques erected during this early period include the Sultan Murat or Hjunkar Mosque, Aladža Mosque and the Mustafa Pasha Mosque.

In 1555 another earthquake hit the town, destroying much of the centre, although the outskirts survived and the town continued to prosper with traders and travellers. Travel reports from the era number Üsküb's population anywhere between 30,000 and 60,000 inhabitants.

For a very short period in 1689, Üsküb was occupied by the Austrian General Piccolomini. He and his troops did not stay for long, however, as the town was quickly engulfed by the plague. On retreating from the town Piccolomini's troop set fire to Üsküb, perhaps in order to stamp out the plague, although some would say this was done in order to revenge the 1683 Ottoman invasion of Vienna.

For the next two centuries Üsküb's prestige waned and by the 19th century its population had dwindled to a mere 10,000. In 1873, however, the completion of the Üsküb–Saloniki (now Skopje–Thessaloniki) railway brought many more travellers and traders to the town, so that by the turn of the century Üsküb had regained its former numbers of around 30,000.

Towards the end of the Ottoman Empire, Üsküb, along with other towns in Macedonia – Kruševo and Manastir (now Bitola) – became main hubs of rebellious movements against Ottoman rule. Üsküb was a key player in the Ilinden Rising of August 1903 when native Macedonians of the region declared the emergence of the Republic of Kruševo. While the Kruševo Republic lasted only ten days before being quelled by the Ottomans, it was a sign of the beginning of the end. After just over 600 years of rule of the area the Ottomans were finally ousted in 1912 during the First Balkan War.

The Balkan Wars and the World Wars

As the administrative centre of the region, Üsküb also administered the *vilayet* (district) of Kosovo under Ottoman rule. This did not go down well with the increasingly Albanian population of Kosovo, who preferred to be ruled by Albanians rather than the ethnic Slav and Turkish mix of Üsküb. Albanians had started to intensify their harassment of Serbs in the area over the past decade, culminating on August 12 1912 when 15,000 Albanians marched on Üsküb in a bid to take over the city. The Turks, already weak from other battles against the united front of Greece, Serbia and Bulgaria during the First Balkan War, started to flee.

When Serb reinforcements arrived some weeks later, the October 23 Battle of Kumanovo (50km northeast of Skopje) proved decisive in firmly driving out the Ottomans from all of Macedonia. Skopje remained under Serbian rule during the Second Balkan War of 1913 when the formerly united front started to fight amongst themselves, until in 1914 the town was finally taken over by the

Bulgarians. By 1918 it belonged to the Kingdom of Serbs, Croats and Slovenes, and remained so until 1939, apart from a brief period of six months in 1920 when Skopje was controlled by the Yugoslav Communist Party. The inter-war period of Royalist Yugoslavia saw significant immigration of ethnic Serbs into the region. An ethnic Serb ruling elite dominated over Turkish, Albanian and Macedonian cultures, continuing the repression wrought by previous Turkish rulers over the region.

During World War II, Skopje came under German fascist occupation, and was later taken over by Bulgarian fascist forces. March 1941 saw huge anti-Nazi demonstrations throughout the streets of the town, as Yugoslavia was dragged into the war. But Nazi war crimes were not to be stopped and on March 11 1943, Skopje's entire Jewish population of 3,286 Jews was deported to the gas chambers of Treblinka concentration camp in Poland. Another year and a half later, on November 13 1944, Skopje was liberated by the partisans, who finally won control after a bitter two-day battle.

The Federal Yugoslav Republic of Macedonia

From 1944 until 1991 Skopje was the capital of the Federal Yugoslav Republic of Macedonia. The city expanded and the population grew during this period from just over 150,000 in 1945 to almost 600,000 in the early nineties. Continuing to be prone to natural disasters the city was flooded by the Vardar in 1962 and then suffered considerable damage from a severe earthquake on July 26 1963. Over 1,000 people were killed as a result of the earthquake, almost 3,000 injured, and over 100,000 were made homeless.

Almost all of the city's beautiful 18th- and 19th-century buildings were destroyed in the earthquake, including the National Theatre and many government buildings, as well as most of the Kale fortress. International financial aid poured into Skopje in order to help rebuild the city. Sadly, the result was the many 'modern' concrete monstrosities of sixties' communism that can still be seen today and hundreds of now-abandoned caravans and prefabricated mobile homes left to rot. Even Mother Teresa's house was razed to make way for a modern shopping centre (the Trgovski Centar). Fortunately, though, as with previous earthquakes, much of the old Turkish side of town survived.

Independence

Skopje made the transition easily from the capital of the Federal Yugoslav Republic of Macedonia to the capital of the former Yugoslav Republic of Macedonia that it is today. The city has livened up considerably since Skopje housed the headquarters of the NATO intervention into Kosovo in 1998 and 1999, and due to its proximity to the protectorate the city will continue to see NATO troops and other international staff for as long as the UN governs Kosovo. The city also saw rioting during the conflict of 2000 and 2001 when internal conflict between the Albanian minority and the Macedonian ruling majority erupted over lack of Albanian representation in government and other social institutions.

GETTING AROUND

Transport in Skopje is plentiful. **Taxis** abound and are cheap at only 50MKD for a minimum fare, which will take you most places in the city. Taxis come in a variety of four-door sizes and makes, from old Skodas, former Yugoslavian Zastavas, Mercedes and BMWs to brand new VW Golfs and Passats. All are marked with lighted taxi signs on the roof, and you can flag them down almost anywhere on the street. Taxi ranks can be found at the main intersections of town, the central one being outside the Blue Café at the pedestrian end of 11 Oktomvri near the Trgovski Centar. Taxis can also be ordered from any of the following numbers: 9183, 9188, 9190, 9192, 9193, 9194, 9195, 9196, 9197, 9198. The dispatchers at 9177 speak excellent English and are accustomed to the expat community phoning them in English. Most taxi drivers also speak good English or German, and those who do will be quick to give you their business card for repeat business in case you prefer to have a taxi driver who speaks English.

Buses can get very crowded during rush hour, but they are frequent and cover a wide area. A bus map and timetable are non-existent, so hop on a bus going in the general direction and bring your own town map. The Inter Town Bus Station is located at the train station (tel: 02 3166 254). There are direct international buses from here to Belgrade, Zagreb, Ljubljana, Priština and Sofia, but there are no direct buses to Greece. A fast bus to Negotino and Lake Dojran leaves at 16.00 every day from Maršal Tito street opposite the Bristol Hotel.

There are no buses to the **airport**. A taxi there costs 900MKD (€15) if flagged down on the street, although sometimes you can get them for less, and often they can be ordered in advance for 600MKD from 9177. You can order a taxi into town from the taxi desk inside the airport, after customs but before you exit into the arrivals lounge. This will cost you only 900MKD, whereas a taxi from outside the airport will be 1,200MKD (€20). When taking a taxi to the airport and if you are unlucky enough to get a driver who does not speak much English, make sure you ask for the '*aerodrom vo Petrovec*' not to be confused with a part of Skopje city which is also called *Aerodrom* after the old airport!

The new **railway station** on Jane Sandanski is 15 minutes' walk southeast of the Stone Bridge (tel: 02 3164 255). It is probably one of the sorriest main stations you will come across in the Balkans and is not located in a very inviting part of town, although it is as safe as anywhere else in Skopje. The information desk staff do not speak much English, but fairly good German. There are two trains a day going to Thessaloniki, one early in the morning and the other late afternoon. Trains to Priština (Kosovo) are due to start again soon.

COMMUNICATIONS

The main post office is the large building immediately to the east of the Stone Bridge on the south side of the river. It is open from 07.00 to 17.30 Monday to Saturday and from 07.00 to 14.30 on Sunday. The telephone centre located in the main post office is open 24 hours. Calls made at the post office or at telephone kiosks on the street need to be made either with tokens or using a prepaid phone card. Both can be purchased from post offices, and in addition phone cards are available at any cigarette kiosk, and tokens can be obtained from any newspaper stand.

There are numerous internet cafés around town and they are very cheap. The newest is Contact Café on the top floor of the Trgovski shopping centre. One hour here costs 120MKD. For half the price you can also use the internet centre opposite La Caffe on Maršal Tito street, or at Ivo Ribar Lola 22. Black-and-white print services are available at both. Some of the smaller internet cafés may not have the latest web browsers and so if you are trying to access a fairly advanced site then you are better off going to the Contact Café.

WHERE TO STAY

Skopje offers a whole range of hotels and private rooms, as well as a youth hostel, and in the summer there are also camping sites.

Hotels

Hotel Aleksandar Palace (135 rooms) Blvd Oktomvriska Revolucija; tel: 02 3092 392/3092 200; fax: 02 3092 152; email: info@aleksandarpalace.com.mk. Located by the river, this is the only five-star hotel in Skopje. All the rooms have air conditioning, satellite and cable TV, minibar and internet connection. Its restaurant is good value, has reasonable food and is open to non-residents. Its fitness centre is also open to non-residents at 380MKD per session (800MKD including use of sauna and lukewarm jacuzzi) and is the best available, although its layout is not the best for privacy. There is no swimming pool, but there is an Olympic-size pool next door to the Aleksandar Palace. Prices from 9,480MKD (US$158) single, including breakfast, to 14,280MKD (US$238) double. There are no seasonal price variations.

Continental (230 rooms) Blvd Aleksandar Makedonski bb; tel: 02 3116 599; fax: 02 3222 221; web: www.contimax.com. A four-star tower-block hotel that houses the Skopje NATO press office on the southeast outskirts of the city. It has good conference facilities and a decent restaurant. Prices range from 8,000 to 12,050MKD.

Holiday Inn (178 rooms) Vasil Agilarski 11; tel: 02 3292 929; fax: 02 3115 503; email: hiskopje@holiday-inn.com.mk; web: holiday-inn.com/skopje. Another four-star hotel conveniently located near the centre of town on the south side of the river. It is next to the Trgovski shopping centre and so is very close to amenities such as restaurants, supermarkets, underground parking, pubs and the new Millennium Cinema. The hotel has an excellent fitness centre, which is not open to the public. Reserve a room well in advance as the hotel is often booked with international conferences. Single room €150, double €258. During August prices can drop by up to 50% when Skopje empties out due to the summer heat.

Best Western Hotel Tourist (85 rooms) Gjuro Sturgar 11; tel: 02 328 9111; fax 02 328 9100; email: bestwestern@hotelturist.com.mk; web: www.bestwestern-ce.com/turist. The hotel's coffee shop entrance is on Maršal Tito near the centre of the city. Maršal Tito Street is a pedestrian zone although there aren't many pedestrians to be seen at this end of the street, which makes it very quiet. This four-star hotel has recently become a part of the Best Western chain and has been completely refurbished. Western four-star standards apply. Single €120, double €150, suite €170.

Hotel Bristol (33 rooms) Maršal Tito bb; tel: 02 3114 883; fax: 02 3236 556. A three-star hotel at the end of Maršal Tito with an older feel to it, this was the original meeting place for the Skopje International Rotary Club starting in 1924 (now held in the Hotel Aleksandar Palace). Rooms here go for 4,450–6,000MKD.

Hotel Jadran (21 rooms) 27th Mart bb; tel: 02 3118 427; fax: 02 3118 334. Formerly the embassy of Armenia, this small three-star hotel is resplendent with 19th-century Turkish style furnishings and is centrally located in the pedestrian heart of the city. A single room costs €60 and a double costs €100.

Hotel Dal Met Fu (6 rooms) tel: 02 3239 584, above the restaurant of the same name in the town square, has recently opened, and is well furnished including internet connection in each room for those who can't afford to get away from work. Single €55, double €85, apartment €145.

Rose Diplomatique (8 rooms) Roza Luxemburg; tel: 02 3135 469; fax: 02 3129 058. A very nice small hotel with an attractive interior and a good restaurant (for residents only). The hotel is often full so book well in advance. Single €70 per night, double €95, apartment €115.

Hotel Ambassador (35 rooms) Pirinksa 38; tel: 02 3121 383 is in the courtyard next to the Russian Embassy. This is the hotel with the statue of liberty on top and a couple of other Roman figures. Simply furnished single/double rooms for €50/€80.

Hotel Tasino Češmice (60 rooms) Belgradska 28; tel: 02 3177 333; fax: 02 178 329. A three-star hotel to the south of the centre of town offering small nicely furnished rooms with fridge, satellite TV and telephone. Single €67, double €83.

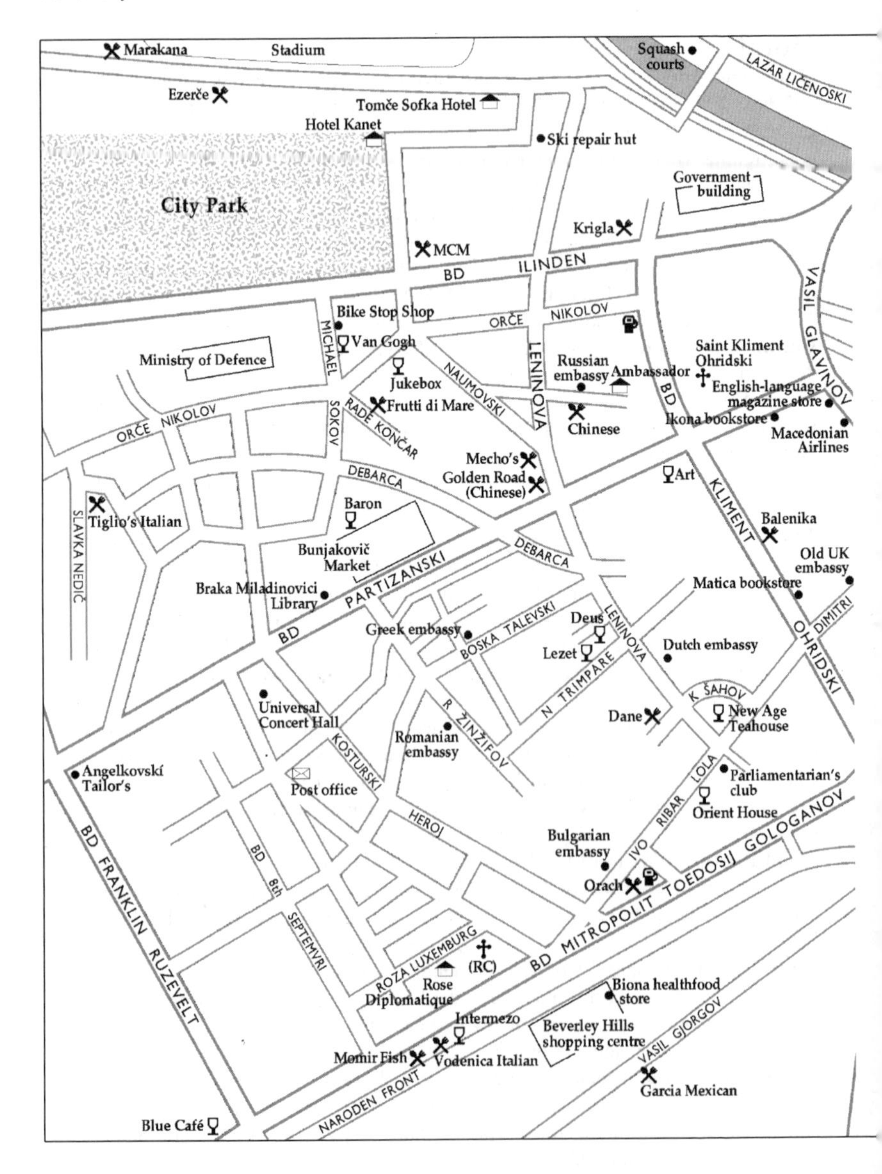

Panorama (72 rooms) Vodnjanska bb; tel: 02 3178 474. This hotel is south of the city on the road starting up to Vodno hill. It offers excellent views of the city and its backyard is the vineries and woods of Vodno. The hotel is still of the classic socialist style in need of refurbishment and a coat of paint. Single €44, double €64.

Private rooms and *pansions*

If you would prefer to stay in a **private room** in order to get a more Balkan feel to your visit then these can be arranged through the Skopje Tourist Information Office, tel: 02 3116 854. Make sure you ask for something near the centre of the city otherwise you may have a long walk into the centre. Private rooms start at

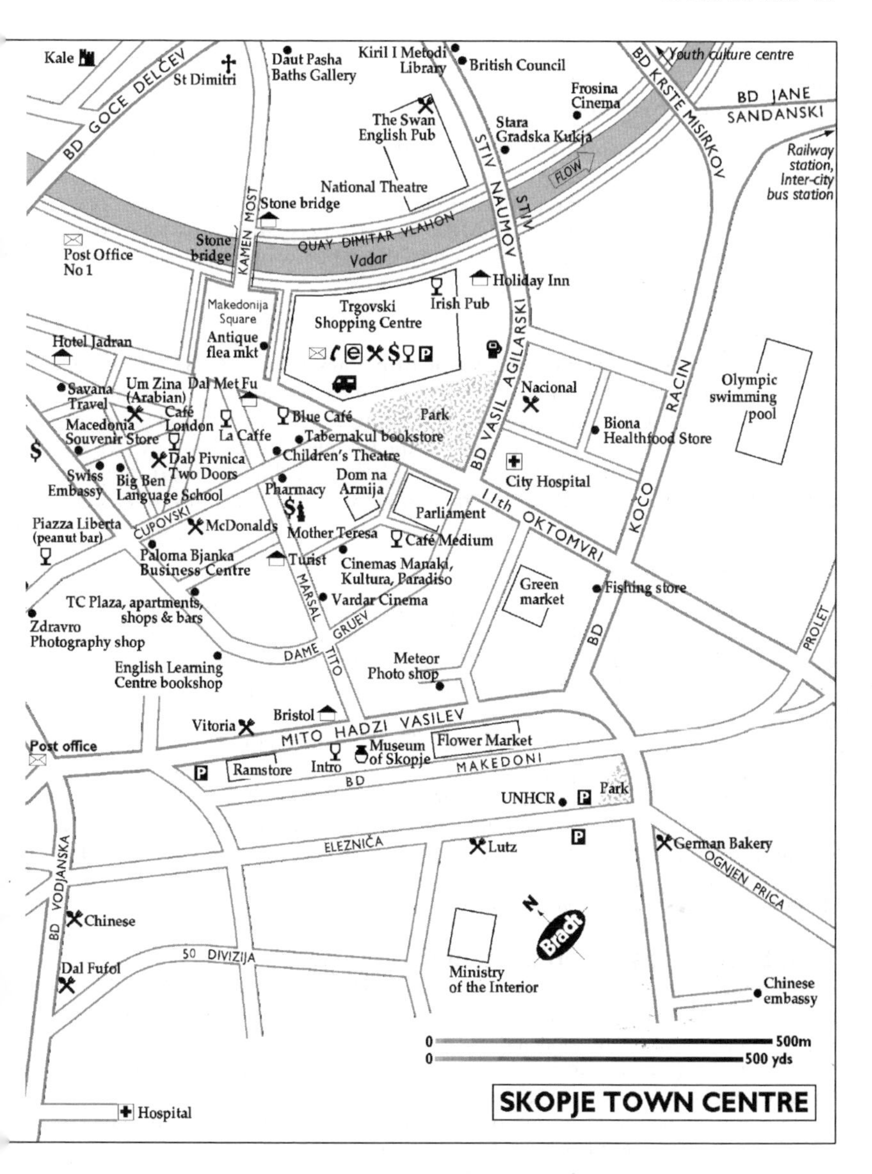

1,200MKD or €10 per person per night, excluding breakfast.

Bed and breakfast type lodges or *pansions* are also available. **Pansion Brateks** at Aco Karamanov 3a (six rooms) tel: 02 3176 606, mobile 070 243 232, is popular and therefore often full. It is a good half-hour walk from the centre but is set at the foot of Mount Vodno among the houses of the rich and the diplomats giving it an airy up-market feel. German is spoken and only a little English. Singles/doubles are 2,000/3,500 MKD. Other *pansions* include:

Boda Ivo Ribar Lola 32; tel: 02 3221 023
Ema Gavril Lesnovski 4; tel: 02 3078 651

Kapištec Mile Pop Jordanov 3; tel: 02 3081 424/425
Mlin Balkan Leninova 79; tel: 02 3110 635
Vuk Skopje Mile Pop Jordanov 1; tel: 02 3081 426/427

There is only one **youth hostel** in Skopje, the Dom Blagoj Sosolcev Prolet 25, tel: 02 3114 849; fax: 02 3235 029. It is not far from the train station and is open 24 hours a day all year round offering clean tidy rooms. A single room costs 1,520MKD for nonmembers, 1,210MKD for members; a bed in a twin room costs 1,210/865MKD; there are also a few three-bed rooms, and apartments. Breakfast costs an additional 65MKD.

Camping

Camping is available at **Feroturist Autocamp Park** (tel: 02 3228 246; fax: 02 3162 677) between the stadium and the river in the city park. It is open April to mid-October at 500MKD per tent space for four. It is located very close to the centre, but also suffers from mosquitoes in the summer. **Belvi** campsite (tel: 02 2751 100) is 5km east of Skopje just off the highway at Ilinden. **Saraj** campsite (tel: 02 2047 307) is on the River Treška just before Lake Matka. It is often very full in the summer.

WHERE TO EAT

The influx of foreigners into Skopje since the NATO intervention into Kosovo has sprouted a host of new café-bars and restaurants, including Chinese and Indian, as well as the usual Italian and Greek, and of course Macedonian and Turkish. For a more in-depth comment on cuisine in Macedonia see *Chapter 3*.

Eating out is still quite cheap, with a lunch dish often as little as 150-200MKD, and evening meals going up to 1,000MKD or more if you eat on the expensive side. Almost any menu in Skopje will appear in English as well as Macedonian. Most places will be very smoky in the winter, but in the summer the abundance of outdoor seating in Skopje makes this point irrelevant — only Dal Met Fu offers non-smoking seating. There are an abundance of eateries in the Trgovski shopping centre, as well as around Orče Nikolov.

The best of Macedonia's traditional mix

Dab Pivnica (also known as Two Doors among the internationals) Gorki Maksim 1. Just off the main square, and would be easy to miss if you were not to look for the two huge dark brown wooden doors. Don't miss a mixed platter of their cold creamed starters (*ordever*), parma ham and chunks of parmesan cheese, with a side basket of their delicious sesame seed pizza bread strips. This is often enough for a meal on its own, but they have lots of other excellent dishes including aubergine and mozarella pizza, mixed grills, and excellent rack of lamb ribs. Usually open at 08.00 for soup if you haven't had breakfast included in your hotel.
Pivnica An Inside the old Turkish inn on Kapan An in the old town; tel: 02 321 2111. Offers a few vegetarian dishes.
Nacional Vasil Agilarski, opposite the park by the Tgovski Centar; tel: 02 3214 200. Has excellent pizza bread but beware the live elevator music.
Krigla On the corner of Ohridski and Ilinden.
Makedonska Kukja Slavej Planina, tel: 02 3216 016. This building, which was the home of Josif Mihaijlovski, the first Mayor of Skopje from 1929 to 1941 who was appointed by the king of royalist Yugoslavi. The building has been a restaurant since 1964, making it the oldest restaurant building in Skopje. The building and restaurant interior have been beautifully restored to give a sense of royal times and displaying a

number of the achievements of Skopje's first mayor. The menu is not extensive but the food is excellent. Try their mince meat stuffed aubergines.
Balkanika Bd Kliment Ohridski. Decked out in true Yugonostalgia with busts of Tito and waiters in red pioneer scarves. Traditional music and food add to the atmosphere.
Lira Nikola Tesla 11; tel: 02 3061 726. Excellent traditional live music every evening.
Idadia M and **Idadia Š** On the corner of Orče Nikolov and Rade Končar streets. This is an old family restaurant once owned by two brothers who split the restaurant in two when they fell out with each other. There is an obvious partition wall down the centre of the main entrance.
Orach At the end of Ivo Ribar Lola opposite the Bulgarian Embassy; tel: 02 3223 933. It's a cosy winter restaurant and serves great beef stroganoff. Sadly its patio seating is very noisy in the summer.
Stara Gradska Kukja (Old City House) Pajko Maalo 14 (opposite the east side of the Macedonian National Theatre); tel: 02 3131 376. This beautifully renovated old-style Macedonian house from 1836 is atmospheric, although the food is average.
Dva Elena (Two Deers) Zagrebska 31; tel: 02 3082 382). An excellent steakhouse.

Slightly further out of town in the City Park on the street dividing the stadium from the park proper are a number of upmarket traditional restaurants, all of which serve good food:

Ezerce Tel: 02 3122 389
Uranija Tel: 02 3118 030
Sofka Tel: 02 3117 250
Marakana Tel: 02 3221 548. Live blues and jazz after 21.30 every evening.

Turkish cuisine can be found in abundance in Čaršija, the old Turkish side of town. *Kebapci* at any of these restaurants is very good especially if accompanied with grilled red peppers. *Burek* and *baklava* are also in abundance. On the south side of the river, the *kebapci* at **Destan**, next to the Blue Café on 11th Oktomvri, is also very good, and claims to use a special family recipe handed down over several generations. Their bread is not as good though and they only offer *kebapci*.

For a traditional Serbian restaurant serving excellent food go to **Lutz** (tel: 3110 306) on Železnička bb, noticeable by the smoke and steam pouring out of the coke stove chimney by the front door. It serves particularly impressive *ražnič* (skewered meats and vegetables) on a small sword, which takes about 40 minutes to cook, so make sure you order a starter to stave off the hunger whilst

FAST FOOD 'NOW, THAT'S WHAT I CALL SERVICE'

McDonald's here is like going out to eat in a fancy restaurant in America ... the décor is straight out of a page from *Ikea* magazine and the people speak English better than they do at a McDonald's in east Harlem. They greet you with a smile, and you order your food; then they kindly ask you to take a seat because they will bring it out to you when it's ready. However, there is one drawback: you have to pay for BBQ sauce, and there aren't any salt and pepper shakers on the table – you have to ask for them. And there isn't any ketchup either – you have to ask for that as well.

Other than that, however, it definitely is an excellent experience.

Abridged extract from 'The Hitchhiker's Guide to Macedonia ... and my Soul' by Carol Cho, Forum Publishers, Skopje, 2002.

wafts of your sizzling *ražnič* tantalise your tastebuds. Also to be recommended is their thinly sliced *džigr* (liver). Fried to perfection in local herbs and seasonings, it is like liver you will never have eaten in an English-speaking country!

Italian

The Trgovski shopping centre offers a whole host of restaurants, especially pizzerias. The best of them all is **Da Gino's** on the second floor (tel: 02 3121 109). This place offers the best pizzas, made true Italian style, and with fresh mushrooms (often more difficult to find in other restaurants). Da Gino's brings all their seafood up daily from Thessaloniki and offers an impressive fresh seafood platter. Pizzas can be ordered ahead ready to go.

Another well-known Italian restaurant is **Dal Met Fu** (tel: 02 3112 482) right on the main square. It has lots of outside seating in the summer and even in the winter the glass-fronted restaurant offers lots of sunlit areas as well as upper seating in a more cosy atmosphere. This restaurant also offers a non-smoking area. The restaurant has an excellent salad bar of some of the best of Italian anti-pastas as well as the best carbonara in town. The owner has two other restaurants, **Dal Fufol** and a fast-food version **Fufufu** both on Vodnjanska street.

A more up-market Italian restaurant is **Tiglio's** (tel: 02 3124 073) at Slavka Nedič 15, opposite the western end of Debarca Street (which most taxi drivers should know). It is difficult to find even with a taxi, but it has excellent food and an atmospheric quiet patio. Rivalling Tiglio's in excellence is **Vodenica** (Mulino in Italian, the Waterwheel restaurant in English, tel: 02 3232 877) on Boulevard Metropolit Teodisij Gologanov. The waterwheel and fishpond make for a pleasant atmosphere and if you want to eat during the popular eating hours after 20.00 you may need to phone in advance to reserve a table. In the same strip as Vodenica is **Momir**, specialising in fish, and also the popular **Café Intermezzo**.

Foreign fare

MCM Boulevard Ilinden. Hidden away and not well signposted, but offers excellent food, especially Greek and seafood (although the grilled squid is the worst to be found in Skopje). Also offers a range of good Greek retsina wines and an up-market atmosphere with attentive silver service staff.

Frutti di Mare Rade Končar 5; tel: 02 3132 145. Specialises in Dalmatian and Mediterranean seafood dishes. Closed on Sunday.

Bombay Serves good Indian food in a traditional setting, although their paneer is not authentic (probably a feta substitute) and their ginger is reconstituted. They also have a take-away menu.

Den i Nokj (Jour et Nuit, Day and Night) Opposite Aleksandar Palace on the other side of the river; tel: 02 309 6069. Serves refreshingly small portions of good French food in a swanky up-market atmosphere. Rather pricey.

Um Zina 27th Mart 5; tel: 02 3129 345. Arabian food. Their patio seating is particularly convivial and the chicken skewers and humus is to die for.

Zlaten Pat (Golden Road) Leninova 36 (cornering Boulevard Ilinden); tel: 02 3228 100. Serves excellent Shanghainese food, especially considering the lack of fresh ginger and Chinese noodles to be found in Skopje itself. The noodles are actually spaghetti pasta but most of the rest of the food is imported from China, and the tofu is exquisitely fresh and made on the premises. Try their salt and pepper fried prawns, fish or pork for something truly Chinese.

Kineski Restoran Vodnjanska 7. More northern Chinese dishes in less traditional surroundings, but cheaper than Zlaten Pat.

McDonald's Dimitri Čupovski 13; tel: 02 3130 131; out of town on Jane Sandanski; and Metropolit Teodosij Gologanov next to the Vero hypermarket. If you or the kids are desperate there's always respite in the familiar double cheeseburger with large fries and a Coke. The last-mentioned is decked out with toys and climbing frames and is a popular place for children's parties.

Vegetarian

There is only one place in Skopje that specialises in vegetarian food. **Harmonija** (tel: 02 241 3023) at Skopjanka Mall 37 behind the railway station offers a feast of macrobiotic meals. The owner and cook, Tanja, earned her degree in macrobiotic cuisine in the US and is able to give you a dietary consultation on appointment. For those who just want a tasty meal and a change from *skara*, this is the place to come. Closed on Sunday.

Aside from Harmonija, some places such as Dal Met Fu, **Kibo Restaurant** in the DC Paloma Bjanka business centre and Dabnica An do have good salad bars and dishes. Pivnica An in Čaršija offer a few vegetarian plates, and most *ordever* choices will be vegetarian. A lot of Italian places will have non-meat pizzas and pastas. **Patis**, next to the DC Paloma, serves excellent vegetarian dishes and smoothies.

Outside the city

Manastirska Pestera at Lake Matka and the restaurant at St Pantelejmon Monastery offer good Macedonian food in a delightful setting. See the next chapter, *Outside Skopje*, for more information. A nice restaurant out of town serving traditional Macedonian food is **Cherry Orchard** (tel: 02 2055 195). The restaurant is set in the grounds of the riding stables *El Kabon*, which has a well-manicured terrace and lawns overlooking the exercise paddocks and a delightful children's play area. The restaurant building itself was used in the Macedonian movie *Dust* by Milčo Mančevski, and was reconstructed at the stables (whose horses were used in the movie) at the end of filming. The well-groomed interior offers fire-side seating in the winter, but is sadly not well frequented, not least because it is complicated to get there by car. The number 22 bus from anywhere on Partizanski ends its journey 700m from the restaurant where it is signposted for the remainder of the dirt track to the stables.

To get there by car take Partizanski all the way to the end and at the crossroads, rather than turn left as if going on to the highway to Tetovo, continue straight ahead. At the next crossroads in 400m turn right opposite the church and go over the railway flyover. Follow this road through the village of Novo Selo for 3km until you cross the railway line again at Volkovo. Turn right immediately after the railway line. After almost 2km turn right at the crossroads and in 600m you'll cross back over the railway line. The road forks in another 400m and you will want to take the left fork to get to Cherry Orchard. From here on there are signs for the restaurant which is only another 700m away.

Coffee and tea houses

Macedonia has more cafés than you can shake a stick at, and Skopje is no exception. Here are some of the more popular daytime cafés. The modern **Blue Café** on 11th Oktomvri near the Trgovski shopping centre is a popular meeting place as it is so easy to find, but it's very noisy and often plagued by begging children. **La Caffe** on Maršal Tito has comfortable sofas and armchairs to lounge around in and an extensive patio on the pedestrian area. On the tracks of the old railway station (Mito Hadzivasilev Jasmin Street) are a number of interesting little cafés and restaurants themed on the old railway.

The **New Age Teahouse** at Kosta Šahov 9 offers a welcome alternative to the many smoke-laden coffee houses in Skopje, offering a rich menu of black, green and fruit teas, milkshakes, kefirs, alternative coffees and cocktails in a garden atmosphere with low seats, floor seating and cushions. This is where you'll find that mix of East meets West, reminiscent of the great Viennese coffee houses, if a little more Bohemian. The teahouse has lots of board games to while away the hours, as well as a pet black cockerel and a female peacock in the garden.

Another good relaxing café is **Café Medium** behind Café Ring (which is more noisy) next to all the city cinemas. The café has lots of eclectic hand-made furniture and a tree-shaded patio. **Van Gogh** on Michael Sokov is more upbeat and popular with art and film types. You might even meet Milčo Mančevski there if you are lucky. **Lezet** and **Art** are also worth a look in.

ENTERTAINMENT

Skopje is certainly not the buzzing hive of evening entertainment that some cities can be. Nevertheless, it has a choice of theatre, dance, concerts and cinema, as well as pubs and nightclubs. The Skopje Tourist Information booklet, available free every month from the main tourist office in the old town and in many travel agencies and hotels, lists a full calendar of events in the city, as well as many useful addresses and telephone numbers.

Theatres and concert halls

Universal Hall on Partizanksi Odredi (tel: 02 3224 158) holds concerts two or three times a week, both classical and modern jazz/rock. Skopje's jazz festival is held there for a week every October. The **Dom na Armija** (Army Hall) on Maršal Tito Street (tel: 02 3118 450) also holds classical concerts once a week on Thursday at 20.00 except in July, August and September.

The **Macedonian National Theatre** has two halls, one on Quay Dimitar Vlahov (tel: 02 3114 060), which holds opera and ballet, and the **Theatre Centre** on Kliment Ohridski (tel: 02 3164 667), which holds modern drama and plays. There is also the **Drama Theatre** on Sekopvski 15 (tel: 02 3063 453) and the **Theatre for Children** on Dimitri Čupovski 4 (tel: 02 3222 619). The **Theatre of Nationalities** on Nikola Martinoski 41 in the old town (tel: 02 3221 570) holds plays in Albanian and Turkish.

Cinemas

Skopje has five cinemas, although only the recently built **Millennium** on the first floor of the Trgovski Centar is really worth going to at MKD150. All the other city cinemas (**Kultura, Manaki, Paradizo** in the same building, and **Vardar 1&2** around the corner) at a mere MKD100 are on Maršal Tito. The Vardar has bad acoustics and you'll probably miss half of the script. All films are shown in their original language and tend to come out a few months after their release in their country of origin. Frosina Cinema at the **Youth Culture Centre** on Quay Dimitar Vlahov (tel: 02 3115 508) often holds art or foreign movies, usually a different movie every evening at 20.00.

Nightlife

Popular bars to hang out in at night are **Havana Club** in the city park, **New Age** (see above), **Café London** just off Ploštad, **Café Art** on Partizanski, the **Peanut Bar** on Dimitri Čupovski and **Jukebox** on Orče Nikolov 99. Jukebox is small and cosy with live jazz on a Thursday night. **Hollywood** on the top floor of the Trgovski Centar above the Millennium Cinema offers dancing most nights, as does **Vega** on the ground floor of the Trgovski Centar. By far the most popular in the summer though are the outdoor nightclubs in the city park. **Colosseum, Cabrio** and **Element** (www.element.com.mk) all hold a mixed programme over the summer inviting DJs from abroad such as Heaven and Pete Tong, as well as modern Balkan artists and sounds. Element retreats to its winter quarters under the TC Plaza when the weather gets too cold for the outdoor club. **Club MNT**, beneath the Macedonian National Theatre, is another lively scene after 22.00, and the old town offers a number of bars, which get busier towards the end of the week. Of course, no major European city would be complete without an Irish bar. **St Patrick** on the ground floor of the Trgovski Centar, riverside at the eastern end, is a hive of good cheer, live music and expats, as well as traditional British fare and a good pint of Guinness.

SHOPPING

Food

The **Vero supermarket** chain and the **Ramstore** on Mito Hadzi Vasilev has the widest range of food available in Skopje, including ginger, fresh limes, mint and horseradish sauce and fresh seafood (from Greece). Another supermarket chain is **Tinex**, which along with Vero and the Ramstore also takes all major credit cards. Local fresh produce is best bought from the big fresh markets either at the Bit Pazar (see below) or the **Green market** on the western corner of Kočo Racin and 11th Oktomvri, or **Bunjakovač market** on Partizanski just after Leninova.

The **Bit Pazar** is the biggest outdoor market in Skopje. Not only does it have fresh vegetables, fruit, meat products, fish, spices, pulses and tea, it also has a large ironmongery section and, in fact, you can buy almost anything there. Now held every day, it used to be held on Tuesdays and Fridays only, following a 600-year-old tradition, when it was first held by the monks of the Monastery of St Gjorgi Gorga. The monastery no longer exists but the market is still in the same spot and has expanded over the former grounds of the monastery.

There are a few **health food** stores in Skopje under the Biotika chain. The closest to the centre of town is behind the hospital on 11th Oktomvri.

Souvenirs

The old town is the best place to get souvenirs and local made handicrafts such as leather slippers, hand-embroidered cloths and ethnic style clothing. There is also a small souvenir shop on the ground floor of the Trgovski Centar, and another on the corner of Maksim Gorki and Dame Gruev. The Roma market in Šutko (see page 118) is the place to get the lavish Roma costumes.

Clothes

Skopje is awash with shoe shops and there are also plenty of clothes shops. Most of these products are mass produced in China and imported. The Trgovski Centar is the main shopping mall, even offering the likes of Benetton, Wolfords and Mango. Local **tailors** in the old town are still cheap especially for repairs and copying, although the choice of materials from which to make clothes is not the best. For a top class men's tailor used by the diplomatic community try Borče on Ivan Kozarov 5, tel: 02 3133 065, 070 230 061 or 070 278 585. He offers prompt service and quality tailoring with a price tag to match.

ACTIVITIES

Aside from sightseeing, Skopje offers a host of sports facilities and outdoor pursuits. The city sports stadium is on the river side of the city park. The

Macedonian national **football** team can often be seen practising and playing there when they're not away playing a match. Tickets for matches can be purchased at the stadium box office or from the Football Association of Macedonia, 8th Udarna Brigada 31a (tel: 02 3235 448, or 02 3229 042).

Another big sports complex, including an outdoor swimming pool and an ice-skating rink in the winter, is Kale Sports Hall below the castle itself, open 09.00–22.00 Monday to Thursday, and 09.00–24.00 Friday, Saturday and Sunday. There is an all-female gym, Vitalis (tel: 070 268 559), at Orče Nikolov 101 near Juke Box bar. It is open every day 11.00–21.00 except Sunday.

The **Olympic Swimming Pool** on Kočo Racin is open to the public 20.00–24.00 Tuesday to Sunday, and 10.00–16.00 in addition on Saturday and Sunday. It is closed on Monday. The pool complex also offers a **fitness centre** open every day 09.00–23.00, although it is not as pleasant to work out in as the fitness centre at the Aleksander Palace Hotel (open to the public). Next door to the Aleksandar Palace Hotel is the Olympic size **Karpoš III Indoor Swimming Pool**. By far the nicest outdoor pool is the recently reopened army pool, **Bazen Biser**, just off Kosta Novakovič in the Aerodrom part of town. It's open 10.00–18.00 and 21.30–01.00 every day and serves drinks and snacks. It's packed after midday so go early or in the evening. 100MKD entry fee.

The numerous mountain ravines and watercourses throughout the country also offer plenty of **fishing**, which is a popular local sport. A walk along the banks of the Vardar in Skopje will show a dozen or more fishermen on any given day, although from the frequency of the catch it looks as though there are more fishermen there than fish. Nevertheless the fishermen turn up religiously every day, so there must be something worth catching and all the local restaurants offer trout (more likely harvested from local fish farms). Streams outside Skopje look like more interesting fishing. The Fishing Association on Kočo Racin (tel: 02 233 539) gives information on licensing and seasons.

Horseriding is becoming increasingly popular around Skopje, especially among the expats. Riding fees are €10 per hour, or €100 per month at the El Kabon stables at Cherry Orchard in Volkovo district (tel: 02 2055 195). To get to El Kabon see the details for Cherry Orchard restaurant above. Other riding stables are in Stenkovec, Hippodrom and Petrovec 20km outside Skopje near the airport.

Tennis clubs abound in Skopje, and private lessons are cheap at 700–900MKD per hour. Courts cost 300–444MKD per hour. Try one of the following:

Tennis Club Forca Tel: 02 306 0333. Two outdoor courts. Pleasant atmosphere.
Tennis Club Jug City Park; tel: 02 3118 530
Tennis Club ABC Ilindenska; tel: 02 3063 622. Also has a popular café and drinks bar.
Tennis Club Hipodrom Tel: 02 2521 444
Tennis Courts Kamnik Tel: 02 252 3522. Excellent restaurant opened 2004.
Squash Club Lazar Ličenoski 31; tel: 02 322 7077. Brand new with a nice café.

Finally, the Aviation Association on Dimitri Čupovski (tel: 02 3227 672) offers private **flying, parachuting and paragliding** courses.

For other sporting events and opportunities try contacting the Sport Association of Skopje at Jordan H Dzinot 12a (tel: 02 3117 687 or 02 3228 624).

The southern bank of the River Vardar to the west of the Stone Bridge is paved all the way to the Aleksandar Palace Hotel. The 3km stretch makes a wonderful **walking, rollerblading** or **running** route on a sunny day, and is a great place to see the locals taking a stroll too. It is hardly built up on either side and continues beyond the Aleksandar Palace Hotel on an unpaved single track to the bank opposite Zlokučani. The single track becomes paved again near Partizanska and is lit at night most of the way along.

WHAT TO SEE

Suggested one-day tours

If you are in Skopje for just one day and do not have your own transport the following itinerary will give you a good overview of the city: Kale, Sveti Spas, Mustafa Pasha Mosque, *kebapci* lunch outside Kapan An, Chifte Amam Gallery, Suli An, Kuršumli Han, Bit Pazar, dinner in Two Doors or Pivnica An.

If you have a car, or can afford a taxi or guided tour then a trip up to Vodno, on to the Monastery of St Pantelejmon and back via Lake Matka in the morning is well worth the extra effort for a taste of the spectacular mountainous scenery of Macedonia (see *Chapter 6* for information on these places). The afternoon should take in at least Kale and Čaršija.

Museums and galleries

The **City Museum of Skopje** (tel: 02 3114 742) is housed in the old railway station on Mito Hadzivasilev Jasmin, opposite the southern end of Maršal Tito. The original Skopje–Thessoloniki railway started from this station in 1873, but the present building was built in 1940–41. The earthquake of July 26 1963 destroyed a large portion of the building and station, leaving the station clock stopped at 05.17 when the earthquake hit. The clock hands have remained at this time ever since and the building became the city museum soon after. The new railway station is now 15 minutes' walk away further east. The museum is open Monday to Saturday 09.30–17.00 and on Sunday 09.30–13.00. The museum exhibits a permanent history of the city through the centuries (although the 20th-century section was closed off at time of writing) as well as temporary exhibitions of local artists, architects and designers. A small brochure in English can be obtained at the front desk.

The **Daud Pasha Baths National Gallery** on Kruševska 1a (tel: 02 3133 102, or 02 3124 219) is the obvious copper cupola building to your right as you enter the old town from the Stone Bridge. It is well worth a visit at 100MKD just for the building itself. Built in the 15th century as a bath house while Skopje was under Turkish rule, the bath house was then one of the most magnificent of its kind, boasting 13 different sized copper cupolas and varying degrees of hot steam rooms and cold baths separated for men and women. Nowadays only the beautiful roof and ceiling architecture remain. The gallery houses mostly contemporary art, although there are a few older pieces, one dating back to the 13th century. The art is an added bonus to the building if you like modern art, although a good working Turkish steam bath in Skopje is sorely missed.

Another old Turkish bath house, the second largest in Skopje, is **Chifte Amam**, built at the beginning of the 16th century under the orders of Isa Bey, the son of Isak Bey. It is now also a national art gallery housing various travelling exhibitions and lies immediately south of Suli An. Another old bath house in Čaršija is Šengul Amam (also known as Gurciler Amam) next to Kuršumli Han. Like Chifte Amam, it was badly damaged in the 1963 earthquake, but this bath house has not been repaired.

The **Museum of Contemporary Art** on Samoilova (tel: 02 3117 735) lies to the west of Kale on top of the hill. It is open every day 09.00–16.00 (closed on Monday).

The **Museum of Macedonia** lies between Mustafa Pasha Mosque and Kuršumli An in Čaršija. It is open Tuesday to Friday 08.00–16.00, Saturday 09.00–15.00, and Sunday 09.00–13.00. It is closed on Monday. Some of the archaeological exhibitions are held in Kuršumli Han, access to which can only be gained through the main museum. The museum is not marked up as the 'Museum of Macedonia' from the outside and the entrance is merely a break in the red railings on the southernmost side of the complex. Sadly, all the text for the exhibits is in Macedonian only. Kuršumli An is usually locked, so ask for it to be opened, or at least look through the cracks in the huge wooden doors in order to get a glimpse inside this former tavern and prison (see below for a history of the inn). If you haven't got much time to visit ancient sites in Macedonia and absorb the history to this country in depth, then the museum is a good way to get an overview of all the civilisations who have passed along the River Vardar. Many of the best iconasteries in the country are also housed here, and there are some excellent exhibits of World War I and II, including weaponry and ammunition.

Another old trading inn, Suli An, houses the **Museum of the Old Skopje Bazaar**, which holds an interesting exhibition on trading life in Skopje during the Ottoman Empire. The museum and exhibits are badly in need of repair and all the text is in Macedonian but it is free of charge to enter. The museum itself is upstairs, and downstairs is the university's Department of Applied Arts. You can walk around the courtyard to see the students working in the downstairs rooms and the entrance hall to the department has a number of interesting modern art paintings. Exhibitions and visiting lectures are advertised in Macedonian on the front door. Suli An lies in the centre of the old bazaar area and the front entrance to the inn often looks closed, but it is usually in fact open.

The **Macedonian Museum of Natural History** is on Ilinden 86 (tel: 02 3117 669) and is open Tuesday to Sunday from 09.00–16.00 (closed on Monday). There is not much to see in the museum and all the text is in Macedonian, but there are some impressive remains of prehistoric animals found in Negotino and other areas of Macedonia, and lots of stuffed eagles and vultures as well as other animals of the region. It's 30MKD to enter and make sure you have small change as the ticket attendant does not. Next door to the Natural History Museum is the **Skopje Zoo**. A visit here is not recommended unless you want to see how bad a zoo can be. Most of the safari animals are dead already, except for one chimpanzee and three baboons. There is also one very lonely white bear, lots of penned-in ruminants and birds, and several stray wild dogs. Entry at 50MKD will make you want to become an animal rights' campaigner.

Churches and monasteries

The Church and Monastery of **Sveti Spas** (Holy Salvation) is the only remaining monastery in the centre of Skopje and houses one of the most beautiful churches. Its main entrance is at Makarije Frckovski 8 (tel: 02 3163 812 and 02 3109 401) although it is easier to visit it from its top entrance on Samoilova opposite Kale. Some of the foundations of the monastery go back to the 14th century before Ottoman times. Under Ottoman rule it became illegal for a church to be taller than a mosque, and so the church was mostly rebuilt below ground in order to accommodate the height of the original church bell tower.

The present three-naved church dates from rebuilding in the 18th and 19th centuries. The iconastry also dates from the early 19th century when three of the most famous wood carvers of the time, Makarije Frckovski of Galičnik and the brothers Marko and Petar Filipovski from the village of Gari, worked for five years from 1819 to 1824 to create the 10m wide and 6m high iconostasis (the intricate

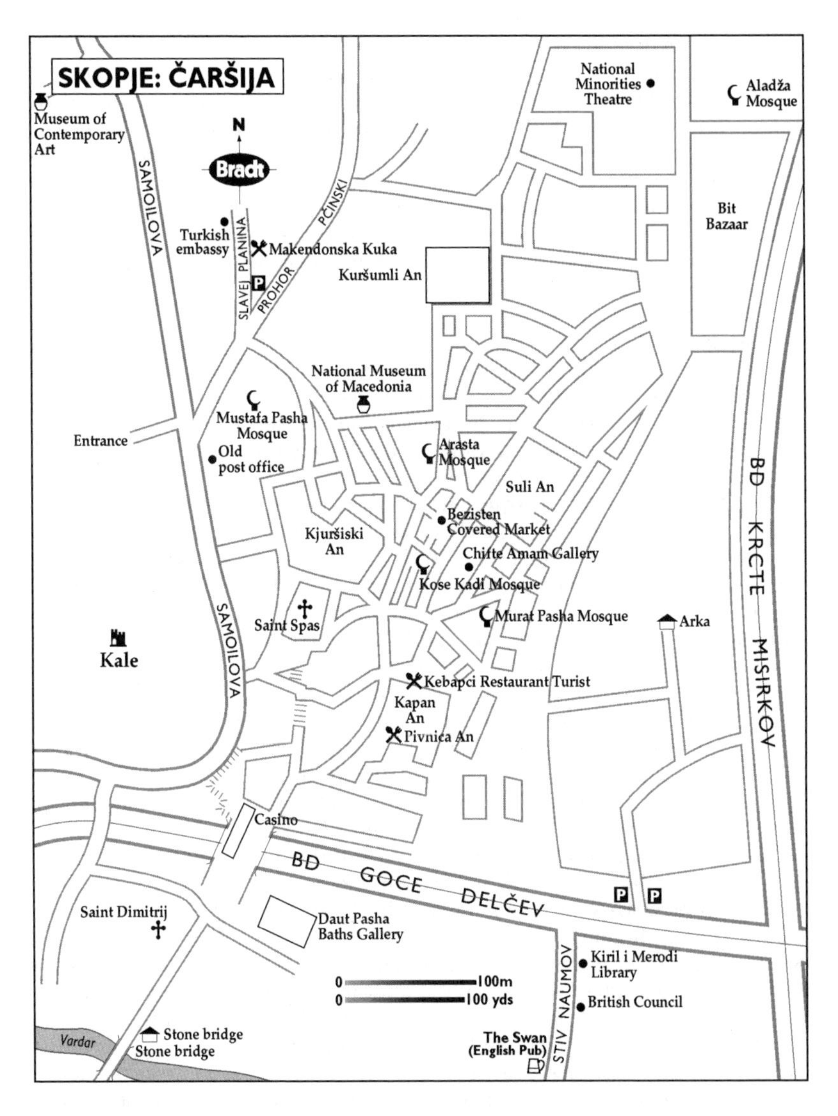

woodwork divider between the nave and the main part of the church). The iconostasis is cut from the wood of walnut trees, and is made up of two rows of partly gold-inlaid icons depicting scenes from the Old and the New Testaments. Many of the scenes have been carved to reflect Macedonian traditions and folklore, such as the figure of Salome, who is dressed in traditional Macedonian garb. Among their more famous works, Frckovski and the Filipovski brothers carved even more stunning iconostases for the Monastery of Sveti Jovan Bigorski in Mavrovo National Park and the Monastery of Sveti Gabriel in Lesnovo.

Sveti Spas is also famous for housing the beheaded remains of the revolutionary Goce Delčev. Leader of the Independence for Macedonia Revolutionary Organisation (IMRO – to which the present-day opposition government VMRO traces its roots) Delčev was beheaded in 1903, but his head, no doubt posted on the Stone Bridge as proof of his execution, was subsequently lost. His remains were only exhumed and moved to the Sveti Spas in 1964.

Also north of the river is the **Church of Sveti Dimitri** just west of the Stone Bridge. It dates from the 14th century and in typical Macedonian fashion, the bell tower is separate from the main building. The present structure dates from the 19th century.

The **Cathedral of St Clement of Ohrid** on the corner of Partizanski and Ohridski is a modern 20th-century building shaped interestingly in the form of a dome with four smaller domes at each corner, making it easily mistaken as a modern mosque at a quick glance.

Mosques

The Čair and Čaršija districts of the old town have over 30 mosques. In the mid 17th century Evlija Čelebi, a famous Turkish travel writer of the time, noted 120 mosques in Skopje. Most were burnt down in the fire of 1689 started by the Austrian General Piccolomini in order to rid the town of a rampaging plague. A few of the mosques from that time remain.

The **Mustafa Pasha Mosque** on Samoilova opposite the main entrance to Kale is the largest and most ornately decorated of all the mosques in Skopje. It was built in 1492 at the order of Mustafa Pasha whilst he was Vizier of Skopje under Sultan Selim I. The entrance to the mosque is through a four-columned porch. The porch is crowned with three cupolas and a 124-stepped white minaret rises from its western end. Inside, the pulpit and prayer recess is made from intricately worked marble. The interior of the mosque is decorated at all four corners with ornate paintings, which rise all the way up to the dome in the ceiling. Light streams into the room from five windows set into each of the four walls. The windows are staggered in the upper half of each wall, two windows over three, and enhanced by a top window crowning the pyramid effect from a row of windows set into the base of the dome. Despite having stood the test of time well, it did have to undergo major restoration after the earthquake of 1963 and still has a cracked dome. In the grounds of the mosque is Mustafa Pasha's mausoleum and his daughter Umi's sarcophagus.

The **Hjunkar Mosque**, also known as the Sultan Murat Mosque, predates the Mustafa Pasha Mosque by some 50 years. It was built next to the Monastery of St Georgi Gorga near the present-day university of St Cyril and Methodius. At the time, the monastery was one of the most important monastic centres in the Balkans, but when Isak Bey, then commander of the Turkish army, built the **Aladža Mosque**, the Pasha Bey Mausoleum (still visible in the grounds of the Aladža Mosque) and a *medresa* (school for teaching the Koran) on the actual grounds of the monastery, he effectively destroyed life at the monastery. The *medresa* no longer exists, nor the monastery, but both mosques remain on either side of Blvd Krste Misirkov. The mausoleums of Sultan Beyhan and of Ali Pasha of Dagestan lie in the grounds of the Hjunkar Mosque.

Further north on Blvd Krste Misirkov is **Yayha Pasha Mosque** built in 1504 for Yayha Pasha, the son-in-law of Sultan Bayazit II. Notable for its modern four-sided roof, it is the imposing mosque visible as you come off the highway from the airport into the centre of town. Originally, the prayer area was roofed with one large and five small domes, but these were destroyed in the last earthquake of 1963.

Opposite Chifte Amam is the modern square-roofed **Murat Pasha Mosque** built in 1802. The original 15th-century structure was burnt down when General Piccolomini set Skopje alight in 1689.

At the western end of *Bezisten* (the covered market) is the 17th-century **Kose Kadi Mosque**. The mosque is upstairs above a passageway of shops leading to the western entrance of *Bezisten*. The mosque was most recently renovated in 1993.

The 16th-century **Hidaverdi Mosque** between Kuršumli Han and the Theatre for Minorities looks more like a half-renovated shop-front than a mosque, despite having been restored in 1995. It lacks the usual distinguishing minaret.

Gazi Isa-Bey Mosque on Čairska used to hold one of the oldest libraries in Skopje. In the grounds of the mosque is a 560-year-old plain tree (*Platinus Orientalis*).

Historical sites

The present-day site of **Fortress Kale** has probably seen some sort of occupied fortification since the Illyrians first came through from Greece to settle in Albania. Excavations of the site revealed artefacts dating back to the Thracian era of 200BC when the Dardanians fought from Kale to defend the surrounding area from the invading Romans.

After the earthquake of 1963, only a few restored walls, the main gateway and two towers remain to be seen to the northwest of the Stone Bridge. The present-day ruins date from the 10th-century enlargement of the fort under Tsar Samoil. The ramp was partly built of stones from the ancient town of Skupi, which was destroyed in 518.

After crossing the Stone Bridge into the old town, the main gateway of Kale can be approached from behind the Bingo hall and tourist office, or a more scenic route can be taken a little further on by following the cobbled street up to the grape-vined café at the top and then taking the steps up to the forecourt of the Monastery of Sveti Spas. The main entrance is opposite the old post office.

Now a well-kept tourist attraction (apart from the piles of rubbish thrown down from the top of the fortified outer wall), Kale served as a barracks to the Turkish army during Ottoman rule, and then to the JNA (Jugoslav National Army) until 1963. The restaurant, open in the summer to tourists, is the old army canteen – not the most comfortable of restaurants, and the otherwise excellent view from the restaurant is obscured by mangy net curtains. A drink there is welcome, however, when the heat and exposure to the sun, making quite a difference in temperature between the river level and the top of the fortress, can parch the thirst very quickly most of the year round.

The 214m **Kamen Most** (Stone Bridge), which joins the old Turkish town to what has now become the centre of town south of the river, was first built in the late 15th century under the orders of Sultan Mehmet II the Conqueror. By then the population of the city was increasing so rapidly, due to the draw of merchants to this important trading town, that people were already living beyond the original town walls. The only bridge across the river was many miles away further west, so a new bridge here, close to the main hub of the town, helped with the problem of overcrowding on the north side of the river as well as easing the arduous trading route into the town from the south.

The original stonework of 13 arches of travertine stone still stands, although the top of the bridge has been changed a number of times since it was built. Originally at a width of 6.33m, it was widened to 9.8m in 1909, and then returned to its original width in 1992. During the conflict of 2001 the bridge was badly damaged, and the fact that it has taken so long to be repaired (due to be completed mid-2003) is a symbol of the difficult reconciliation between what has become the largely Muslim community in the old town and the remainder of the Macedonian community to the south of the bridge. Damage to the old watchtower during the first attempt to repair the bridge in 2002 has not helped matters, and even the Turkish Embassy has demanded an explanation.

The bridge was originally built with stone pillar railings, used by the Turkish rulers of Skopje to spike the heads of those disloyal to Turkish rule. The Turks favoured the bridge as a public execution place, and amongst many others before and after him, the Turks sentenced Karpoš, the 'King of Kumanovo', to die a particularly gruesome death by impalement on the bridge in 1689.

Little is left of the old city walls today except for the bottom half of the **Saat Kula**, the dark red brick clock tower near Hjunkar Mosque (Sultan Murat Mosque). Erected in the mid-16th century, the top half of the clock tower was originally made of wood and housed a clock brought over from Hungary. In 1904 the wooden structure was replaced with stone and a new clock was procured. That clock was then destroyed in the earthquake of 1963 and has not been replaced since.

The covered marketplace, **Bezisten**, of the Old Bazaar area is a courtyard-type building with more stores built inside the courtyard itself. It is located behind Chifte Amam to the northwest. Originally built in the 15th century for trading cloth and material, the store soon spilt outside the original structure, forming narrow little cobbled lanes between the one- and two-storey shops, which lent on to each other. The old bazaar was soon made up of 18 different trading houses: goldsmiths, cobblers, ironmongers, corn exchange etc, and the remnants of these can still be seen today. The *Bezisten* of today is a 19th-century structure, housing some tourist shops and cafés, but is no longer reminiscent of its former glory.

Čaršija has a number of **Turkish trading inns**, which are well worth a visit, including Kuršumli An belonging to the Ragusan merchants, Suli An and Kapan An. These inns usually have one or two entrances and no windows on the outside. The entrances lead into a large courtyard, which is surrounded on all four sides on the first floor by wooden-balconied guest rooms looking out on to the courtyard. Underneath these, on the ground floor, were the stabling quarters for animals and goods. There was often a well in the centre of the courtyard where guests would usually gather to while away the evening.

As you go past the old bazaar area of Čaršija from the Stone Bridge the first inn you will come to is **Kapan An**. It now houses a number of restaurants and bars and the inn is also surrounded on the outside by other restaurants, which lean on to it.

Further down the street towards Bitpazar is **Suli An**. It now houses the Museum of the Old Skopje Bazaar (see above).

Kuršumli An, meaning Bullet or Lead Inn, to the northwest of Bitpazar is probably one of the most impressive inns of its period. At the time it was designed to stable up to 100 horses, and of course house their traders and owners. Some of the rooms even had their own fireplace, which was deemed quite a luxury in those times. In 1878 the building became the town prison. It now holds archaeological exhibitions from the Museum of Macedonia, which is the white building lying to the southwest of the inn.

Monuments and statues

Unlike many former communist cities, Skopje does not display the usual array of statues to communist heroes, although there are still plenty of communist/late '60s and '70s style buildings to be seen, such as the main government building, main post office and the Macedonian National Theatre. There is a quite nice, larger-than-life-size statue of Mother Teresa on Maršal Tito, which was put up shortly after her house near the main square was demolished to make way for the Trgovski shopping centre. The site of her former house is marked with a small plaque at the western entrance to the shopping centre.

6 Outside Skopje

Most of Macedonia is accessible from Skopje in one day, depending on how long you want to spend at a place, and whether you're prepared to return after dark. Aside, then, from places covered in this book elsewhere, here are a few suggested day trips closer to Skopje.

MOUNT VODNO

Mount Vodno at 1,066m is the prominent summit to the south of Skopje topped by a huge 75m yellow steel cross, which is lit up at night. It takes almost three hours to walk up to the summit from the centre of town, and is a very popular walk with Macedonians on a sunny weekend. It is possible to drive up to the summit during the day in the winter or between 20.00 at night and 09.00 in the morning in the summer, but on a popular walking day the road is firmly closed at Hotel Vodno, and parking can often overflow from the hotel car park for more than half a kilometre down the road.

The view of Skopje from the summit is quite spectacular and all the main sites can be viewed easily. The **mountain hut Dare Djambaz** (50 beds) tel: 02 3234 365 or 02 3143 236, at the summit offers basic food, a collegial atmosphere, and welcome shelter if the weather has turned foul on the way up the mountain. It's well worth the visit just for the numerous photos of Macedonians who have climbed mountains around the world to proudly fly their flag, and also for the hot sweet mountain tea (*planinski čaj*) at a mere 15MKD per cup.

The steel cross at the top is quite the monstrosity and evoked a lot of controversy among Albanians when it was first erected in 2002. The cross is an overt sign of antagonism to the Albanian minority, who populate the opposite side of the valley, and who have been struggling for years to assert their own identity and symbolism. Their frequently thwarted attempts to build their own monuments, such as in Tearce and Šemševo, and institutions, such as the Albanian university in Tetovo have often resulted in opposition from the government which has ended in violence on more than one occasion. For them this cross simply serves as a reminder of their domination by the ethnic Macedonian majority.

At the time of writing the cross could not yet be climbed to the top, but the stairs and viewing platform should be finished by 2004. Lit up at night, the cross is a convenient orientation marker denoting the south of the city if ever you are lost at night in the streets of Skopje.

The easiest and most popular route to the summit is from the entrance to Vodno National Park on Salvadore Aljende street. The westernmost road opposite the turn- off to the Hotel Panorama takes you over a couple of small bridges, up past a modern apartment block to your left, and then past some

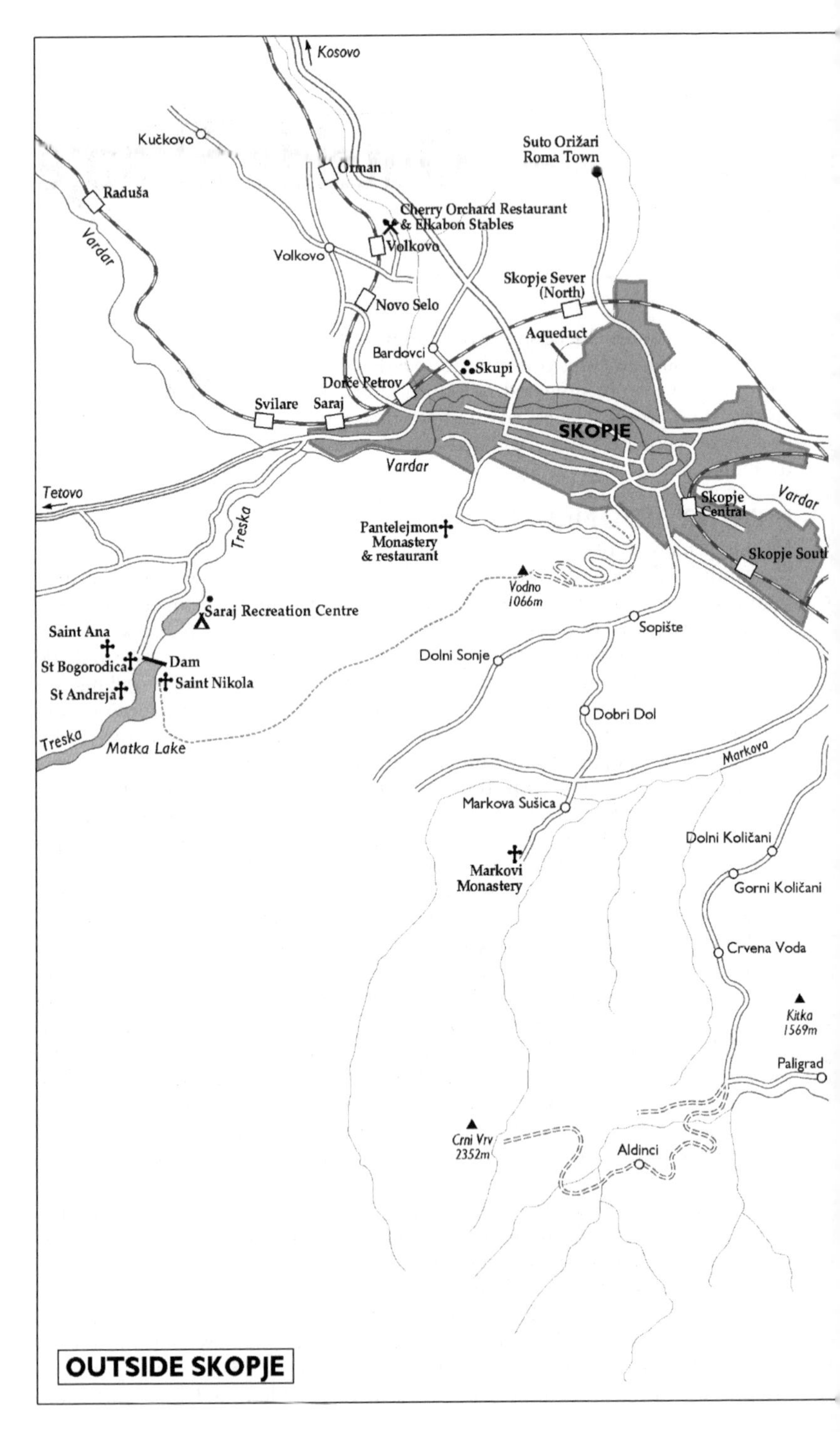
Kosovo
Kučkovo
Orman
Suto Orižari
Roma Town
Raduša
Cherry Orchard Restaurant
& Elkabon Stables
Vardar
Volkovo
Volkovo
Skopje Sever
(North)
Novo Selo
Aqueduct
Bardovci
Skupi
Dorče Petrov
Svilare
Saraj
SKOPJE
Vardar
Tetovo
Treska
Skopje
Central
Vardar
Pantelejmon
Monastery
& restaurant
Skopje South
Vodno
1066m
Saraj Recreation Centre
Sopište
Saint Ana
St Bogorodica
Dam
Dolni Sonje
St Andreja
Saint Nikola
Dobri Dol
Treska
Matka Lake
Markova
Markova Sušica
Dolni Količani
Markovi
Monastery
Gorni Količani
Crvena Voda
Kitka
1569m
Paligrad
Crni Vrv
2352m
Aldinci
OUTSIDE SKOPJE

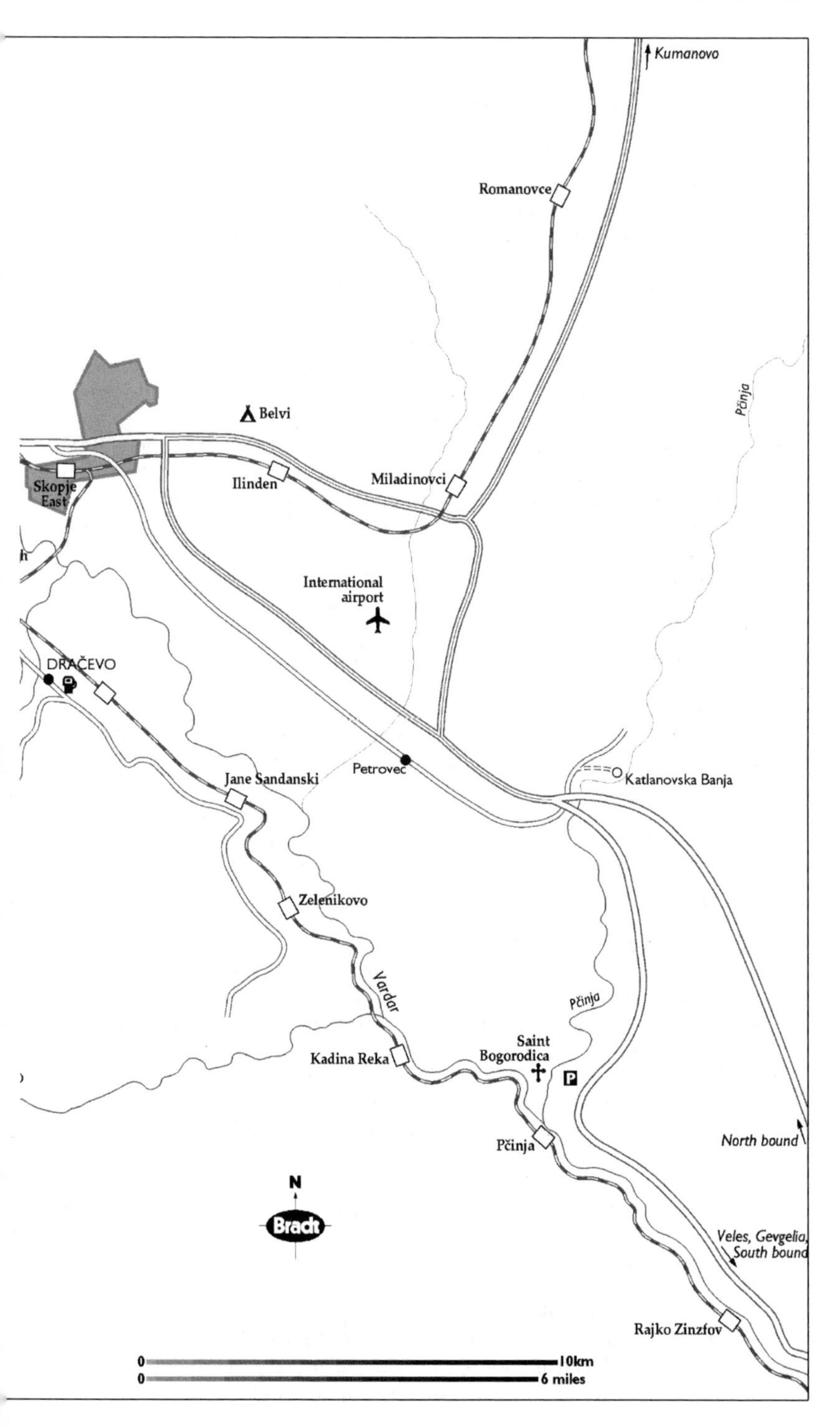
Kumanovo
Romanovce
Belvi
Skopje East
Ilinden
Miladinovci
Pčinja
International airport
DRAČEVO
Petrovec
Jane Sandanski
Katlanovska Banja
Zelenikovo
Vardar
Pčinja
Saint Bogorodica
Kadina Reka
Pčinja
North bound
N
Bradt
Veles, Gevgelia, South bound
Rajko Zinzfov
0
10km
0
6 miles

lovely old farmhouses. This quickly leads up into the woods above the town, and the main path is easy to follow. There are numerous diversions off the main path, and almost all diversions heading upwards will pop out at the summit eventually.

The main path is marked with red and white paint stripes on trees, and joins the road again just before the turn-off to St Pantelejmon Monastery. A short walk along the road past the Hotel Vodno will reveal a number of paths into the woods and up to the summit although the main path actually starts again only 200m up the road after the turn-off to Hotel Vodno. This upper path is steep, badly eroded and desperately in need of maintenance before a major landslide causes some serious environmental damage. The path joins the road again about 1,200m from the road's end at the mountain hut and cross, although by now the road is no longer paved, but simply a gravel path. There is talk of this last section of the road being paved in 2003, although critics say that this will only detract further from the natural beauty of the summit.

An alternative route from Hotel Vodno up to the cross starts a mere 100m after the barrier to the upper asphalt road, and is marked with yellow and green painted stripes on the trees. This path keeps to the left of the main path; it is more shaded and less eroded, making it a thoroughly more pleasant hike. You are also more likely to get your share of chestnuts in the autumn on this route.

A walk up to the summit in late autumn is spectacular for its vistas of vivid red and yellow foliage laced with clouds and evergreens. Sweet chestnuts can be harvested in abundance on an early morning walk up the mountain, but be prepared to compete with the many locals with the same idea. Mushrooms are also plentiful at this time, but be sure to pick only those you know are safe to consume. All mushrooms can be eaten, but some only ever once!

Numerous routes lead from the top of Mount Vodno, including a lovely day-hike to Lake Matka (see next). The route is about 10km mostly downhill and ends with magnificent views of Lake Matka. The route is well marked until about the last 4km when the trails are lost in overgrown fields and poor markings, so it is best to take a guide, such as one from **Korab Mountaineering Club**, tel: 070 712 573, email: contact@korab.org.mk, where the club president, Kotevski Ljubomir, can set you up with a guide.

LAKE MATKA

Lake Matka is the beloved quick getaway retreat of most Skopjites. It is a mere half- hour drive from the city and the number 60 bus from anywhere on Boulevard Partizanski goes there hourly. The lake itself has been manmade by damming the River Treška, which lies in the steep sided ravine of the Treška Valley. The cliffs really are quite spectacular and are popular with the sport climbing crowd. Small boats at €10 a boat will take you down the lake, where you can see a number of caves, and there is lots of hiking in the surrounding hills.

Before the dam itself is the **Restaurant Pestera** (tel: 02 2052 512) also known as the Bear Cave in English, which has a nice outdoor patio and a small indoor restaurant set into the rock walls, making it extremely cool inside. The food is traditional Macedonian and does a good house stew and allegedly you can eat bear steak too. Near the restaurant the bridge over the river takes you to a path leading up to the **Church of St Nikola.**

Above the restaurant is the **Monastery of St Bogorodica**. It is a working monastery with inns which are not open to the public and a small church. Above the entrance to the church is an interesting inscription reading:

> By the will of the father, the son and the holy ghost and the divine temple of the Mother of God came Lady Milica. She found this church unroofed, built a roof for it, painted its frescoes and built a wall around it. Mention, Lord, that this took place in 1497.

Presumably the church itself is older than this if she found it already without a roof.

To the left of the entrance to the monastery is a path marked red which leads up to the churches of St Spas (80 minutes) and St Trojica (85 minutes) and the ruined Monastery of St Nedela (95 minutes). The walk to these churches is beautiful, although the trail is steep and badly marked so patience is required to get there. **St Spas** was built in the 14th century on the foundations of an earlier church, and renovated in 1968. To the right of the church as you approach it (ie: to the northeast) are the large and overgrown limestone blocks of an ancient fortress. The site continued to be populated into Ottoman times when it was known as *Markov Grad* (Marko's Town). It was also a hideout for Macedonian revolutionaries, until it was discovered by the Ottomans and ransacked.

An alternative rendition to the end of this fortress comes in the form of a love story. Allegedly, an Ottoman *bey* fell in love with the beautiful Bojana from Marko's Town, and when she refused his overtures, the *bey* decided to take her against her will. The citizens of the fortress helped her and killed almost a hundred Turk soldiers before Bojana realised her fate was sealed and threw herself to her death from the steep cliffs of the canyon into the River Treška. Sadly for the rest of the citizens, the soldiers took revenge by razing the fortress to the ground. The only building still left standing (just about) is the **Church of St Nedela** (St Sunday) with its ruined archway and old fresco of St Sunday. Take care going up to this church as it stands on precariously steep ground.

There are two paths from here back down to the lake at St Andreja. The longer path marked yellow goes via *Matkin Dol.* It is very steep and should be walked with care. The name *Matkin Dol* means Torture Valley, which might give you an idea of how difficult it is. There are a few small caves along this path where monks retreated in order to find union with God.

The main path to the lakeside St Andreja leads along the River Treška from the parking area to the foot of the dam, and then once past the dam, the path opens up to the grounds of the **Church of St Andreja**. The church, dedicated to St Andreja, was built in the 14th century by another Andreja (not the saint) who was the brother of King Marko (see next). Next door to the church is mountaineering hut **Matka** (30 beds) tel: 02 3052 655 or 02 3022 922. There is a small café at the hut which also offers paddle boats for hire. During 2003 the river was being flooded further so the water level may rise up even closer to the edge of the monastery. Before the river was turned into a dam at this section, the church and hut used to stand 20m above the river. Take a look inside the café downstairs to see some excellent photos of the nearby churches and caves.

To the left of the hut are several boards showing the walks, animals and sites to be found in the area, as well as a climbing guide board showing the climbing routes on the large rock face on the opposite side of the lake. For those wishing to do some serious climbing or extended hiking and mountaineering in Matka or anywhere else in Macedonia or Bulgaria, **Matka Climbing Club** can offer experienced guides as well as rock climbing lessons at all levels of experience. The club can also provide most of the necessary equipment such as ropes, helmets, and other safety devices, but you will have to provide your own shoes. Prices vary from €20 to €80 depending upon the duration and location of climbs and the amount of equipment hired. Anela Stavrevska, president of the club and an excellent English-speaker, can be reached on 02 2533 877, or 070 528 237.

The path along the river continues after the monastery past a huge memorial of a carabiner hung on a piton stuck into the rock. The memorial was put up to commemorate the lives of climbers lost in a climbing accident at that spot in the early nineties. The rest of the path along the lake is mostly good, but in some places it is crumbling and requires a bit of careful footwork. Again, not a walk for those with severe vertigo.

Eventually, the hike comes to the end of the lake and continues up the River Treška, which it is still being flooded at the time of writing. Parts of the river cliffs are also being quarried for rock, and so you may not be able to walk more than the first 3km as the cliffs' sides become unsafe. The middle reaches of the Treška between Makedonski Brod and Lake Matka are meant to be good fishing, and these can be reached more quickly by driving around via Sopište.

SARAJ CAMPSITE AND WATER PARK

A few kilometres before Lake Matka, is the Saraj recreation centre. Right at the foot of the Matka cliffs, it looks as if it should be heavenly, and USAID has poured a lot of money into getting it back into some semblance of order. It is also very popular with the local Albanian community, who spend large portions of their weekends at their caravans on the site. You can also set up a tent on the site. Call 02 2347 307 to book a space.

There are plenty of swimmers diving off the edge at the deep end, but about half the large expanse of water is not even adult knee deep, so your young ones can splash about in it in relative safety. There are a few snack bars and ice-cream stalls about, but a distinct lack of public toilets. There are much cleaner pools in Skopje, and if you can get to Mavrovo or Ohrid lakes, the water there is much more inviting. The poor River Treška which skirts around the edge of the recreation park is sinking under trash, despite the new bins supplied by USAID, proof that 'Keep Macedonia Tidy' has yet to become a firm part of the Macedonian psyche.

PANTELEJMON MONASTERY

In the village of Gorni Nezeri, half-way up Mount Vodno, is the Monastery of Pantelejmon. The present church dedicated to St Pantelejmon is built on the foundations of an older church dating back to 1164. The church is surrounded by inns (see below) and a restaurant offering traditional Macedonian fare. The restaurant has excellent views of the Vardar Valley, with a long outdoor patio area which promises a good sunset on a summer evening.

It takes about 20 minutes by taxi to the monastery from the centre of Skopje, which should cost in the region of 250MKD. There are two routes to Pantelejmon Monastery from Skopje: the easiest route is to take the road just below Hotel Vodno around the mountain; the shorter route is to take Kozle Street all the way to the end past the long blue factory on the right, and at the end of the factory complex take a left turn marked Gorni Nezeri all the way up to the monastery.

Rooms at the **Hotel Pantelejmon** (12 rooms) tel: 02 3081 255, cost €75 per person including breakfast for an apartment, or €50 per person including breakfast for a twin room.

ŠUTO ORIZARI ROMA SETTLEMENT AND MARKET

Šuto Orizari, or Šutka for short, is the home of the sizeable Roma minority (see page 40) who live in Skopje. It is a part of Skopje that is little visited by tourists,

Above Sveti Jovan at Kaneo, Ohrid (AT)

Left St Michael Archangel Monastery (AT)

Below Frescos outside the church of St Jovan Bigorski (TE)

Above View of the Radika Valley (TE)

Below left Smolari Waterfalls (TE)

Below right Kukla Stone Dolls (TE)

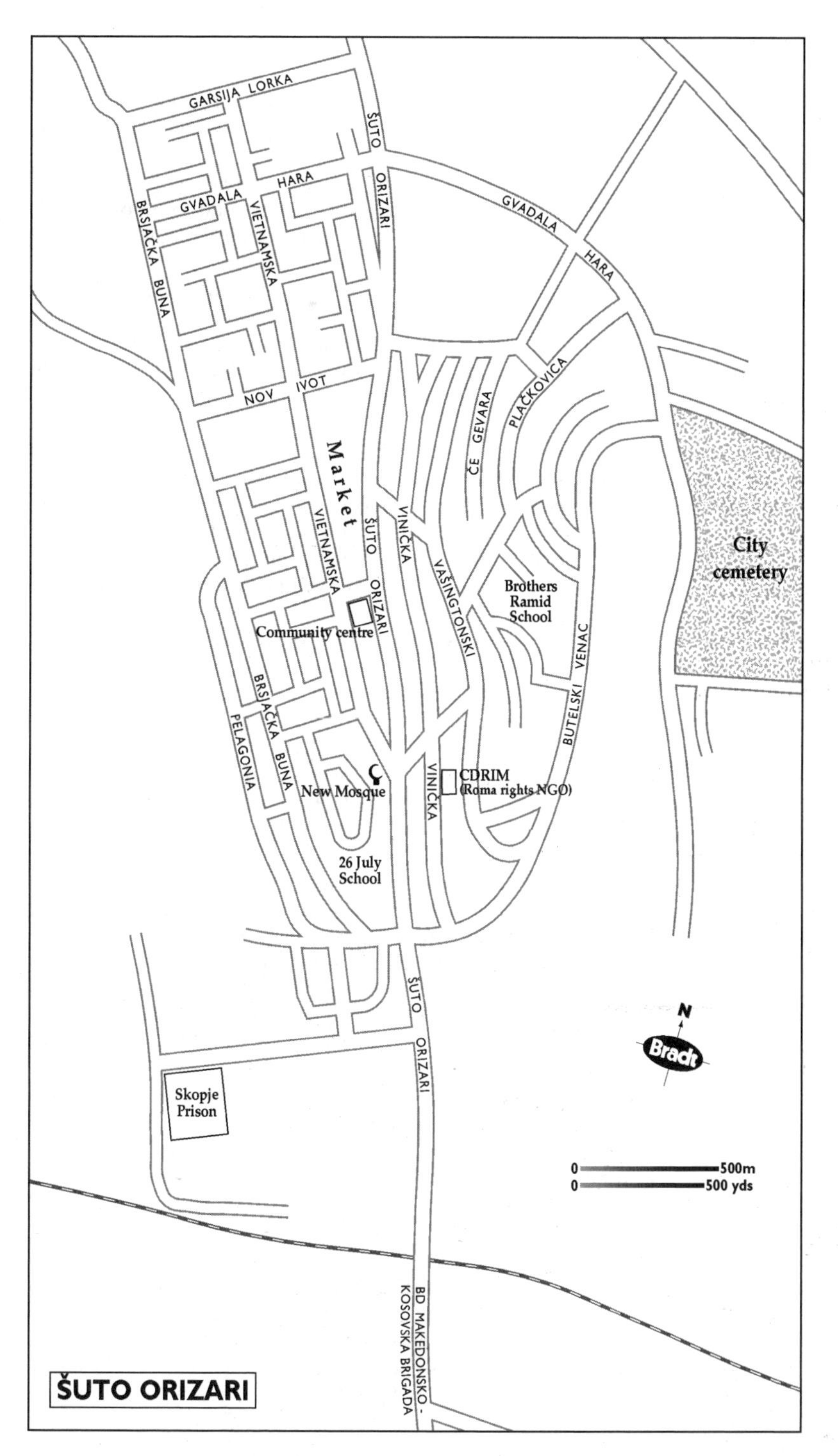
GARSIJA LORKA
ŠUTO ORIZARI
GVADALA HARA
BRSJAČKA BUNA
VIETNAMSKA
NOV IVOT
Market
ČE GEVARA
PLAČKOVICA
VINIČKA
VAŠINGTONSKI
Brothers Ramid School
City cemetery
Community centre
BUTELSKI VENAC
PELAGONIA
New Mosque
CDRIM (Roma rights NGO)
26 July School
Skopje Prison
N
Bradt
0 500m
0 500 yds
BD MAKEDONSKO - KOSOVSKA BRIGADA
ŠUTO ORIZARI

and most Macedonians would think you were a little bit crazy to want to go there. However, this is the equivalent of London's Little Venice, Greece or Turkey, where the daily **market** is super-cheap (and filled with a lot of junk) and it's the only place you can get some of the hand-sewn and embroidered Roma clothing and shoes.

More interesting than a wander through the market (where even the Roma will tell you to keep a tight hold on your wallet) is a walk around some of the side streets off the northern end of Vietnamska. This area of their settlement will give you a feel of how the Roma live and love a carefree and artistic life. The closely packed one- or two-storey houses are usually immaculately whitewashed with a decorative fence of moulded concrete or ironwork, topped with whitewashed lions and pekinese dogs pawing a ball. Wooden caravan wheels, harking back to the nomadic days of the Roma, adorn the walls and fences. Many of these lovely homes are not built from money earned here in Macedonia, but are the result of years away working in Germany and Austria.

The atmosphere and surroundings are not unlike a Chinese or Indian neighbourhood in Malaysia or some other southeast Asian country. Children laugh and play in the streets and this is a world away from the Roma who beg on the streets with their half-naked, half-drugged babies. But behind the laughter of children, the concerns of adults are not difficult to find.

In a community where education is not always highly valued, it is difficult enough to get the really poor of the Roma community to attend school. It is even more difficult when the main school in Šutko, Brothers Ramid School, is filled three times over capacity and has few facilities and insufficient teaching staff. The school gymnasium has no heating in the dead of winter and most of the windows are broken. Water runs down the walls of the changing rooms and many of the corridors in the school. The school received its first ever photocopier and five reams of paper on November 15 2002, through the donation of five churches in Dorset, England. The Macedonian government has no money for such basics, and where the school will continue to get its paper from is as yet unanswered.

On the bright side, the Roma are outstandingly musically talented (Django Reinhardt was Roma). The school has a few musical instruments of its own, but most of the children bring their parents' instruments into school, the very instrument that their parents earn their living from by playing in bands for hire at parties and festivals. In recent years, despite the poor teaching conditions and the other overwhelming concerns of poverty, Brothers Ramid School has repeatedly won the first prize in the annual Skopje school choir and school orchestra competitions.

To find out more about the Roma or to help in any way see the *Giving something back* section on page 86. To get to Šutko take the number 19 or 20 bus heading north from Dame Gruev outside the main post office, or take the ten-minute taxi ride for less than 100MKD. Ask to be dropped off at the *Šutko Bazaar*, which is on the main street through Šutko.

THE RUINS OF SKUPI

This small site of the ruins of 4th-century Skupi are hardly worth the time to visit, as they are barely uncovered, lack any information at the site, and you cannot gain access to the grounds. But this may change, and if you are staying at the Aleksandar Palace Hotel and fancy a walk over the river, or are eating at the new French restaurant, Day and Night (see page 102) then you might take a look at what is there.

THE LAST ORTHODOX KING OF MACEDONIA

After the death of Serbian Tsar Dušan in 1355, a mere ten years after he had been crowned king in Skopje, the Serb kingdom started to fall apart at the seams. Tsar Uroš took over, helped by the Mrnjavčevič brothers, Volkašin and Ugleša. They headed up feudal kingdoms within the empire and in 1365 Volkašin proclaimed himself co-Tsar and ruler of the western side of the empire with its seat of power at Prilep.

Volkašin had four sons by his wife Elena, and several daughters. Marko, the eldest, was born in 1335. Twenty-six years later in 1371, when Volkašin and his brother were killed fighting against the Ottomans in Thrace, Greece, the crown of the empire passed to Marko, as neither Tsar Uroš nor Volkašin's brother Ugleša had any heirs. Even though he was of Serb origin, King Marko is often viewed by the Macedonians as the stepping-stone for Macedonian nationhood between Tsar Samoil (967–1014) and the ten-day Kruševo Republic of 1903.

Prilep was centrally placed within Marko's kingdom, which reached from the Šar mountains in the northwest down the western bank of the River Vardar to Kastoria (in present-day Greece) in the south. Rarely did his kingdom include Skopje or Ohrid, however, and eventually even Prilep fell to the Ottomans in 1394. A year later King Marko was killed in Romania whilst forced to fight for the Ottomans against the Vlachs.

The site is 1.5km from the Aleksandar Palace Hotel and to get there take the bridge over the river and take the next left turn at the traffic lights 200m after the river. Take the second right turn 1km down this road heading toward Bardovci, and the ruins are on the right another 100m down the road. They are fairly easy to miss if you are driving any faster than snail's pace as there are no signs and the place could easily be mistaken for an abandoned building site. For a brief summary of the history of Skupi see page 92.

THE OLD STONE AQUEDUCT

The 55-arched aqueduct on the other hand is worth going out of your way for, as at least there is something there to see and to photograph. Some sources say the aqueduct goes back to Roman times; others, however, say it was built during Ottoman rule by Isa Bey in the 16th century. It was certainly used then, when the Ottomans required more water for the many Turkish baths in town, such as Chifte, Gurciler and Daut Pasha Amam, and maybe they built the present structure on the ruins of a Roman original. It is now in disrepair and completely unprotected, although attempts have been made in the past to keep it from falling down completely.

To get there, cross the river at the Aleksandar Palace Hotel and join the E65 highway (Motorway 2) going north to Kosovo. Just over 1km after turning on to the E65, turn right immediately after the railway flyover on to a dirt track. Pass back under the railway flyover for a few hundred metres until you reach the gates of the army barracks and then turn left, or park here if you do not have 4WD. From the barracks gates it is a 500m walk to the aqueduct which will have been visible from the E65 highway. You may not be allowed to take photos of the aqueduct with the barracks in the background, so position yourself with the barracks behind you to take photos.

MARKO'S MONASTERY

Tucked in the foothills of Jakupica Mountains, south of Vodno Mountain, is the village of Marko Sušica, at the southwestern end of which is King Marko's monastery. The **monastery church dedicated to St Dimitri** was started by Marko's father, King Volkashin in the mid-14th century, and then finished by Marko after his father's death in 1371. This may have been as close as Marko's kingdom got to Skopje, and from here the border probably went through his brother's monastery of St Andreja at Matka and on to the Šar Mountains in the east.

The monastery has frescos of the king himself, as well as an interesting fresco of the three wise men visiting baby Jesus, and a fresco of St Clement, the first archbishop of Ohrid. Although Ohrid was never a part of Marko's kingdom, the Archbishopric was always behind the fledgling kingdom, and the absence of Serbian saints and church figureheads in Marko's monastery are seen as a good indicator that Marko adhered to the church of Ohrid rather than the new church of Serbia.

To get there, take 11th Oktomvri Street southeast out of town and keep on this road as it becomes Sava Kovačevič street and leads on to the village of Sopište. Take care to keep going straight on Sava Kovačevič and do not follow the main road around to the left when it turns into 1st Maj street. After Sopište bear left toward Dobri Dol and Markova Sušica (signposted). At the crossroads just before the village, go straight on over the bridge and into the village until you reach the monastery on the other side. You will require shoulder and leg coverings to enter the church itself.

The small stream running below the monastery is a popular picnic site with Macedonians.

MOUNT KITKA

Mount Kitka is the beginning of the next mountain range behind Vodno, south of Skopje. At 1,569m the peak has a mountain hut and lots of adventurous hiking trails in the beautiful forests of the Jakupica mountain range.

To get there, take 11th Oktomvri heading southeast out of town until it becomes Sava Kovačevič and follow the road around to the left as it becomes 1st Maj street (Sava Kovačevič continues straight on to Markova Sušica – see above. This road will take you to the village of Dračevo where you should turn right (south) opposite the village petrol station to get to Kitka Mountain. The turning is signposted in Cyrillic for Kitka and the Količani villages, and the road will take you past the Dračevo village graveyard and the red-and-white radio mast.

Just before the village of Dolni Količani are many old marble Muslim gravestones. Keep right when you get to the village itself in order to continue on to Kitka. Two hundred metres before the crossroads after the village of Crvena Voda are a number of trails heading up to Mount Kitka, which is another 3km by foot, but the trails are badly marked. The hut warden at **mountain hut Kitka** (60 beds) tel: 070 246 419, or 02 3117 100 is Sašo Popovski.

The asphalt road continues south and at a prominent crossroads on the crest of a hill turns left along the steep Kadina ravine to the Albanian village of Paligrad. Here the asphalt road runs out and a 4WD is required to take the rest of the track up towards the summit. Back at the crossroads there is a dirt track turn-off on the right which is signposted for mountain hut Karadžica, and the road ahead, signposted for Solunska Glava, becomes a dirt track going to the village of Aldinci and beyond. The hut wardens at **mountain hut Karadžica** (50 bed) tel: 02 3112 199 ext 630 are Atanas Ovnarski and Blagoja Petrusevska.

KATLANOVSKA BANJA

The **hot springs** at Katlanovo Banja (*banja* is the Macedonian for 'thermal baths') are well known to the denizens of Skopje. Anyone past the age of two can remember being brought out there for a picnic, a walk in the wilderness, a fishing trip, or to visit an ailing relative who was staying at the sanitorium. There are two approaches to Katlanovo; one from the north side and one from the south. The difference is that most of the good **picnic areas** are on the north bank of the river, and the best rock climbing and fishing seem to be on the south.

To get to the south side, go east out of town, past the airport as if going to Greece, and then take the Katlanovska Banja exit on the right. Keep following the signs (watch for the goats) and when you run out of signs, follow the river. If you get disoriented or lose the river on your right, just open the window and follow the sulphur smell. It is faint, but it will lead you to the Banja area.

You can park either in front of the bathhouses or in a lower parking area closer to the river. Also watch for the water carriers on the final approach to the baths. There are many natural springs coming from the rock walls along the drive and the older folks in the area consider the water to be medicinal and stock up regularly. A fun side trip is to bear left on the final approach to the baths and go up, away from the river.

Katlanovska Banja is situated on the Pčinja River, which empties into the Vardar. The fish are plentiful but it is neither clean enough nor deep enough to swim in. It has easy, natural rapids that would be perfect for an intermediate in a kayak/canoe and nice pools for the fisherman (hip waders seemed to be essential clothing for this area). The river is 10m wide at the smallest point and too deep to ford, so the only dry place to cross is a bridge that runs from the baths over to a 'suburb' of Katlanovo (it is hardly big enough to call a suburb really). This enclave set into the hillside has several holiday-type homes and a new monastery under construction. There is not much to do amongst these new homes (a couple of old cafés are no longer working), but it does get you to the north side for an extended hike.

Good **hiking** and views can be found all along the ridge which runs behind the baths and eventually all the way back to the highway. You can find **old bath pits** there and the water channels that used to supply them with water, as well as some easy bouldering rock face. A small bat cave tops one of the rock faces.

There are only two formal picnic gazebos near the baths since the banks on the south side of the river are somewhat damp and swampy. There is also a healthy number of stray dogs and cats on the south bank near the baths so keep a look out if you have your lunch on the south side. There is a little shop there for snacks but no *skara na kilo* so you need to pack your own food.

On the north bank of the river is dry, flat land that is suitable for spreading a blanket and having a picnic with plenty of room for festivities. To get to the north side, stay on the highway past the Katlanovo exit, cross the big gorge that follows it, bear right at the next exit and double back along the north side of the river. You'll find a dense, relatively steep forest as you walk from the river into the mountains on the north side and one really inviting rock climbing face for the intrepid.

The baths themselves are open to the public at 50MKD entry, but they are a little bit Hannibalesque to say the least. The doors to all the dorm type rows of ceramic baths are falling off and the lighting is extremely dim if there is any at all. The main bathing pools are separated into men's and women's.

ST BOGORODICA MONASTERY NEAR KOŽLE

On the drive down to Veleš from Skopje, the road south follows the River Pčinja from Katlanovska Banja until it joins the Vardar. The road winds around the sides of a steep gorge making interesting driving and fantastic scenery. Fortunately, at this section there are no oncoming cars as the road north takes a completely separate route further east. On this southerly road, a couple of kilometres before the River Pčinja joins the Vardar, there is a spacious stopping place on the right-hand side of the road with a couple of holy roadside shrines and a water fountain. This place also marks the stop for the Monastery of St Bogorodica which can be seen across the river from the roadside.

The 500m hike starts through a metal entrance to the left of the fountain and the bus shelter, goes across a small wooden bridge crossing the river, and ends up in the courtyard of the monastery. It is no longer a working monastery, but is kept by two wardens who live there. They might join you at this juncture to explain more about the monastery.

The site was originally just a shrine in the rocks and, like many rock shrines in Macedonia, it eventually became a cave church. This one was built using old train rails from 1918 to help support the roof, but by the 1930s it was completely abandoned. It took another 40 years for the church to be rebuilt in 1976, thereby saving some of the original roof frescos, and replacing the old iconostasis.

If you spy the monastery on the way down south, but don't manage to stop, remember you won't be able to see it on the way back north as the north road does not pass that way.

Ohrid architecture

7

Lake Ohrid and Galičica National Park

Ohrid is the jewel of the Macedonian crown. Both the town and the lake are under the protection of UNESCO as a site of rare environmental, scientific and cultural significance. And not without due reason: the lake itself is one of the oldest in the world, belonging in the ranks of Lake Baikal in Russia and Lake Titicaca in Peru/Bolivia; the town has historic roots going back to Neolithic times, much of which is still to be seen in the museum or in the form of churches, castles and other architecture. Allegedly, there are 365 churches, monasteries and holy sites around the lake, one for every day of the year. Aside from these attractions, Macedonians love Ohrid because it is their seaside: the waters are beckoning in the long hot days of July and August, and there is many a festival to while away the time, should you ever get bored of all the other activities around the lake or in Galičica National Park. The two main towns situated on the lake are Ohrid and Struga.

And once you have partaken in the festivals and seen the sites of the town, **Tsar Samoil's fortress**, **St Sophia's church** and the **Robevi house** to name a few, there are plenty of things outside the town too: the lake **springs** at Sveti Naum, **cave churches** at Kališta and Radožda, hiking in **Galičica National Park**, the Twelfthtide **carnival** in Vevčani, and day trips to mountain villages around the lake.

OHRID

History

The shores of one of the oldest lakes in the world have undoubtedly been inhabited since prehistoric times. The earliest signs of mankind in the area have been found in Dolno Trnovo, to the north of the main town, dating from Neolithic times (around 6000BC). Some of these artefacts can now be seen in the Ohrid museum.

Later, tribes known as the Brigians, Ohrygians and Enhelians settled in the area. These tribes neighboured the Illyrians of Grecian origin, who at that time had moved through Ohrid into areas further west (now Albania). They were displaced by the Desaretes, and it is as the capital of Deseratia that Lychnidos (present-day Ohrid) is first mentioned.

Lychnidos, meaning 'town of light' (in ancient Greek *lychni* = light, *dos* = town), was so named by Phoenician Cadmus, a Theban who settled in the town after he was banished from Greece. Later, in the 4th century BC, the town was inhabited by the Macedonians of Philip II, and then the Romans in the late 2nd century BC. The town developed during Roman times from traders travelling along the Via Egnatia (see page 29), which passed through Lychnidos, and with the travellers also came the preachers of Christianity.

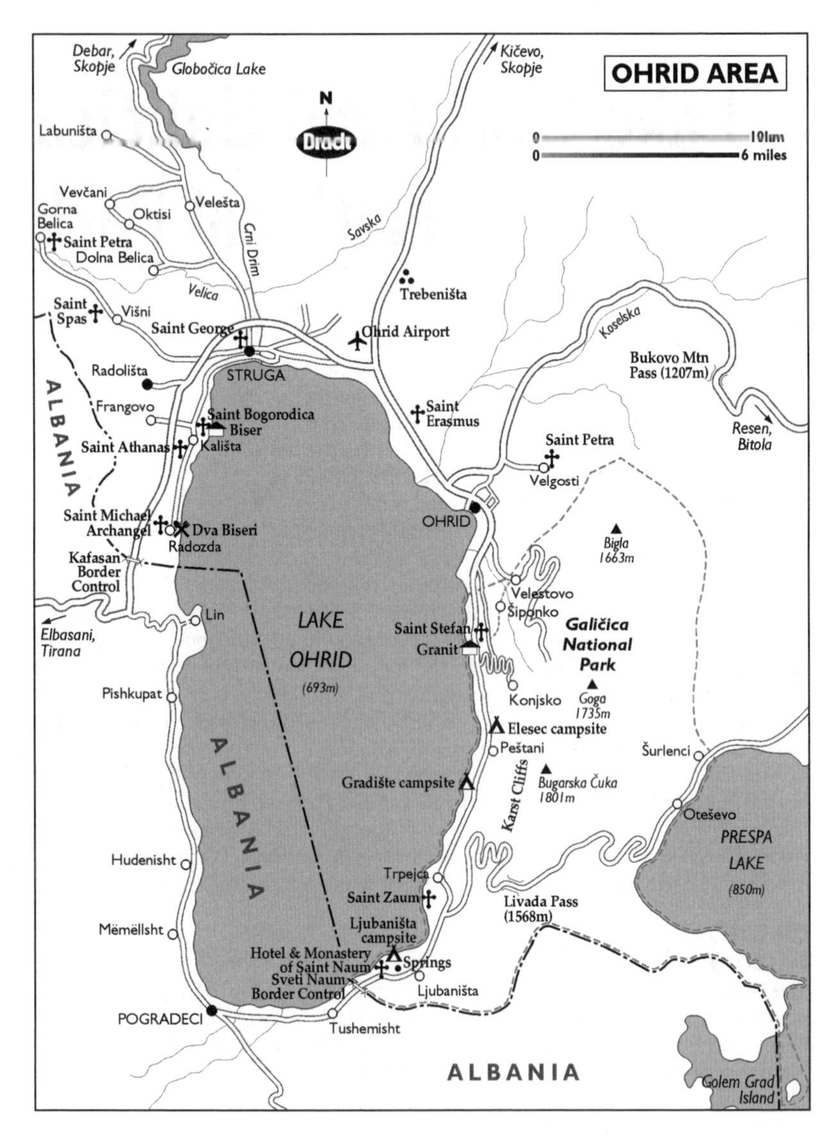

By the 5th century AD, the first early basilicas were being built in Lychnidos. Twelve are believed to have been built altogether, although only six have been found so far. The largest and most significant of these is at the site of today's Monastery of St Clement at Plaošnik. The size of the basilica indicates the importance of this church and of the bishops who resided here, whose work was cut out for them when the pagan Slav tribes started arriving in the town in the 6th century.

By 879, the town was no longer called Lychnidos but was referred to by the Slavs as Ohrid, possibly from the Slav words *vo hrid*, meaning 'on a hill' as the ancient town of Lychnidos was at the top of Ohrid Hill.

A few years later, the missionaries Clement and Naum came to Ohrid and set

THE FIRST UNIVERSITIES OF CLEMENT AND NAUM

Clement (840–916) and Naum (835–910), like the brothers Kiril and Metodi, were native Macedonians. Both had been disciples of the brothers and travelled with them on their pioneering journey to Moravia in Hungary, to teach the Slavs in their own language which brought about the invention of the Glagolitic and Cyrillic scripts. Due to their heavy involvement in language and writing and the teaching of these to their pupils, there are also extensive diaries of the two men that have been passed on through the ages, the best known of which are the *Extensive Hagiography* and the *Short Hagiography of Saint Clement.*

Clement would have been 22 when he accompanied Kiril and Metodi to Moravia, and 46 by the time he came to the Ohrid region to teach the scriptures there. In 893 at the age of 53 he was appointed Bishop of Velika, a large swathe of land reaching up to the River Treska around Kičevo, by Tsar Simeon of the new Bulgarian state recently freed from Byzantine. As a result of his new duties he had to move from his original monastery up in the wilds, north of Ohrid, into Ohrid itself where he founded a new monastery, the Monastery of St Clement, and asked for his former fellow disciple, Naum, to join him in order to help teach the scriptures to their ever-increasing audience. They mostly taught in the Glagolitic script, which only fully died out to be replaced by the dominant Cyrillic script in the 12th century.

It is recorded in the diaries that over 3,500 pupils passed through the monastery of St Clement, and numbers became so demanding that Naum set up another monastery, the Monastery of St Naum, in AD900 at the other end of the lake. When he died in 910, he was buried in the vaults of the church, and it is believed that if you stand over his crypt and put your ear to the wall, you will hear Naum's heart beating even today.

up the first monasteries to teach in Slavic (see box above). This strengthened the already strong religious tradition in the town, and a century later, when Tsar Samoil (see box, page 9) moved the capital of his Macedonian empire to Ohrid, he also made Ohrid the head of its own autocephalous archdiocese.

Tsar Samoil's fortress city at Ohrid is still visible today, although parts of it were destroyed when Samoil was defeated by the Byzantine Emperor Basilius II in 1014. Ohrid then became a part of the Byzantine Empire again and the archdiocese of Ohrid was reduced to an archbishopric. But it remained an influential archbishopric nonetheless, whose reach extended from the Adriatic in the west as far as Thessaloniki to the south and all along the River Danube in the north to the Black Sea, and the Archbishop of Ohrid was always a powerful political appointee.

The Archbishopric of Ohrid, although nominally under the patriarch of Constantinople, went from strength to strength as well as growing in geographical influence even under the Ottoman Empire (see box, page 44). By the end of the 16th century the jurisdiction of the Archbishopric of Ohrid went as far as the Orthodox communities in Dalmati and Venice in mainland Italy, as well as to Malta and Sicily.

Ohrid's privileged position within the Ottoman Empire through its seat as the Archishopric was rarely challenged, although in 1466 this was jeopardised when the citizens of Ohrid sided with the Albanian Lord Skenderbey (see box, page 186) against their Ottoman rulers. Several high-ranking church officials and the archbishop were jailed as a result and died in prison.

When the Archbishopric of Ohrid was abolished in 1767 at the behest of the Greek patriarchate, Greek influence on Ohrid's religious life became pronounced, much to the dislike of the locals. It took just over a century for the locals to then convince the Ottomans to shut down Greek teaching in Ohrid in 1869. Thereafter, Ohrid's history follows a very similar pattern to the rest of northern Macedonia. VMRO's branch in Ohrid rose up on Ilinden in 1903 like the rest of the land, and was brutally put down again afterwards. Under Yugoslavia, Ohrid saw a big development in tourism, and Tito even had a summer residence on the lake, now reserved for the President of Macedonia.

Sadly, the amount of money and concrete that was poured into socialist-type tourism throughout the country has yet to be updated, and Ohrid is no exception, although improvements are happening faster here than elsewhere in Macedonia. A few gems are opening up, and it should not be too long before the slow revolution in catering and accomodation that is happening in Skopje will catch up with Ohrid too.

Getting there, around and about

Macedonia's only other **international airport** is at Ohrid, tel: 046 262 503. There are only a few flights a day in and out of the airport, which is 14km north of the town, and closer to Struga than it is to Ohrid itself. Macedonian Airways (MAT – tel: 046 263 375 or 046 254 151; fax: 046 254 241; email: matohrid@freemail.org.mk; www.mat.com.mk) fly once a day to Vienna and Zurich from Skopje, and Slovenian Airways also flies in from Ljubljana. There are no flights from Skopje to Ohrid. Full flight details for Ohrid airport can be viewed at www.airports.com.mk.

If you are not driving the two hours down from Skopje, then there are frequent **buses** to Ohrid at least every two hours, and in the summer even more. The inter-town bus station, tel: 046 262 490, is at Dimitar Vlahov Street in the centre of town, from which frequent buses go towards Sveti Naum and Struga. If you are driving to Ohrid from Skopje, you should consider taking the back road via Debar, which is stunningly beautiful in the autumn when the trees are turning colour. There is no train to Ohrid.

Once in Ohrid the best way to get around is by taxi, which has a minimum fare of 10MKD. If you can't flag one down on the street, try calling one of the following numbers: 9166, 9180, 9181, 9183, 9184, 9189, 9190, 9191, 9192, 9193, 9198.

Another good way to get around the lake is by boat. There are lots of **boat taxis** which will take one or a whole boatload of passengers for a ride for a minimum of €10. This is a great way to get from the centre of town to the church of St Jovan at Kaneo on a hot day if you do not fancy the 1km hike over the hill. You'll see many a boat-taxi driver along the harbour and wandering the streets, usually wearing a sea captain's hat and holding a bottle of beer, and they will probably ask you if you want a ride long before you have got around to asking them. €20 will take you for an extended tour around the harbour, €30 will take you to Struga, Kališta or Radožda where the view of the cave church from the water is quite striking (at least one hour's boat journey), and €45 will take you the two-hour journey to Sveti Naum.

For **larger boats** contact Vladimir Stojoski, tel: 046 277 221 or 046 277 222, email: vstojosk@macedonia.eu.org, based in the Hotel Ohrid, who will be able to sort out hiring a boat for the day or half-day. A 30-passenger boat, for instance, including lunch on board with drinks, works out at about €30 per person. Unfortunately, demand is not yet enough for a regular passenger boat service which would take passengers individually, and so it is the whole boat or nothing.

A 1:6,000 **city map** of Ohrid can be bought in most supermarkets and bookstalls, both in Skopje and in Ohrid itself. The Trimaks map also includes a 1:65,000 map of the lake on the back side of the city map, as well as some useful information on sites, telephone numbers, and street names.

For help with bookings, tours and further information, contact one of the following **travel agencies** in Ohrid: General Tourist at Partizanska 6, tel: 046 262 071; fax: 046 260 415; or Mergimi Air at Turistička 50, tel: 046 254 576. Mišo Yuzmeski (tel: 070 507 424; email: yuzmeski@msn.com; web: yuzmeski.bizhosting.com) will give tours of Ohrid and Macedonia in English, Italian and Spanish.

Where to stay

Upmarket

Villa Sveta Sofia (5 rooms) Kosta Abraš 64; tel: 046 254 370. For style, comfort, excellent value for money and that finishing touch, this is the place to stay. Exquisite service accompanies every room. They have one single room for €35; one twin room for €60; two doubles at €80 each; and one luxury apartment for €120.

Millenium Palace (60 beds) At the eastern end of the town next to the shoreline; tel: 046 267 010 or 046 265 414; fax: 046 263 361; email: millenium_palace@mt.net.mk. New and smart, and every room has minibar, air conditioning, TV, phone and internet connection. The hotel also has its own sauna, fitness centre and restaurant. €49 for a single, €66 for a double. A great buffet breakfast is 200MKD for non-residents.

Riviera (36 rooms) Tel: 046 268 735 or 046 251 912; fax: 046 254 155; www.hotelrivieraohrid.4t.com. The hotel also has a restaurant with patio seating, a piano bar and mini-shop. Rooms cost €40 per person per night including breakfast.

Hotel Sveti Naum (30 rooms) Tel: 046 283 080. Your chance to stay in the holy grounds where St Naum himself taught and preached. Situated at the south end of the lake, the monastery is tranquil at night but can be just as busy as Ohrid during the day with visitors. The hotel was newly built in 1999, so it is thoroughly up-to-date. All rooms are en suite, with TV, air conditioning and telephone. A single room is €56 and a double is €36 per person. The peacocks crow loudly in the morning.

Mid level

Hotel Granit (233 rooms) Tel: 046 277 886/887; fax: 046 277 888; email: hotelgranit@hotmail.com; www.hotelgranit.com.mk; is a favourite for conferences on the eastern edge of the lake, with direct access to the lake and a jetty for boats to come up to. Rooms are ensuite with TV and balcony lakeside and hillside. Occasionally noisy depending on the conference. Paddle boats on the beach are 150MKD per hour. There are plenty more conference-style hotels in the vicinity if the 233 rooms here are miraculously full. €28 per person for bed and breakfast.

Villa Rustica (5 apartments) Hristo Uzunov 1; tel: 046 26 55 11, or 070 212 114; www.villarustica.com.mk. Fantastic 270° view of the lake from the top suite. €15 per person per night in the four-person apartments. €100 for the top suite.

Budget

Lucija's (7 rooms) Kosta Abraš 29; tel: 046 265 608 or 070 352 804; fax: 046 266 396. Excellent value for money for its range and location. The patio is right on the water so you can go for a quick swim before breakfast, and the house is right opposite the Jazz Inn, so you don't have far to stumble in the evening either! Her rooms are often booked a week or two in advance during the summer, so reserve early. €15 for a single, €25 for a double or €40 for an apartment with two twin rooms and its own bathroom on the lake side of the house. €4 extra per person for breakfast.

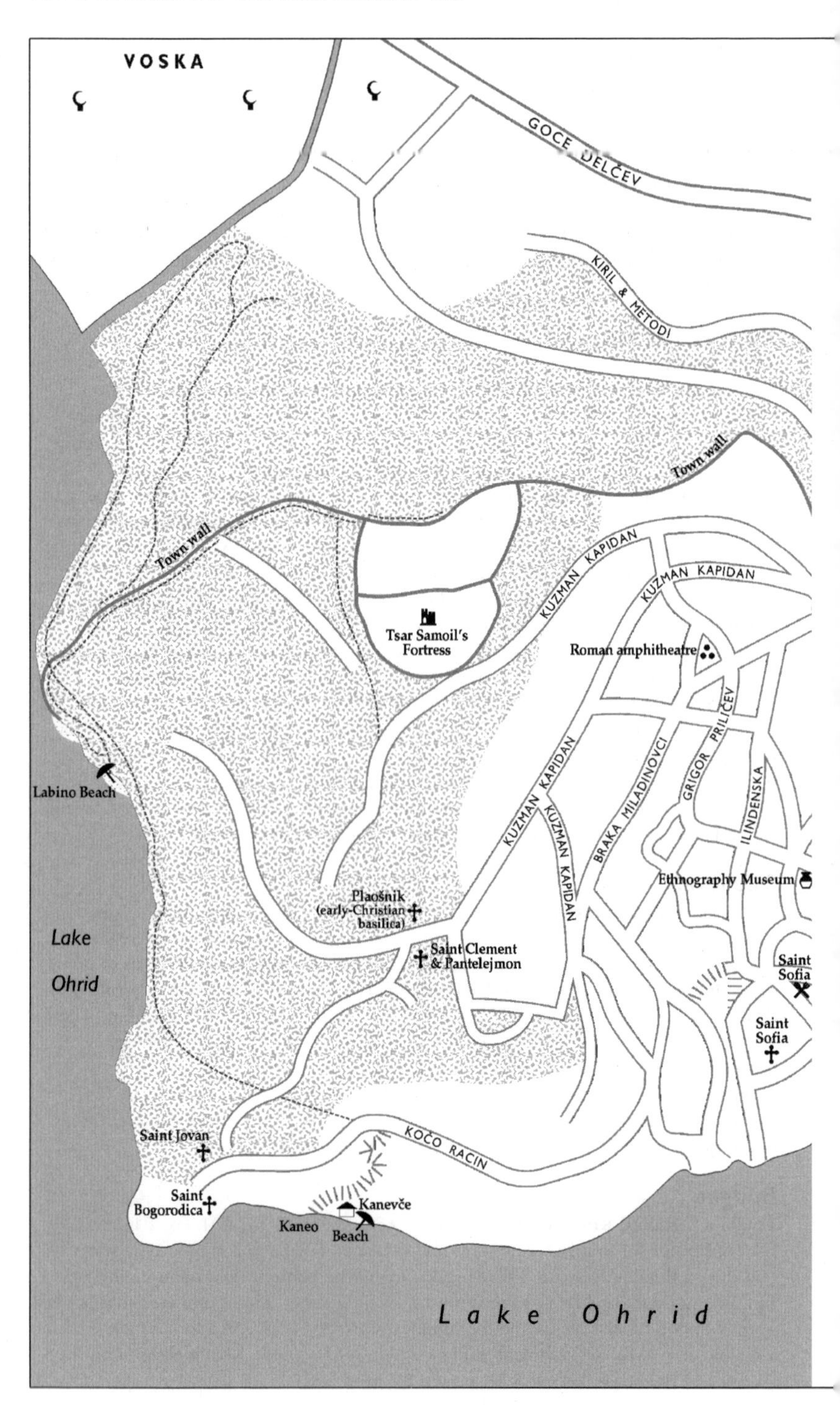
VOSKA
GOCE DELČEV
KIRIL & METODI
Town wall
Town wall
KUZMAN KAPIDAN
KUZMAN KAPIDAN
KUZMAN KAPIDAN
KUZMAN KAPIDAN
KUZMAN KAPIDAN
Tsar Samoil's Fortress
Roman amphitheatre
GRIGOR PRILIČEV
BRAKA MILADINOVCI
ILINDENSKA
Ethnography Museum
Labino Beach
Plaošnik (early-Christian basilica)
Saint Clement & Pantelejmon
Saint Sofia
Saint Sofia
Lake Ohrid
KOČO RACIN
Saint Jovan
Saint Bogorodica
Kanevče
Kaneo
Beach
Lake Ohrid

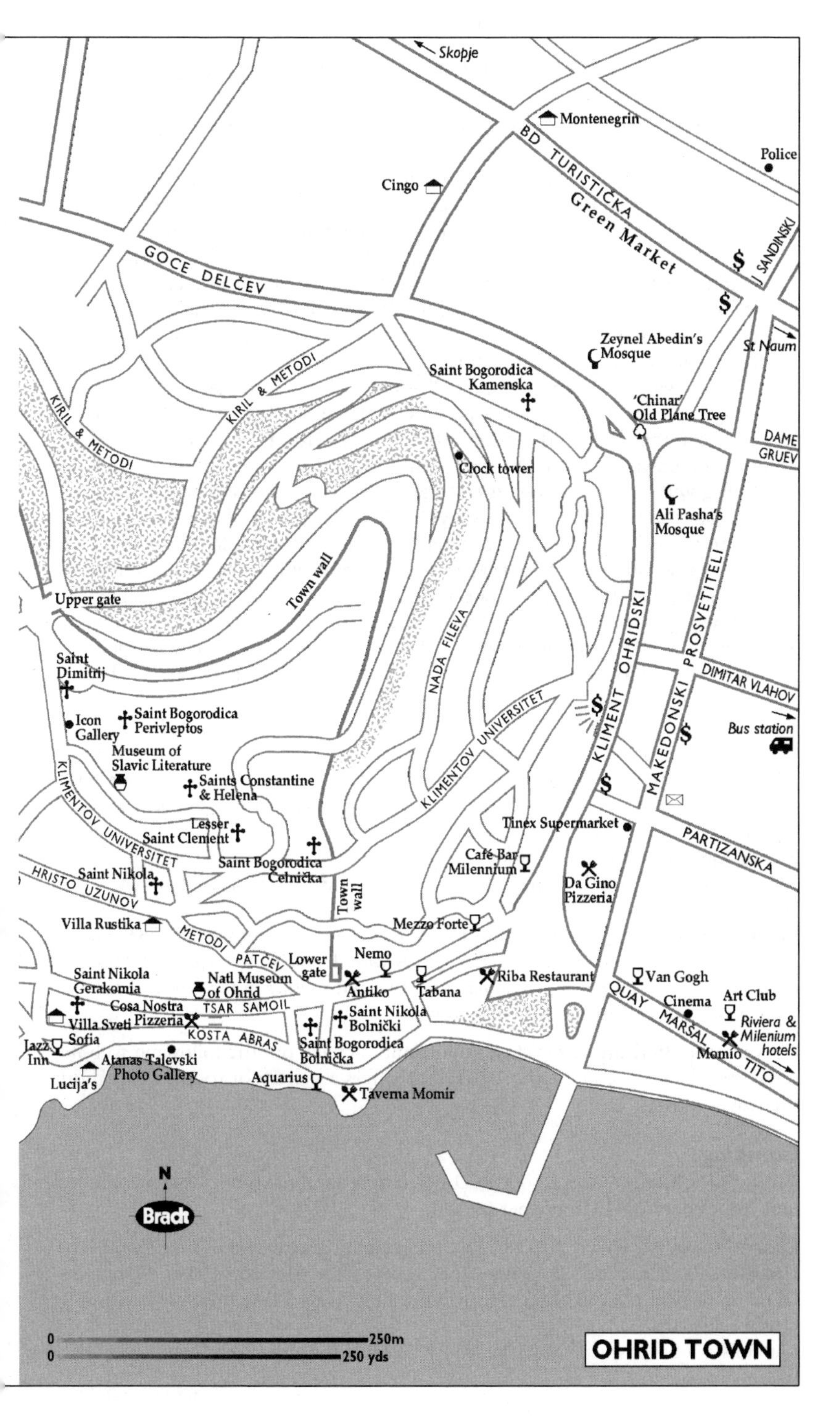
Skopje
Montenegrin
Police
Cingo
BD TURISTIČKA
Green Market
J SANDINSKI
GOCE DELČEV
Zeynel Abedin's Mosque
St Naum
KIRIL & METODI
Saint Bogorodica Kamenska
'Chinar' Old Plane Tree
DAME GRUEV
Clock tower
Ali Pasha's Mosque
Town wall
Upper gate
NADA FILEVA
KLIMENT OHRIDSKI
MAKEDONSKI PROSVETITELI
Saint Dimitrij
DIMITAR VLAHOV
KLIMENTOV UNIVERSITET
Icon Gallery
Saint Bogorodica Perivleptos
Bus station
Museum of Slavic Literature
Saints Constantine & Helena
Tinex Supermarket
Lesser Saint Clement
PARTIZANSKA
Saint Bogorodica Čelnička
Café-Bar Milennium
Saint Nikola
HRISTO UZUNOV
Da Gino Pizzeria
Villa Rustika
Mezzo Forte
METODI
PATČEV
Lower gate
Nemo
Riba Restaurant
Van Gogh
Saint Nikola Gerakomia
Natl Museum of Ohrid
Antiko
Tabana
Cinema
Art Club
QUAY MARŠAL TITO
Cosa Nostra Pizzeria
TSAR SAMOIL
Saint Nikola Bolnički
Riviera & Milenium hotels
Villa Sveti Sofia
KOSTA ABRAS
Saint Bogorodica Bolnička
Momo
Jazz Inn
Atanas Talevski Photo Gallery
Lucija's
Aquarius
Taverna Momir
N
Bradt
0
250m
0
250 yds
OHRID TOWN

400 YEARS OF THE KANEVČE FAMILY AT KANEO

The Kanevče family came to Kaneo from Kičevo over 500 years ago in the late 1400s. They settled in the sheltered nook of the rocks of Kaneo still protected within the town walls, and quickly became wealthy lake fishermen after they bought the fishing rights for the northern half of the lake from Peštani to Kalište from the Ottomans. The family soon outgrew the small settlement at Kaneo and expanded into Ohrid itself where some of the early 19th-century style houses still belong to the family, such as the one below Sveti Sofia Church, and their older houses on Kaneo beach. Ohrid's abundant fishing and its position on a major trading route kept the Kanevče family busy up until the beginning of the 20th century.

Then with the Balkan wars, the division of Macedonia, the closed door policies of early communism, and the disastrous effect of bloated and over-centralised socialist policies, the luck of the Kanevče family has gone steadily downhill. Stefan Kanevče, who remembers those days of good fishing with his grandfather, is still a keen fisherman, and will happily take you out fishing on the lake if you want. He's also a mine of knowledge on anything in Ohrid or even Macedonia. But the fishing trade isn't what it used to be, and he and his family have little money now to renovate the beautiful but crumbling houses at Kaneo. His, however, are the few rooms in Macedonia where you can actually stay in an original 19th-century house, complete with intricate wooden ceiling, closets and wardrobes. No heating, and no TV, only the sound of the waves of the lake to lull you to sleep.

Dimče Kanevče (3 rooms) Kaneo; tel: 046 262 928 or 070 579 359. Very nice rooms, simple and clean, right on the lake with a private jetty to swim from. €10 per person without breakfast.

Stefan Kanevče (9 rooms in various houses) Kaneo; tel: 046 260 350, or 070 212 352; stefan_kanevce@yahoo.co.uk (see box). €10 per person per night without breakfast.

Ljupka Maslova (4 rooms and 2 apartments) tel: 070 353 999 or 046 265 583; email: maslova@ohrid.com.mk. One of the few places with double beds. Nice tasteful rooms in two houses, one in Kaneo overlooking the lake and another in the centre of town. €15/30 per room/apartment excluding breakfast.

For the other **bed and breakfast** opportunities check out the following website: www.magiclakes.com/indexEn.asp, which offers a variety of rooms throughout the town.

Camping

All the sites listed here are 500MKD per tent space (maximum four people per tent space) plus 20MKD tax per person.

Elesec (70 tent spaces) Tel: 046 285 926. 10km on the eastern road of Lake Ohrid.

Gradište (400 tent spaces, 25 caravans, 8 bungalows) Tel: 046 285 945/845. 17km from Ohrid on the way to Sveti Naum. Huge, but with it comes a long stretch of beach, and several ball courts.

Ljubaništa (65 tent spaces) Tel: 046 283 240. Very close to the Sveti Naum end of the lake.

Where to eat

Ohrid has a host of little pizzerias and fish restaurants along Tsar Samoil and Kosta Abraš, and fast food joints and cafés galore along the main drag. They can quickly become much of a muchness, and once you've eaten through the good few, trout *again*, can become a bit boring. Ohrid is begging for some cuisine alternatives and a really good breakfast bar. Here are some of the best available:

Taverna Momir Kosta Abraš; tel: 046 255 999. The third Momir restaurant to open in Ohrid but the first in the old town. Interesting table and chair stuck to the ceiling. Great lakeside seating.
Antiko Tsar Samoil 30; tel: 046 265 523. Another up-market place to eat, with a nice wooden interior and traditional Macedonian food.
Restaurant Sveta Sofia Tsar Samoil 88; tel: 046 267 403. On the uphill side of Sveta Sofia Church, has a wonderful outdoor patio overlooking the church and even more wonderful food. They serve the best fried squid after Croatia, the homeland of magnificently delicious grilled and fried squid, and a good freshly squeezed lemonade to go with it. Also excellent trout soup.
Da Gino's pizzeria in Skopje has a branch in Ohrid right on the main square. Excellent pizza and the only place in Ohrid to serve pizza with fresh mushrooms rather than tinned.

Nightclubs and bars

These are abundant in Ohrid. Here are a few favourites:

Jazz Inn Open from 22.30 to 01.00. Has live music on Thursdays, Friday and Saturdays. Very popular and good music.
Mezzo Forte Tsar Samoil 4. A happening little place.
Tabana Tsar Samoil 11. Has a fantastic rooftop pub overlooking the town.
Aquarius Kosta Abraš . Right on the lake, trendy and lively.

What to see

Unlike the rest of Macedonia, Ohrid is cottoning on to how to make money from its tourist attractions, and almost all the cultural and historical sites require an entry fee of 100MKD per person. In those few churches which do not charge an entry fee it is usually customary to leave some money at the altar or icons anyway, and the money is definitely needed if Macedonia is to preserve these historical sites.

Churches and monasteries

Of the 365 holy sites around the lake, here are seven of the most important within the town to start you off. Details of many more of the lesser churches can be found in *Ohrid, Macedonia*, a 91-page booklet available in most of the church shops and bookshops in Ohrid.

St Clement's Monastery Church, dedicated to saints Clement and Pantelejmon, is a newly built church, which was only completed in 2002. It stands, however, beside the original site of St Clement's very own monastery school, started in AD893. Clement had built the original church on the ruins of the early 5th-century basilica at Plaošnik, and had even built his own tomb into the church, in which he was buried upon his death in 916. Almost 150 graves recently found at the church show that the church was also a hospital during Clement's time.

The church was renovated and enlarged three times in the 12th, 13th and 14th centuries, but during the time of Ottoman rule the church was transformed into the Imater Mosque. St Clement's relics were then hastily moved to the 10th-century church of St Bogorodica Perivleptos. The mosque did not survive the end of the Ottoman Empire and after its destruction only legend remained that St Clement's monastery and his tomb used to stand at Plaošnik.

Excavations to find the church and tomb were started in 1943, and it was not long before the foundations of the church, the basilica and the tomb were found. Frescos from the renovation and enlargement periods have also been found, but none from the original 9th-century church. The foundations of the 5th-century basilica have been preserved and are on display in front of the new church.

The **Church of St Sofia** was built in the early 11th century as a cathedral church for Archbishop Leo of the Archbishopric of Ohrid. It was also built on the remains of a former basilica and later became a mosque and then a warehouse during the Ottoman Empire. In 1912 it was re-converted to a church.

As a mosque the inside of the cathedral had been completely whitewashed and so it took extensive work during the second half of the 20th century to retrieve the 11th-century frescos which lay underneath the whitewash. Most of these are now on display again, as well as some of those from later renovations of the church in the 12th and 14th centuries. St Sofia Church is one of only two churches in the world to display such a high number of well-preserved 11th-century frescos. The other is St Sophia Church in Kiev.

St Clement's Church of the Holy Mother of God Most Glorious *(Sveti Bogorodica Perivleptos)* is a late 13th-century church which started out simply called by the second half of its present name, but took on the St Clement prefix when St Clement's relics were transferred there during the Ottoman Empire. At the same time the church became the cathedral of the archbishop when the original cathedral at St Sofia was converted into a mosque. By the end of the 15th century the cathedral had started to become a collection point for historical records and artefacts saved from other churches around Ohrid. In 1516 the cathedral's collection and its library became the archbishopric museum, which is now the National Museum of Ohrid housed in the Robev Residence (see below). In the 1950s, centuries of smoke and soot from candles and incense were carefully cleaned from the frescos to reveal some interesting examples of late medieval painting. Look out for the fresco of the Last Supper which is being eaten outside rather than inside, and note the use of perspective in this new style of painting which emerged in the late 12th century as opposed to the older style of more traditional churches.

The **Church of St Jovan** at Kaneo is one of the most frequently visited churches in Ohrid because of its beautiful location on the cliffs directly above the lake (see front cover photo). It was built at the end of the 13th century by an unknown benefactor, but shows signs of both Byzantine and Armenian influence. Inside, a group fresco of the 3rd-century St Erasmus, believed to be one of the first missionaries to the area, together with the 9th-century St Clement and the early 14th-century Archbishop Constantine Kavacila of Ohrid betray the eclectic nature of the church, which although built later than St Clement's Church of Sveti Bogorodica Perivleptos, was painted in the older style of 11th- and 12th-century frescos.

This church features visibly in Mančevski's film *Before the Rain*, which is a must-see film about Macedonia (see page 47). Behind the church a small path leads up to St Clement's Monastery at Plaošnik. Tucked away in the rock below the entrance to the church grounds is also the very small cave church of Sveti Bogorodica. If you are lucky and can bump into Stefan Kanevče at Kaneo (see page 132), his mother might be able to find the key to the church for you.

The **churches of the Holy Mother Bolnički** and **St Nikola Bolnički** are to be found on either side of a small lane leading from the Lower Gate of the town wall to the lake. Both were built in the 14th century and were originally hospital churches (*bolcnica* in Macedonian), separated into the women's hospital of the Virgin Mary, and the men's hospital of St Nikola. The men's hospital is some 70 years older than the women's hospital and is an interesting construction of an older church inside a newer church. Both originally backed on to the town wall, parts of which can still be found in the church grounds. The St Nikola church is usually closed, but well worth a look into – ask Slavica next door at the women's hospital to open the heavy walnut doors for you.

Museums and galleries

The **National Museum of Ohrid** (tel: 046 267 173) was first established in 1516 in St Clement's Church of Bogorodica Perivleptos as a museum to the Archbishopric of Ohrid. This must make it one of the oldest museums in the world. Now the collection is divided into the archaeological display housed in the Robev Residence and the ethnographic display housed in the Urania Residence. The Robev house on Tsar Samoil is the gleaming white and wooden three-storey house which has obviously just been renovated. It is a museum piece in itself, and one of the finest examples of 19th-century Macedonian architecture in the land, well worth a visit. Open every day 10.00–14.00 and 18.00–21.00.

The **Icon Gallery** (tel: 046 251 395) at the top of Klimentov Univerzitet Street shows a range of some of the most valuable icons from the 11th to 19th centuries saved from churches all over Macedonia. It is open every day 09.00–13.00 and 17.00–20.00.

The **Museum of Slavonic Literature** is an interesting place to go if you can read any Cyrillic. The exhibits cover the development of the Glagolitic and Cyrillic scripts from their invention by St Kiril in the 9th century through to their present- day use. The museum is tucked away behind St Clement's Church of Sveti Bogorodica Perivleptos in an old primary school.

Ohrid is home to a lot of painters, sculptors, woodcarvers and other artisans, and they are hidden away in many of Ohrid's tiny streets. Try the following: Živko Pejoski at **Atelier Gallery** (Tsar Samoil 52); **Gallery Ohridska Porta** for the work of Vangel Naumovski (29th November 3); **Gallery Upevče** (7th November 10); **Gallery Bukefal** (Sveti Kliment Ohridski 54); **Gallery Marija** (Dame Gruev 28) for Ohrid pearls made using the scales of local fish; **Barok woodcarving workshop** (Tsar Samoil 24); **Porta woodcarving workshop** (Tsar Samoil 32); **Vangel Dereban silver filigree workshop** (Sveti Kliment Ohridski 40); **Vasil Malezan packsaddle workshop** (Goce Delčev 40); **Milan Belevski cobbler** (Goce Delčev 26) for handmade shoes and repairs.

Other sites of interest in Ohrid

Tsar Samoil's fortress dates only from the end of the 10th century, but records from Livy and other ancient historians tell that a fortress has stood on the top of Ohrid Hill since at least the 3rd century BC and other findings go back even further. In 2002, a golden mask and glove similar to those found in Trebenište (see below) from the Paeonian period were found behind the fortress walls.

Today much of the 3km fortified wall which enclosed the fortress can still be seen, although the inside of the fortress itself is mostly destroyed and still awaiting restoration. Up until the Ottomans arrived in Ohrid in 1395, the town was completely enclosed within these great city walls, and only two gates, the Upper Gate and the Lower Gate, existed by which to enter the town. The people of

Ohrid must have put up an almighty fight against the Turks from within the walls. Once taken though, the town expanded beyond the walls as the Turks and Ottomans moved into the Ohrid area. As in other towns like Skopje, the Ottomans kept the Christian population within the town walls. The town walls must then have felt more like a prison barrier than a defensive structure.

The Turks meanwhile built up what came to be known as the Lower Town of the **Mesokastro** area, which continues today to have a much more Turkish feel to it. There you will find two working **mosques**, the Zeynel Abedin Mosque and Ali Pasha's Mosque, astride the **900-year-old plane tree** (*Platanus Orientalis*) known locally as *Činar* in the middle of Kruševska Republika Square. Allegedly, this tree's hollow trunk used to house a barber's shop at some time in its history and later a very small café. As the old Turkish town winds around the back of the town wall you will see a number of old Turkish shops which are no longer in use, but their dust-covered artefacts and tools are still on display. These may not be around for much longer as a few new buildings are beginning to be moved in.

The **Roman amphitheatre** near the Upper Gate is just over 2,000 years old, but had been buried for centuries until, in the early 20th century, trial excavations confirmed its location. The next few decades of turmoil put the full excavation on hold, until in the sixties the excavations finally got going again. By the 1990s the amphitheatre was fully uncovered and is now once again being used in the summer as in days of old for outdoor concerts and performances. If you manage to attend a concert there, take a close look at your seat to see if you can decipher the name of the season ticket holder who owned that seat some 2,000 years ago.

A walk along **Maršal Tito quay** toward's **Tito's summer residence** is particularly pleasant in the evening when the sun is setting on the lake. Sometimes there are buskers and street performers on the quayside. Tito's summer residence sits atop the promontory which marks the south end of Ohrid Bay. It is now used as a summer residence by the President of Macedonia and so it is not open to visitors.

Festivals and events in Ohrid

Summer is the big festival season for Ohrid. In early July is the **Balkan Folklore Festival.** From mid-July to mid-August is the **Ohrid Summer Festival** now over four decades old. Classical concerts and plays are held in historical and outdoor locations around the town, such as in the amphitheatre, basilicas, churches and Tsar Samoil's fortress. Simultaneously through August there is also the **Ohrid Troubadour Festival** of popular and folk music. The last weekend in August is reserved for the **Ohrid International Swimming Marathon** when, since 1962, swimmers have been invited to test their strength against the 30km course from St Naum to Ohrid. In September Ohrid holds the musical and folklore festival entitled '**Songs of the Old City**'.

OUTSIDE OHRID

The **Monastery of St Naum** stands right at the other end of the lake practically on the border with Albania. It is a beautiful and popular site, with well-kept grounds that are the home to a flock of peacocks, including an albino, and a source of the waters for Lake Ohrid. New inns built in the last decade make up the Hotel of Sveti Naum, and are a good place to stay when the rest of Ohrid is getting overcrowded (see above).

The actual early 10th-century church of the Holy Archangels built by St Naum is in fact buried beneath the present 16th-century church, which stands in the middle of the monastery courtyards. The church had been destroyed during

Ottoman rule and its remains were only rediscovered in 1955 when excavations beneath the present church floor were carried out. The original church was a typical trefoil or clover-leaf design and contained the tomb and relics of St Naum himself. These have been preserved and re-interred beneath the new floor of the present church, which is now marked with black and white marble to show the floor plan of the original 10th-century church.

The present church was enlarged in the 17th and 18th centuries, and in 1799 the tiny chapel over St Naum's underground tomb was built. When you enter the chapel, which is to the right as you enter the narthex, and listen very carefully above the tomb, you are meant to be able to hear St Naum's heart still beating. Touching the stone above the tomb is also meant to make a wish come true.

A **boat trip down to the springs**, which feed Lake Ohrid, is available from St Naum. Trips and boat numbers are limited by the Galičica National Park authorities as the springs are rare natural phenomena and therefore it is important not to disturb the ecological balance in the waters. This doesn't stop unlicensed boat men from trying to take surplus visitors in the busy summer months, so make sure you take a legal ride. The 45 springs, which bubble up from the bottom of the crystal clear stream bed, mostly bring water from the neighbouring lake of Prespa on the other side of Galičica National Park. Prespa lies another 157m above Lake Ohrid and so the water is effectively syphoned off through the bed of Galičica Mountains into the spring on the other lower side of the mountain.

A good boatman to go with is Nikola Pavleski. For 100MKD on your half-hour trip into the springs and back, he will give a constant stream of information in English and Macedonian, as well as convenient stops just to listen to the tranquillity and the orchestra of birds, allow for photos and of course see the bubbling springs themselves. He tops it off with a round of *rakija* for everyone.

Biljana springs at Studencista also feed the lake, but are better known for their refreshing drinking water which is bottled and sold throughout Macedonia.

Just 5km outside Ohrid is the **Monastery and Cave Church of St Stefan**, hidden away above the lake a short 500m hike from the lake road. The little old lady, Raina, a wizened *baba*, almost bent in half from years of sweeping and caring for the grounds, is the only person now living in the monastery. She will tell you that the original cave church here was built in the 9th century at the time of St Clement. Villagers from the surrounding settlements of Šiponko, Gorica and Konjsko up the hill have since built the present walls and in the 15th century the church was painted with frescos.

The best reason to go to the church is for Raina. She'll serve you coffee if you have time to stop and chat, and will try to sell you postcards from the last Taiwanese people who stopped by. She doesn't like having her photo taken though.

To get there take the path uphill from opposite the Hotel Beton, 4.5km from the petrol station on the eastern edge of Ohrid. The path is marked with a hand-painted sign saying Sveti Stefan in Cyrillic.

At the gateway into the monastery the path continues up above the monastery to the villages of Šiponko in the north and Konjsko in the south, and further hiking into Galičica National Park. Beware the *Šarplaninec* sheepdogs in Šiponko – the farmers in this old and dying settlement are not used to keeping their dogs chained up, and the villagers don't like strangers wandering around on their own.

There are two more cave churches on the eastern side of the lake, one at St Erasmus between Ohrid and Struga, and one at Peštani halfway to St Naum.

North of Ohrid airport, outside the village of **Trebenište**, are the burial tombs of what have become some of the most important and rich

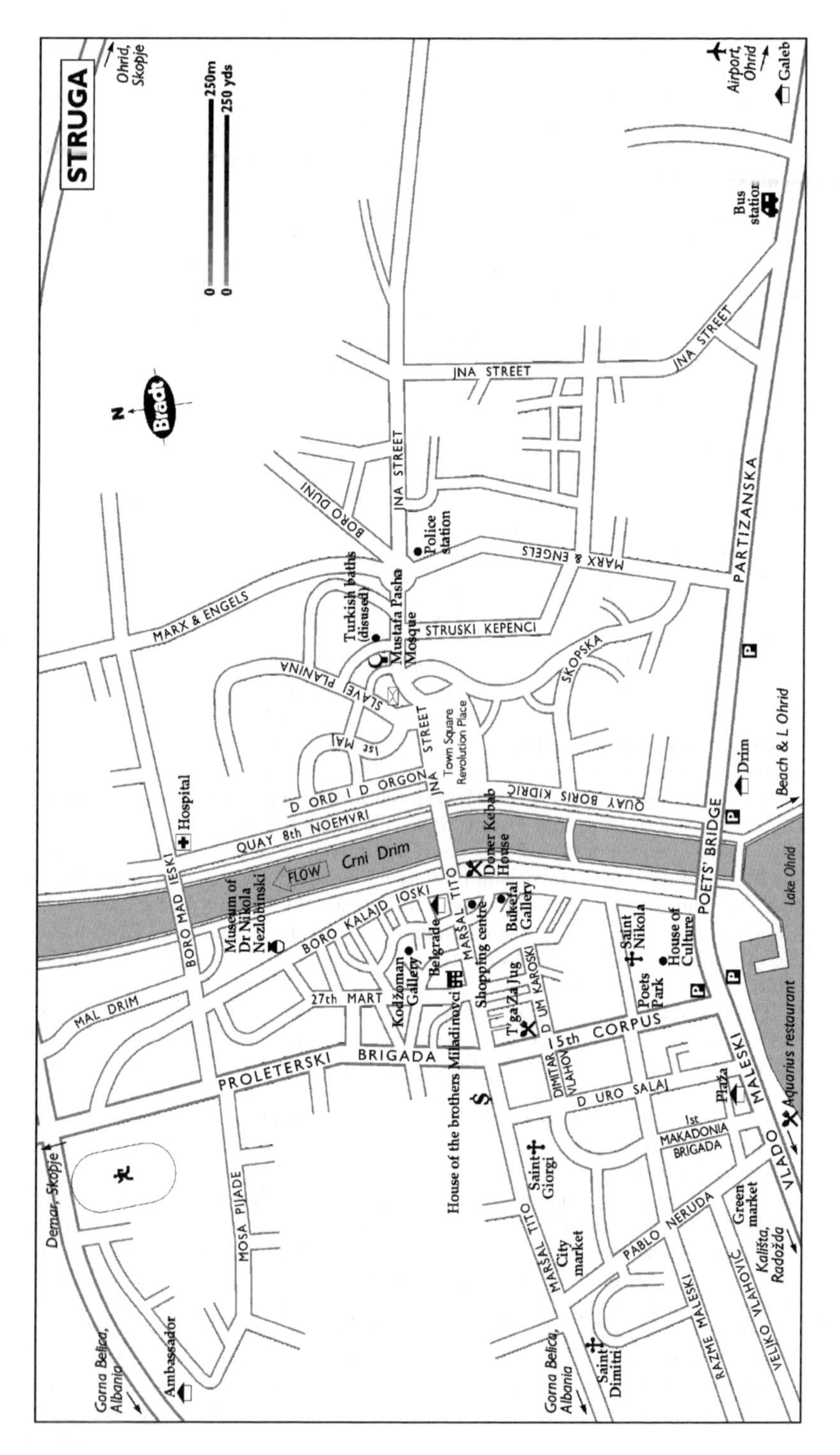
STRUGA
Ohrid, Skopje
0 250m
0 250 yds
N
Bradt
JNA STREET
MARX & ENGELS
BORO DUNI
Police station
Turkish baths (disused)
Mustafa Pasha Mosque
STRUSKI KEPENCI
SLAVE PLANINA
1st MAJ
SKOPSKA
PARTIZANSKA
Bus station
Airport, Ohrid
Galeb
Town Square Revolution Place
D ORD I D ORGON
QUAY 8th NOEMVRI
QUAY BORIS KIDRIC
Hospital
Crni Drim
FLOW
Doner Kebab House
POETS' BRIDGE
Drim
Beach & L Ohrid
Lake Ohrid
Museum of Dr Nikola Nezlobinski
BORO MAD IESKI
BORO KALAJD IOSKI
MARŠAL TITO
Belgrade
Kodžoman Gallery
Bukefal Gallery
Shopping centre
Saint Nikola
House of Culture
Poets Park
MAL DRIM
27th MART
House of the brothers Miladinovci
T'ga Za Jug
D UM KAROSKI
15th CORPUS
PROLETERSKI BRIGADA
DIMITAR VLAHOV
D URO SALAJ
Plaža
MALESKI
Aquarius restaurant
1st MAKADONIA BRIGADA
VLADO
Saint Giorgi
City market
Green market
PABLO NERUDA
Kališta, Radožda
RAZME MALESKI
VELJKO VLAHOVIĆ
Saint Dimitri
Gorna Belica, Albania
MOSA PIJADE
Ambassador
Debar, Skopje

archaeological discoveries ever to be made in Macedonia. The unearthing of ten burial chambers in 1918 revealed the lavish burial ceremonies of the ancient Paeons and Macedonians of the 1st millennium BC. Four golden masks were found in the graves as well as jewellery, pottery, ceremonial clothing and shoes. The burial chambers belonged to rich princes of the region who were cremated at death, so only the burial riches remain. Two of the masks are now in Belgrade and the other two in Sofia. A fifth mask has been found at the Petilep tomb in Beranci, near Bitola, and more tombs, long since ransacked, exist all over Macedonia. Little but age-old scars in the ground exist at these tombs now, or at the sites of the impressive Paeonian palaces that used to adorn the prominent hills in the region. On the way to Trebenište are the churches of St Erasmus, and St Ekaterina, from which there is a good view of Lake Ohrid.

STRUGA

With just over 16,000 inhabitants, Struga is less than half the size of Ohrid. Even if it had a lot of investment poured into it, Struga does not have the historical significance and attractiveness of Ohrid, but it could become an alternative getaway in the future. In the meantime, the many cafés along the river make a pleasant half day or night out away from Ohrid.

There are regular buses to Struga from all over the country, and it is less than half an hour's drive from Ohrid. Ohrid airport is only 15 minutes away.

Struga has a number of lake-front hotels ranging from 50 to 250 rooms. None of them are anywhere near as nice as what is available almost anywhere else on the lake, so I would not advise a stay in them unless you are really stuck. In years to come, when Ohrid really is bursting at the seams, then these hotels may come into their own, but until then they have some catching up to do.

What Struga does have to offer is a **long pebble beach** right in the centre of town, a lovely **riverside walk** from the lake through town along the Crni Drim River, and a small compact pedestrian and **old town** area. Aside from wandering around the narrow streets, there are a few sites worth popping into if you are interested.

The **Natural History Museum** (Boro Kalajdžioski bb; tel: 070 786 644 or 070 782 487) of Dr Nikola Nezlobinski (deceased) has over 10,000 examples of flora and fauna from the Ohrid and Prespa regions. Mostly from his own collection and displayed in his original house, the collection is the best available on the region. Dr Nezlobinkski, a Russian doctor who immigrated here in 1924 during Royalist Yugoslavia when Serbia encouraged many Russians to move to Macedonia, first put his collection on display in 1928. The display is open every day from 09.00 to 17.00 but it is best to phone ahead to make sure or arrange for the museum to be open as it is often closed despite its alleged opening hours.

The **Brothers' Miladinov house** (see box, page 141) in the old town houses the **Struga Poetry Evenings**' collection from the international festival of the same name held every year at the end of August. Always opened with Konstantin Miladinov's famous *Longing for the South*, the poetry evenings were started in 1962, exactly 100 years after the death of two of the brothers. Recitals take place throughout the town on the bridges over the Crni Drim.

Near the Miladinov house is the Vangel Kodjoman art gallery, with his paintings of old Struga, and on the western outskirts of the old town is the **Church of St Gjorgi**, built in 1835 on the grounds of an older 16th-century church, which contains a number of icons dating back to the 13th century, including one of St George from 1267. Next to the post office on JNA Street is the town mosque and Turkish baths.

MILADINOV — PROSE, MUSIC AND POETRY AND 'LONGING FOR THE SOUTH'

The Miladinov brothers, Dimitrija (1810–62), Naum (1817–95) and Konstantin (1830–62), were pioneers in re-establishing the supremacy of the Macedonian language in Macedonia during a time when Greek had been forced into Macedonian schools and sermons (see page 45). Dimitrija was a prominent Macedonian-language teacher and struggled daily with the Ottoman authorities to recognise the Macedonian language. His brother Naum was a distinguished musician, and his youngest brother Konstantin became one of Macedonia's most famous poets with his poem *Longing for the South* (*T'ga za Jug* in Macedonian), written whilst studying in Russia. *T'ga za Jug* is now the name of a popular Macedonian wine and of numerous restaurants throughout Macedonia. Dimitrija and Konstantin both died in prison in 1862 for their efforts to bring the Macedonian language officially back to Macedonia. Their efforts were not wasted, however, and seven years later, in 1869, the Greek schools in the Ohrid region were finally shut down.

Longing for the South

If I had an eagle's wings
I would rise and fly with them
To our own shores, to our own climes,
To see Stamboul, to see Kukuš,
And to watch the sunrise: is it
Dismal there, as it is here?

If the sun still rises dimly,
If it meets me there as here,
I'll prepare for further travels,
I shall flee to other shores

GALIČICA NATIONAL PARK

Founded in 1958, Galičica National Park extends from Ohrid Lake shore immediately west of Velestovo, through Velestevo village, around the peak of Bigla at 1,663m and then down to the shores of Lake Prespa just east of the village of Šurlenci. It includes all the land south of this line to the border of Albania. The park also includes the island of Golem Grad (see page 166) in Lake Prespa.

The park offers endless hikes in pristine countryside, although few of them are well marked, and there are no good hiking maps, so be confident of your orienteering skills before you go into the park, or take a guide. The highest peak, Bugarska Čuka meaning Bulgarian peak, lies in the middle of the park, where there is some off-piste skiing in the winter if you have access to a 4WD vehicle and skins to hike up the rest of the peak with your skis. From the peak is a panoramic view including both Lake Ohrid and Prespa.

Three kilometres south of Trpejča village is the turn-off to the southern mountain pass of Livada at 1,568m. The winding asphalt road gives spectacular views of Lake Ohrid on one side and Lake Prespa on the other. On the Prespa side the road continues past the dishevelled holiday resort of Oteševo and on to Carev Dvor and Resen. The road is partly cobbled and partly badly paved.

Where the sunrise greets me brightly
And the sky is sewn with stars.

It is dark here, dark surrounds me,
Dark fog covers all the earth;
Here are frosts and snows and ashes,
Blizzards and harsh winds abound.
Fog everywhere, the earth is ice,
And in the breast are cold, dark thoughts.

No, I cannot stay here, no,
I cannot look upon these frosts.
Give me wings and I will don them;
I will fly to our own shores,
Go once more to our own places,
Go to Ohrid and to Struga.

There the sunrise warms the soul,
The sunset glows on wooded heights;
There are gifts in great profusion
Richly spread by nature's power.
Watch the clear lake stretching white
Or bluely darkened by the wind,
Look upon the plains or mountains:
Beauty's everywhere divine.

To pipe there to my heart's content!
Ah! let the sun set, let me die.

Konstantin Miladinov (1830–62)

Translated by Graham W Reid

DAY TRIPS IN THE AREA

Around the lake into Albania

A good half-day trip in the area if you have a car and car insurance to cover you in Albania (most hire-cars from Macedonia will not be covered for Albania) is to drive around the lake. If it ever crossed your mind that Macedonia's economy was bad, then this corner of Albania will take the biscuit. It doesn't matter which way round you go, although the anticlockwise direction appears more of an eye-opener to me than the other way around.

Most countries at their borders with other countries become a bit frayed at the edges and neglected, and Macedonia is no exception here. Just as the edges of towns are often rubbish dumps in any country, so is the edge of the country near the Kafasan border crossing into Albania. The stench, smoke and eyesore don't say much for the Macedonian view of Albania, but then again the rest of Macedonia is littered with rubbish too.

The border crossing itself is relatively painless, and a short wait and €10 will get you the requisite visa. Once on the other side the full effect of former communist Albania's paranoia with foreign influence and invasion comes into full view. The countryside is strewn with concrete dome lookouts and troop defences, which appear like giant molehills from a mole gone mad all over the hills. These defensive positions complete with rifle lookouts do not cease until you are back in Macedonia on the other side of the lake. Most have now fallen into disrepair, and some have even fallen into the lake.

Along the lake in summer, boys will hold up strings of fresh trout caught from the lake, and a number of nice-looking lakeside restaurants on the way around will serve freshly caught fish and local vegetables. There are allegations that fish caught on this side of the border are sometimes caught using dynamite, but I have certainly seen no evidence of this on my way around.

You are more likely to get food at these little cafeterias outside lunchtime than in Pogradec town on the south side of the lake. Pogradec has a few shops and buffet-bars along its main street and a lot of money changers who will buy your euros and dollars from you. Not a soul seems to speak anything other than Albanian, and unless you've practised a lot, they probably won't understand your accent. On your way out of Pogradec on your way back to Macedonia make sure you head towards the lakeside road shortly after the centre of town before you go veering off on the main road into the wilds of central Albania.

Gorna Belica

Another good day trip away from the lake is up to the village of Gorna Belica, 16km northwest of Struga. The village is now mostly the weekend residence of Strugites, but it has a fine Vlach church, a high view on to Lake Ohrid, proximity to the Via Egnatia and good hiking up to a glacial lake and a cave church. The village first became a settlement in 1769, when the Vlachs of Moskopole, southern Albania, were driven out of that town by the destruction wrought by the local Ottoman *bey*, and moved up here with all their animals, belongings and families. They chose this spot along the River Belica, where villagers believe that the old crumbling **Church of St Clement** is no less than his actual 9th-century summer monastery from before he moved to Ohrid permanently as bishop.

The Vlachs built their own church, **St Petka**, or *Paraschevia*, in Vlach, up above St Clement's Church, and it is a fine example of an early 19th-century Vlach church. By that time, 1829, the Greek influence on the old Ohrid archbishopric was all pervasive and so all the original inscriptions on the church are in Greek. The church is cared for by the Dunoskis and if they are around they will be happy to tell you more about it. Look out for the **wooden hawk** above the central lantern in front of the iconostasis. This original pulley-system still flaps the wings of the hawk as the lantern is pulled up and down, making a loud clapping noise.

The village celebrates two **festivals** in honour of both patron saints, St Petka on August 8 and St Clement on August 9. This double whammy fills the village up with visitors on those two days and it is well worth a visit if you can make it. Other patron saint festivals exist for neighbouring churches and holy sites, one of the most interesting being that of the dedication to the **Church of the Perumba** (meaning white dove).

The tiny cave church was built in 1998 in honour of a local legend about a girl who, several centuries ago, was being chased by the local Ottoman thugs. The girl ran up against the steep cliff rocks where the church is now and fell to the ground exhausted, knowing that there was nowhere for her to escape. She prayed to God for deliverance and just as the thugs were catching up with her, they saw her fragile body fly up into the air as a pure white dove. The dove flew away and locals have honoured the place as a holy site ever since.

The locals walk up to the site once a year on the first weekend in June. Due to the proximity of the site to the Albanian border, the hike only takes place with the accompaniment of local Macedonia Army soldiers. For more information on how to join in the hike, ask in Gorna Belica or contact **Ohrid Climbing Group** (Abraš 22, Galičica; tel: 046 262 458). Any other hikes west of Gorna Belica and up to the glacial lake in the north are also best accompanied by a professional guide or other Macedonian who knows the area. The tracks are not well marked and encounters at the border could become difficult.

To get to Gorna Belica take the main road west out of Struga for about 2km and take the turning to the right signposted Zagračani. After 1.5km you will come to a T-junction immediately after a very small bridge. Turn right and then almost immediately left along an unmarked road. This road leads first of all up to the village of Visni. After the village follow the asphalt road around to the right and continue on another 5km to the village of Gorna Belica.

Oktisi, Vevčani and Vajtos

Less than half an hour north of Struga are the villages of Oktisi and Vevčani. The pretty old village of Oktisi lies along a tributary of the Crni Drim and has a number of old watermills hidden along its banks. On the outskirts of the village is a 5th- century Christian basilica with some excellent examples of late Roman mosaics. Above the village in the hills is also an overgrown site called Kale with a number of large stone blocks which marks **Vajtos**. Some say this is the eighth stopping place on the Via Egnatia, and the last stop before Ohrid, but it is much more likely that this was a stop on the Crni Drim road to northern Albania. The crumbling stone blocks here tell of the Cyclopean masonry (see page 48) used in ancient times when this area must also have been a Paeonian fortress.

Turning right before the mosque, go over the bridge to get to the next village of **Vevčani**. Allegedly the villagers of Vevčani held their own referendum during the break-up of Yugoslavia for their very own republic. Although they didn't manage to gain independence, they nevertheless created their own coat of arms and even printed specimen currency. The village is beautiful, with babbling brooks, old-style houses and proud people. Here there are a number of old *babas* and *tatkos* in traditional dress, who will be happy to have their photos taken. A great traditional restaurant to eat in whilst you are there is **Domakjinska Kukja** near St Nikola Church (tel: 046 790 505 or 070 815 950). The restaurant has a fireside atmosphere, good food and a few rooms to overnight in.

The town holds a **Twelfthtide carnival** on January 13 and 14 every year, which has been going since the middle of the 6th century. The 12 days after Christmas, which in the Orthodox calendar is on January 7, are meant to be a time when evil spirits are at their most active with regards to wreaking havoc on the coming year. On New Year's Eve (January 13 in the Orthodox calendar), the locals start a two-day event designed to banish evil spirits from entering into the new year. People dress up in costumes and masks representing all things evil and unlucky in the hope that if evil is faced with its own reality this will scare it away. The costumes and disguises are a testament to what Macedonians find evil or unlucky. Typical costumes include policemen, soldiers, pregnant brides, an old groom, a funeral procession as well as ghoulish monsters of all varieties. This has recently started to become a popular national event, attracting over 2,000 visitors every year.

Radožda and Kališta

Radožda is the last village before Albania on the western side of Lake Ohrid. It's a sleepy fishing village right on the shores of the lake which is renowned for the very best fish from the lake and for its **cave church** high on the cliffs overlooking the village. The cave church is dedicated to the Archangel Michael. Amongst the frescos on the cave rocks is one of the Archangel at the Miracle of Chonae. Some of the frescos in this church date back to the 13th century. It's quite a steep hike up the steps to the church, and the door to the cave itself is usually kept locked. Ask for the key in the Restaurant Dva Biseri at the bottom of the steps.

Once in the village there are a number of small restaurants along the shore road where you can stop for lunch. Looking on to the village square below the cave church is the small and cosy restaurant of **Dva Biseri** (Two Pearls). The two old ladies who cook here hold the secrets of their fresh-cooked lake trout close to their heart. It really is the most divine trout you'll ever taste, as good as if you had caught it yourself and whisked it straight on to the barbeque. Further down the shore road is a village shop, the village hall, and a small dingy café called **Albatross**. The next restaurant worth a stop in is **Letitca** (Little Diver) which has a spacious glasshouse upper deck for a good view of the lake. Between Letitca and the next restaurant, Ezerski Raj, is a small basic ten-bed hostel called **Lebed** (Swan – although at the time of writing there was no sign outside indicating this). Rooms vary between two and three beds and cost €15/person/night including breakfast, which you can take outside right on the shorefront. There is also a small swimming deck inviting you for a dip into the crystal clear waters. The hostel (and all the other restaurants in town) are run by the Slavkovski family. Their parents, Maria and Branko, are often to be seen sitting in traditional dress on the benches outside the hostel. They are very amenable to having their photo taken if you ask nicely and especially if you can offer to send them a copy. They only speak Macedonian. The last restaurant on the shore road is the **Ezerski Raj** (Heavenly Lake). It has a beautiful wooden deck overlooking the lake as well as views on to the Albanian peninsula of Lin village. It is the last restaurant before the entrance to the campsite and the footpath to Albania.

Five kilometres from Struga, on the way to Radožda is the small settlement and monastery complex of **Kališta**, located right on the shores of the lake. The monastery is the summer residence of Archbishop Naum, the highest church official in the Holy Synod of the Macedonian Orthodox Church. Within the monastery complex is the cave church of **Sveti Bogorodica**, whose frescos date back as far as the 15th century. Access to the church is often closed, so ask at the Hotel Biser if they can open it for you.

The **Hotel Biser** (230 beds; tel: 046 785 700; fax: 046 780 404) is open all year round and also has a restaurant downstairs set into the cave wall. All rooms are en suite with TV and central heating, but need refurbishing at 1,500MKD per person per night including breakfast.

A short 500m walk from the monastery, south along the shore of the lake, leads to the tiny **cave church of St Atanas** set up high in the lake cliffs. The steps up to the church are not for those with severe vertigo, and one would be hard pushed to deliver a service inside the church to a congregation of more than half-a-dozen people.

Both villages can be reached by car from the turn-off at Frangovo on the E850, or by taking the coastal road from Struga through Kališta. By far the most picturesque way to get there though is by boat taxi from Ohrid, as it is quite impressive to see the cliffs and church loom up over the village. A boat taxi will cost you €30 round trip whether there is one passenger or six, but the boat will wait for you and your party to finish your half day round Radožda to take you back to Ohrid. There are infrequent bus services to the villages from Struga.

8 Pelagonia, Lake Prespa and Pelister National Park

This southeastern corner of Macedonia, known as Pelagonia in ancient times, is rich in history both natural and manmade. The **Via Egnatia**, a monumentally long Roman road joining the Adriatic crossing from Rome with Constantinople (now Istanbul in Turkey), passes through the area, which has traditionally been rich in trading towns. **Pelister National Park**, on the Baba mountain range, is the oldest national park in Macedonia. It conserves some rare **glacial lakes**, the Pelister Eyes, and is a haven of hiking and hidden Vlach villages. From up in its hills you can see both major and minor **Prespa lakes** (the latter lies in Greece and Albania) as well as the mountain range of Galičica National Park on the other side of the lake. In the north of the region is the **biggest cave** in Macedonia, Slatinksa Izvor, where the ruins of cave houses can be seen.

There are a number of initiatives to revitalise the Pelagonia region with tourism and so you will sporadically find pockets of convenience and good signage (usually a rarity in the Balkans). Hopefully this will only improve with time, making the area more accessible to the unaccompanied traveller and those who speak little Macedonian. If you visit nowhere else in this region, spend at least a couple of days in Prilep to see the ruined **Towers of King Marko** and the remote **Monastery of Treskavec**. The scenery at these two sites is magnificent and is the setting of the films *Before the Rain* and *Dust* by Macedonia's most famous film director, Milčo Mančevski.

BITOLA

The main town of the region is Bitola. Once a major trading town, it is now more of a backwater, although it remains the second largest city in Macedonia with over 80,000 people, and is the seat of Macedonia's second university. It has managed to maintain its pretty 18th- and 19th-century architecture in the centre of town, and these old buildings tell of the former glory of Bitola when every major European country had a consulate here due to the amount of trading and business conducted in the town. The River Dragor divides the old Turkish town from the 18th-century town and conjures up a beautiful tree-lined canal effect, drawing in the cool air of the Baba Mountains. Despite being further south than Skopje, Bitola is usually cooler than Skopje all year round, sometimes up to 12 or 15° cooler – lovely in the summer when Skopje can get up to the high 30s, but bring an extra sweater in the winter.

History of the region

It is believed that a tribe known by the name of Linkestris were the first to inhabit the area south of Bitola around 4500BC. Just over 4,000 years later the

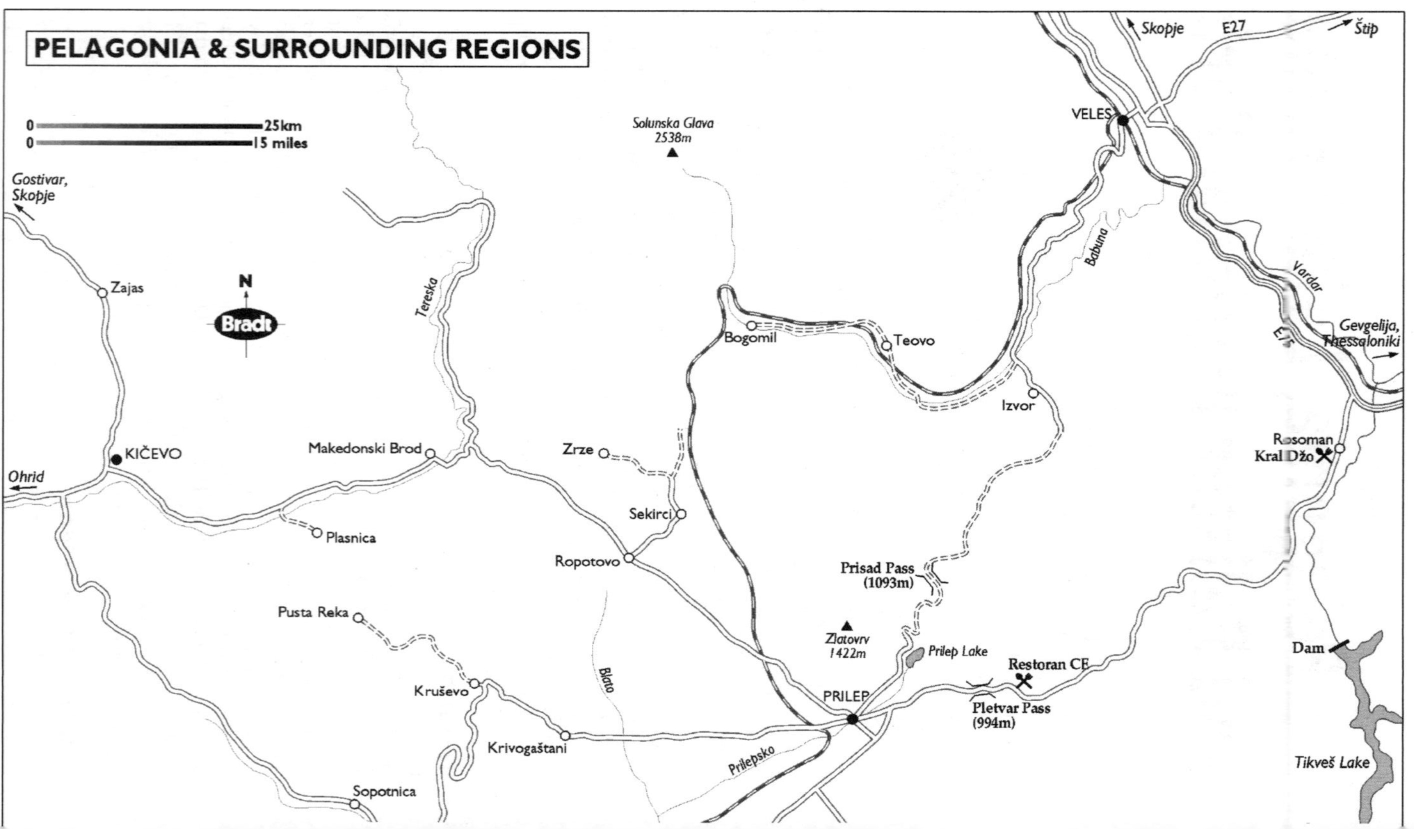
PELAGONIA & SURROUNDING REGIONS
0 25km
0 15 miles
N
Bradt
Gostivar, Skopje
Zajas
KIČEVO
Ohrid
Tereska
Makedonski Brod
Plasnica
Pusta Reka
Kruševo
Krivogaštani
Sopotnica
Solunska Glava 2538m
Zrze
Sekirci
Ropotovo
Blato
Prilepsko
Bogomil
Teovo
Izvor
Babuna
VELES
Skopje
E27
Štip
Vardar
Gevgelija, Thessaloniki
Rosoman
Kral Džo
Prisad Pass (1093m)
Zlatovrv 1422m
Prilep Lake
Restoran CE
Pletvar Pass (994m)
PRILEP
Dam
Tikveš Lake

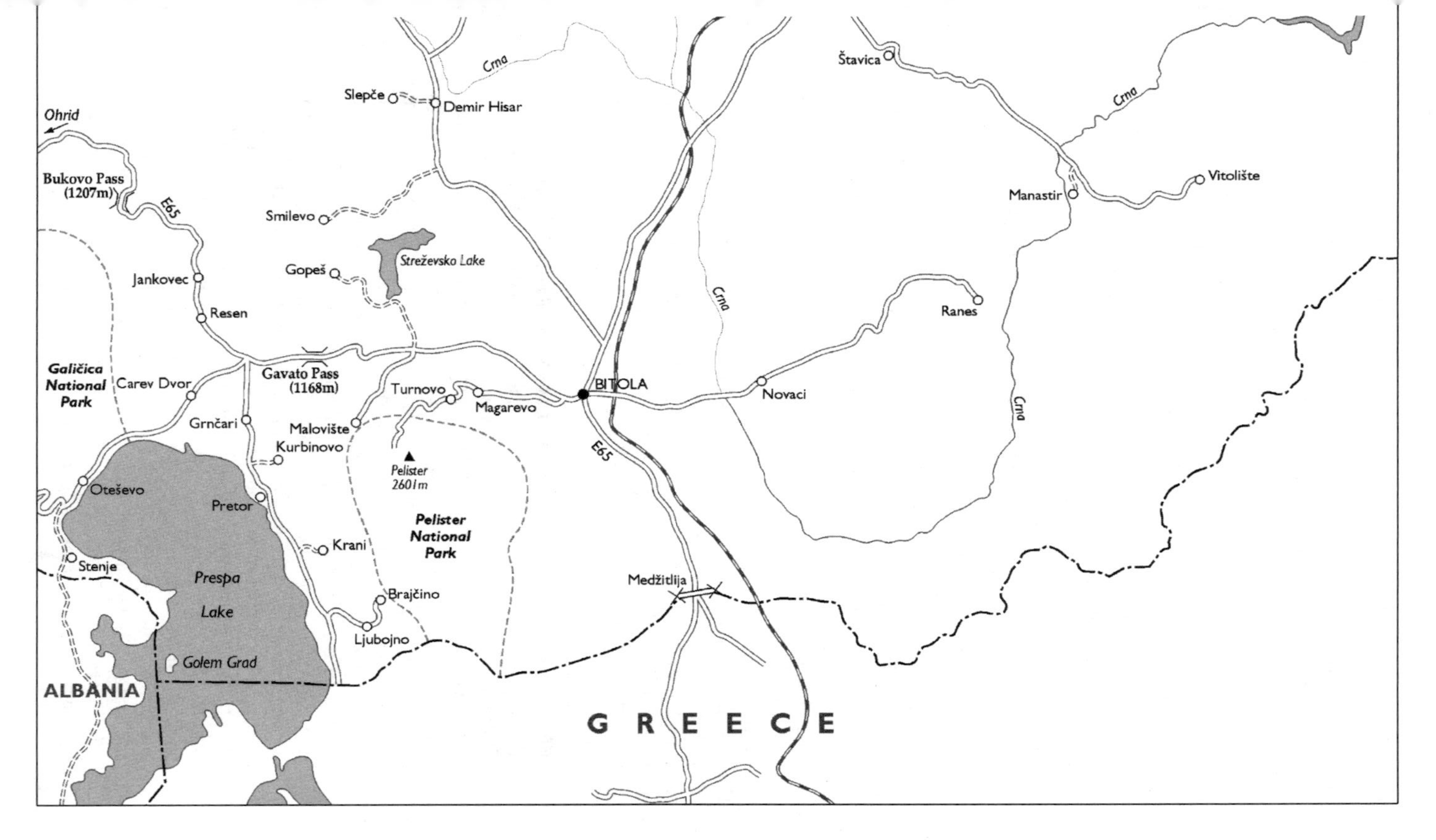
Crna
Štavica
Slepče
Demir Hisar
Ohrid
Crna
Bukovo Pass (1207m)
E65
Manastir
Vitolište
Smilevo
Streževsko Lake
Gopeš
Jankovec
Resen
Crna
Ranes
Galičica National Park
Carev Dvor
Gavato Pass (1168m)
Turnovo
BITOLA
Novaci
Magarevo
Crna
Grnčari
Maloviště
Kurbinovo
E65
Pelister 2601m
Oteševo
Pretor
Pelister National Park
Krani
Stenje
Prespa Lake
Medžitlija
Brajčino
Ljubojno
Golem Grad
ALBANIA
G R E E C E

first major town to be established in the rich Pelagonia valley was the ancient Macedonian town of Heraclea Lyncestis. The town was founded by Philip II of Macedon (the father of Aleksandar III of Macedon) in the middle of the 4th century, and named in honour of the ancient tribe of Linkestris. Although Philip lived there for some time, his son was eventually born in Pella over the present-day border in Greece.

With the fall of the ancient kingdom of Macedonia, Heraclea came under Roman rule in the 2nd century BC and continued to grow as an important trading town. By this time the Via Egnatia passed through Heraclea and crossed at Heraclea with the Diagonal Way, another major north/south road joining Heraclea with Stobi, Štip and then Kustendil (now in Bulgaria).

Julius Caesar used Heraclea as a supply depot during his campaigns and many of the veterans of his campaigns settled there. Later, during the time of early Christianity in the 4th century, Heraclea developed as the seat of the regional bishopric. By the 5th century, Roman rule was in decline and Heraclea was ransacked several times by marauding Avars, Goths and Huns from the north. When a large earthquake struck in AD518, the inhabitants of Heraclea abandoned the city for other towns.

Later, in the 7th century the Dragovites, a Slavic tribe pushed down from the north by the Avars, settled in the valley and gave the river its present name of Dragor. Eventually a new town was established immediately north of Heraclea, mentioned under the name Obitel in one of the charters of Tsar Samoil, showing that even then the town was closely associated with churches and monasteries (*obitel* means family chamber of a monastery). The town continued to prosper from trading and eventually became the third largest city in the Balkans after Constantinople and Thessaloniki. The surrounding area also thrived as a centre of Christian worship, so that by the time the Ottomans came at the end of the 14th century they named the town Manastir due to the number of monasteries in the surrounding hills, which served the monks of the 500 churches in the region.

YA NAKI (1878–1960) AND MILTON (1882–1964) MANAKI

The Manaki brothers were born in the Vlach village of Avdela, near Grevena in present-day Greece, where they first got into photography and opened their first studio. Wanting to expand their work, however, they moved to Bitola in 1904, then the centre of the western Macedonian region. After opening their new studio in 1905 they went on to win the gold medal in the Big World exhibition in Sinaia, Romania, became the court photographers for King Karol of Romania, and started to travel Europe widely on photographic assignments. In 1907 they brought back the 300th Bioscope cinecamera from London, allowing them to start making films in the Balkans. Thus began their historical recording of the tumultuous events in Macedonia in the lead-up to and during the Balkan Wars and the two World Wars. Unfortunately, there is no museum dedicated to their work, but their photos can be seen in every museum in Macedonia, depicting the life and times of events such as the Ilinden uprisings, the Turkish reprisals and state visits by kings and ambassadors, as well as the simple life in villages and of everyday people. For more information on the Manaki brothers go to www.manaki.com.mk.

Soon, Manastir became so important that the French set up a consulate there. Eleven other countries quickly followed. The influx of 18th- and 19th-century architecture can still be seen in Bitola today, despite artillery fire and bombing during World Wars I and II. Mixed with the influence of Ottoman architecture in the form of mosques, covered markets and bath houses, Bitola has a very cosmopolitan feel to it even today, and its inhabitants still pride themselves on their international heritage.

At the beginning of the 19th century, Manastir was at the zenith of its trading history and the railway even came to town, linking southern Macedonia with Skopje, Belgrade and beyond. French was widely spoken in the town, which included a number of foreign and international schools as well as a military academy that was attended by Turkey's pro-reform leader, Kemal Ataturk. The town boasted 2,000 households, and every second household owned a piano, on which many a song about Bitola was composed. Allegedly there are over 200 songs about Bitola.

The Manaki brothers (see box, page 148), famous for their pioneering work with the camera, opened their Studio of Art Photography in Bitola in 1905. In honour of their work in photography and later cinematography, Bitola started the first international film camera festival in the world, which continues every September. 2004 will be the 25th Manaki film camera festival.

At the end of the 19th century, revolution against the Ottomans was taking hold all over Macedonia, and Bitola was no exception. The Internal Macedonian Revolutionary Organisation (IMRO) was very active in Bitola and there are those who say that some of the guerilla warfare tactics developed in Bitola during those years were even exported to other nations rising up against dictatorial foreign rule. The Ilinden Festival every August 2 (a national holiday) celebrates the Ilinden uprising of 1903 against the Ottomans. The Republic of Kruševo which was proclaimed the next day in nearby Kruševo only lasted ten days before it and all other regions of dissent were sharply put down.

The Balkan Wars of 1912–13 put an end to Ottoman rule in Bitola and all of Macedonia, but many more years of foreign rule still followed. Reprisals against the Turkish community were high and over 40 of the 60 Turkish mosques in the town were destroyed. Nazi occupation in the early 1940s annihilated Bitola's thriving Jewish scene when 3,011 Jews were deported on March 11 1943 to Treblinka gas chambers in Poland.

While Bitola has languished in Balkan obscurity during the 20th century, modern lines of communications and transport have bypassed the once important trading centre. To add insult to injury, the provincial town of Skopje was made capital of the Socialist Republic of Macedonia in Federal Yugoslavia. Since then, Bitola, far from the heart of Yugoslavia, has only ever been given secondary consideration. It has little chance now of regaining its importance in trade, but it may still become a prime cultural destination.

Getting there

There is no airport at Bitola, so your main choice of public transportation is bus or train. There are many buses to and from Bitola, including international buses. Inquire at the **bus station** on Nikola Tesla Street (tel: 047 231 420) opposite the **train station** (tel: 047 237 110). There are only three trains a day to Bitola from Skopje and three back out. The train is slow and decrepit, but the journey at least between Prilep and Skopje is scenic. Average train journey from Skopje to Bitola is 3½ hours for 370MKD return.

There were no trains from Greece at time of writing but, with a new Greek consular office opening in Bitola in 2004, the line may reopen again soon.

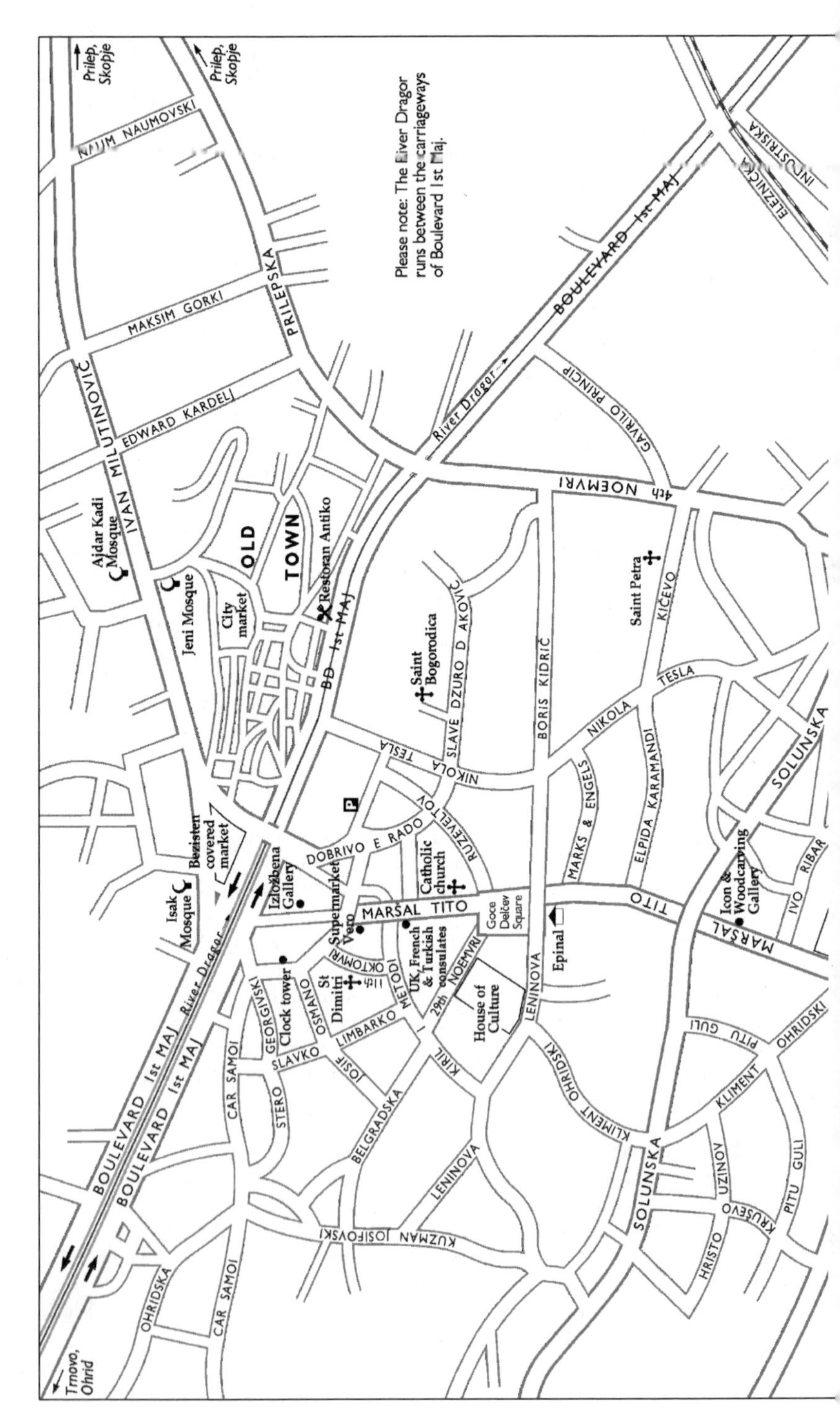

Prilep, Skopje
Prilep, Skopje
NAUMOVSKI
MAKSIM GORKI
PRILEPSKA
EDWARD KARDELJ
IVAN MILUTINOVIĆ
Please note: The River Dragor runs between the carriageways of Boulevard 1st Maj.
BOULEVARD 1st MAJ
INDUSTRISKA
ELEZNICKA
River Dragor
GAVRILO PRINCIP
4th NOEMVRI
Ajdar Kadi Mosque
Jeni Mosque
OLD TOWN
City market
Restoran Antiko
BD 1st MAJ
Saint Bogorodica
DZURO D AKOVIC
SLAVE
BORIS KIDRIĆ
Saint Petra
KIČEVO
TESLA
NIKOLA TESLA
SOLUNSKA
MARKS & ENGELS
ELPIDA KARAMANDI
Bezisten covered market
Isak Mosque
Izložbena Gallery
DOBRIVO E RADO
RUZEVELT OV
Catholic church
Supermarket Vero
MARŠAL TITO
Goce Delčev Square
Epinal
Icon & Woodcarving Gallery
IVO RIBAR
OKTOMVRI
St Dimitri
UK, French & Turkish consulates
29th NOEMVRI
House of Culture
LENINOVA
Clock tower
OSMANO
GEORGIVSKI
SLAVKO
LIMBARKO
METODI
JOSIF
KIRIL
KLIMENT OHRIDSKI
PITU GULI
OHRIDSKI
KLIMENT
CAR SAMOI
STERO
BELGRADSKA
LENINOVA
KUZMAN JOSIFOVSKI
UZINOV
KRUŠEVO
HRISTO
BOULEVARD 1st MAJ
OHRIDSKA
Trnovo, Ohrid

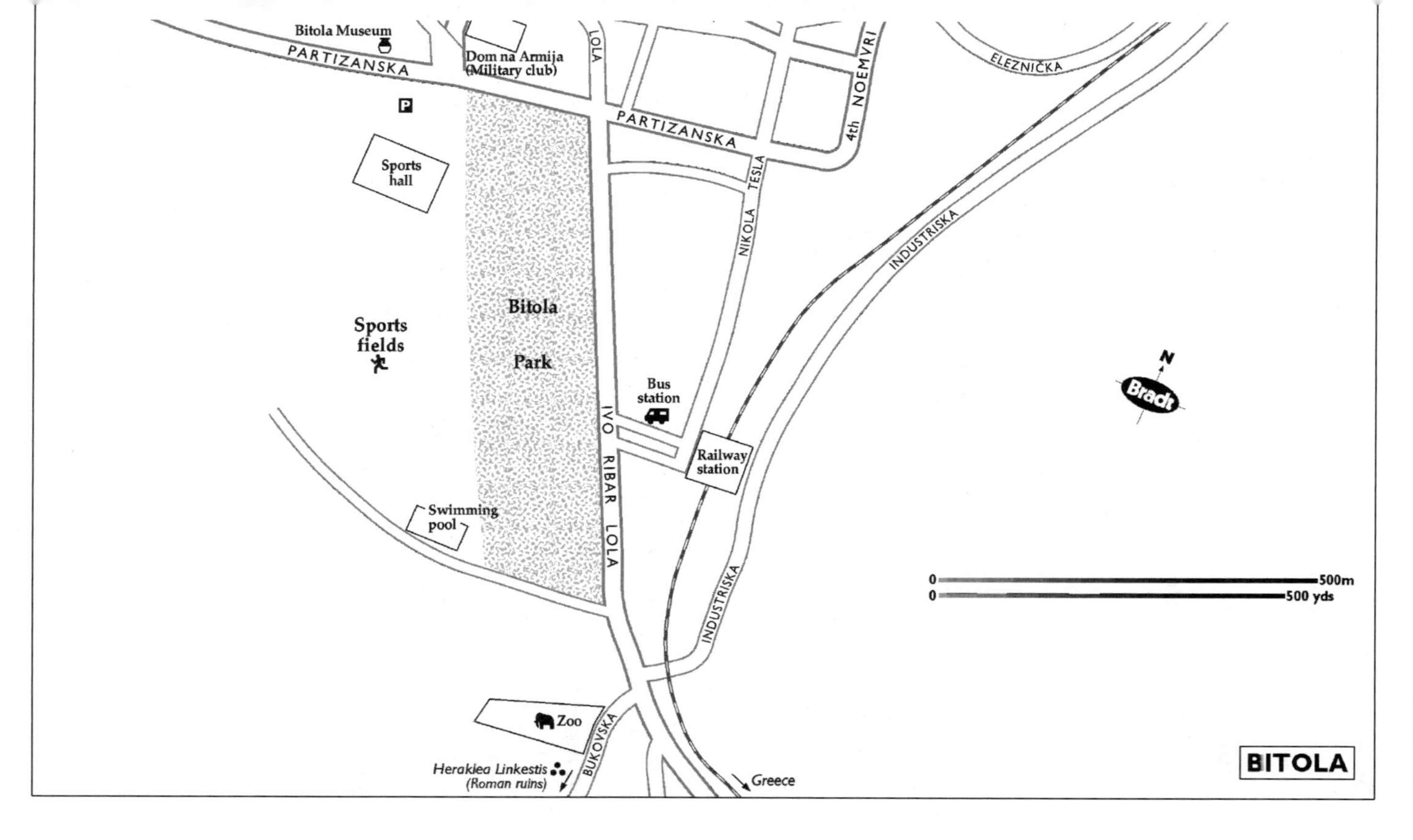
Bitola Museum
PARTIZANSKA
Dom na Armija
(Military club)
LOLA
P
PARTIZANSKA
4th NOEMVRI
ELEZNIČKA
Sports hall
NIKOLA TESLA
INDUSTRISKA
Bitola Park
Sports fields
Bus station
IVO RIBAR LOLA
Railway station
N
Bradt
Swimming pool
INDUSTRISKA
0
500m
0
500 yds
Zoo
BUKOVSKA
Heraklea Linkestis
(Roman ruins)
Greece
BITOLA

Getting around

The main areas of Bitola are very walkable. Buses do exist but like most town buses in Macedonia their destination is not always well marked although they are frequent. Taxis are cheap and abundant. Minimum fare is 10MKD.

Tour operators

There are many tour operators in Bitola, some are even linked with operators in Skopje, such as **Mergimi**, tel: 047 237 401; email: mergimi@mt.net.mk. By far the most helpful, avant-garde and caring of the environment is **Isidor Travel**, Solunska 111-d, 7000 Bitola; tel: 047 220 204; email: isidor@mt.net.mk. This travel agency was set up by the Balojani brothers, Gorki and Isidor, in 1989 and has expanded links particularly between Greece and Macedonia by organising tours on both sides of the border for groups and individuals. Within Pelagonia the Balojanis have good contacts to set up your travel, accommodation and outdoor pursuits such as biking, hiking, paragliding, skiing, photo safaris, rock climbing, hunting and birdwatching, as well as monastery tours, and wine tours in the Tikveš region. They will also organise visas to other countries as well as international travel.

Originally of a Vlach family from Magarevo, their parents remain dedicated to preserving the region for future generations. Their father, Dimitar, is working on building up an eco-tourism co-operative for Magarevo and surroundings called 'Village House'. They offer bed and breakfast for €12–18 per person per night, and can organise tours and guided hikes. Working hand-in-hand with her husband and sons, Dimitar's wife, Ljubica, heads up a local ecological society called Ecowomen, who work on maintaining the area as well as working with local refugees and the orphanage at Bitola. If you are interested in finding out more about the work of Village House and Ecowomen, or would like to help in any way, get in contact with them through Isidor Travel.

Where to stay and eat

De Niro (6 rooms, 2 apartments) Kiril i Metodij 5; tel: 047 229; fax: 047 207 233; email: hotel-deniro@mt.net.mk. Right in the centre of town. Nice bar and restaurant downstairs. Beautiful rooms if a bit small for €50 including breakfast. Apartments include jacuzzi bath and breakfast €80.

Šumski Feneri (4 doubles, 4 singles and 4 apartments of 5 beds each) Near Trnovo; tel: 047 293 030; fax: 047 293 131; email: sfeneri@mt.net.mk. Set around a cosy foyer and landings laden with well-kept plants and flowers. The hotel also has conference facilities for 40 and restaurant seating for 140. The Vlach family Musulanov have run the hotel for many years now, and their daughter, Ljubica, speaks good English and will give guided tours of Bitola and Malovište on request. To get to the hotel, head west out of Bitola along the river and turn left at the battered sign for Pelister Park, and then right on to a cobbled road for 1km. The hotel is on the left. Price per person per night is €30 including breakfast.

Epinal (375 beds including 4 apartments) On the cross of the pedestrian zone Maršal Tito and Leninova; tel: 047 224 777. Recently renovated and popular with tour groups of Greek visitors. All prices include breakfast. Standard single €65, standard double €100, de luxe (including TV, central heating, and jacuzzi bath) single €78, delux double €120.

Bed and breakfast stays can be arranged through Isidor Tours, see above.

The main pedestrian area, **Maršal Tito Street**, hosts a number of café bars and restaurants. These change owners and names as frequently as the wind, so the best bet is to take a stroll with all of the other Bitolans and pick whichever looks the best. Don't forget to look up at the 18th-century architecture as you walk by. There is a good **supermarket** at the north end of the Maršal Tito if you want to buy provisions for a day out or simply a snack and drinks. For a traditional restaurant with live music and good food, try **Restoran ANTIKO**, Bulevar 1st Maj 229, on the left bank of the river next to the old town.

What to see and do

Although a little dilapidated, Bitola is a pretty town to walk around. The long pedestrian area on **Maršal Tito Street** is lined with 18th- and 19th-century buildings and leads down past the town **museum** and Dom na Armija concert house and club to the pretty **park** south of the town. Beyond the park the road leads to Greece and a turn-off clearly marked shortly after the park leads to Heraclea, half an hour's walk from the centre of town.

Heraclea (see *History of the region* above) is barely uncovered, so visits in future years may be more fruitful, but for now there are a number of important finds to be seen there including the amphitheatre, baths, basilicas and some impressive mosaics. There is a small museum and sometimes a snack and drink shop on the site, but most of the more important finds are in the town museum or in the National Museum in Skopje. Entry to the ruins costs 150MKD and permission to photograph the site costs another 500MKD.

The tree-lined **Boulevard 1st Maj** runs the length of **River Dragor** and skirts the south side of the **old Turkish town**. Along the boulevard going west out of town are a number of the old consular residences. The **present consulates of Great Britain, France and Turkey** are on the corner of Maršal Tito Street and Kiril and Methodius Street.

In the centre of town at the north end of Maršal Tito Street is the **Clock Tower**, the **Izložbena Art Gallery** housed in a former mosque, and the covered **Bezisten**, which still houses one of Bitola's markets and whose gates are still locked at night.

Dating back to the Turkish period of Bitola's history are the **Isak Mosque**, built in 1508–09, the **Yeni Mosque**, built in 1559, and the **Yahdar-Kadi Mosque**, built in 1562 by Kodja Sinan, a prominent Ottoman architect. There are a number of churches in Bitola, the most significant being that of **St Dimitri**, renowned for being one of the biggest churches in the Balkans. It was built in 1830 during Turkish times when churches were not allowed to be ornate or ostentatious on the outside. As a result the builders lavished the inside of the church, which has been well preserved to this day. The opulence of the church is captured in the opening scenes of *The Peacemaker* (1997, George Clooney and Nicole Kidman), which were filmed in St Dimitri.

There are a number of **festivals** that take place in Bitola every year. Interfest is an international festival of classical music, held in August every year. Heraclea Evenings are a series of outdoor theatre and musical events held over the summer in places like the amphitheatre in Heraclea as well as other outdoor venues. Over the summer there is also the International Graphics Convention, the international children's festival The Small Monmartre and others.

PRILEP

If you are venturing beyond Skopje and Ohrid and are wondering where to go next, and/or want a compact representation of Macedonian life through the ages, then look no further than Prilep. The town is situated under the Towers of Marko, a medieval fortress, and has two worthwhile monasteries in the vicinity. The town also has a well-preserved, if small, old Turkish town and a pedestrian area where it is simply nice to drink coffee and relax. The area is so symbolic of Macedonian culture that it has been used twice by Macedonian film director Milčo Mančevski, as settings for his films *Before the Rain* (1995) and *Dust* (2001).

Aside from driving, there are frequent buses to Prilep and four trains from Skopje every day. If you don't manage any other train journey in Macedonia, this is the one to do, as it takes you through some great mountain scenery. The section from Veles to Prilep is in parts not even accessible by road and midway between the towns of **Sogle** and **Bogomila** offers a fantastic view of the Solunska Glava Mountain with its 800m drop from the summit.

A return train trip to Prilep costs 300MKD and takes approximately two hours each way. The morning train (06.45, but don't be surprised if it leaves late and arrives even later, especially in the winter) is also the fishermen's train in the summer and will stop at a number of unscheduled stations in order to let out fishermen on to the River Kadina. The drive to Prilep between the **Babuna and Dren Mountains** is also very pretty, although the road is often only one way in each direction and blocked with tractors, lorries or expansion work. The pass at Pletvar lies at 994m above sea level. For the back road from Veles to Prilep see page 217. If you are taking it from Prilep to Veles, take the lake road out of town and at the marble statue of a cannon above the lake take the right-hand fork on to a dirt track.

Once in Prilep, the best form of transport if you get tired of walking through the small town is one of the numerous taxis. Minimum fare is 10MKD and you can call a taxi on 9188. Two helpful tourist agencies are **Miro Trans Travel** tel: 048 410 166; fax: 048 415 392; email: mirotrans_prom@yahoo.com; address: Joska Jordanoski 3, Prilep; and **Info Tours** tel: 070 741 275, near the bus station, open 08.30–13.30 and 17.00–19.30 every day, except Wednesday and Saturday when opening hours are 08.30–15.00. Closed on Sundays.

Where to stay and eat

The **Crystal Palace** (22 rooms) Lenin 184; tel: 048 418 000, near the railway station, is modern and the best place to stay in town. All rooms are en suite with satellite TV and air conditioning. Their rooftop swimming pool was not working at the time of writing. As it is the nicest place in town, it is also the hotel for wedding receptions which can get a bit noisy in the evening. A double room with *fransuski krevet* (double bed) for two including breakfast is €40.

The Hotel Lipa (130 beds) Aleksandar Makedonski 4/3; tel: 048 435 791, has basic rooms for €13 per person per night including breakfast, although breakfast is taken at the more upmarket **Makam Sunce Palace** (15 rooms; Aleksandar Makedonski 43; tel: 048 401 720) which is on the old road from Bitola. Rooms are available here for €20 per person including breakfast.

The pedestrian area and the old town offer a lot of places to eat. Recommended are: **Café Pizza Square** offers a selection of hot and cold dishes and has a cavernous interior; **Café Pizza Di Caprio** has nice upstairs seating and a balcony which overlooks the old town; **Restoran Biser** is on Spase Quay and offers good traditional Macedonian cuisine and accompanying traditional music; **La Strada** is a happening bar on Goce Delčev Street with a nice raised balcony off the street, and is also the sister company of **VIP Nightclub** (tel: 048 414 212; www.v-i-p.com.mk), on Quay 9th December, opposite the bus station which plays live music on Thursdays, Fridays, Saturdays and Sundays, and has its own pizzeria and bar food. If you are driving down to Prilep from Veles/Skopje

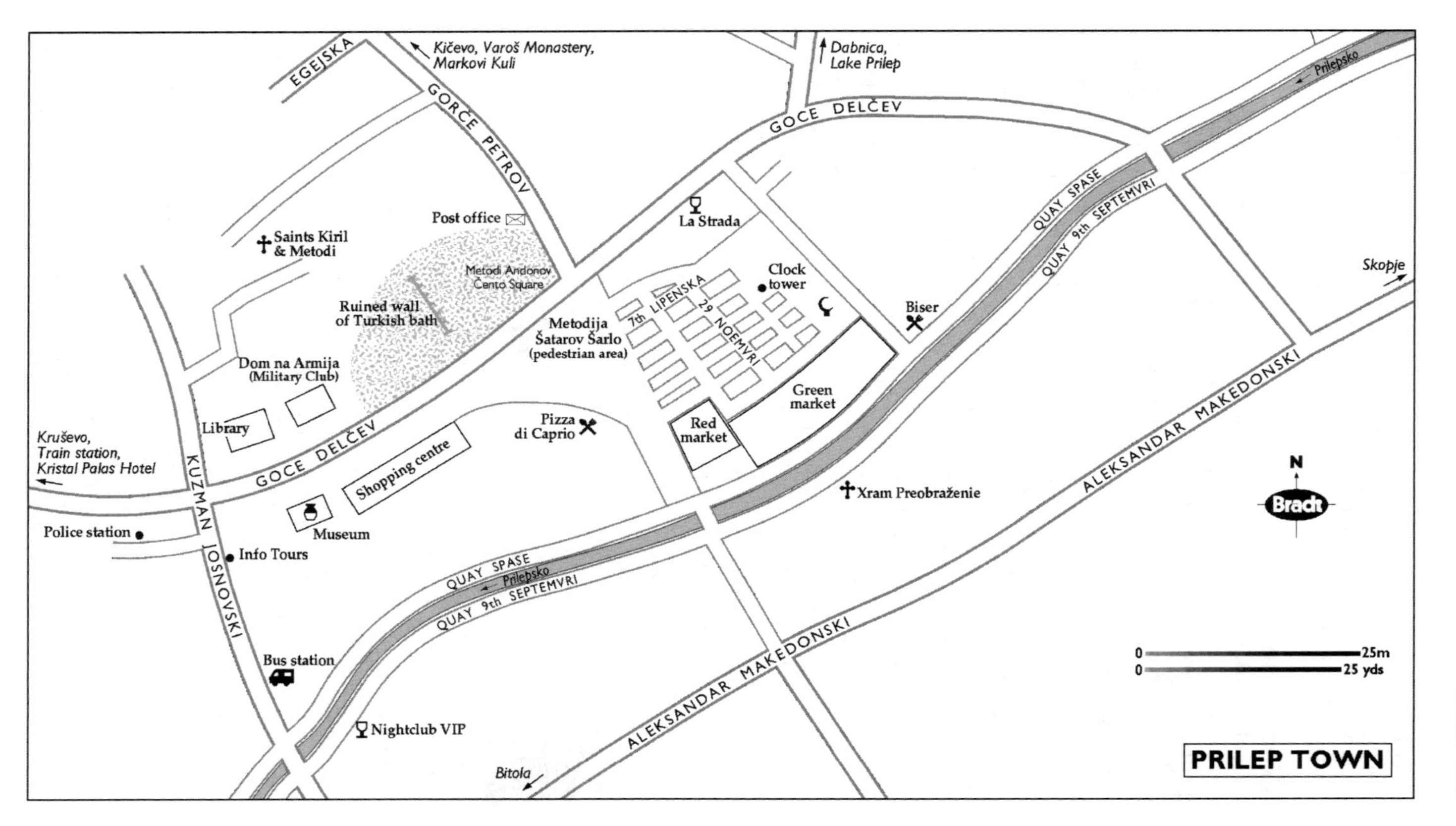
EGEJSKA
Kičevo, Varoš Monastery, Markovi Kuli
Dabnica, Lake Prilep
Prilepsko
GORČE PETROV
GOCE DELČEV
Post office
Saints Kiril & Metodi
Metodi Andonov Čento Square
Ruined wall of Turkish bath
La Strada
Clock tower
Biser
Skopje
QUAY SPASE
QUAY 9th SEPTEMVRI
7th LIPENSKA
29 NOEMVRI
Metodija Šatarov Šarlo (pedestrian area)
Dom na Armija (Military Club)
Green market
Red market
Pizza di Caprio
Library
Kruševo, Train station, Kristal Palas Hotel
Shopping centre
KUZMAN JOSNOVSKI
Xram Preobraženie
ALEKSANDAR MAKEDONSKI
N
Bradt
Police station
Museum
Info Tours
0 — 25m
0 — 25 yds
Bus station
Nightclub VIP
Bitola
PRILEP TOWN

and can't wait to get to Prilep to eat, there is the traditional **Restoran Ce** at the stopping place 5km before the mountain pass of Pletvar which serves good Macedonian food. The stopping place is recognisable not only by the cars which are parked there, but also by the large shining white marble cross.

What to see

The **old Turkish centre** of Prilep is small and can be walked around in about ten minutes, so it is best enjoyed over a drink break or lunch. It borders on the **pedestrian area** of Metodi Šatarov Šarlo Street, and towering over the old town is the **Clock Tower**. Next to the Clock Tower are the **ruins of an old mosque**, and the one remaining wall of another can be found in the **Metodi Andonov Park.**

There are two churches near Prilep's centre. Behind the library is the **Church of St Kiril i Metodi**, which dates from 1926. It is a fairly modern church, with no frescos. The **Church of *Xram Preobraženie*,** built in 1871, is located opposite the **Green Market** on Quay 9th December. The church is dark, no frills, and mostly locked although you can look through the glass doors. The courtyard, however, provides a welcome place to sit down and there are taps in the courtyard for water.

The **Fortress Towers of Marko** stand prominently on the hill above Prilep. The fortress is named after King Marko (see box, page 156), the last Macedonian king, who fought bravely against the Turks. There is no information available at the site itself, but archaeological findings show that parts of the fortress date back to the Iron Age, the 3rd and 4th centuries BC and later periods during the Ottoman Empire. Most of what remains to be seen today is from medieval times. It is sadly mostly in ruins, but still well worth the hike, and the views from the top over the ruins and beyond are quite magnificent.

To get there take the road from the centre of town up towards the hill and turn off to the right after about 1km where the road levels off. Unfortunately, there is no sign at this point, but the turning lies opposite some conference halls, and if you follow your nose you won't go far wrong. After another 100m you will come to a crossroads. Go straight on, and if you are lucky the handwritten sign for *Markovi Kuli* will still be there pointing you in the right direction. This road leads you to the famous stone called ***The Elephant***, which marks the beginning of the site and continues on in a blaze of white crushed marble (Prilep is also a mining town for marble) around the back of the hill. This is the easy route up, suitable for a high clearance vehicle, although whether you will find parking at the top on a busy weekend is another thing.

Alternatively, you could take on a frontal assault of the towers and go straight up the middle of the rocks. A path eventually forms itself if you bear right of the entrance. As you make your way up, imagine what a nightmare it must have been as a foot soldier, possibly with armour and weapons, to attack the towers from this direction: hard work all the way up and arrows raining down at the same time! Bring plenty of water with you, at least half a litre per person on a hot day, as there is none at the top and the lack of water would spoil an otherwise lovely gambol among the rocks.

The frontal assault and parts of the towers are steep, require some scrambling and have no hand-rails, so this is not advisable for those with severe vertigo, and keep children well reined-in. A watchtower has been recreated at the eastern end of the rocks using concrete and looks decidedly out of place. Inside at the time of writing were a makeshift bed and solid fuel stove: an interesting overnight option which may already belong to somebody. The highest part of the rock formation is marked by a huge Meccano-style cross, similar to the one in Skopje but smaller.

From the top it is also possible to hike 8km over to the next obvious rise of rocks, Zlatovrv, to the north. This is where the village of Treskovec lies and the monastery of the same name.

On the southeastern edge of the Marko Towers' rock feature, in a part of Prilep called Varoš, is the **Monastery of St Michael the Archangel**. It is perched between the rocks looking out to the Pelagonia plains, and now houses five nuns. As you enter the monastery take note of the 15th-century iron doorway. Little remains of the original church, built in the early 12th century, but two partial remains of frescos and some of the original walls can be seen in the vaults underneath the present church.

The church now standing in the monastery courtyard is made up of two parts built during medieval times and of three classical period marble columns, which were found by the monks who built the first monastery. The second oldest Cyrillic inscription to be found in Macedonia is carved at eye-level into the far right pillar as you stand in the exonarthex (the oldest inscription is the epitaph dedicated to Tsar Samoil's mother and father). The remaining housing for the nuns was erected in the 19th century. Underneath the main inn is a deep well which is entered via a small doorway.

Allegedly there used to be 77 churches in the Prilep area, but only six were left standing after the Ottoman Empire moved in. The **Church of St Atanas**, which no longer has a roof, can be seen on the road approaching the monastery of St Michael.

To get to Varoš take Gorče Petrov out of town past the turning to Markovi Kuli. At this point the road turns into Orle Čopela, and very quickly you'll come to a bust of Orle Čopela on the right at the top of the rise in the road. Take the right turn just before this monument on to Borke Dopačot (in typical Macedonian fashion this is not marked as such at the turning!). Follow this asphalt road all the way to the monastery.

Outside Prilep

The remote **Monastery of Treskovec** is 10km outside Prilep under the summit of the impressive Mount Zlato. It is a magnificent old complex, which has a central role in the Macedonian film *Before the Rain*, directed by Milčo Mančevski. The monastery is built on the ancient town of Kolobaise, which existed from the 3rd century BC until the 7th century AD. The name of the town is written in a long inscription cut into a stone used as the base of the cross on top of the central dome of the church. There are also other inscriptions around the church that date back to the 1st century BC, when a temple to Apollo and Artemis was first built on this site.

Further remnants of the town under Roman rule can be found in the present 14th- century church of St Bogorodica, which was built on the foundations of the original 6th-century basilica. There is a **baptism font** on the left of the narthex as you enter, and the walls of the narthex have a number of stone carvings and sculptures. As there are few lights in the church, it is a good idea to remember to **bring a torch** with you or a lighter for the candles so that you can see the artefacts. The narthex goes around to the right covering two sides of the church, at the end of which is a separate confessional room. The confessional room is interesting for its fresco depicting the donors who paid to have the church built. The two old men dedicated their life to God and are shown, as is typical of frescos of the original church donors, holding the church between them.

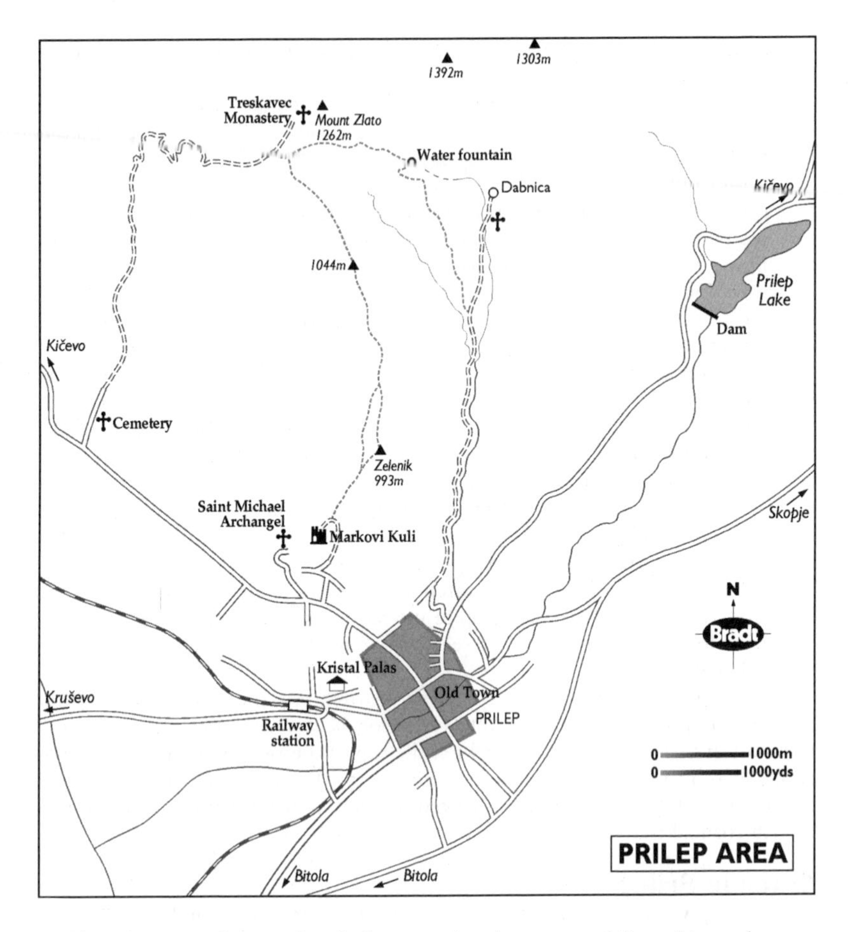

There is a secondary narthex before entering the nave, and from this narthex are some steps on the right that lead into a small chamber. Inside the cupola there is one of the few frescos of **Christ as a young boy** (there is another in the Monastery of St Eleusa, also in the right-hand chamber). The church has a number of 16th-century frescos with the typical greenish sheen on the face of the figures that was the hallmark of Macedonian rather than Greek artisans. Also in the nave is a **casket of the skulls** of seven monks from the monastery who were executed, along with almost 200 other monks who lived there at the time, by the Ottomans.

To the right of the entrance into the monastery is the **old dining hall**. It contains the old stone tables and Roman jars and vats, but it is in a terrible state of repair, and the last fresco at the end of the hall is in dire need of help if it is to remain intact on the wall. The chips in it show that it is an older fresco which was deliberately chipped in order to apply new plaster for a new fresco. The newer fresco has long since gone.

Despite its former glory in the early Ottoman period, only four monks returned to the monastery in 1999, after it had lain abandoned for decades during the communist era. Father Sofrajni, who speaks quite good English, welcomes visitors to the monastery; make sure to introduce yourself before wandering around his home. It is forbidden to enter the monastery scantily clad, so make sure you **bring coverings** for shoulders and legs before you get all the way there only to find you are improperly dressed and refused entry.

Father Sofrajni has meagre income from this remote monastery with which to do much-needed renovation work, and he charges nothing to stay in the inns, so give generously at the altar when you visit the church. Like all modern monks these days, he has internet access at the monastery, email: treskavec@mt.net.mk; and excellent mobile phone coverage (there are mobile phone relay stations right outside the monastery). The landline number is 048 800 120.

Outside the monastery are **ancient graves cut into the rock**. Water wells are encased in the stone wall to the left of the monastery main gate which leads to the ancient graves. There are also caves and monks' cells up on Mount Zlato. Allow yourself plenty of time once you get up there as the stone outcrops and the views are worth it.

There are two ways to get to the monastery, by 4WD along a dirt track to the southwest, or by foot along an old cobbled road to the southeast. To reach the dirt track head out of Prilep on Gorče Petrov, then turn into the new town cemetery a couple of kilometres out of town, but turn immediately left and follow the road around to the back of the cemetery. At the junction where you lose the tarmac (500m from the main road) is a small sign, marked *Manastir Sveti Bogorodica, Treskavec,* pointing the way straight ahead. Follow this road, always going uphill, to get to the monastery in about 8km.

By far the more **scenic and rewarding way** to get to the monastery though is to hike the 8km on the **old cobbled road**. The stones along this walk are what make Prilep famous and the scenery really is fantastic. The easiest way to get to a good starting point is to get a taxi to take you towards Dabnica. This will take you through the Roma slums of Prilep. The conditions here are utterly appalling for a country like Macedonia which claims to be at least halfway developed, and I can find no excuse valid enough for why this road through a busy part of town is untarmacked, allowing run-off water to create rivulets in the mud street.

From the end of the tarmac, ask the taxi driver to count off 2.8km (if his tachometre even works) or stop when the road is no longer fenced off on the left and comes to the obvious opening on to the foothills of Mount Zlato. At the end of the fence there is another dirt track to the left leading to a nearby house. The cobbled track you require, which is not obvious at first, heads straight up the ridge of the spur leading up to Mount Zlato. It lies directly between where the dirt track divides, and if you have a compass, set it to 6,000 mils or 340° and follow this bearing until you come across the obvious path uphill.

After an hour, the path, with large chunks of cobbling still intact, starts to wind back and forth and comes upon a water fountain. From the fountain the path is practically straight until you get to the back gate of the monastery. A while before the back gate you can see the monastery nestled between Mount Zlato and the next rock hill to its left. Follow the path around to the left and to the front of the monastery. As you walk around to the front of the monastery, the 10km hike from here directly to Prilep over Markovi Kuli is the obvious spur to the south.

If you drive yourself to the start point of the hike, then take the lake road out of Prilep, and exactly 500m from the turn-off Goce Delčev take the fifth right turn at house number 47. Follow this road as it winds through the Roma part of town until after 800m you reach a T-junction in front of a lion-fenced house. Turn right on to the mud road through Roma town and follow the remainder of the directions as above.

To the southeast of Prilep towards the border of Greece is the region of **Mariovo**. This rugged, beautiful area straddles the River Crna, which is flooded to the north (forming the manmade Tikveš Lake), and to the south comes from Pelister National Park through Bitola and the ancient Paeonian city of Lynk, whose exact location is still not known. The river must have been an important one to the ancient Paeons, for outside the small village of Manastir is one of the finest examples of what little remains of their ancient cities. Built out of finely cut limestone blocks using what has become known as Cyclopean masonry (ie: a masonry technique which uses no mortar, but precision cuts and the size of the blocks to keep a construction together), these fortified cities date back to Aneolithic times.

Evidence of other such cities have been found in Demir Kapija, Vajtos near Ohrid, Debar, Tetovo, Prilep and Skopje amongst other places, usually in high locations that are easy to defend. The site at Mariovo is unusual for being in the river valley, and archaeologists are still researching the site to see if they can find clues as to why it was located there.

To get to the site, take the road south out of Prilep towards Bitola and turn off southeast towards the town of Vitolište (signposted). After 5km the road passes the village of **Stavica**, a picturesque village used by Milčo Mančevski in *Before the Rain*. Another 25km later the road crosses the River Crna at the new bridge which replaced the old Ottoman bridge of Hasin Bey. The river crossing is **popular with picnickers** and fishermen, and parts of the old bridge can still be seen. After another kilometre the old road to Manastir village is signposted from the opposite direction. Turn south to follow the dirt track (4WD only or walk) upstream for 4km towards the village of Manastir. The site of large old limestone blocks can be seen from this track. At the village the site is known as *stari grad* (old town) *arxeološko naogjalište* (archaeological site), and although the two very old men who live here know about the site they are past the age to be able to take you there. It is admittedly just a site of old limestone blocks, but if you want to see for yourself the closest thing you'll get to Cyclopean masonry built by the Paeons, then let your imagination build the rest of the city for you. The new road to Manastir, 4km from the bridge, does not allow a vantage point on to this site.

Around Makedonski Brod

Another interesting monastery, halfway between Prilep and Kičevo, is the **Monastery of Zrze**, near the village of the same name. Quite spectacular to see from the approach, it is set into the cliffside as if it hangs there only by the will of God. The monks' cells are built precariously into the cliff walls under the monastery. The monastery inns and church are built at the site of an earlier Christian basilica, whose foundations can still be seen, as well as a number of marble pillars and other artefacts.

The church dedicated to **St Petar and Pavle** contains frescos from the 14th century, and an additional nave, known as the Shepherd's Church, to the left of the main nave. The main church is famous for its icons, which show the Virgin Mary in profile rather than face on and on the right of Jesus rather than the left. Legend says that when the icons first came to the church they were placed, as is usual, with Mary on the left of Jesus. Every morning, however, the church's monks would come for morning prayers to find the icons reversed. Bewildered by this phenomenon the father prayed to Mary for enlightenment on the issue. She told him that she had to be placed on the right of Jesus because otherwise her profile depiction would turn her back rather than her face to her son, which she would never do herself.

The depiction of Mary in profile is unusual in Macedonia, but common in Russia. There are also the graves of two Russian nuns in the grounds of the monastery (recognisable by the Russian Orthodox style gravestones), and so it is believed that these icons originally came from Russia with the nuns.

To get there, turn off the road to Kičevo from Prilep at the village of Ropotovo. The turn-off is signposted for Peštalevo. Go through these next two villages until you reach the first left turn in the village of Kostinci at what appears to be the Mayor's house. There is a hand water pump at this corner. Here the road turns into a dirt track and leads only to the village of Zrze and straight on to the monastery which you'll be able to see long before you come to the village. The last turn before the monastery is very rutted, so park at the corner unless you have 4WD.

Just before Makedonski Brod is the turn-off to Modrište. This area of Macedonia, like Matka and Lesnovo, is riddled with **caves** and underground tunnels. At the end of this road at Belica are a couple of impressive caves, but the most awe-inspiring in Macedonia has to be the **cave of Slatinski Izvor** on the way to Lokvica. It is no longer inhabited, but the ruins of former residents there still exist and the cave goes back a long way. In 2003 French caving teams were still exploring new tunnels as the back of this extensive cave system.

In Makedonski Brod itself there is the **Church of St Nikola,** which used to be a Bekteši Teke (monastery of the Muslim order of the Bekteši), and some pleasant walks along the river. In the nearby Plasnica the village restaurant is renowned for its excellent fish dishes straight from the River Treška.

KRUŠEVO

Macedonians will rave about Kruševo, but there is not actually that much there: no Roman ruins, no fortress, no pedestrian area, and relatively few churches! It is, however, the town with the highest number of old-style houses and the fewest number of high-rise blocks, making it a thoroughly pleasant place to walk around. At 1,250m, the town is the highest in the entire Balkans, and is a ski town in its own right, with ski lifts connecting the town to the slopes on Musica, Golomanica, Kozjak and Ručalo.

A century ago on August 2 1903, the holy day of St Ilija, the Internal Macedonian Revolutionary Organisation (VMRO) rose up all over Macedonia to fight for independence from the Ottoman Empire. This day is known as Ilinden, literally *Ilija den* or Ilija's day. After fierce fighting Kruševo succeeded in wresting power from the Ottomans and on August 3 the new government of Dinu Vangeli announced the independence of the Republic of Kruševo to a population of 14,000 (today there are only 10,000 in Kruševo). Nikola Karaev was made president.

However, it lasted only ten days before the Ottomans brought the new government to its knees and the Republic of Kruševo was no more. In 2003, the celebrations commemorating the centenary of independence (even though Macedonia has been shackled for most of the intervening years) were of the utmost national and cultural significance. For the Macedonians, August 2 is like July 4 for the Americans or July 14 for the French, although much more solemn, and no suggestions that the intervening years of lost statehood annul the count are entertained.

The only way to get to Kruševo, if you are not driving yourself, is by bus. The main **bus station** (tel: 048 477 102) is on the far side of town on the road out to Demir Kapija. Two good places to stay in Kruševo are the hotels Montana and Ilinden at the ski side of the town (west). ***Hotel Montana*** (200 beds; tel: 048 477 121 or 048 447 522; email: montilin@mt.net.mk; www.montana.com.mk) has recently been refurbished. The Montana towers over the town and is well

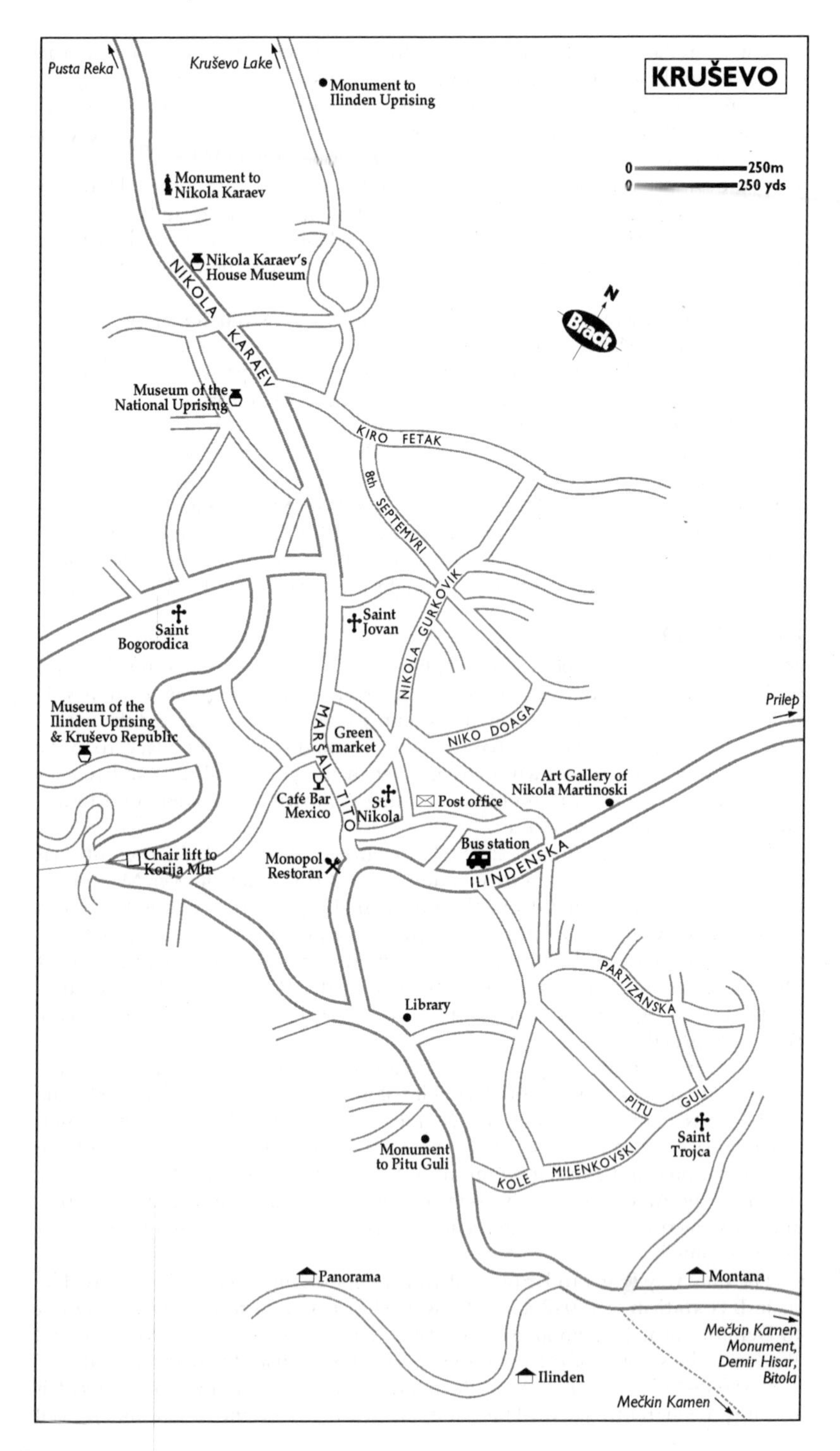
KRUŠEVO
Pusta Reka
Kruševo Lake
Monument to Ilinden Uprising
0 250m
0 250 yds
Monument to Nikola Karaev
Nikola Karaev's House Museum
NIKOLA KARAEV
N
Bradt
Museum of the National Uprising
KIRO FETAK
8th SEPTEMVRI
NIKOLA GURKOVIK
Saint Bogorodica
Saint Jovan
Museum of the Ilinden Uprising & Kruševo Republic
MARSAL TITO
Green market
NIKO DOAGA
Prilep
Art Gallery of Nikola Martinoski
Café Bar Mexico
St Nikola
Post office
Bus station
Chair lift to Korija Mtn
Monopol Restoran
ILINDENSKA
PARTIZANSKA
Library
PITU GULI
Saint Trojca
Monument to Pitu Guli
KOLE MILENKOVSKI
Panorama
Montana
Mečkin Kamen Monument, Demir Hisar, Bitola
Ilinden
Mečkin Kamen

signposted, to the left when the main road through town forks just after the centre. Rooms in the refurbished part of the hotel, including breakfast and jacuzzi bath are €30 per person. ***Hotel Ilinden*** (50 rooms; tel: 048 477 072) is much more down-market and can be found on the right fork after the centre, next to the ski lift. Sadly, there are no good places to eat in the town, choices being either your hotel, the main dilapidated *restoran* in the centre, or a few *skara na kilo* places.

What to see and do

Aside from taking in the architectural beauty of the old houses, the main attraction for Macedonians is the **Ilinden Uprising Monument** containing the tomb of Nikola Karaev. It's easy to find, just head for the large white concrete monument on the northern hill of the town. The **house of Nikola Karaev** is now preserved as a museum, and is well worth a look inside for the rich decoration of the era. Like most of the intellectuals who made up VMRO, Nikola was obviously not from a poor background. Two more museums in the town are the **Museum of the Ilinden Uprising** and the Kruševo Republic (tel: 048 477 177 or 048 476 756) and the **Museum of the National Liberation War** (tel: 048 477 126/197). There is also an **art gallery** of the paintings of the local painter Nikola Martinoski.

An hour's hike uphill from the Hotel Montana is **Mečkin Kamen**, the site of one of the battles. There is a large statue there of a fighter throwing an extremely large boulder. This is where Macedonians gather on August 2 every year to pay homage to the independence of Macedonia.

On the holy front, the **Monastery of St Spas** in Trstenik, on the outskirts of Kruševo, is relatively young by Macedonian standards having been built in 1836. The monastery stands out on the hill as you approach Kruševo from Prilep, but the turn-off for the monastery (signposted) is low down in the valley before you start climbing up into Kruševo on the main road. The monastery is a popular place for Macedonians to stay. Churches in the town itself include the **Church of St Jovan**,

A TALE OF TEARS

Legend has it that a town once stood in place of the great Lake Prespa. Whilst walking through the local woods one day, the son of the king of the town chanced upon a wood nymph whose beauty surpassed that of any girl he had hitherto laid eyes upon. On asking her name, she replied in the most beautiful voice that her name was 'Nereida'. The king's son fell immediately in love with the nymph and came to the woods many times to woo her hand in marriage, offering her all the riches of his father's land and a place by his side as the queen of the kingdom. But the nymph turned down his generous offer, saying that she could not marry a mortal being without sinister consequences befalling the groom and his homeland. Unable to imagine a deed so awful and unable to supress his love for the nymph, he chose one night to have her kidnapped and kept her in confinement until she accepted his offer of marriage. Upon their pronouncement as husband and wife, however, the heavens opened and a downpour of rain ensued. The rain did not stop until the whole town was under water and every citizen had drowned. The result is the present-day Lake Prespa. The moral of the story is that when a woman says 'no' she really does mean it.

built in 1904, which houses a collection of old icons from Kruševo, the **Church of St Nikola** in the centre of town, which was built in 1905 during the restoration of the town after the Ilinden uprising, and finally the youngest **Church of St Bogorodica**, built in 1967.

DEMIR HISAR

Halfway between Bitola and Kruševo is the small town of Demir Hisar. There is not much, if anything, worthwhile stopping for in the town itself, but nearby are some historical villages and monasteries. Four kilometres to the west, outside the village of **Slepče**, is the monastery dedicated to St Jovan Preteča. The monastery was established in the 14th century although a newer church, dedicated to **St Nikola**, was built in 1672. Further south into the Plakenska Mountains is the village of **Smilevo** where, at the Congress of Smilevo, the decision was taken to carry out the Ilinden uprising that brought about the ten-day Republic of Kruševo. Nearby is also the Vlach museum village of **Gopeš**, practically in ruins and barely lived in now. There you will find what was once the biggest church in Macedonia 200 years ago. North, halfway between Demir Hisar and Kruševo, is the **Monastery of Zurče** near the village Zurče. Its church, dedicated to St Atanas Aleksandriski, was built in 1617, although it took another century for the iconostasis to be put in.

LAKE PRESPA

Lake Prespa offers a peaceful, cooler and cheaper alternative to Lake Ohrid, and is well worth a visit in July and August when even Ohrid can get blisteringly hot and the festivities can be too much. Combined with Pelister Mountain, which is exactly 800m higher than the Galičica Mountains running the length of Lake Ohrid, the area offers a lot for those who love the outdoors.

The lake is situated 850m above sea level, making the surroundings quite cool from the mountain air. But due to the relatively shallow depth of Prespa, only just over 50m, the lake itself can get quite warm, up to 25°C in the summer. This is also helped by a shallow sandy shoreline that allows children to play and swim safely where their feet can still touch the bottom.

Sharing its borders with Greece and Albania, the lake is in fact closely connected on the Greek side to a smaller lake of the same name situated between Greece and Albania. The two lakes are separated only by a narrow strip of land in Greece, and in centuries gone by the two lakes used to be one. During that time, the name Prespa, meaning blizzard, came about because of the illusion created of an almighty blizzard when the lakes would freeze over; covered in snow, the lake would appear like a white-out to anyone looking in their direction. Other legends abound as to how the lake actually came into existence (see box, page 163).

Where to stay on the shores of Lake Prespa

Hotel MVR (56 rooms, including 3 apartments with double bed, sink, cooker and fridge; tel: 047 483 247) is on the shores of Lake Prespa at Krani. This is arguably the safest hotel in Macedonia as it belongs to the Ministry of the Interior and is reserved primarily for use by the police. It is rarely anywhere near full, however, and its good location on the lake with a small exclusive beach for hotel customers makes it a good place to stay for the price. Rooms are basic in that very 'socialist' style, all en suite but no TV or air conditioning (it rarely gets that hot there anyway). The hotel has a restaurant which seats over 100 guests and is sometimes booked up for weddings, but usually you will have the terrace to

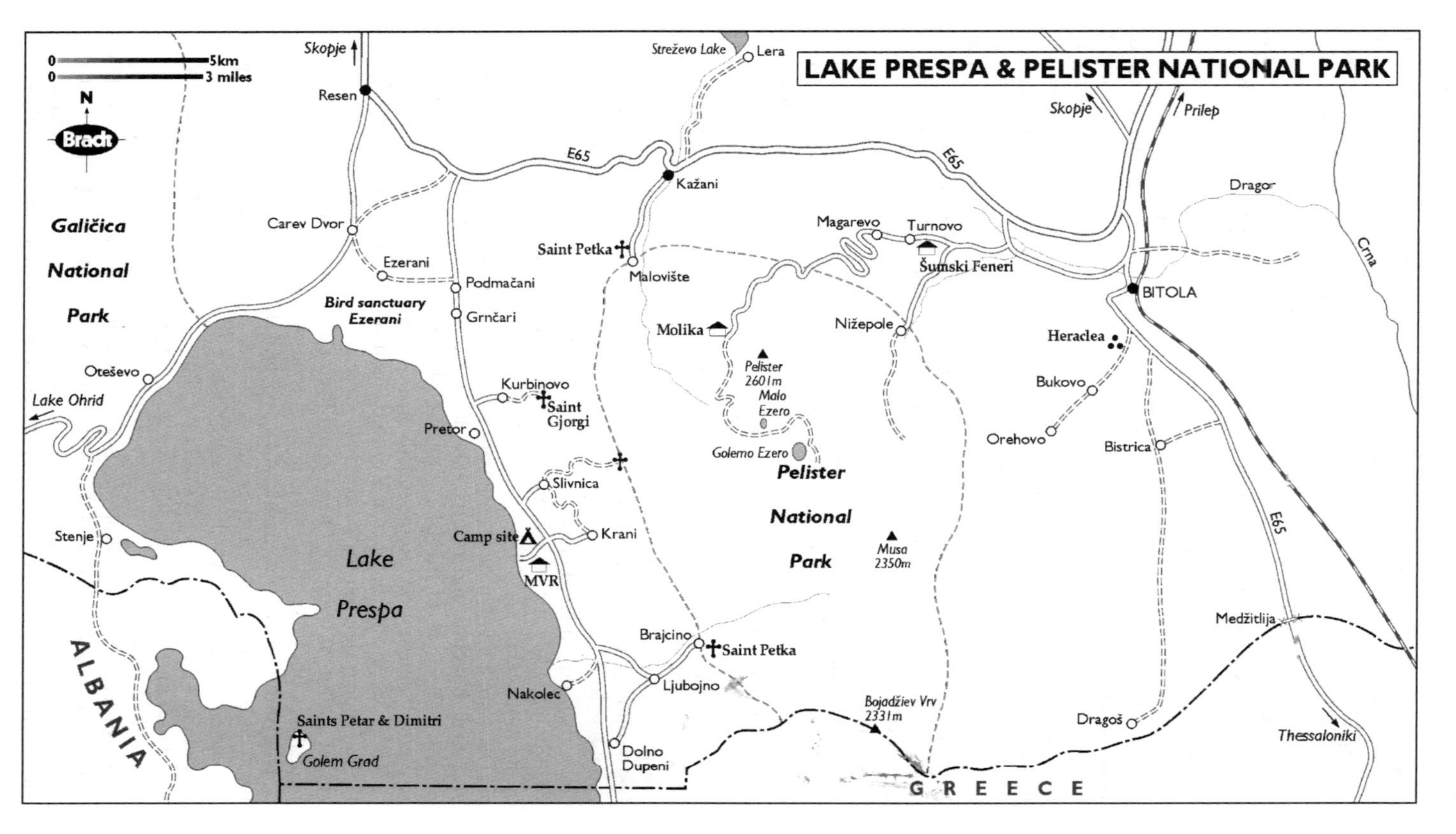
LAKE PRESPA & PELISTER NATIONAL PARK
0 5km
0 3 miles
N
Bradt
Skopje
Resen
Streževo Lake
Lera
Skopje
Prilep
E65
Kažani
E65
Drago
Crna
Galičica
National
Park
Carev Dvor
Ezerani
Podmačani
Grnčari
Bird sanctuary Ezerani
Saint Petka
Maloviště
Magarevo
Turnovo
Šumski Feneri
BITOLA
Molika
Nižepole
Heraclea
Pelister 2601m
Malo Ezero
Golemo Ezero
Bukovo
Orehovo
Bistrica
Oteševo
Lake Ohrid
Kurbinovo
Saint Gjorgi
Pretor
Slivnica
Pelister
National
Park
Musa 2350m
Camp site
Krani
MVR
Stenje
Lake
Prespa
E65
Medžitlija
Brajcino
Saint Petka
Ljubojno
Nakolec
ALBANIA
Saints Petar & Dimitri
Golem Grad
Dolno Dupeni
Bojadžiev Vrv 2331m
Dragoš
Thessaloniki
GREECE

yourself. The hotel also has about 20 hook-ups for caravan and camping with block showers and toilets. To get to the hotel turn towards the lake (signposted *Ezero*) from the main lake road where it is also signposted Krani in the opposite direction. This road will also take you to **Autocamp Krani** (which is not as nice as the hotel but is cheaper) but turn off left before you reach the gated entrance of the Autocamp. Full board at the hotel is 650MKD per person, bed and breakfast is 380MKD per person, apartments are 833MKD per person full board.

What to see and do

Aside from swimming in the lake and enjoying the cooler temperatures of Pelister Mountain, the must-do thing at Lake Prespa is to visit the **island of Golem Grad**, sometimes known as 'Snake Island' for all the water snakes which live around the shores of the island. The island is now uninhabited and is part of the nature reserve of Galičica National Park. The island contains rare flora and fauna protected by the island's lack of contact with the rest of the world, so if you do get the chance to go, be sure not to disturb the valued ecosystem here.

The island has been inhabited over the centuries. It is believed that Tsar Samoil was crowned Tsar on the island in 976, and the remains of two 14th-century churches, dedicated to St Petka and to St Dimitri, as well as the ruins of an old village can be still be found there.

If you can't find a local to take you out to the island, then boat trips can be arranged by Isidor Tours in Bitola (see *Local tour operators* above). When you go back to your boat, look for all the water snakes which will have gathered around the boat. As soon as you step into the water or move the boat, they will disappear and are perfectly harmless.

If you are approaching the lake from Ohrid via the E65 then it is worth a look into the **Women's Monastery of Jankovec**, a few kilometres before the town of Resen. This was the first women's monastery to be brought back to life after several decades of neglect during communist times. Sister Kirana, who heads the best group of fresco painters alive today in Macedonia, brought the nuns to the rundown 16th-century monastery in 1998. They have done a lot of work to it since then and their skills as fresco artisans are in high demand throughout Macedonia. They also weave, and sometimes you can purchase their handicrafts at the monastery.

There are a number of access points to the shores of Lake Prespa where there are small **beaches** and resorts. The largest of these is at **Oteševo** on the northwestern side of the lake. Oteševo also houses the national centre for respiratory illnesses, due to the superb quality of the air at Lake Prespa.

There are smaller beaches at Konjsko, Asamati, Pretor, Krani, Nakolec and Dolni Dupeni right on the border with Greece (the road-crossing here was still closed at time of writing). Oteševo and Pretor also offer hotels and beach-style bungalows, but these are in some need of renovation.

Konjsko is on the western side of the lake near the border with Greece. It has a lovely little public beach, which is quite secluded, and the village itself is the site of an ancient settlement which is largely intact and now protected as part of Macedonia's cultural heritage. A small cave church dedicated to St Elias can also be found near the village. The asphalt road does not go all the way, so be prepared for a hike or take 4WD.

Krani has a lovely small private beach available to those staying at the Hotel MVR (see *Where to stay* above), whereas the beach at **Dolni Dupeni** is larger and public, but also has a small food and drinks hut. The beach at **Nakolec** has the added attraction of being right next to this small mixed-ethnicity village, one of the few in the area along with Krani, Grnčari, and Arvati. The **Church of St Atanas** on the shores of Nakolec used to stand practically in the water, but now lies some way away due to the water loss from the lake. The receding shoreline has allowed for some excavation, however, which has revealed the foundations of buildings further into the lake. As measures are now being taken to refill the lake these excavations will undoubtedly be covered over once again but hopefully not before the research on them has been finished. Nakolec also used to have a number of wooden houses on stilts, but these are no longer standing.

At the northern end of the lake the village of Podmočani has a small **museum of national dress** and artefacts in a small house on the main road. Still the private collection of a local farmer, Mr Jone Eftimoski, it is now open to public viewing for a small entry fee. There are over 140 costumes from all over Macedonia along with jewellery, weapons and coins. Just as you get to the start of the cobbled part of the road there is a small green sign marked 'museum' pointing to the house on the right of the main road. It may not look open, but there is usually someone around in the front garden who will let you in and give you a guided tour.

Further along the lakeside road is the **bird sanctuary of Ezerani**. As with any bird watching it is best to go early during the day or in the evening, otherwise you may only find a herd of cows among the rushes eating discarded apples. The bird sanctuary is home to over 115 different species of bird including wild geese, pelicans and local moorhens. It is a part of the University of Skopje and internationally protected by EURONATUR. University members can stay at the sanctuary for a discounted price, but non-members pay €15 per night for bed and breakfast. The rooms and facilities are in great need of attention.

The next turn-off on the left leads to the village of **Kurbinovo**. This is a typical working local village along a pot-holed tarmac road crowded with meandering sheep, goats and cows. At the second house on the left, a two-storey white house with a railed front lawn, ask for the key to the **Church of St George** (*kluč za Sveti Gjorgi*), and continue on up the road. At the crest of the hill in the village turn right through a narrow row of houses and continue another couple of kilometres until you turn into a large tarmacked parking area, obviously out of keeping with the surroundings. Above the car park is the 12th-century church of St George. The roof has recently been repaired and there are a number of medieval frescos still to be seen inside dating from when the church was first built in 1191. Unfortunately, of the many frescos depicting the life of St George, there are few to be seen now.

PELISTER NATIONAL PARK AND ECO-TOURISM

Opened in 1948, Pelister National Park is the smallest (12,500 hectares) but oldest national park in Macedonia. It is famous for its ancient *Molika* pine trees, as well as some rare species of lynx, bearded eagle, gentian plants and many other different types of flora and fauna. Mount Pelister, at 2,601m, is the summit of the Baba Mountains which are in fact a part of the Rhodope range of mountains usually more closely associated with Bulgaria.

Where to stay

Hotels and guesthouses

Gorsko Oko (14 beds) Tel: 047 232 865. This is a private mountain guesthouse 14km south of Bitola set in its own grounds and close to a ski lift and good hiking trails. Each room is en suite with TV and telephone, and the guesthouse common areas offer a TV room with pool table, a library, a bar with fireplace, and a restaurant. The guesthouse can also organise professional guided hikes and excursions, both summer and winter, by foot, jeep, ski or sled, and also offers lessons in many summer and winter outdoor sports. In addition they also offer 'ecological safaris' giving tips on how and when to gather wild fruits, mushrooms and herbs. Rooms are priced at 1,650MKD per person (bed and breakfast), 50% discount for kids aged up to 7 years, and a 30% discount for kids aged 7–14 years.

Hotel Molika (56 rooms) Tel: 047 229 406. This hotel, commanding amazing views, is at the bottom of the ski lift. All rooms are en suite with TV and central heating. 1,700MKD (single, bed and breakfast), 2,700MKD (double, bed and breakfast).

Mountain huts

Golemo Ezero (45 beds). This hut lies 600m below Pelister peak at 2,000m. To arrange an overnight stay contact Sterjov Zlatko, tel: 047 221 605 (afternoons only).

Kopanki (110 beds) 1,600m Mountain Baba; tel: 047 222 384. 200MKD per person per night without breakfast, so bring your own food.

What to see and do

Skiing is the favourite winter pastime in Pelister. To get to the ski lifts from Bitola, drive west out of Bitola and turn off for the park after about 3km towards Trnovo. Keep driving through Trnovo and Magarevo until you get to the end of the road. Unfortunately, there is no public transport to the ski lifts, other than a taxi. Make sure you fix the price of the journey before you set off.

Hiking is the popular summer sport. The walk from Hotel Šumski Feneri in Trnovo village to Magarevo further up the mountain takes you along part of the Via Egnatia. Parts of the road still have the cobbles laid down by French troops fighting in the area during World War I. The Hotel Ris (tel: 047 293 901) offers a good stop for a drink (although rooms were not ready for accommodation at time of writing) and the giant pet rabbit offers hours of entertainment.

A Vlach village that is well worth a visit and is a real museum piece is **Malovište**. The village was once a rich Vlach trading village, and it is not difficult to see that some of the houses were once very stylish in their time. Most are now in various states of decay. The **Church of St Petka** is usually open and, unusually for most churches in Macedonia, its exonarthex is on the left of the entrance rather than on the right (it is also on the north side and a good place to cool off in the hot summer). The church sometimes allows stranded travellers to stay overnight in a couple of makeshift beds in the upper gallery. Behind the church is a graveyard containing some gravestones as old as the church itself. Forty minutes hike from the village is the **Monastery of St Ana** which houses guests for the moderate price of 150MKD per night per person.

Malovište has had some funding from the EU to spruce itself up and put out some advertising. There is a small information room just where the tarmac runs out (ask in the village to be let in) where you can buy a well laid-out book on the village (also available from Hotel Šumski Feneri). Unfortunately, the village is literally dying, as very few if any young people live there now, and although the EU has injected some much-needed funds into advertising the village, not much seems to have been done regarding follow up. No further money seems to be coming into the town and there isn't even a village shop or somewhere to buy a coffee, although there are drinking fountains near the church.

To get to Malovište from Bitola take the highway towards Resen for almost 20km and take the exit marked *Kazani*. At the crossroads turn left and then take the next left at the village shop. Follow this one-lane road some 5km until you get to the village. Back at the crossroads, if you take the road straight on north, you will drive along the River Šemnica to **Streževo Lake**, and turning left at

EATING AT HOME

Brajčino offers the chance to eat with the locals. Some friends and I ordered a day ahead for the set menu to be served at 19.00 upon our arrival in the village. There is no à la carte menu, but vegetarian food or other dietary requests can be included, if the order is placed in advance.

We arrived in good time and walked up the narrow winding roads of the village to Jadranka's little farm at house number 144 (the village is so small that there are no street names). The family were waiting for us and ushered us into their tiny Sunday room, the one reserved for guests and special occasions.

Sitting at the neatly laid table we were offered a shot of *rakija* or *liker* as an aperitif to welcome us to their home. I chose the *liker* made of a *rakija* base re-distilled with blueberries and sugar. Fortunately, the Macedonians take their time over their liqueurs, and this one was well worth savouring: accompanied by salad fresh from their garden, I could have drunk two or three glasses, but saved myself for the home-made wine which was to come with the main course.

We moved on to a country veal soup, so delicious that I asked the origin of the calf. 'Yes, it is our cow,' Jadranka replied. Feeling slightly guilty that I was eating from their larder, I continued the conversation enquiring if the cow had had a name. 'Rusa,' came the reply. 'Ah yes, well Rusa is indeed most delicious,' I added in my best Macedonian. Everyone burst out laughing at this point, probably at my attempt to speak Macedonian.

The next course included more of Rusa's melt-in-the-mouth offerings, accompanied by sweet roasted peppers and sautéed potatoes. Their homemade wine was fruity and mild, quaffable by the jugfull, although we restrained ourselves to fit in some of their home-made peach juice, while we chatted away with the family about each other's lives. Formerly the area had lived well from sheep farming, but now Macedonia's depressed economy could not support the high price of sheep. With so little work in the locality, Jadranka and Jontsche were glad to receive the extra income that eco-tourism might bring their way. Jontsche could be hired as a mountain guide by the day or half-day (1,500/800MKD), and in addition to set meals, Jadranka sells dried boletus mushroom (350MKD/500g), *liker* (400MKD/litre), *rakija* (150MKD/litre) and other home-made products such as jam, juice and wine.

We finished the meal with some home-made marble cake, cherries from their garden and a cup of coffee or mountain tea, then meandered back down the hill to our beds.

The next evening we ate at Milka's house. We were greeted with the Macedonian tradition of candied fruits (locally grown and produced, of course) and shots of mint or cherry *liker*. More home-made courses followed and then ended with a *baklava* made of walnuts and poppy seed that was so tasty that I'll be ordering a whole tray in advance next time to take home to freeze.

the village of Lera and then left again at Sviništa, you can take a dirt track up to another formerly rich Vlach village, **Gopeš**. Gopeš has not had as much funding as Malovište, but is also a good potential museum town showing a glimpse of life back in the rich Vlach days.

Eco-tourism development in Pelister National Park

Less than 5km from the border with Greece, the village of **Brajčino** is courting an eco-tourism initiative offered through the Swiss non-governmental organisation ProNatura. Brajčino was chosen for its pristine picturesque setting on the edge of Pelister National Park and for its idyllic location away from the hustle and bustle of city life, protected by the *Baba massif* and with a view on to Lake Prespa. It has good access to the glacial lakes atop the range and from there to Pelister summit and the mountain huts, and it is easily accessible by car or direct bus from Skopje (two buses every day from the main bus terminal via Veles, Prilep and Bitola for 400MKD) or Resen (several buses every day).

Formerly a rich trading village, it still has a small population of mixed ages despite the emigration of many of the villagers in the middle of the 20th century to Canada and Scandanavia due to lack of employment or in order to escape communist persecution. The departure of the vast majority of business know-how from the village has left it in hard times, even more so since the break-up of Yugoslavia which has taken its toll on the village's formerly prosperous apple trade through the imposition of border controls and taxes. Now the villagers, through the help of ProNatura and the local non-governmental organisations of DEM (Ecological Movement of Macedonia) and BSPM (Bird Society Protection of Macedonia), are trying to revive the local economy by offering visitors access to their pristine lifestyles in return for keeping it so. Ten percent of the income of the guides, accommodation and the village shop is reinvested into preserving the local area.

Where to stay and eat

Accommodation is either bed-and-breakfast style in a local house at 900MKD or €15 per person per night (or bed only for 420MKD) or dormitory style in the old Monastery of St Petka (24 beds) for 350MKD. The monastery is no longer a working monastery, but was renovated by the villagers in 2003 under the eco-tourism project in order to accommodate visitors. It is set in a meadow above the village and offers utter tranquility, a view on to Pelister and a fantastic night sky. The accommodation price at the monastery includes bedding and use of the bathrooms, but you will have to pay 30MKD extra for a towel if you need one, and another 60MKD for use of the kitchen. There is so far no heating, so once the weather turns cold you may prefer to seek accommodation elsewhere. Breakfast is not provided.

There is a small village shop and café just off the main square, that also provides information on the village guides and tours, but no restaurants. A village lunch or evening meal can be arranged in one of the local houses, giving you that extra special local experience, eating almost entirely locally grown and produced food (see textbox). You can order three types of menus: a basic menu for 350MKD (three courses), a standard menu for 450MKD (four courses) and a special menu for 550MKD (for special occasions). Children aged between five and 12 years pay half price, younger than five years are free. Wine with your meal is not included in this cost.

To book accommodation, a meal or a guide in Brajčino call 070 497 751 or 047 482 444.

What to see and do

The village has done a lot of work to tidy up local hiking trails and to keep them well marked and signposted. **Hiking guides** can be arranged for 800–1,200MKD for a half- day or 1,500–3,600 MKD for a full day (depending on the number of people) to take you on less-well-trodden trails and to give you an insight into local flora, fauna and history. It's a five- to six-hour hike to the mountain hut of Golemo Ezero at one of the 'Eyes of Pelister', and then another three-hour hike from there to the summit of Pelister.

The village itself is pretty to walk around and an ideal setting for **walks with children**. There are many animals to be seen in the village farmyards and a number of buildings are marked with information plates on the usage, architecture and previous owners of the building. Much of this information is from the book *Brajčino Stories* by the writer Meto Jovanovski from Brajčino, a former chairperson of the Macedonian Pen Club. He is now retired and returns to the village every summer. The **bey's house** (*Begot Kukja*), the house of the last Ottoman commander for the area from the end of the 19th century, can be viewed inside if you ask for the key in the neighouring houses or at the village shop.

There are **six churches** near the village dating from medieval times through the beginning of the 20th century. The medieval churches are those dedicated to St Petka, St Bogorodica and St Atanas. It's not known exactly when these churches were built or even in which order, but all contain frescos of the same era and, like so many churches in Macedonia, are in various stages of disrepair.

The **Church of St Petka** lies in the grounds of the old monastery 15 minutes' walk outside the village. St Petka's holy day is August 8, when as many as 600 of the local villagers gather in the monastery with food and drink to celebrate.

The small **Church of St Bogorodica** leans against a cliff above the village. The cliff can be seen from the village and, although the church itself is obscured by trees, the rock face is marked out with a cross at the top of the cliff. Set into the cliff are a number of 'cells' where local monks used to stay overnight in days of old, which shows that the rock here makes for an excellent if small **rock climbing wall**. It can be top-roped from the cliff top, but be sure not to disturb the walls of the monk's cells as these are part of the ancient village heritage.

The medieval church 15 minutes' walk to the south of the village, is dedicated to **St Atanas**. It is mostly in ruins but has some graves possibly dating back to medieval times.

The church closest to the village and still used by its inhabitants is the **Church of St Nikola.** Built in 1871, it is in a pretty location with a good view on to Lake Prespa. The main nave of the church is usually locked, although you may be able to access the glass-fronted exonarthex. Ask in the village for the key. The bell tower is a recent addition, made of a simple metal frame but in the traditional Macedonian style of being separate from the church itself.

The churches of **St Ilija** (1915) and **St Archangel** (1919) are located outside the village and are very simple. They are also rarely used, making them musty and damp.

Further down the valley is the larger village of **Ljubojno.** It is made up of houses similar in style to Brajčino, although a few 19th-century town houses have also made it into the village square. The square is begging for a few good outdoor cafés and a piazza lifestyle … maybe in a few more years. Clearly seen above the village are the two churches of **St Petka and St Pavle**, which watch over Ljubojno vigilantly.

Oleander

The Northwest

9

The northwest of Macedonia along the Vardar and Radika rivers is edged by the **Šar mountain range** bordering Kosovo, and by the **Korab** and Dešat mountains bordering Albania. The main towns of Tetovo, Gostivar and Debar are predominantly Albanian and if you don't speak any Albanian for the most part you'll be more warmly welcomed if you speak German rather than Serbian or Macedonian. German is more widely spoken here than English as a second language. This area is the home of **Mavrovo National Park**, preserving some stunning mountain scenery and wildlife, and where the **wedding festival** of Galičnik takes place every July. The back road to Ohrid from Gostivar goes past Mavrovo Lake and down the Radika River into the manmade dammed valley lake of Debar and up the Black Drim River past the dammed Globočica Valley on to Struga. In the autumn it is probably one of the prettiest routes in Macedonia, when the densely wooded mountainside becomes a riot of red, orange and yellow. This is the area of Macedonia which could earn itself the name of 'Little Switzerland'.

TETOVO

Tetovo is the gateway to the Šar Mountains and to the popular Popova Šapka ski resort. Towering above the town, often covered in snow as late as June and as early as September is Macedonia's second-highest mountain, Titov Vrv (Tito's summit, 2,748m). This is in fact the highest mountain which lies completely in Macedonia (and was also the highest in the whole of Yugoslavia, earning it the title of Tito's summit). The higher peak of Mount Korab (2,764m) lies further to the south above Lake Mavrovo and marks the border between Albania and Macedonia.

Nestled close to the Muslim strongholds of Kosovo and Albania, Tetovo is the de facto capital of Macedonia's significantly sized Albanian minority. It is also the headquarters of the main Albanian-centred political parties, the Democratic Union of Integration and the Democratic Party of Albanians. Just outside Tetovo is the South East European University, Macedonia's third university after Skopje and Bitola.

History of Tetovo

Tetovo is a relatively new town by Macedonian standards, although there are archaeological discoveries found near the town which date back to the Bronze Age (2200–1200BC). Macedonia's oldest artefact, a Mycenae sword from this period, was found outside Tetovo. Copper and gold in the local streams first attracted Greek settlers but during Roman and early Slav times there were few

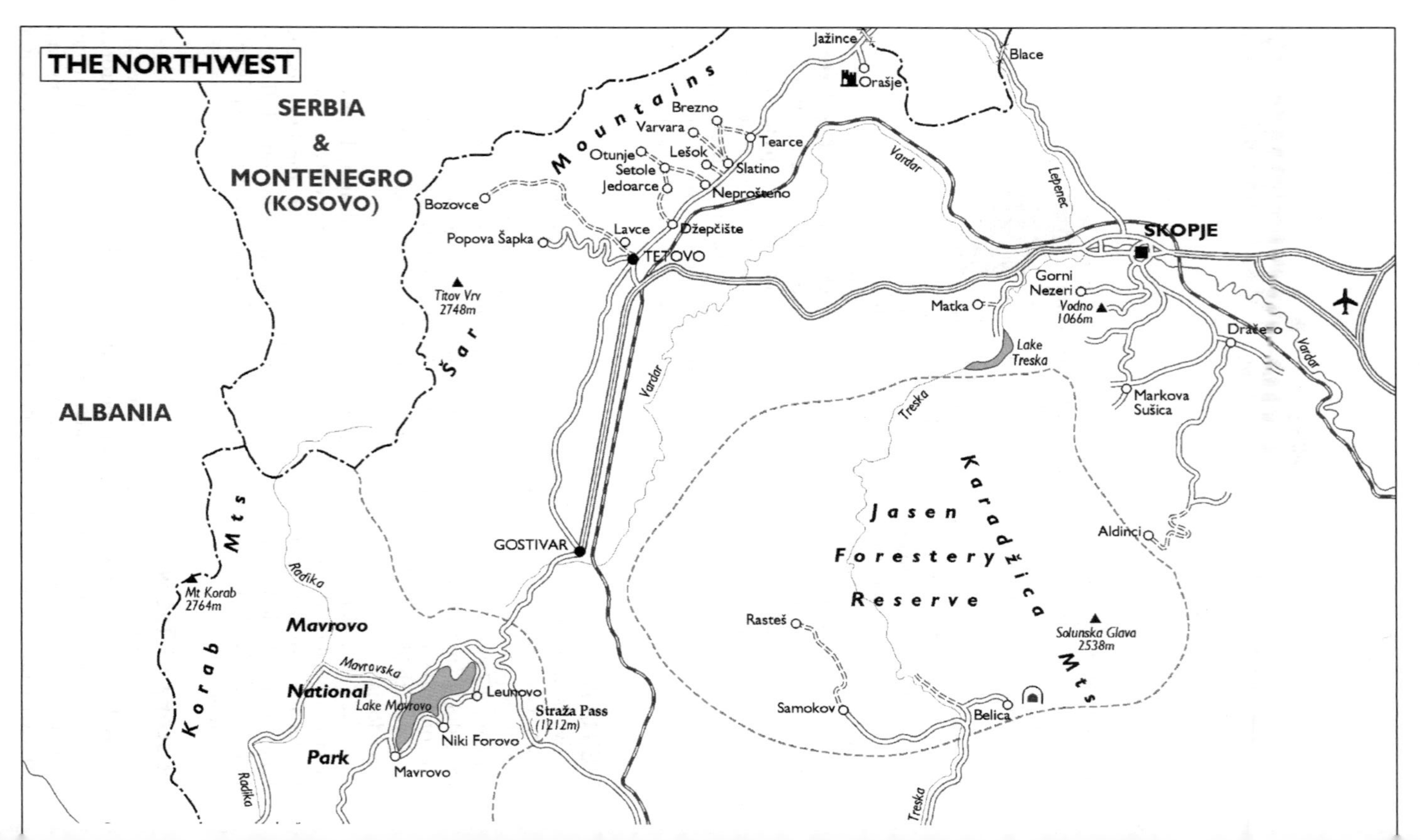
THE NORTHWEST
SERBIA & MONTENEGRO (KOSOVO)
ALBANIA
Šar Mountains
Jažince
Orašje
Blace
Brezno
Varvara
Tearce
Otunje
Lešok
Slatino
Setole
Jedoarce
Neprošteno
Bozovce
Lavce
Džepčište
Popova Šapka
TETOVO
Vardar
Lepenec
SKOPJE
Titov Vrv 2748m
Gorni Nezeri
Matka
Vodno 1066m
Drače
Lake Treska
Markova Sušica
Treska
Karadžica Mts
Jasen Forestery Reserve
Aldinci
GOSTIVAR
Korab Mts
Mt Korab 2764m
Radika
Mavrovo National Park
Mavrovska
Lake Mavrovo
Leunovo
Straža Pass (1212m)
Niki Forovo
Mavrovo
Rasteš
Solunska Glava 2538m
Samokov
Belica

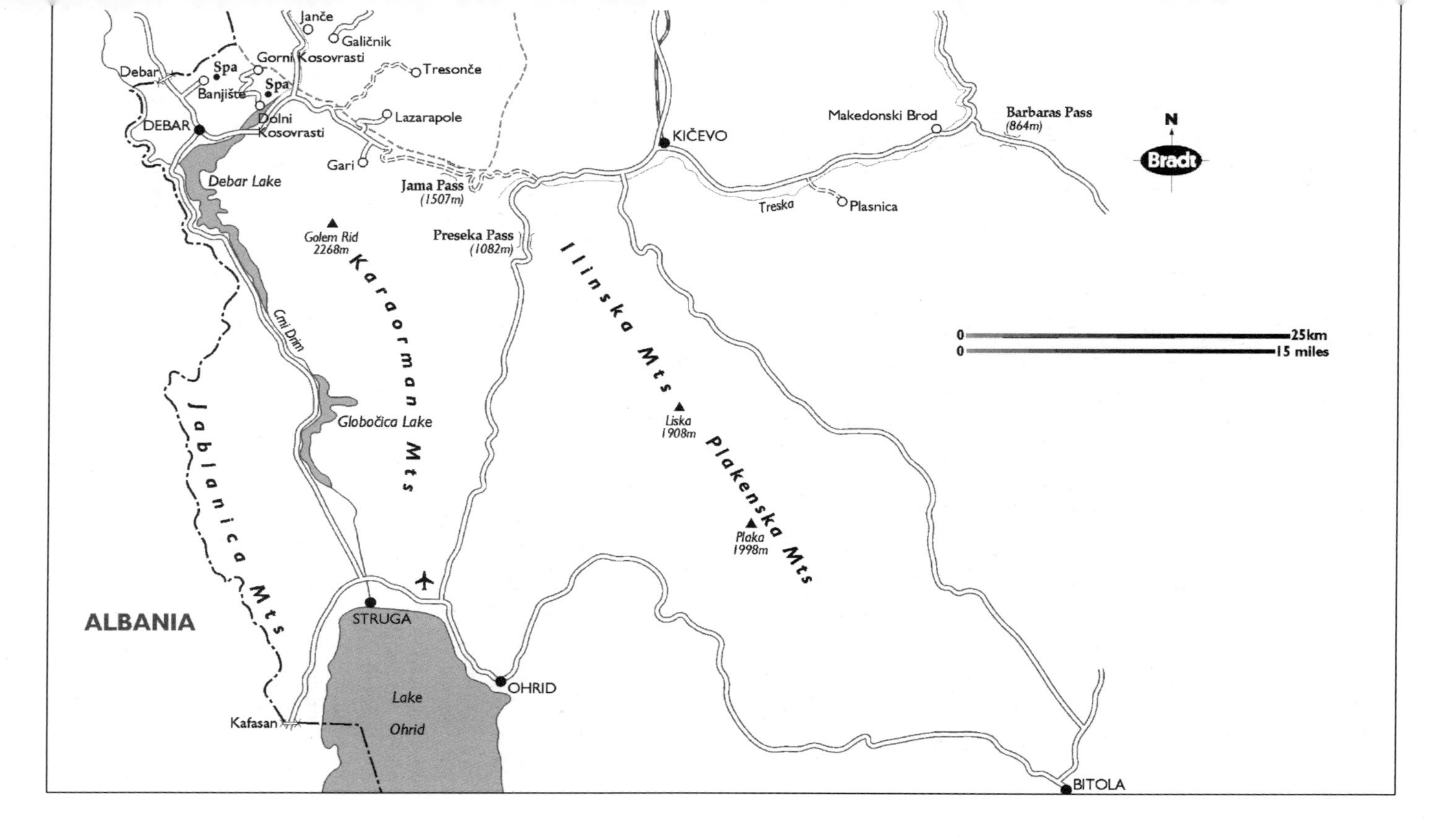
Janče
Galičnik
Gorni Kosovrasti
Spa
Spa
Debar
Banjište
Tresonče
Dolni
Kosovrasti
Lazarapole
DEBAR
Gari
Debar Lake
Jama Pass
(1507m)
KIČEVO
Makedonski Brod
Barbaras Pass
(864m)
N
Bradt
Treska
Plasnica
Golem Rid
2268m
Preseka Pass
(1082m)
Karaorman Mts
Ilinska Mts
Crni Drim
0
25km
0
15 miles
Liska
1908m
Plakenska Mts
Globočica Lake
Jablanica Mts
Plaka
1998m
ALBANIA
STRUGA
OHRID
Lake
Ohrid
Kafasan
BITOLA

MULTI-ETHNICITY IN EDUCATION

In the early nineties, the Albanians, self-selectedly disenfranchised from the democratic process in Macedonia, tried to start the first university in the country to offer courses in Albanian. The Macedonian authorities disapproved of the move, repeating that Macedonian was the only official language allowed under the constitution (the writing of which the Albanians had not participated in), and with that the battle for the right to learn in one's own mother tongue ensued. Eventually, after intense mediation from the international community, both sides settled on naming the university 'The South East European University' (SEEU) offering courses in a variety of southeast European languages and English.

In many ways SEEU was set up to be independent of the government by being a fee-paying estabishment built with international money. In the academic year of 2003, SEEU enrolled 3,800 students, of whom 78% spoke Albanian as their mother tongue. But neither community is completely happy with the compromise, and the Albanian community is still trying to set up its own university, the Tetovo University in the Tetovo suburb of Mala Rečica, in order to strengthen teaching in Albanian. It was only in mid-2003 that the Macedonian authorities recognised some of the faculties and courses at Tetovo University, which is now trying to strengthen its ties to SEEU.

SEEU has the potential to be a role model for education among mixed ethnicities around the world, and could make for a valuable exchange year for students of Balkan history and language. It remains to be seen if these ideals will really prosper.

inhabitants here. The first signs of a significant settlement appeared as a small rural village served by the Church of St Bogorodica during the 13th and 14th centuries. At that time the village was called Htetovo. Legend says that the village got its name after a local hero Hteto succeeded in banishing snakes from the village. Thereafter it became known as Hteto's place, or in Macedonian, Htetovo.

Tetovo remained under Ottoman control from the end of the 14th century until the Ottomans were ousted from Macedonia in 1912. During that period the town was named Kalkandelen, which means 'shield penetrator', in honour of the local smithies' excellent weapon making. Their superior craftsmanship extended also to the advent of small firearms and cannons, which were traded all over the Balkans. The small hill above the town, near the present-day village of Lavce, has been fortified since Paeonian times and the Ottomans also built a substantial fortress there.

A number of mosques were built in the town, the most beautiful of which is the Šarena Mosque, built in the 16th century, which fortunately escaped the fire of the middle of the 17th century that destroyed most of the town. In the 16th century, the *Bekteši* order also settled in Tetovo, and the seat of the order can still be found in the town today.

During Turkish times Tetovo came under the *vilayet* of Kosovo and was strongly oriented towards its Albanian brothers and the Albanian struggle for independence from Ottoman rule. But the Serb victory in the Balkan Wars of 1912 and 1913 left the entire *vilayet* of Kosovo, including Tetovo, Gostivar and Debar, under the control of Royalist Yugoslavia. The resulting crackdown on Islam forced many Muslims from Tetovo to emigrate to the USA and Canada, while thousands of Serbs were encouraged to move into the town to develop the mining and hydro-electric industry.

The town prospered, however; orthodox churches were built, skiing and pony trekking started in the Šar Mountains, and White Russian settlers even found their way to Tetovo. The 1930s were good for the new Slav settlers of Tetovo; and then came World War II and Tetovo became a part of fascist Albania. In resistance, some of the new Serb settlers set up the Macedonian Communist Party, founded on March 19 1943 in Tetovo, but by then the Albanian Communist Party was also fighting for the town.

Eventually, the town fell to Tito under the Socialist Republic of Macedonia (SRM), and Albanians in Tetovo were subject to much the same repression as the Albanians of Kosovo in Yugoslavia. More Muslims emigrated and those who remained demonstrated periodically but violently against the communist regime, notably in 1957 and 1968. When the troubles in neighbouring Kosovo began in 1981, Tetovo had to be put under the control of paramilitary police due to the rioting and show of sympathy with the Kosovar Albanians. The same happened again in 1989.

When it became obvious in 1990 that Yugoslavia was about to fall, over 2,000 ethnic Albanians marched through Tetovo demanding secession from the Socialist Republic of Macedonia and unity with Albania. Self-determination of an ethinic minority within a state was not a right under the SRM constitution, and protesting their lack of representation under the constitution of a new Republic of Macedonia (RM), the Albanians of Macedonia boycotted the referendum on independence from Yugoslavia and were thus excluded from almost any representation in the new government. Tetovo became the headquarters of the new Albanian political parties, which were regarded as unconstitutional by the new RM. Tensions grew worse, and were fuelled by increasing lawlessness in neighbouring Kosovo. Prior to the NATO bombing of Serb forces in Kosovo, Tetovo became the rear supply base for the Kosovo Liberation Army, and then later home to thousands of Kosovo refugees.

In 1997, Ajladin Demiri, the mayor of Tetovo, was jailed for raising the double- headed eagle flag of Albania from Tetovo town hall, and by 2000 the outbreak of hostilities in Tanuševci, north of Skopje on the border with Kosovo, had spilled into the towns of Tetovo and Gostivar. Even after hostilities had ceased and a peace deal had been brokered by the international community, there was still inter-ethnic tension in the area. The old Tetovo–Gostivar–Debar highway, linking these predominantly Albanian towns, was the scene of many blockades and armed hold-ups in 2001/2002.

Today, although some tensions remain, they tend to be of a political nature, and Tetovo is a safe and welcoming place to visit.

Getting there, around and about

Tetovo is a 40-minute drive from Skopje on the E65 highway (Motorway 2). There is also a railway service to the town three times a day, and buses run frequently every hour. The inter-town bus station (tel: 044 339 130) is on B Kidrič Street next to the train station (tel: 044 336 660). Tetovo itself is a fairly small town to walk around and taxis run for a minimum fare of 10MKD.

Where to stay and eat

There are few good places to stay in the town of Tetovo itself, and you may prefer to opt for Skopje only half an hour away, or go right up into the mountains and stay at the Popova Šapka ski resort (see next).

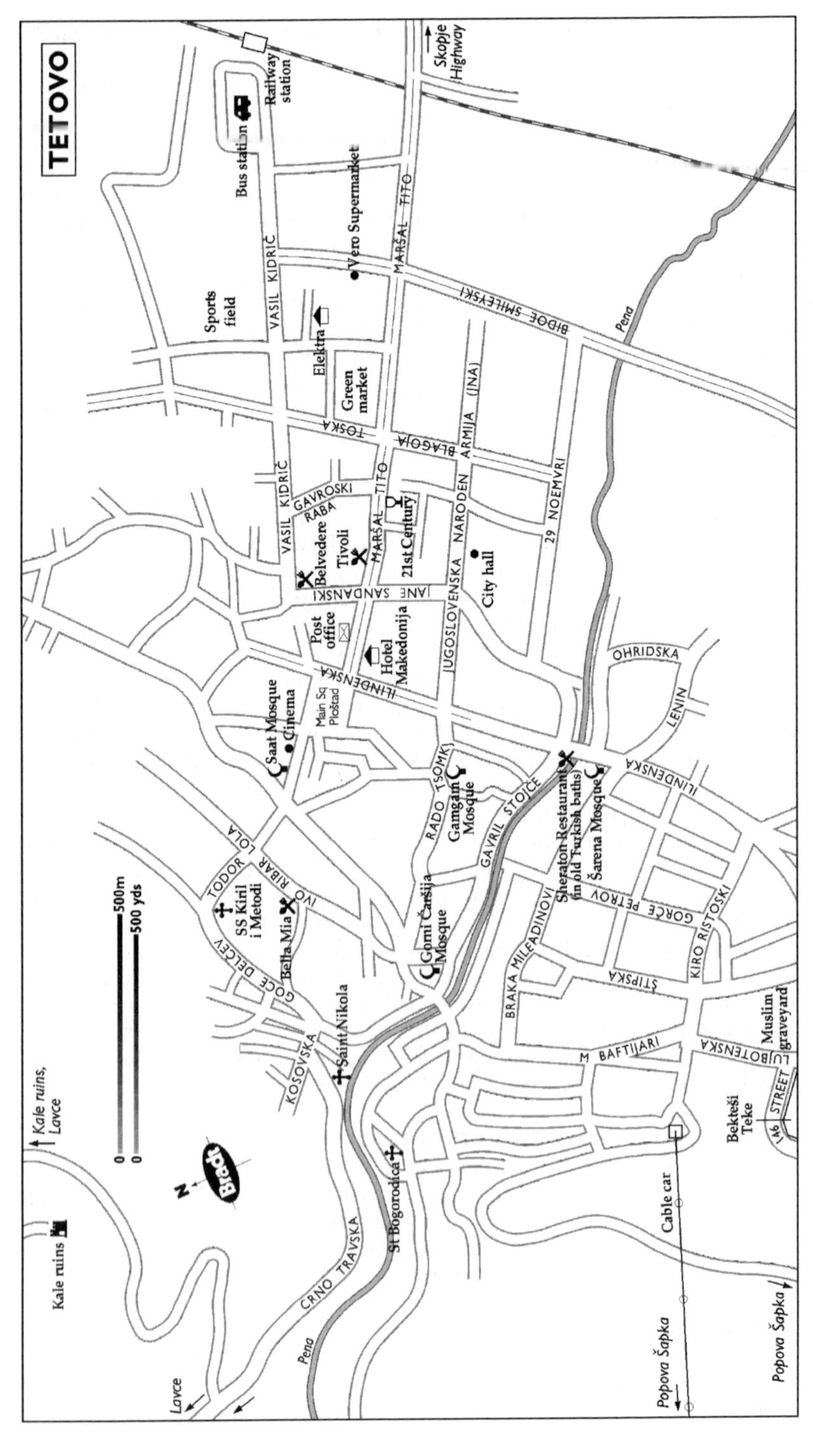
TETOVO
Skopje Highway
Railway station
Bus station
Vero Supermarket
Sports field
Elektra
Green market
VASIL KIDRIČ
MARŠAL TITO
BIDOE SMILEVSKI
TOSKA
BLAGOJA
NARODEN ARMIJA (JNA)
GAVROSKI
RABA
Belvedere
Tivoli
21st Century
JANE SANDANSKI
29 NOEMVRI
City hall
Post office
Hotel Makedonija
JUGOSLOVENSKA NARODEN
ILINDENSKA
Main Sq Ploštad
Saat Mosque
Cinema
OHRIDSKA
LENIN
RADO TSOMKI
Gamgam Mosque
GAVRIL STOICE
Sheraton Restaurant (in old Turkish baths)
Šarena Mosque
ILINDENSKA
Pena
IVO RIBAR LOLA
TODOR
SS Kiril i Metodi
Bella Mia
GOCE DELČEV
Gorni Čaršija Mosque
BRAKA MILEADINOVI
GORČE PETROV
KIRO RISTOSKI
ŠTIPSKA
Muslim graveyard
M BAFTIJARI
LJUBOTENSKA
Saint Nikola
KOSOVSKA
Bektesi Teke
146 STREET
0 500m
0 500 yds
Kale ruins, Lavce
Kale ruins
N
Bradt
St Bogorodica
CRNO TRAVSKA
Cable car
Pena
Lavce
Popova Šapka
Popova Šapka

Hotel and Restoran Elektra (5 rooms) 120 Street, number 2; tel: 044 339 190; fax: 044 339 455. Close to the centre of town and in a quiet area behind the OSCE offices. The restaurant offers the traditional Macedonian fare, but for atmosphere you would be better off going into town. Basic, but clean and tidy rooms, en suite with TV. 1,700MKD for a double room for one night, 1,200MKD for a single.
Hotel Makedonija (39 rooms) Tel: 044 338 586. In the centre of town, this hotel is well located but rather noisy and very run-down. Single €17, twin €30.

The high street offers a number of places to eat and drink, but by far the most popular is **Tivoli**. It is one of the few places in Macedonia which approaches anything like a breakfast culture, serving excellent breakfast omelettes, and their salads include a home-made mayonnaise dressing, also practically unheard of in Macedonia. Next door is **Restaurant Delfin**, and over the road is **Pizzeria Palma**, both serving tradional Macedonian food and pizza. **Belvedere** (tel: 070 240 392) at Jane Sandanski 1 also has good food. In the old town two atmospheric places to eat are the old Turkish bath house, now called the **Sheraton**, and **Bella Mia**, both of which serve traditional Macedonian fare. The favourite café-bars in town are **21st Century**, and **Madison**, both on the high street. They offer good music and plenty of space to sit outside in the summer.

Tetovo has a wonderful green market on the high street if you are yearning for fresh fruit in the summer.

What to see and do

The **Arabati Baba *Bektaši teke*** is one of the prettiest sites in the town, with well-kept gardens and old-style inns and meditation platforms. A *teke* is the Sufi equivalent of a monastery belonging to the *Bektaši* order of *dervishes* (Muslim mystics). Sufism is derived from the Sunni branch of Islam. This *teke* in Tetovo was built at the end of the 18th century and remained the seat of the *Bektaši* until 1912 when the Ottomans were driven out of Macedonia.

With the departure of the Ottoman rulers from the area in 1912 the *dervishes* were no longer welcome and most fled to neighbouring Albania or elsewhere. Although the *teke* saw a small revival between 1941 and 1945, the lands were taken as state property during Yugoslav times and made into a hotel and museum. In recent years, however, the *Bektaši* order has regained access in the *teke* and the site is being slowly refurbished. Although in considerable disrepair it is still the largest and most well-preserved *teke* in the western Balkans.

The prayer room and library are open to visitors if accompanied by the *baba* (priest), who will welcome any library donations of Islamic books to replace the many burnt in 1948 when partisan forces set light to the library.

At present Baba Tahir is head of the *teke* and can often be found in the buildings in the opposite corner from the main entrance, and is happy to chat if you would like find out more about the *teke*. He speaks Macedonian and Albanian, but the *dervishes* hope to have a booklet on their *teke* available in English soon. Next to the Baba's courtyard is the *meydan*, which used to be the main place of worship for the *Bektaši*. Now it has been converted into a Sunni mosque (much to the annoyance of the *dervishes* who would like to see their *teke* completely returned to the Sufi order).

The **Šarena Djamija** (meaning coloured or painted mosque and often called the Motley Mosque by English speakers) is known locally as Pasha Djamija (Prince's Mosque). Its colourful exterior makes the building look like it is clad in a deck of playing cards. Over 30,000 eggs were used to manufacture the paint and glaze. The site used to include an inn as well as a bath house on the other side of

ALI SERSEM BABA AND THE ARABATI BABA TEKE

Ali Baba (not Ali Baba of the *Tales of 1001 Nights*) was the brother-in-law of the Sultan Suleijman the Magnificent, and had been a high-ranking *baba* in the important Dimotika Teke (now in Greece) when his sister (who was one of the Sultan's wives) fell into disfavour with her husband. This did not bode well for Ali Baba, who was sent to Tetovo at the outer fringes of the Ottoman Empire to live the simple life of a *Bektaši* monk.

Another version of the story goes that Ali Baba was an official of the Ottoman Empire who gave up his position in order to live the simple life of a *Bektaši* monk. The Sultan, angered by the departure of one of his favourite officials, yelled after Ali as he departed Constantinople, 'If you will be a fool, then go.' *Sersem*, the old Turkish for 'fool', became Ali Baba's nickname thereafter.

Whichever the true story (the Turks favour the first story), Sersem travelled through the vast empire of Turkey until he came upon the River Pena among the tranquil mountains of Tetovo. There he settled until his death in 1538, quietly practising the 'way' of the *Bektaši* order. After his death, his only pupil to survive him, Arabati Baba, founded the present-day monastery in Tetovo to commemorate Sersem's life.

The present-day buildings were built at the end of the 18th century by Rexhep Pasha, also a *dervish*, whose tomb lies next to that of Sersem's in the mausoleum of the *teke*. Not all the buildings are still standing today: in the courtyard can be seen the foundations of what might formerly have been the *teke* stables; still to be seen are a fountain, the meditation platform and the tower, painted blue, next to Baba Tair's courtyard, which was probably a lookout tower or fortification, but some say was built to house the sick daughter of Abdulrahram Pasha. The reception inn is still in disrepair, although the library is being refurbished. One of the buildings has been turned into a Sunni mosque, but the inns around the *Bektaši* graveyard have been preserved for the Baba.

Many Sufi/Dervish orders include a ceremony or dance ritual called *zikr*. This involves swaying movements in time to music and/or the repetition of Islamic texts by the lead *dervish* or *zakir*. The ceremony requires a lot of control and concentration in order to empty the mind of all but God himself, and can appear to result in an almost trance-like state. The *zikr* is preformed on a meditation platform like the one at the *Bektaši* Arabati Baba Teke. (For the *rufa'i dervish* order, renowned for their feats of walking on hot coals and swallowing swords, the *zikr* often appears quite frantic and it is from this order of *zikr* that the phrase 'whirling *dervish*' comes.)

At the Arabati Baba Teke another ceremony takes place once a year in recognition of the martyrdom of the Shia Imam Hussein family, who were stabbed to death in Kerbela, Iraq, for their religious beliefs. As seen recently in Iraq, worshippers beat themselves in order to re-live the martyrdom of the Imam and his family.

the river, but the bath house is now a restaurant named the Sheraton (see above). The grounds of the mosque contain an octagonal *turbe* (grave) of Hurshida and Mensure, the two women who paid to have the mosque built in 1459.

Other mosques in Tetovo include the **Saat Mosque** which as its name implies used to have a clock in its minaret, the **Gorni Čaršija Mosque** so called for its proximity to the upper bazaar area, and the **Gamgam Mosque**. Churches in town include the **Church of Sveti Bogorodica** near the river, the **Church of Sveti Nikola** also close to the river, and the **Church of Kiril and Metodi** dedicated to the founders of the Macedonian Orthodox church.

In the village of **Lešok**, 8km to the northeast of Tetovo is a monastery of the same name housing the two 14th-century **churches of the Holy Virgin** (1326) and of **St Atanas** (mid-14th century). The Church of the Holy Virgin contains frescos from three different dates: the time of construction, the 17th century, and lastly 1879. The original iconostasis and several marble columns from the original church are now on show in the city museum. The monastery was one of several in the area so-favoured by the 19th century Pasha Abdulrahman, who donated money to the upkeep of the churches. Later, he attempted an uprising against the Sultan and failed (it wasn't just the locals who were unhappy with the Ottoman elite) and was packed off to fight in the Crimea, where he died. Unfortunately, during the conflict of 2001, the Church of St Atanas was severely damaged by a bomb. It is now being reconstructed with the help of international finance and work on new frescos should start in 2004. In the yard of the Monastery of Lešok is the tomb of the Macedonian educator Kiril Pejchinovik, who was born in 1770. In his honour, the monastery hosts an International Meeting of Literary Translators every year.

Just outside the small village of Lavce, further up the River Pena from Tetovo, are the ruins of the **Ottoman fortress**. The fortress and its accompanying mosque were destroyed in the 1912–13 Balkan wars. Little remains now except magnificent views, but in its heyday it was quite the construction with a series of tunnels from all the main Ottoman houses in the town leading to the fortress. The thinking behind the tunnel system was to allow the defenders of the fortress to escape behind enemy lines if the fortress was beseiged, allowing the beseigers themselves to be encircled. The last tunnel collapsed in the sixties. The site remains strategically important and was used in the last conflict of 2001, as was the valley behind, for shoring up troops and supplies. In World War II the valley was bombed repeatedly by the Germans.

The paths up the River Pena lead to a number of mountain villages and past the **Iron Cave**, a large underground system popular with cavers and pot holers. There are also attractive villages along the Tetovo road to Prizren in Kosovo. In villages such as Brezno and Varvara, you can still see good examples of traditional village architecture – wattle and daub houses with stone roofs. Some villages, such as Jedoarce, Setole and Otunje, are weekend house retreats which were damaged during the conflict and are now slowly being rebuilt. While you are unlikely to come across many people, there are wonderful views over the Polog Valley and mountain walks through mature beech and sweet chestnut forests on to the top of the Šar range.

POPOVA ŠAPKA SKI RESORT AND MOUNTAIN RANGE

Povova Šapka lies to the west of Tetovo a full thousand metres above the town. In days gone by it was the most successful ski resort in Macedonia, but now its location in the heart of the predominantly Albanian region of the country has caused many non-Albanians to shun the resort. During the conflict of 2001 mines were laid along strategic routes into Kosovo, and although these have now all been cleared by de-mining teams, the fear that a few may remain still lingers in the minds of those determined not to return to the area. This and the continued closure of the cable car from Tetovo town centre to Popova Šapka has meant that local economic renewal has been slow.

Nevertheless, the road to Popova Šapka is well paved if long and zigzaggy and the snow at the top is well worth the drive, although parking remains at a premium. Even if you don't ski or snow-shoe the views from the drive of the Vardar Valley are outstanding.

In the summer the Šar mountains offer a host of **hiking** trails for which a 1:60,000 map can be bought in bookshops such as Tabernakul on Dimitri Čupovski street in Skopje. The range has a number of **lakes**, such as Golemo Ezero, Belo Ezero, Bogovinsko Ezero, and Crno Ezero, and there are also **rock climbing** sections at Crnen Kamen, Kobilica, and below Mount Plat.

For most though the attraction is to reach the top of Tito's summit at 2,747m. The superfit can achieve this in a day, with an early-start drive up to Popova Šapka or Dolna Lešnica. But for those who wish to take a more relaxed route and enjoy sunrise and sunset over the mountains there are several **mountain huts** which offer basic accomodation. On the edge of Popova Šapka is mountain hut **Smreka** (100 beds; tel: 044 361 101; or contact Duško Boskovski on 02 322 5958). Further up the mountain at 1,750m is mountain hut **Jelak** (55 beds; tel: 044 361 101; or contact Zoran Kostadinov on 02 308 6235).

MAVROVO NATIONAL PARK

Ten kilometres outside the sleepy town of Gostivar on the road south is the turn-off to Mavrovo National Park and lake. The park itself extends over the Bistra plateau across the Radika Valley and all the way up to the Dešat mountain range which forms the border with Albania. In the little town of Mavrovo there are a number of places to stay and the town makes a good base for hiking, skiing, water sports or simply just a quiet getaway.

Where to stay and eat

By far the most luxurious place to stay is the **Hotel Bistra** (42 rooms; tel: 042 489 027/219; fax: 042 489 002; email: bistra@bistra.com; web: www.bistra.com). This hotel at the end of town on the hill overlooking the lake is a true ski resort hotel, with spacious lounges and reception areas, welcoming open hearth fire, good restaurant and bar, fitness centre, pool and conferencing facilities. All the rooms are en suite with air conditioning and TV. They also have overflow acommodation down by the lake for the same price, but it is not nearly as luxurious even though you get to use all the facilities of the main hotel. All prices are per person: standard double €65, single €95; de luxe double €75, single €105; de luxe with jacuzzi bath double €95, single €130.

The Hotel Bistra also runs the **Hotel Ski Skola** (same contact details as for the Bistra) which offers access to the Bistra facilities and is located right at the bottom of the ski lift. All prices are per person and include breakfast: standard double €55, single €85; de luxe with jacuzzi bath double €85, single €115.

Hotel Srna (62 beds; tel: 042 388 083) is very good value for money. All rooms have newly refurbished bathrooms, TV and central heating. All rooms are €20 per person.

The village of Galičnik offers the **Hotel Neda** (25 rooms; tel: 070 596 114) during the summer from July 1 to October 1. Rooms are basic with no TV or air conditioning, and aside from four rooms which are en suite, bathroom facilities are on the corridor. Price per person is €10, and €15 for the en-suite rooms.

Camping is also available in Mavrovo town campsite, and many people camp almost anywhere in the surrounding hills.

Mavrovo does not yet offer a wide range of places to eat, and for the price you are best off eating at the Bistra for atmosphere and quality. For those determined

Left Grounds of the Šarena (Motley) Mosque, Tetovo (TE)

Below Wall detail of Šarena (Motley) Mosque, Tetovo (TE)

Above Roman aqueduct, near Skopje (TE)
Right Ohrid Museum (TE)
Below Elegant period house, Ohrid (LM)

to try something really local, the village of Trnica on the River Mavrovo just before it joins the Radika offers **sour cheese and ground corn** as a speciality, allegedly the best in the region. The modest restaurant is nothing to write home about nor is the food.

Activities in the park

Mavrovo is a small but popular local **ski** resort, offering black, blue and green runs accessible by chair lift. A day ticket to ski in the park is a mere 650MKD, a week ticket is 3,200MKD and a season ticket is 12,500MKD. **Hunting** trips can be arranged through the Hotel Bistra, which also sells **fishing** permits. Fishing on the lake is from February 1 to October 30, and on the River Radika it is from January 15 to October 30.

There are many **hiking** trails throughout the park although they are not always well marked, and for **mountaineering** enthusiasts Mount Korab beckons alluringly above the lake. Due to the lack of good hiking maps of the area it would be best to take a guide with you on such trips (see *Chapter 4*). As Mount Korab is on the border with Albania, it is out of bounds except for once a year when Mountaineering Club Korab arranges the annual climb on the weekend closest to Independence Day (September 8). It is a big event escorted by the Army of the Republic of Macedonia (ARM) and many enthusiasts go for the day out even if they don't make it to the top. To find out more phone Korab's English-speaking secretary, Slobodan, on 071 564 086, or email contact@korab.org.mk.

Places to visit

The most famous village in Mavrovo National Park is undoubtedly **Galičnik**. In this cliffside Vlach village, tradition goes that the travelling traders of the village would return once a year in July in order to marry their sweetheart. Now a national festival, couples must apply in advance for the limited number of weddings on the mid-July weekend. The village is accessible by road only from Mavrovo town (15km) over the Bistra plateau, or by foot from Janče. The hike from Janče takes almost two hours and gives spectacular views of the Mount Korab and the Radika Valley. Once the asphalt road ends in the village, head left along the 4WD track that curves around the mountain. After about 45 minutes by foot the 4WD track turns right and is blocked off, whilst the footpath heads left. After another five minutes there is a water fountain. The path is mostly shaded and levels out at Markovi Nogi, a small stone site with a foot-size depression in the stone, from where King Marko is alleged at the end of the 14th century to have flown to the other side of the valley. From here it is a few more minutes until you round the corner to view the village.

Other old Vlach villages worth visiting in the area are **Gari**, home of the famous iconostasis woodcarvers the Filipovski brothers; **Lazaropole**, a hunting village with a small ski lift; and **Tresonče**. All these villages are increasingly abandoned and with this the once-rich architecture of the Vlach inhabitants is slowly being lost. Gari and Tresonče are accessible only by 4WD or a 10km hike along the beautiful River Mala in the case of Tresonče.

To get to all of these three villages turn off the Debar–Mavrovo road at the southern entrance to the park. Less than 2km on this road on the left-hand side watch out for the 600-year-old **Deer Leap Bridge**. Legend has it that the bridge was built by the local *bey* (Ottoman lord) during the 14th century to commemorate the gallant death of a deer which he and his army had been hunting. Badly wounded, nevertheless the deer continued to elude the *bey* and his army, until it reached the Garska River. The deer leapt over the river but died on the other side. To commemorate the deer's bravery, the *bey* ordered a bridge to be built in the likeness of the deer's last leap.

DEBAR

The road past Mavrovo Lake through the Mavrovo National Park snakes its way along the River Radika to the town of Debar (Diber in Albanian and also seen in older writings on the town as Dibri or Dibra). It is a fairly small town of some 1,300 inhabitants, tucked away in the crook of the Black Drim and Radika rivers. Although it lies in Macedonia and is only 137km from Skopje and 67km from Ohrid, its traditional cultural and economic orientation has been towards towns further afield in Albania. As a result of today's more open borders with Albania, town life in Debar is reviving again, but the town is still in need of significant repair and rejuvenation. There is not much of note in the town itself, but it has a rich strategic history and lies in magnificent countyryside. This is an area well worth exploring for the intrepid and is sure to be developed in time.

History of Debar

The earliest recording of Debar is under the name 'Deborus' on a map drawn by the Greek astronomer and cartographer Ptolomy in the 2nd century. After Tsar Samoil was defeated in 1044 (see box on page 9) by the Byzantine Emperor Vasilius II, Debar was administered under the Bishopric of Bitola. In the latter half of the 14th century Debar was ruled by the Albanian Kastrioti clan, but fell under the rule of the Ottoman Empire in 1423 when the local Albanian ruler Gjon Kastrioti died shortly after his four children were taken hostage. His son, Georgj Kastrioti Skenderbey survived to take back his father's land and unite all of Albania in 1444. A larger than life statue of Skenderbey adorns the central square in Debar, showing the fondness which the locals have for his cause (see box, page 186).

Only a few years later in 1449, Debar was overrun once again by the Turks, and became known as Dibri or Debra in Turkish. The city constantly rebelled against Turkish rule, however, not least because of the wealth of the many Turkish *bey* and *aga* who lived there off local taxes and the fat of the land. But Turkish rule also bought trade to Debar and the city centre grew and became known for its crafts industry. Much of the architecture from that period still survives and if you can get a look into some of the older houses you will still find the distinctive Turkish woodcarved *dolapi* (wardrobes), *minderliki* (built in benches) intricate ceilings and doors as well as *cardaci* (enclosed porches on the second floor).

During the Balkan wars of 1912–13 Debar was taken back by the Albanians, but was then handed over to the Kingdom of Serbs, Croats and Slovenes as a reward for helping the Allies during World War I. Thereafter many Serbs and Montenegrins were encouraged to settle in Debar, a common tactic to ensure that newly acquired land became more integrated with the motherland.

During World War II Debar was again fiercely fought over by various partisan groups and their Great Power backers (see box, page 185) but in the end the Federal Republic of Yugoslavia won out, and Debar became part of the Socialist Republic of Macedonia in Federal Yugoslavia. Socialist Yugoslavia helped to develop the economy of the regions by building hydro-electric dams (Debar and Globočica Lakes), local mines and quarries and developing tourism.

Sadly, the transition to an independent Macedonia has not helped Debar's economy in the same way the transition to communism did initially (not that

BRITISH OPERATIVES IN DEBAR

By 1943 the Axis advance into the Balkans threatened Macedonia. Albania was already held by the fascist Italian powers and the Allies were concerned that without help from special forces, the Macedonian region would also fall into fascist hands. As a result the British Special Operations Executive (SOE), a secret military branch set up by the British government in the forties to help defeat the enemy through sabotage and subversion, parachuted operatives into the Debar region. Their mission was to liaise between anti-Axis elements of the local resistance and the Allied forces in order to advise and see how best to help the resistance.

Major Richard Riddell, Captain Anthony Simcox, Flight Lieutenant Andy Hands and Lieutenant Reginald Hibbert were four such British SOE officers. They had been given only a few weeks' notice of their impending insertion into Debar and barely received enough language training or in-depth political background briefings, not least because their mission was to aid the resistance and not report on political developments.

And the political situation there was complicated. Albania had divided into two main political factions, the pro-fascists of the puppet government under King Zog (who was living in London at the time) and the republicans, and the anti-fascist resistance of the National Liberation Movement (LNC) headed by Enver Hoxha. To complicate this otherwise clear division there were various tribal chieftains in the hills around the Debar region who were prepared to go with either party depending on who would give them the most autonomy. And then there was the Communist Party of Albania (CPA), an offshoot of the Communist Party of Yugoslavia (CPY), which had joint control with the LNC over the Albanian National Liberation Army (ANLA) otherwise known as the Partisans. In addition, having lost the Debar, Gostivar and Tetovo regions to Royalist Yugoslavia after the Great War, many Albanians were wary of the ANLA and their political masters the CPA and LNC for their close links to the CPY. It was difficult to know in the end who would help whom.

By early 1944 Debar was firmly in the hands of the Germans and it was impossible to drop supplies into Albanian territory to help any potential pockets of resistance. Nevertheless in July 1944, Mehmet Shehu, commander of the 1st Brigade of the ANLA, now holed up north of Peshkopia in the foothills of Mount Korab, decided to march 1st Brigade into Macedonia in order to try to regain Debar from the east. The British SOE officers went with him. In four days the brigade marched over Mount Korab, down to the Gostivar-Dibra road, then up to the Bistra plateau above Mavrovo and back down to the Dibra-Kiševo road, possibly close by Tresonče, Lazaropole and Gari. Finally, marching up again towards Struga and Ohrid, the British officers heard of a supply-drop base for the Macedonia partisans only four hours' march away from their position. They convinced HQ Balkan Airforce to drop 'Albanian' supplies into Macedonia from where they could reinforce the ANLA with ammunition, arms and equipment. With additional help from the Royal Air Force, Debar was finally brought back into the hands of the Allies on August 30 1944.

For a lengthier account of this operation read Sir Reginald Hibbert's piece in *The New Macedonian Question* edited by James Pettifer (see *Further Information*, page 233).

much of former Yugoslavia has benefited from socialist over-centralisation and the collapse of the Yugoslav dinar). Debar has seen a drop in its population from 15,000 in its heyday at the end of the 19th century to a mere 10,000 today. Many non-ethnic Albanians left the town after the independence of Macedonia, and this trend was exacerbated by the conflict of 2001. Such high emigration has further dampened the town's chances of economic revival.

Where to stay and eat

Whatever was developed for tourism in Debar on the accommodation and eating front, it is not there now. Five kilometres out of town is the scenic hotel at **Banjište Spa** (75 rooms) tel: 046 831 092/832 680. Rooms at present are basic, with some converted to en suite with a TV, but as yet no air conditioning. The hotel side of the spa is being privatised but it will take some time for the hotel to see the benefits of this. Here they will give you full board and entry into the spa (see page 188 for futher details on the spa itself) for €20.

Even more basic at 250MKD (€3.50) per night are the dormitory beds at the tranquil **Monastery of St Jovan Bigorski** (35 beds; tel: 042 478 675). See page 189 for more on the monastery.

A place to eat offering a wonderful scenic view is **Restorant Cami** (tel: 046 833 721 or 070 241 205). The turn-off to the restaurant is exactly 3km southwest of town immediately after the dam. The food is average Macedonian, but the atmosphere is pleasant.

GJERGJ KASTRIOTI (SKENDERBEY)

Gjergj Kastrioti is known as the greatest hero of the Albanians for freeing and uniting all Albanians against the Turks in 1444.

Born in Kruja, Albania, to the Lord of Middle Albania, Gjon Kastrioti, Gjergj was one of Gjon's four sons who were kept hostage by the Turks in return for loyalty from the Albanian lord. When Gjon died, the Turks poisoned the four sons, but Gjergj managed to survive. He went on to convert to Islam and attend military school. He so excelled in swordsmanship and other military skills that he earned himself the title of Iskander Bey, meaning Lord Alexander. He then successfully led several Ottoman campaigns in Europe and Asia Minor, and was appointed General and then Governor General of several provinces in Middle Albania.

But Gjergj missed his homeland, and in 1443, after being defeated by the Hungarians at Niš in Serbia, he deserted the Ottoman army and went back to recapture his home town of Kruja. On raising the Albanian flag, red with a double-headed black eagle, the flag that remains today, Gjergj claimed, 'I have not brought you freedom, I have found it here among you.' Less than a year later, having reconverted to Christianity, he united the Albanian princes against the Turks at the Assembly of Alesio (Lezha in Albanian) with an army of a mere 20,000. He won 25 out of his 28 battles against the Turks and received a lot of aid from the Italian princes and popes across the Adriatic for staving off the Turkish assault from Catholic western Europe for 25 years.

In 1468 Gjergj died of fever, but his army kept the Turks out of Albania for another 12 years. Debar was retaken in 1449, and so only enjoyed five years of freedom under Skenderbey.

ST GEORGE THE VICTORIOUS

Sveti Gjorgj Pobednoset, or St George the Victorious in English, is indeed the same patron saint of England who slayed the dragon from his gallant white horse in order to save the princess. St George is a legend in many countries and it is quite astounding that his benevolence should reach as far as the Russian, Greek and Macedonian Orthodox Churches as well as the Church of England and many other churches around the world.

George was born in AD280 in Cappadociea, now in modern-day Turkey. He joined the Roman Cavalry at the age of 17 and rose to become a great swordsman and favourite of the then Roman emperor, Diocletian. George had converted to Christianity whilst Diocletian was a firm believer in the pagan traditions. Eventually this rift in their beliefs brought George to his death. After doing his best to save Christians who had been sentenced to death by Diocletian, George was cast in prison to be tortured until he renounced his belief in Christ. Despite extreme forms of torture he did not renounce his faith and finally he was beheaded on April 23 AD303 in Nicomedia near Lydda, Palestine.

He became the patron saint of the little church in Debar because that church contains the only replica of St George's original icon that stands in the Zograf Monastery at Mount Athos in Greece. When the original icon appeared miraculously in the Zograf monastery shortly after it was built, the local monks claimed that it had been sent from Lydda by St George himself. The local bishop did not believe in the veracity of this story and so touched the icon to check for telltale signs of fresh paint. As soon as he touched the nose of the icon his finger stuck fast and eventually it had to be chopped off when all other efforts at removal failed. It is claimed that the finger remains stuck to the original icon and a bloody digit represents this on the replica icon at St George's church in Debar.

The frescos in the church at Debar reveal the life and times of St George, including his many miracles. Depictions of the terrible Emperor Diocletian show him wearing a Turkish turban, indicating the locals' views of the Turks at the time.

Many of the nuns at the nunnery speak English and will be able to tell you much more of the history of the church and the frescos if you have time.

What to see

Debar is sorely missing a small museum which could tell the history of this strategically important town and its various rulers. There are two orthodox churches, whose priests can tell you a lot about the town, however, if you want to take the time. As you come to the centre of town from the Skopje road you will be faced by a larger-than-life size statue of **Skenderbey** (see box, also written as Skenderbeu, Skenderbeg, and not to be confused with the Skenderbeg fascist troops of World War II). This is the town's main street and continues on to Banjište skirting the edge of the old town of Upper Debar.

Just before you exit Debar on the Skopje road is the **Nunnery of St Gjorgj Pobedonoset** (see box, page 187). The nunnery was completed in 2001 and is dedicated to the church of the same name. The grounds of the nunnery are small, but very well-kept and hang on the edge of the cliffs of Lake Debar. If the main vehicle gate is closed, enter through the house door a little further down the nunnery outer wall. The effect of entering the door on a sunny evening accompanied by the ding-a-ling-ling of the door bell is like being transported to another world or a secret garden. The church itself is one of the best preserved in Macedonia, with all its 19th-century frescos intact, giving it a much richer feeling than many of the churches in Macedonia which are obviously in great need of repair. Although this church dates back to only 1835, it is built on the foundations of a 16th-century church which was later destroyed by the Arnaut invasion. The 16th-century church had in turn been built on the grounds of the 11th-century castle of St George.

Lake Debar, spread out magnificently below the town of Debar, is a 22km artificial lake built in 1964 as a means of producing hydro-electricity. It's a popular lake for fishing and swimming although it is little visited outside the local area. At the southern end of the lake is the Globočica Power Station which also serves Globočica Lake further upstream towards Struga. At the northern end of the lake, where the Radika River enters, is Kosovrasti spa. This is also a favourite fishing spot for the locals, as the lake fish come up to the mouth of the Radika to feed. At the time of writing it's the largest artificial lake in Macedonia (of which there are ten) and at its deepest point the lake is just less than 100m deep. The reservoir at Lake Treška, which is still being filled, should surpass the Debar Lake by 8km when it has been fully flooded.

Outside Debar

Dolni Kosovrasti hot springs

These hotsprings like all the others in Macedonia are indoors. There are separate baths for men and for women (no mixed bathing) and each bath is about 3x4m. One hour in the bath will cost you a mere 10MKD. The baths are open every day 08.00–21.30. Sunday evenings tend to be pretty busy. Banjište hot springs (see below) is a better experience.

To get there turn off the Debar Gostivar road at the northern end of Lake Debar, and cross the bridge back over the Radika River. Follow the dirt track on the left and over the small hill for 200m back towards the lake. Over the hill is the hot springs, now inside a concrete one-storey building. Next to it is a ramshackle old Turkish house which used to cater for the hot springs, but has long since fallen into disrepair. There is a small outdoor pool available occasionally.

Gorni Kosovrasti village

If you follow the tarmacked road straight up the side of the mountain for 20 minutes (two hours by foot), you'll come to the ethnic Albanian village of Gorni Kosovrasti. There's not much here except excellent views of the valley floor, the terraced fields on the way up and some fascinating wooden houses and barns. You'll get a real taste of mountain village life here, with cattle and goats wandering around in and out of houses and stables, and the local herdsman riding mules and donkeys. There is a small mosque in the village.

Banjište hot springs

Banjište, 5km outside Debar, close to the Albanian border (so close that your mobile phone is more likely to pick up an Albanian signal than a Macedonian one) lies in the foothills of the Gole Krčin Mountain (2,341m). As you approach the village you can see the run-off from the hot spring tumbling down the ditch on the side of the road, and where it burbles over the hill the water minerals have formed deposits of calcium, lime and sulphur. The smell of sulphur is strong.

The springs themselves, of which there are three (Nova Kaptaža, Goren and Dolen) are quite well kept compared to a lot of other hot spring facilities in Macedonia, although the paint is still falling off the walls and the experience is a far cry from anything you will find in Switzerland or Colorado. But the baths themselves (separated for men and women) are nicely sunlit, and the small lawn area outside the entrance to the baths is a pleasant place to sip a coffee and take in the magnificent view of the surrounding mountains.

The baths are open 07.00–21.00 every day, and cost a mere 30MKD to enter. Until 15.00 every day the baths are reserved for medicinal bathing and relaxing, but after 15.00 the spring turns into the local bath house, and the local community turns up *en masse* to scrub down with soap and shampoo and washcloths. This makes for a very convivial atmosphere, and the front lawn is filled with ethnic Albanian women in their scarves and long dresses chatting away with friends and neighbours.

The Monastery of Sveti Jovan Bigorski (St John the Baptist)

This is a fully working monastery. It was first established in 1020 when the miraculous icon of St John the Baptist (also know as St John the Forerunner) first appeared at the spot where the church now stands. The present-day structures of the church and the surrounding monastery were built, however, in the 18th and 19th centuries. The church closely resembles those of Mount Athos in Greece, characterised by two octagonal domes, the smaller of the two near the main entrance, and the larger residing over the area of worship.

In its day this church's influence stretched over a large part of the region and into present-day Albania as far as Elbasan. Today the church is renowned for containing the final one of only four iconostases carved by the famous Makarije Frčkovski from Galičnik and the Filipovski brothers from Gari (two are in the monastery at Lesnovo – see page 207 – and the Church of the Holy Saviour in Skopje, the third in a church in Krušero was burnt down after the Ilinden Uprising of 1903). The iconostasis has over 500 humans and over 200 animals carved into it depicting scenes from the Old and New Testaments, and also includes a representation of the woodcarvers themselves. Many of the people depicted in the iconostasis are wearing the traditional 19th-century Macedonian costumes despite the fact that the scenes herald an era many centuries earlier. The bishop's and prior's chairs are also carved by the Filipovski brothers and Frčkovski.

The chest of relics in the church contains a fragment of bone purporting to be part of the right humerus of St John, as well as bone fragments of the bodies of other saints. They are apparently preserved by their holy nature. The remainder of St John's forearm lies in the Cetinje Monastery in Montenegro.

Pine marten

10 The Northeast

The northeast of Macedonia is little visited, although it also contains some great scenery, its fair share of churches and monasteries, hot springs and an **Aneolithic observatory** near Kokino. The region's mountains rarely reach above 2,000m except in the Osogovski mountain range, which reaches 2,252m at the border with Bulgaria. But the valleys boast rolling hills and rich paddy fields, and are the wheat basket of Macedonia.

The main river dividing the region is the Bregalnica. Roughly running its course was the ancient road of the Diagonal Way joining Heraclea (near Bitola) with the valley of the River Vardar at Stobi to the valley of the River Struma near Pautalija (now Kustendil in Bulgaria). Another ancient road through the region was the Serres road, joining Ovče Pole in the north to Serres (now in Greece) via Štip, Radoviš and Strumica. Both roads crossed at Štip, making it an important trading town in times of old. Although there are fewer Roman ruins in the north of Macedonia compared to the south, a **Roman amphitheatre** was unearthed near Klečevce in August 2003, adding to the list of important Roman ruins already found in the region.

The two most visited sites in this part of the country are the **Monastery of Sveti Joakim Osogovski** outside Kriva Palanka, and the region of **Berovo** for its lake setting and forest hiking in the cool mountains. In the vicinity of the extinct volcanic crater of **Kratovo**, there are interesting rock formations at **Kuklica**, and caves near the **Monastery of Gavril Lesnovski**.

ŠTIP

Today Štip is still seen as the capital of the east of Macedonia, but it is a relatively sleepy town, worth a stop on the way to places further east, but probably not worth an overnight stay unless you are coming for the international music festival *Makfest* in October. The town is associated with two older names, that of Astibo during the Kingdom of Macedonia, and Stipion during the early Byzantine era. In the 14th century, prior to the Ottoman Empire taking over the whole of Macedonia, five important churches were built in and around the town, the Church of St Archangel Michael, the Church of St Jovan, the Church of St Nikola, the Church of St Spas, and the Church of St Vlasie. In 1689 large parts of the town were burnt down during the Karpoš Uprising.

Like many Macedonian towns, Štip has its claims to its own crucial role in forming a consciousness of independence in the minds of Macedonians and in so doing contributing to the struggle for that independence. Three hundred years after the town was set alight during the Karpoš Uprising, the founders of the next

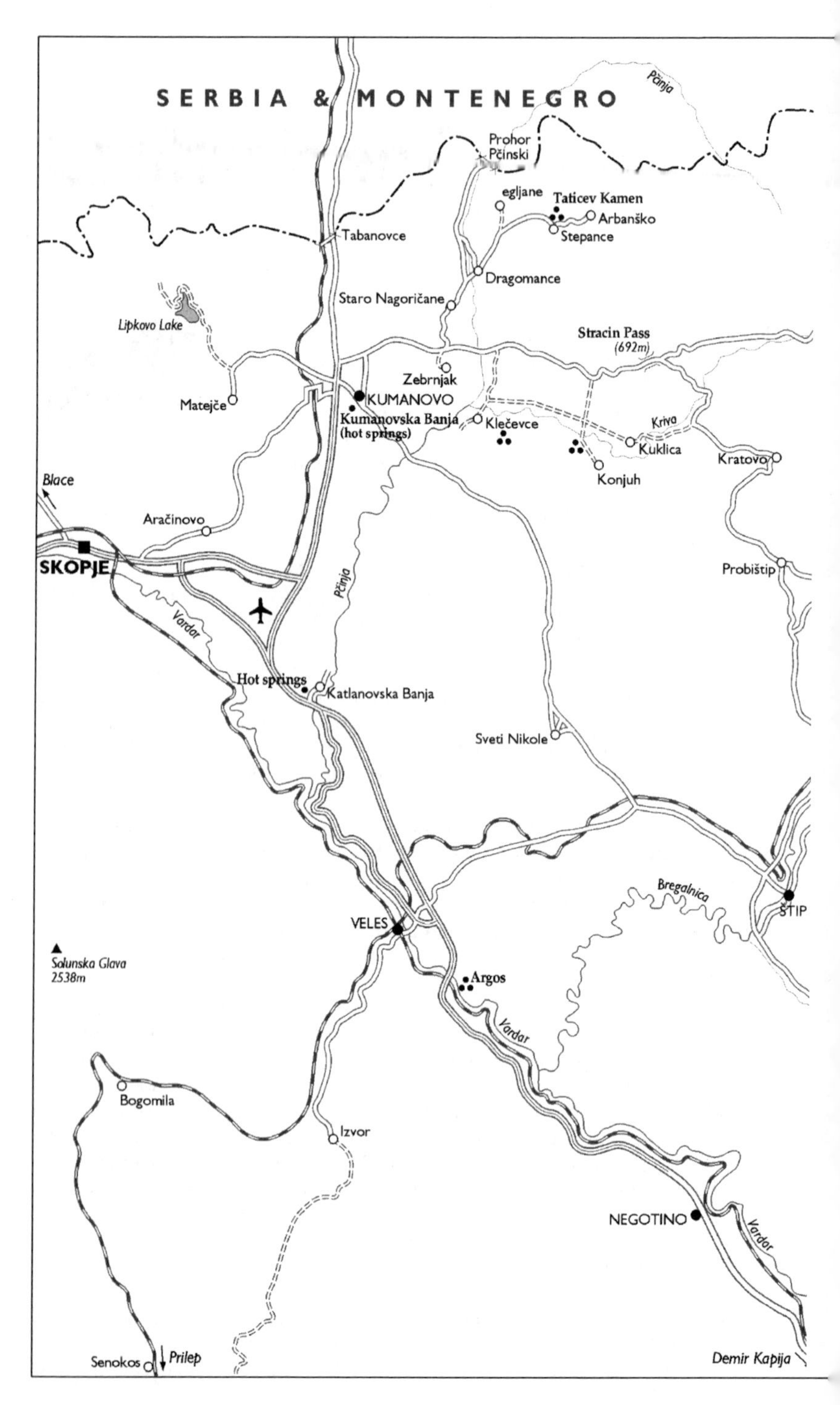
SERBIA & MONTENEGRO
Pčinja
Prohor Pčinski
egljane
Taticev Kamen
Arbanško
Stepance
Tabanovce
Dragomance
Staro Nagoričane
Lipkovo Lake
Stracin Pass
(692m)
Zebrnjak
Matejče
KUMANOVO
Kumanovska Banja
(hot springs)
Klečevce
Kriva
Kuklica
Kratovo
Konjuh
Blace
Aračinovo
SKOPJE
Probištip
Pčinja
Vardar
Hot springs
Katlanovska Banja
Sveti Nikole
Bregalnica
ŠTIP
VELES
Solunska Glava
2538m
Argos
Vardar
Bogomila
Izvor
NEGOTINO
Vardar
Senokos
Prilep
Demir Kapija

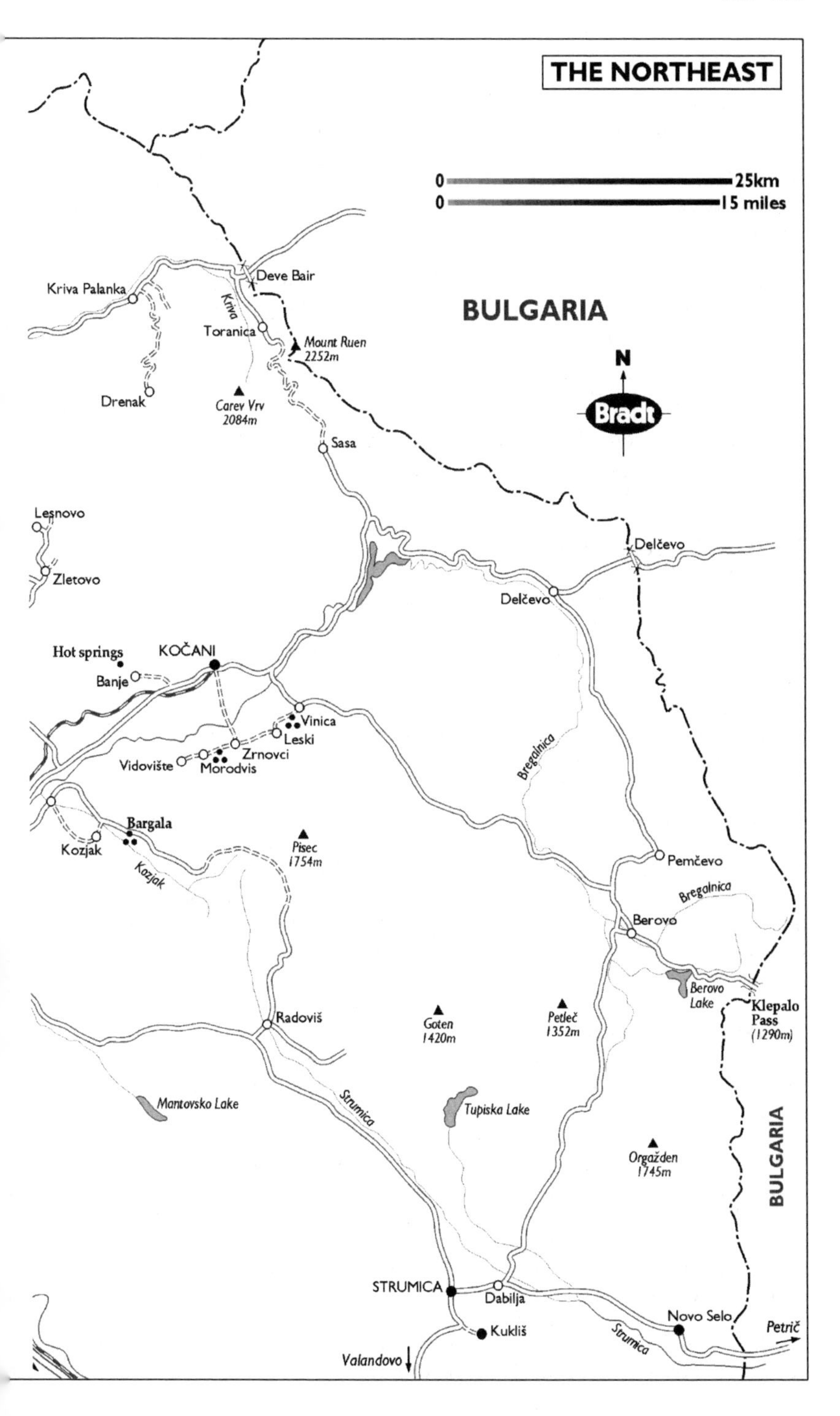
THE NORTHEAST
0 25km
0 15 miles
BULGARIA
N
Bradt
Deve Bair
Kriva Palanka
Kriva
Toranica
Mount Ruen 2252m
Drenak
Carev Vrv 2084m
Sasa
Lesnovo
Zletovo
Delčevo
Delčevo
Hot springs
KOČANI
Banje
Vinica
Leski
Zrnovci
Vidovište
Morodvis
Bregalnica
Bargala
Kozjak
Kozjak
Pisec 1754m
Pemčevo
Bregalnica
Berovo
Berovo Lake
Klepalo Pass (1290m)
Radoviš
Goten 1420m
Petleč 1352m
Mantovsko Lake
Strumica
Tupiska Lake
Orgažden 1745m
BULGARIA
STRUMICA
Dabilja
Kukliš
Novo Selo
Petrič
Strumica
Valandovo

big uprising for Macedonian independence, Goce Delčev and Dame Gruev, both taught at schools in Štip.

The stream running through the centre of Štip brings running torrents in the spring when the snow melts off the Plaškovica Mountains, but by May it is practically dry and turns into a welcome bed of green river plants. The stream is built up on either side to prevent the spring torrents flooding the town, and a pleasant walkway runs alongside. On the south side of the stream is the old cobbled road which forms part of the ancient road joining the valleys of the the rivers Vardar and Struma.

The centre is where Kiril and Metodi Street join Vančo Prke Street. Legend has it that the saints Cyril and Methodius travelled along the River Bregalnica through Štip on their way to Moravia (now in the Czech Republic) in order to preach the gospel to the locals in their mother tongue. For this purpose Cyril invented the Cyrillic alpahabet.

There are regular buses to Štip from skopje and the surrounding towns and two trains a day from Skopje. The train station (tel: 032 392 904) is about 1km out of town on the other side of the River Bregalnica, while the bus station (tel: 032 392 377) is closer to the centre.

Where to stay and eat

Hotel Oaza (72 rooms) Tel: 032 390 899 or 032 394 899. In the centre of town, this establishment is well located and recently completely refurbished. Formerly called the Astibo, it still had the old sign outside at time of writing as well as the new sign for Oaza. All rooms have air conditioning, minibar, TV, hairdryer and telephone. Singles are €20 per night, doubles €30 and twin rooms €40.

Hotel Izgref (7 rooms) Tel: 032 394 919 or 032 394 918. Basic en-suite rooms with TV, phone and air conditioning. Located 1km outside the centre near the railway station, it is also close to the Olympic-sized outdoor pool and has its own restaurant. Twin rooms are €20 per night.

Cafés and restaurants can be found in the centre of town, although much more than *skara* is difficult to find. The **Square Pub** is the main hang-out, but offers no food. **King Sandwich** over the road on Kiril i Metodi offers the standard Macedonian one-type-fits-all sandwich, or the **Biser** *skara* house on Bančo Prke offers something a little more substantial. **Mal Odmor** (tel: 032 380 187) restaurant outside town, owned by the Oaza hotel, has patio seating, an outdoor grill and serves traditional Macedonian food.

What to see and do

Isar fortress on top of the prominent hill overlooking Štip is little more than ruins now. However, it does afford an excellent view of the modern-day town and of the inappropriately named Novo Selo (meaning 'new village' of which there are literally hundreds so named in Macedonia), which is now in fact older than most of the modern-day town of Štip, but in its day was the new settlement in the shadow of Isar. There is ongoing work to restore some of the fortress ruins and to build a stone path up to the fortress but, unless significant restoration is carried out, one can only stand on the top of the hill, imagine the grandeur of the fortress and gaze in awe at the magnificent view that the hill still commands of the surrounding countryside.

To drive there take the obvious road up the hill side as soon as you have passed over the flyover leading from the main highway into town. This road will lead you past the little **Church of St Michael Archangel** built in 1332. It is set in

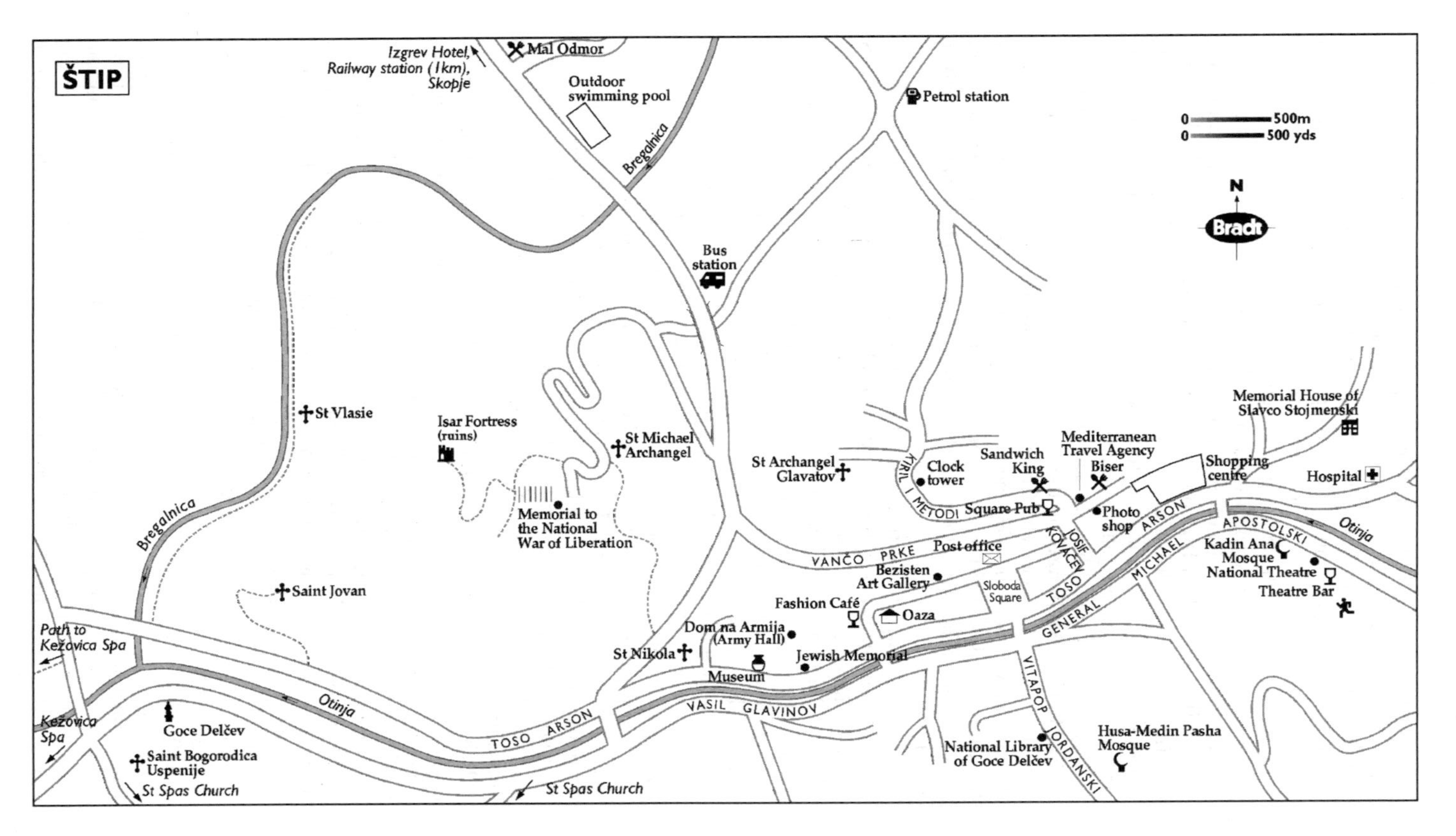
ŠTIP
Izgrev Hotel, Railway station (1km), Skopje
Mal Odmor
Outdoor swimming pool
Bregalnica
Petrol station
0 500m
0 500 yds
N
Bradt
Bus station
St Vlasie
Isar Fortress (ruins)
St Michael Archangel
Memorial to the National War of Liberation
Bregalnica
Saint Jovan
St Archangel Glavatov
Clock tower
KIRIL I METODI
Sandwich King
Square Pub
Mediterranean Travel Agency
Biser
Photo shop
Shopping centre
Memorial House of Slavco Stojmenski
Hospital
Otinja
APOSTOLSKI
ARSON
Kadin Ana Mosque
National Theatre
Theatre Bar
VANČO PRKE
Post office
JOSIF KOVAČEV
Bezisten Art Gallery
Sloboda Square
TOSO
MICHAEL
GENERAL
Fashion Café
Oaza
Dom na Armija (Army Hall)
St Nikola
Jewish Memorial
Museum
Path to Kežovica Spa
Otinja
TOSO ARSON
VASIL GLAVINOV
VITAPOP JORDANSKI
Husa-Medin Pasha Mosque
National Library of Goce Delčev
Kežovica Spa
Goce Delčev
Saint Bogorodica Uspenije
St Spas Church
St Spas Church

small but beautiful grounds, but is rarely open to the public. The path then leads on to the bottom of the National War of Liberation memorial site. There is limited parking here if you come by car, and only just enough space to turn and avoid the drinking fountain. Take the steps up to the war memorial and then go on to the fortress remains. You'll get a great mobile phone signal up there, but sadly the two mobile phone towers also detract from the enchantment of the site.

On each of the four sides of Isar is a church built during the Middle Ages to help protect the fortress. To the south at the bottom of the hill is the **Church of Saint Nikola**, rebuilt in 1876 on the site of an older church dating back to 1341. It is the only church that is open every day, and if you ask inside, one of the priests should be able to take you to the other churches. The upper floor of the church has an extensive gallery of icons.

Opposite the church there are several sets of steps leading up past the **Church of St Michael Archangel** on the east of the fortress, which was the first of the four churches to be built. The **Church of St Vasilie**, on the northwest side of the fortress, was built in 1337, and little remains of it today. The last church, **St Jovan**, was built in 1350 on the right bank of the River Otinja. Opposite it on the left bank of the River Otinja is the **Church of the Holy Saviour (Sveti Spas)** built in 1369.

Walking along the riverbank into town from the Church of St Nikola, the next main building is the renovated **memorial house to the Arsovi brothers**, two local heroes. It was converted into the city museum in 1956 (tel: 032 392 044; fax: 032 385 369). There was no sign outside at time of writing indicating that it is the museum, as it is not ready for show yet, but you can't miss it for all the marble Roman artefacts on display outside on the lawn. If you go in and speak to the museum curator, Zoran Čitkušev, he may be able to furnish you with a bilingual Macedonian/English guidebook to the town, and if you phone in advance he can also arrange a visit to the Roman ruins at Bargala (see opposite). The museum is open Monday to Friday from 07.00 to 15.00.

Between the museum and the neighbouring Dom na Armija military club is a small memorial to the 561 **Jewish citizens** of Štip who were deported to Treblinka gas chambers in Poland on March 11 1943. Like many towns in Macedonia, Štip had a thriving Jewish community prior to the war and though the lives of these citizens are well documented, little remains to be seen of their lives now.

Behind the Oaza hotel is the **Bezisten**, the old covered market built in the mid- 17th century. It is now a modern art gallery open Tuesday, Wednesday, Thursday and Saturday 09.00–12.00 and 17.00–19.00, Friday 09.00–13.00, and Sunday 10.00–12.00. It is closed on Monday. Štip's two mosques are south of the River Otinja. The **Kadin Ana Mosque** built in the mid-19th century, is by the river next to the **national theatre** (built between 1924 and 1936). It is unclear when the older **Mosque of Pasha Husa-Meda** just off Vitapop Jordanski Hill was built. Some say as early as the 14th century, others say not until the 16th century. What is clear, however, is that it was built on the foundations of the much older church of St Ilija. Within the grounds of the mosque is the *turbeh* containing the remains of the mosque's architect.

Kežovica Spa (tel: 032 308 560) is located just off the River Bregalnica past Novo Selo. The water emerges at the L'gji spring at a temperature of 66.8°C, and is then mixed with cold water before it enters the baths. The baths themselves are separated for men and women, and are relatively pleasant and spacious. Entrance to the baths is 40MKD per person, and showers are an extra 50MKD. The baths are open 06.00–20.00 every day, except on Monday when the women's bath is closed for cleaning until 09.00, and on Friday when the men's bath opens at 09.00.

Aside from 100 beds for those booked in for physical therapy and treatment, the spa also offers 40 beds in 15 rooms to those wishing to stay overnight. Although the rooms are extremely basic and cheap at 250MKD per person per night, the spa setting alongside the River Bregalnica is very tranquil, and makes a good base for those on a shoestring budget to explore other places in the region. The spa also offers limited buffet facilities, but you are better off eating in town. It's a 3km walk from the spa along the river through Novo Selo to the centre of Štip.

Remains of the ancient city of Bargala can be found in the foothills of Plackovica mountains near the village of Goren Kozjak, 18km northeast of Štip. The city dates back to the 4th century BC and continued to thrive into the 6th century AD before being overrun by the Avars. During its heyday the city was enclosed in fortified walls some 300m by 150m, whose main entrance in the northwest wall can still be partly seen. Of the many antique and Roman structures to be discovered in the city, the most impressive are those of the antique bath house, which had a number of baths of differing temperatures as well as a sauna, and also the early Christian Church of St Gjorgi.

Plačkovica mountain range offers a whole host of hiking opportunities and beautiful scenery. Take the Kozjak road from Karabinci to access the Plačkovica summit of Lisec (1,754m), Crkvište peak (1,689m), and the mountain villages of Šipkovica and Vrteška. At the village of Vrteška you can stay at the mountain hut **Vrteška** (64 beds; tel: 032 384 788, or 032 384 299). The hut warden is Marjan Ljubotenski. Beds are 200MKD per person per night.

Štip hosts a number of events and festivals throughout the year. On the **first day of spring**, Štipites walk to the top of Izar fortress, where they throw a pebble off the top of the hill and make a wish for the future. In July is the Štip **international film festival**, and in October is the **Makfest**, a music festival featuring a variety of world music. This is a popular event in Macedonia and so book a room early if you want to stay over for the festival. For more exact information on festival artists and films contact **Mediteran Travel Agency** Vančo Prke bb, 2000 Štip; tel: 032 397 001.

KOČANI

From Štip Highway 27 follows the River Bregalnica to Kočani. There is not much in the town itself as, until communist industrialisation, it had mostly been a farming settlement since the time of Aleksandar III of Macedon. Around 330BC, Aleksandar brought back rice from India, which was planted in these fertile fields. The ancient **paddy fields** are still worked today, many by hand, and they provide most of Macedonia's rice.

The more important town in the 5th and 6th centuries BC was the town of **Morodvis**, 7km almost directly south of Kočani on the south side of the River Bregalnica. The **ruins of four early Roman Christian basilicas** have been found at the site as well as almost 80 necropoli (graves). This town was probably on the ancient **Diagonal Way**, as was the neighbouring town of Vinica.

Vinica, named after its reknown in Byzantine times for wine growing, is famous for the **terracotta icons** found at the **fortress** on the hill above the town. There are none left to be seen now at the site, as they have all been moved to the National Museum of Macedonia in Skopje. Since the Bregalnica was dammed at **Kalimansko Ezero** in early communist times, Vinica has given up wine for rice and tobacco. From Vinica, the road east-southeast leads along the River Osojnica to Berovo.

To the west and east of Kočani are the usual dilapidated communist-style hot springs of **Istibanje** (7km to the east) and **Banja** (10km to the west) allegedly good for healing stomach problems.

Continuing along the River Bregalnica, Highway 27 passes the manmade Kalimansko Ezero. Then, 10km before the border crossing of Arnautski Grob (meaning 'grave of the Arnauts') into Bulgaria is the small town of **Delčevo**, named after the Macedonian revolutionary leader Goce Delčev. As a leader of the Ilinden Uprising of 1903, Goce Delčev is resoundingly honoured every year with a festival in his name on August 2, the day of the uprising. Prior to its renaming in 1950, the town had been known by the name of Carevo Selo, meaning 'Tsar's Village' and in Ottoman times it was called Sultania. If you need to stop to eat in Delčevo there is fantastic kebab house called **Buffet Cinco**, on the other side of the bridge across from the centre of town. The buffet is well located with an outside terrace from which to watch the town market on Saturday afternoon, and serves the best, most succulent *ražnič* in all of Macedonia.

Three kilometres to the southeast of Delčevo are the ruins of the Byzantine village of **Vasilevo**, which was named after the Byzantine Emperor Vasilie II. Three kilometres to the southwest on the road to Golak is the new **Monastery of St Bogorodica**. The small church has bright new frescos of all the familiar saints, but check out the new dance moves of Sts Eleuša and Ana on the right-hand side as you go in. The monastery inns are nowhere near complete at the time of writing, but even if you can't overnight there, it's a great place for a picnic as the rock formations along the stream bed are a sight unto themselves and many have been converted into covered eating areas with tables and benches.

The road to Golak leads to the **Golak Recreation Centre** (256 beds; tel: 033 411 733), and Mount Čavka at 1,536m. The views of the Delčevo Valley on the way up are superb.

Places to stay

The best places to stay are outside Kočani itself. **Motel Dončo** (10 rooms; tel: 033 294 343) is 2km outside Kočani in the village of Orizari. The hotel has an unexciting restaurant, and their very basic rooms cost 450MKD per person per night. Less than 1km on the turn-off to Vinica is the much nicer **Hotel Sliv** (30 rooms; tel: 033 360 502 or 033 362 502), with restaurant, outdoor swimming pool and plenty of greenery. Each room is en suite with a TV. A twin room with breakfast costs €30. A single without breakfast costs 600MKD. Six kilometres outside Kočani, very close to Vinica, is the **Hotel Šagal** (18 rooms; tel: 033 361 165), at the petrol station on the main road. The hotel has indoor and outdoor restaurants, and an indoor pool heated with water from underground hot springs, as well as a minuscule fitness centre and a casino. Rooms are €20 per person including breakfast. **Motel Gratče** (21 rooms; tel: 033 274 202; web: www.motelgratce.com.mk) is well worth the difficult 4km drive. 800MKD per person per night.

BEROVO

Turning south at Delčevo, following the River Bregalnica part way, the road comes to the quaint eastern village of Berovo. Unlike most villages and towns in Macedonia, this one does not hark back to Roman, medieval or Byzantine times, but first resembled something like a village only in the late 19th century, barely 150 years ago. It got its name from the Macedonian word *bere* meaning 'to gather', probably because outsiders were so surprised that anyone would gather in a place where there wasn't already a significant settlement.

Now people come here because of the outstanding beauty of the mountains and for the cool, refreshing mountain air. At almost 900m above sea level, Berevo lies in the Maleševo Valley of the upper reaches of the Bregalnica River. Sheltered by mountains, this valley records the coldest average temperatures in winter, and it is fairly cool here in the summer too, rarely getting into the high 20s. This makes it an excellent getaway from the scorching heat of Skopje in June, July and August, but bring an extra sweater for the evenings.

Where to stay

There are three choices of accommodation in the vicinity of Berovo: hunter's lodge, recreation centre or bed and breakfast.

The **Loven Dom**, or Hunters's Lodge in English (4 rooms; tel: 033 470 454), which is less than ten years old, is an excellent choice for the money. Each room is en suite, with TV and a beautiful view out to the mountains. The lodge also has its own tennis courts and restaurant serving traditional Macedonian food. To get there turn north uphill between the church in the centre of village on the cobbled road and City Pub café. Keep following the road uphill for another 2km until you reach the spacious well-kept grounds of the Hunters' Lodge with its distinctive black-and- white, almost Tudor-style house. In the summer is it often booked up with wedding parties so reserve well in advance for a weekend slot. Double room with breakfast is 1,500MKD for two, or 800MKD for a single person. Full board for a minimum of three days is 1,200MKD per person per day.

The **Recreation Centre Maleševo** (44 rooms; tel: 033 471 212, 033 471 555, or 070 206 850) is well designed for large groups of people, and beautifully situated on the edge of Lake Berovo. It is often used for group and company retreats so ask for a discount if you are more than ten people. A room for three is 1,200MKD including breakfast.

For **bed and breakfast** options in the area phone Atlantis Travel Agency in Strumica (tel: 034 346 212). Prices are around 600MKD per person per night.

What to see and do

Aside from **hiking** in the beautiful mountains, there is **skiing** in the winter from the Maleševo Recreation Centre, and **fishing** in the summer in **Lake Berovo**. The lake used to be known as Ratevo Lake, because it lies near the village of Ratevo, but now as Berovo draws more visitors it has come to be known by that village's name and the only road access to the lake is in fact from the village of Berovo. To reach the lake take the turning downhill at the entrance to Maleševo Recreation Centre. The high road continues on to the border crossing at Klepalo. The Bulgarian side has not yet reciprocated the desire to open the border and so the road on the Macedonian side simply leads to an empty border and customs building. The lake itself is completely natural, unlike many of the reservoir lakes in Macedonia, and stays cold year round as it draws its water from the surrounding mountains.

The **Monastery of St Michael the Archangel** is at the eastern edge of the village, and predates the village by less than half a century. The site was originally built in order to train teachers in Macedonian, away from the watchful eyes of their Ottoman rulers, who feared that the development of Macedonian language and literature would lead to revolt. A famous Macedonian literary figure, Joakim Kršovski, taught here. The monastery is surrounded by some inns where the nuns live and has a small informative

museum. You will need to phone ahead for the museum keeper, Dvonko, tel: 033 472 733, if you want to look inside, as it is usually shut.

Nine kilometres north of Berovo is the village of **Pehčevo**. The village started out as an **iron mining town** in Roman times and continued to produce iron-ore throughout Ottoman rule. Remains of the mine at the foot of Mount Bukovik can still be found. Hiking in the vicinity is a popular pastime and there are a number of rooms for accommodation along the River Ravna.

KUMANOVO

The third-largest town in Macedonia after Skopje and Bitola is Kumanovo with almost 70,000 inhabitants. It is not an especially historically significant town, as it lies in the upper reaches of Macedonia, which did not see much development in Roman times, and only saw a settlement of any size when the Kumani tribe settled there in the Middle Ages, hence its name Kumano, the place of the Kumani.

One incident in history that does stand out for Kumanovo is the Karpoš uprising of 1689, when Petre Vojnički-Karpoš, advancing from Kriva Palanka against the Turks, took Kumanovo and was then declared the King of Kumanovo by the Austrian Emperor Leopold I (see box, page 11). Unfortunately for Karpoš and his men, the tale ends in Skopje, where they were beheaded by the Turks and Karpoš' head was displayed for all to see on the Stone Bridge in Skopje as a deterrent to other upstarts.

More recently Kumanovo has made the news because of fighting which broke out in surrounding villages in the conflict of 2001 between National Liberation Army guerillas and the local Macedonian authorities. The border to the northwest of Kumanovo neighbours Kosovo, and Kumanovo's large Albanian population have more often looked to Priština in Kosovo for leadership, trade and cultural ties than to Skopje. In the Kosovo crisis of 1998 and 1999, thousands of Kosovar Albanian refugees fled into the Kumanovo area as well as other parts of northwestern Macedonia over Macedonia's porous border with Kosovo. Although security in the area has improved significantly since the Ohrid Framework Agreement of August 2001, this border area is still proving difficult to police, and so if you are planning any hiking in the border regions check with the British Embassy first for the latest security status. Unexploded ordnance is still possible.

Areas around Kumanovo which have seen bad tension and armed conflict include: Tanuševci (see page 177) on the border with Kosovo, where fighting here marked the beginning of the conflict of 2001; Matejče 17km to the west of Kumanovo, where the 14th-century monastery has been ransacked and reprisals inflicted on local villagers; and Sopot, less than 3km from the border crossing into Serbia north of Kumanovo, where two Polish soldiers and two civilians were killed on March 4 2003 by a land mine laid by former insurgents in an effort to destabilise the region. The investigation for the perpetrators and the court case against some of the accused is ongoing.

Getting there, around and about

There are regular buses and seven trains a day to Kumanovo, including two direct trains from Skopje. The **train** station (tel: 031 423 480) is located at the end of 11th Oktomvri, a good 2km out of town. There are plenty of **taxis** waiting at the station, and if perchance they are all out with passengers then you can call 9182 or 9197 for a taxi. The **bus** station (tel: 031 422 880) is at the northern edge of the town, just off Done Bozinov, but close to the centre.

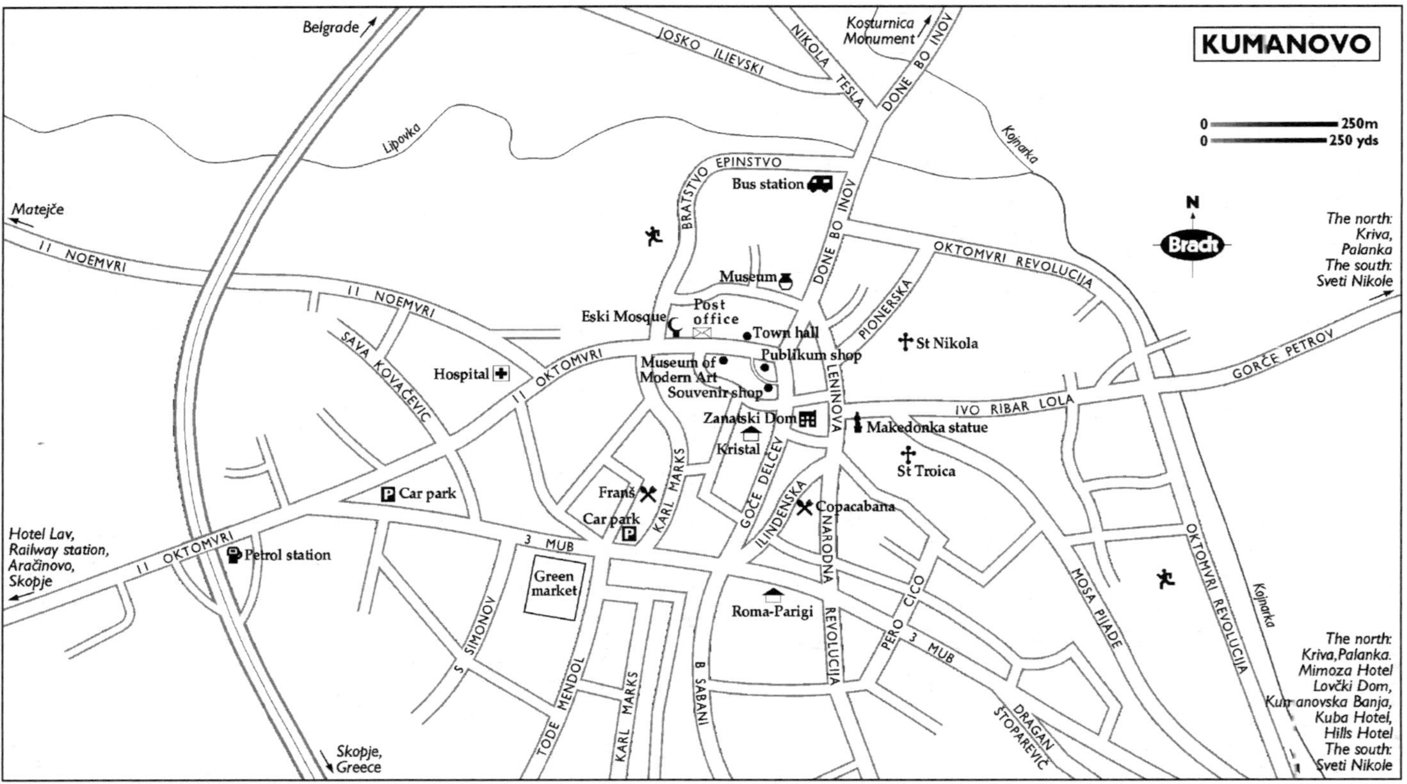

KUMANOVO
0 250m
0 250 yds
N
Bradt
Belgrade
Kosturnica Monument
JOSKO ILIEVSKI
NIKOLA TESLA
DONE BO INOV
Lipovka
Kojnarka
EPINSTVO
BRATSTVO
Bus station
Matejče
11 NOEMVRI
The north: Kriva, Palanka
The south: Sveti Nikole
OKTOMVRI REVOLUCIJA
Museum
PIONERSKA
Eski Mosque
Post office
Town hall
St Nikola
Publikum shop
Museum of Modern Art
Souvenir shop
SAVA KOVAČEVIC
Hospital
11 OKTOMVRI
LENINOVA
GORČE PETROV
IVO RIBAR LOLA
Zanatski Dom
Makedonka statue
Kristal
St Troica
Car park
Franš
KARL MARKS
GOCE DELČEV
ILINDENSKA
Copacabana
Car park
Hotel Lav, Railway station, Aračinovo, Skopje
Petrol station
3 MUB
Green market
NARODNA REVOLUCIJA
Roma-Parigi
PERO CICO
MOSA PIJADE
S SIMONOV
TODE MENDOL
B SABANI
DRAGAN ŠTOPAREVIČ
Skopje, Greece
The north: Kriva, Palanka. Mimoza Hotel Lovčki Dom, Kumanovska Banja, Kuba Hotel, Hills Hotel
The south: Sveti Nikole

Where to stay and eat

Since the conflict of 2001 and the increase in the numbers of foreigners in the Kumanovo area, a few new hotels have opened up. **Hotel Roma Parigi** (6 rooms; tel: 031 415 800), above the pizza restaurant of the same name, is on the busy III MUB Street. Centrally located, it offers a single room for €25 and doubles for €50. **Hotel Mimoza** (8 rooms; tel: 031 413 232) on the southwest edge of town is discreet, quiet and recently refurbished. Rooms include minibar, satellite TV and air conditioning. Single €30, double €45. In the same area of town but even further out is **Hotel Hills** (5 rooms; tel 031 452 536). Singles €35, twins €50. **Lovečki Dom** (tel: 031 452 773) is also at the southwest edge of town, but close to the main thoroughfare III MUB. **Hotel Lav** (Lion – tel: 031 412 999) is opposite the train station, and although a bit eighties in style, it is at least quiet and is building an outdoor swimming pool at the time of writing.

Nearby at Kumanovo Hot Springs is **Hotel Kuba** (110 beds; tel: 031 452 777). At time of writing the hotel is still housing internally displaced people (IDPs in international speak, ie: nationals of Macedonia who have been forced out of their home town by war and conflict), but hopefully they will have been able to return to their home town by 2004. Basic rooms go for 800MKD per person. **Hotel Kristal** (102 rooms; tel: 031 425 355), right in the heart of Kumanovo, was also still being used to house refugees in 2003. A single room goes for €15, and a twin for €18.

The best places to eat in town are **Copacabana** (tel: 031 422 027) at Ilindenska 5 and **Fransh** (tel: 031 428 842) on Narodna Revolucija 1, both serving good salads, pizza and Macedonian food. There are lots of cafés to choose from, especially around the Zanatski Dom and Ilindenska.

What to see and do in and around Kumanovo

There is not very much of note in the town itself, although it is a pleasant town with a bustling centre and some impressive 19th-century buildings, such as the **Zanatski Dom** and **Sokolana**. There is a small **Museum of Modern Art** opposite the town hall, and the **Museum of Kumanovo** (tel: 031 422 495) just off Done Bozinov is small, but interesting if you can read Macedonian, and if you can get the curators to let you in. They are busy documenting artefacts (as most of the museums in Macedonia seem to be) and so may turn you away rather than interrupt their work to show you around.

To the east of the centre of town are two **churches** dedicated to St Troica and to **St Nikola**. The Church of St Nikola was built in 1851 and houses icons from many other older churches in the Kumanovo region.

Outside Kumanovo, and by far the most interesting and unique find in recent years, is the **ancient observatory** of Taticev Kamen (grid 34 T EM 7862 7947) near the village of Kokino. Finally confirmed at the end of 2002, the use of the location as a primitive research station to track the sun through the year goes back almost 4,000 years. Artefacts dating back to 1815BC have been found on the site which lies at 1,000m above sea level on the flat peak of a rock cropping. Macedonian astro-physicists claim the site is equal in historical significance to the UK's Stonehenge, but you'll find no man-made stone structures here and for all intents and purposes it does just look, at best, like an interesting rock feature. The site lies about 30km outside Kumanovo. Take the Prohor Pčinski exit off the E871 (Highway 2) heading north for 7km until you get to the turning for Dragomance. Take this turning, heading northeast for another 14.6km. At the rise of a hill after Slepenče village is a small new sign for the observatory. Turn north on to the dirt road for 100m and the observatory is the obvious rock feature 300m to the west (unless it is foggy and then you won't see it at all, but if you keep heading uphill you will unmistakably get there).

Going back to the more usual Macedonian sites, to the east of Kumanovo north of Highway 2, the **Monastery of Staro Nagoričane** in the village of the same name, houses the early 14th-century **Church of St Gjorgi**, which was built in 1313 by the Serbian King Milutin on the foundations of an 11th-century church. The church's frescos are almost completely intact, but the narthex has been destroyed. The monastery is surrounded by a low stone wall and has no inns. The yard, containing a few old graveyards, is unkempt and the site is usually locked. To get the key ask the police officers in the small police station opposite the church. They will contact the church warden, 80-year-old Kostaldin, who should be able to come over with the key in a few minutes.

To get to the site, take the Prohor Pčinski exit off the E871 (Highway 2) heading north. After 100m, turn left at the T-junction and then immediately right signposted for Prohor Pčinski. Follow this road north for 2.5km, and at the top of a small hill take the new road left to the village of Staro Nagoričane (unsignposted). You will come across the monastery in a few hundred metres at the edge of the village.

Before you get to the turn-off from the E871 for Prohor Pčinski, you will make out in the middle distance to the south a large ruined building on top of a hill. It stands out for many miles like a nipple on the landscape. This modern ruin is what is left of the once six-storey Kosturnica monument of Zebrnjak, commemorating soldiers who died here fighting against the Turks in the Kumanovo battle of the First Balkan War of 1912. The monument was erected on the 25th anniversary in 1937, but blown up six years later in 1943 by the Bulgarians during their occupation of Vardar Macedonia. The 360° view from the monument across the Pčinja plain is the reason why this point was such a strategic location for occupying armies. There is no signage leading you to the monument, but you can get there by turning south off the E871 at a large white house almost 4km after the start of the E871. Turn left past the house for 1km and take the first right. This road leads straight to the monument.

Forgotten in the delta of the River Kriva near the village of Konjuh (best accessed by 4WD drive or a 6km hike) is an ancient cave village and a **Roman rotunda** from the 6th century. The place makes for an interesting half day out and, unlike Kokino observatory, there are lots of obvious man-made rooms, water holes, stairs and windows. To get there continue another 15.1km on Highway 2 (E871) beyond the exit to Prohor Pčinski to grid 34 T EM 7980 6640 where a dirt-track road heads south. At 4.8km, just after the tunnel under the yet-to-be-constructed railway, take the turning to the south across the Pčinski river. The rock formation on the left after the river is the cave settlement (grid 34 T EM 7972 6122). The rotunda is another 100m to the southwest and the old church of St George is 200m to the southeast of the settlement.

There are probably 100 more Roman ruins in this valley, which was a route linking Skupi to Kustendil. In August 2003, a **Roman amphitheatre** was unearthed near the village of Klečevce. The **Kumanovo Hotsprings**, also popular in Roman times, are near the village of Proevce, 4km southeast of Kumanovo. There is a small outdoor pool heated by thermal waters. Entry is 50MKD.

KRIVA PALANKA

Kriva Palanka is now most famous for the 12th-century **monastery dedicated to St Joakim Osogovski** 3km to the east of the town. The town is named after the river it straddles, the River Kriva, which is the Slavic translation of the name first given to the town when it was founded by the Ottomans in 1633. Then it was called Egri Dere, meaning 'Winding River'. The town was originally built as an important stronghold for the Ottomans on the road from Usküb to İstanbul, but despite its supposed impregnability, it was taken by Karpoš (later given the title of King of Kumanovo, see box page 11) during the Karpoš uprising of 1689. When Karpoš and his men were captured and beheaded six weeks later, the town returned to Ottoman rule.

Where to stay and eat

By far and away the best place to stay in the vicinity is the Big Inn at the **Monastery of St Joakim Osogovski** (100 beds; tel: 031 375 063). The monastery is well frequented and usually fully booked within a day or two of the day of stay, so book a few days in advance. Monastery life closes down after evening prayers, so phone during the day and make sure to speak to the innkeeper, Velin, as he deals with all the bookings. Sister Igoumina, who answers the phone in his frequent absence, can only defer to him on questions of bookings. You will need to register yourself at the local police station at the bottom of the hill soon after your arrival at the monastery.

There is no food available at the monastery so bring your own, but there are indoor kitchens, an outdoor grill, and a small shop that sells a few soft drinks, tea and coffee. The monastery is popular with locals as a site for Sunday breakfast before church. Macedonian music from a ghetto blaster may accompany breakfast as well as the evening meal, so don't count on your stay there always being tranquil. Often, however, due reverence to the sanctity of the courtyards is observed, and you'll also see people playing a quiet board game to watch the evening sunset by. A night in the original monks' quarters cost 250MKD for a bed in a twin room with a wood stove burner. A simple en-suite twin room in the new inn costs 500MKD for each occupant.

If you get turned away from the inn, try the **Hotel Turist** (30 rooms; tel: 031 375 209) in the town centre. Classic dilapidated socialist tourism, a shower you can't stand up in, live cockroaches and breakfast are included in the 1,000MKD per person. Definitely a rip-off and not even a TV in the room. Other hotels are

THE BROTHERS OSOGOVSKI, PČINSKI, LESNOVSKI AND RILSKI

Sketchy details going back to the 10th and 11th centuries claim that the four brothers Joakim Osogovski, Prohor Pčinski, Gavril Lesnovksi and Jovan Rilski were amongst God's most dedicated monks. In order to serve God better, they all decided to follow a hermit's life and so they went their separate ways, each ending up in the place of their namesake monastery. Today, the beautifully painted Rilski Monastery is in Bulgaria, the Pčinski Monastery is in Serbia just over the border from Kumanovo, the Lesnovski Monastery containing the third iconostasis of Frčkovski and the Filipovski brothers is in the village of Lesnovo near Probištip (see page 207), and Osogovski Monastery is near Kriva Palanka.

Although the four are said to have been brothers, historical data shows that Rilski lived at least a century earlier than the others, and so it is believed that he was, in fact, a teacher of the other three rather than an actual brother.

being renovated at the time of writing so contact Mergimi Travel Agency (tel: 031 411 697) for the latest information.

What to see and do

St Joakim Osogovski

The Monastery of St Joakim Osogovski probably takes number one position as the most visited monastery in Macedonia. The location was first sought out as a monastery during the middle of the 12th century, and now houses **two churches**, the older one dedicated to the Virgin Mary (St Bogorodica), and the new church of the mid-19th century is dedicated to St Joakim Osogovski himself (see box opposite).

The monastery was founded in the middle of the 12th century by the priest Teodor from Ovče Polje who decided to dedicate his life to God at this spot after the death of his wife. Located on a major thoroughfare to Constantinople (*Carigrad*, town of the Tsar, in Macedonian) the monastery was frequented and honoured by Muslims as well as Christians. In 1585 the *bey* of Kriva Palanka received permission to renovate the dilapidated buildings. The old church was first converted into a mosque and then later a church. Some of the original 12th-century walls and 14th-century frescos still exist, although most of the church is now being completely re-frescoed.

During the Austro-Ottoman War, led in Serbia and Macedonia by General Piccolomini in 1690, the monastery buildings and original church suffered extensive damage, and the Ottomans even ordered it to be destroyed as a punishment against local Macedonians who had sided with the Austrian general. Legend claims that on arrival at the monastery, the Ottomans were so overpowered by the spiritual force of the monastery that they turned back leaving the buildings undamaged. One of them, however, had taken a bone out of the tomb of St Joakim Osogovski, which proceeded to make the thief nauseous the further he took the bone from the monastery. It did not take long for the thief to realise that, for his own well-being, he needed to take the bone back to its rightful resting place, and so he returned it. The Sultan was so overwhelmed by this account when he heard it that he ordered a protective marker of stone to be delivered to the monastery, which would signify to all Ottomans, Turks and Muslims that this monastery was not to be harmed in any way. The stone still stands on the wall near the new church, to the right as you enter the exonarthex, and is usually blessed by the residing Turkish ambassador to Macedonia at least once during his term in office.

The new church is an intricate complex with 12 cupolae in the main nave, two further naves and an exonarthex on two sides of the church. The 12 cupolas represent the 12 apostles, one for each containing a fresco of the apostle, and the remainder of the main nave is brimming with well-kept frescos. Frescos of the four brothers (see box opposite) can be found, as well as of the church donors, and on the outside wall to the right of the main entrance are some interesting frescos of hell and Satan. In the base of the belfry, on the western side of the new church, is the ossuary of the senior monks and priests.

Nearby the monastery is an ancient **milk pipeline**, which used to transport milk from the surrounding mountains to the monastery dairy. The pipe still exists although it is no longer used, and Pop Dobri, the father of the monastery, requests that visitors refrain from visiting it as the pipeline requires some repair renovation to prevent further damage by careless visitors. Pop Dobri is happy to talk to visitors about the monastery although he can't always be found there as he lives in Kriva Palanka. The only monastic inhabitant is Sister Igoumina.

TOWERS WITHOUT STAIRS

Originally there were 12 towers in Kratovo, but now only six remain. The last to be damaged in 1929, the Hadži Kostova tower, was rebuilt in 1957. The remaining towers, Saat (meaning 'clock'), Simitčeva, Krsteva, Emin-beg and Zlatkovičeva towers have stood the test of time well, and it is unfortunate that they are not kept in good repair and open regularly to the public. If you ask nearby one of the towers, one of the villagers might be able to get hold of the keys to the towers and let you in.

Now they are mostly abandoned although a couple are still used for storage. If you manage to get a look inside you will see that they all have wooden stairs going up to the higher floors. It is interesting to note that the towers originally had no stairs at all, following an architectural trait also seen in similar defensive towers in the Caucasus, so that access to higher levels was only by ladder. If the town was overrun by the enemy then villagers could hide in the upper levels of the tower and drag the ladder up with them. If the enemy succeeded in blowing the floor of a lower level then the villagers could again ascend to a higher level, from which they would normally defend themselves by throwing rocks, using weapons or pouring hot oil.

At the end of August every year the monastery holds a young artists' convention. The week includes the saints' days of August 28 dedicated to St Bogorodica (the Virgin Mary) and August 29 dedicated to St Joakim, when the monastery is visited by several thousand visitors who come to pay their respects to the saints. Their generous offerings have allowed over €4 million to be invested into the church since the revival of monastic life in Macedonia in 1995.

Osogovske mountain range

Starting from the entrance to the monastery is the hiking path up to **Mount Carev** (2,084m). It is the highest point in this range completely in Macedonia, and has an excellent all-round view at the summit. An almost 20km hike from the monastery, it is not to be attempted in a single day, and even in two days only by the fit. For the less fit with 4WD, the last turning before the Bulgarian border, towards Toranica village, turns into a fair-weather dirt track which comes to within 6km of the summit and then makes its way back down the other side of the mountain via the **Sasa Zinc Mine** and on to Highway 27 at Lake Kalimansko. The same road also comes within 4km of **Mount Ruen** (2,252m) on the border with Bulgaria. The road takes you above the tree line so the views of the surrounding mountains and into Bulgaria are extensive, and it is a popular place for wild berry pickers in the summer.

If you do take this road, you may need to present identification to the mine wardens at either Toranica or Sasa where the road is gated. From Toranica gates, make sure you turn off left on to the dirt track (unsignposted) almost 3km after the gate, just before an old building on the left and a white building on the right. For those with GPS, this is at grid FM225695. Do not continue on the tarmac until it becomes dirt road as this simply takes you into a logging maze. The dirt track becomes tarmac 1km before Sasa mineworks. At the time of writing, Sasa mine is out of commission awaiting sale to a private bidder.

KRATOVO

Midway between the start of the E871 (Highway 2) at Kumanovo and Kriva Palanka is the turn-off for Kratovo and Probištip, which joins Highway 2 to Highway 27. On this road, deep in the belly of an ancient and burnt-out volcanic crater is the small village of Kratovo. In Roman times this mining town was known as Kratiskara, meaning crater, and variations of its name, Koriton and Koritos in Byzantine times, have centred around this meaning.

The River Tabačka runs deep at the bottom of the crater and four of the **stone bridges** across the river, named Radin, Johčiski, Caršiski and Krajniot, date from the early Ottoman period. Unfortunately, the first and most obscure of these bridges, the Radin, was destroyed and, although it has been repaired, it is not in its original likeness.

On either side of the river are a number of **defensive stone towers**, which were also used in Ottoman times by the local mine owners to store iron-ore (see box opposite). It is the miners of Kratovo who first rallied to Karpoš' call in 1689 (see box, page 11) when he went to fight on the side of the Austrians against the Ottomans. The ***bey*'s house**, on the lower side of town between the bottom two bridges, has been renovated in recent years but is rarely open to the public.

Where to stay and eat

Kratovo only has one hotel, the **Kratis** (25 rooms; tel: 031 481 201), which is another state-run rip-off at 900MKD per person including breakfast. Much nicer accommodation is available outside Kočani. Kratovo does not have a lot of eating establishments to offer, and your only choices are at the village square or along Partizanska Street. The **Café Amor** at the top end of Partizanska Street outside the last tower up the river has a pleasant atmosphere and good music.

What to do outside Kratovo

There is a lovely hike up the River Tabačka to **Gorni Kratovo** and beyond to the villages of **Muškovo** and **Stari Muškovo**, which give further access to the Osogovski mountain range.

To the south just above the village of Lesnovo is the **Monastery of St Gavril Lesnovski**, built in 1341 by the feudal lord Tyrant Oliver. The monastery is one of only three to contain an iconostasis by the famous wood carvers Makarije Frckovksi and the brothers Filipovski (the other two are in the monasteries of St Jovan Bigorski near Debar, and the church of St Spas in Skopje; a fourth in Kruševo was burnt down after the Ilinden uprising). The church stands on the foundations of an earlier 11th-century church, whose mosaic floor is still the floor of the present church, and contains many interesting frescos from the time it was built. The donor fresco of Tyrant Oliver holding the church is still in good condition to the left in front of the chancel, and frescos of King Dušan, his wife, and Tsar Uroš can be found on the left wall of the narthex above the baptism basin. Unfortunately, the fresco of Tsar Uroš has practically been lost. To the right on the ceiling of the narthex are frescos of the sun and the moon and 12 animals or people seen in the night sky. Despite their amazing likeness to the zodiac signs, the friar will tell you that these are not designed to depict them.

To get there, head for Zletovo and ask there for the turning for Lesnovo. The Lesnovo road winds up the mountain and at a fork in the asphalt road follow the road to the right going up to get to the monastery rather than down to the village. This road takes you past some interesting rock outcrops and the entrances to some caves, which may be worth an explore if you have a torch with you.

On the way back out to Highway 2 from Kratovo are the *kukla* or **stone dolls** near the village of Kuklica. They are difficult to get to and if the road were tarmacked and well signposted it might be worth the stop-off, but unless you have children old enough to enjoy a picnic there and not injure themselves down the steep ravines, then it probably isn't worth the visit. For those determined to take a look, make sure you have a high-clearance vehicle or be prepared for a one-hour hike. At the halfway point between Kratovo and the E871 highway (about 10km either way) are two bridges that cross the River Tabačka before they empty into the River Kriva. At the southerly end of the northern bridge (grid EM89406233) is a turn-off to the west. Turn immediately left on the dirt track and keep going past a bridge on your right (do not cross the bridge) until you get to a fork in the road and turn right. Follow this road along the river valley until you get to a stone factory where a right turn will take you across a bridge. Turn left once over the bridge and in less than 1km you will see the stone formations to your right (grid EM866619). The formations extend some way back and could be more interesting if there were some safer paths to them.

SVETI NIKOLE

This small town lies on top of a hill in the middle of the fertile Ovče Pole plain. Known as the 'sheep fields' the plain has been inhabited since Neolithic times and remains have been found in the vicinity of the town, mostly around the villages of **Amzibegovo** to the south of Sveti Nikole, and **Gorobinci** to the northwest on the road back to Skopje. Sveti Nikole takes its name after the **church** of that name built by Serbian King Milutin in 1313. The church stands prominently on top of the hill and can be seen on the approach to the town. It is enclosed within the **monastery** grounds, which are often closed, so ask in the town for the key if you would like to have a look in.

11

The Southern Wine Region

The rich Tikveš Plains running from Veles along the River Vardar to Gevgelija are renowned for their wines. Kavadarci is the wine capital where Macedonia's biggest vineyard, Tikveš Wines, named after the plains themselves, is based. The climate is mild, being only 45m above sea level at the lowest point of the River Vardar at Gevgelija border town. Macedonian wines are little known but very good, and **vineyard visits** are becoming more frequent if you want to find out more about the wines you drink with your meal in Macedonia.

The south of Macedonia was well populated by the Romans so there are lots of Roman remains, including the town of **Stobi** on the crossroads of the Axios and Diagonal Ways, and the best-preserved **Roman baths** at Bansko. There are also working **Turkish baths** at Bansko, a waterfall at **Smolari**, a tectonic lake at **Dojran**, rock climbing at the **Iron Gate** and throughout the region you'll find the usual assortment of monasteries, good hiking and pleasant swimming holes. A good town to stay at in order to explore the region further is **Strumica**.

STRUMICA

Between the Belasica and Ogražden mountain ranges is the town of Strumica. It lies in a little-visited area which is teaming with history, sites and natural beauty. The town itself is one of the oldest in Macedonia to have remained in its original location and not be moved by earthquake or ransacked by marauding invaders. The town started out in the 2nd century BC under the name Astraion, meaning 'City of Stars' and named after the Astrai tribe of the Strumica valley. The starry night sky above the valley is, of course, still visible today, although from Strumica's fashionable pedestrian area the only bright lights to be seen are those of the café bars.

If you are not driving to Strumica, there are several buses everyday from Skopje, Bitola and Gevgelija. The bus station (tel: 034 346 030) is next to the post office.

Where to stay and eat

Strumica does not have much to offer in the way of accommodation, but there are a variety of offers outside the town. The **Hotel Sirius** (38 rooms; tel: 034 345 141), named after the star, is near Kukliš on the Valandovo exit out of town (or left at the first traffic lights if you are coming from Berovo direction). Recently renovated, it is the high end of what's on offer in Strumica. As a Macedonian four-star, it is a long way from a Best Western four-star standard. Rooms are en suite, with TV, phone and air conditioning, and the hotel does

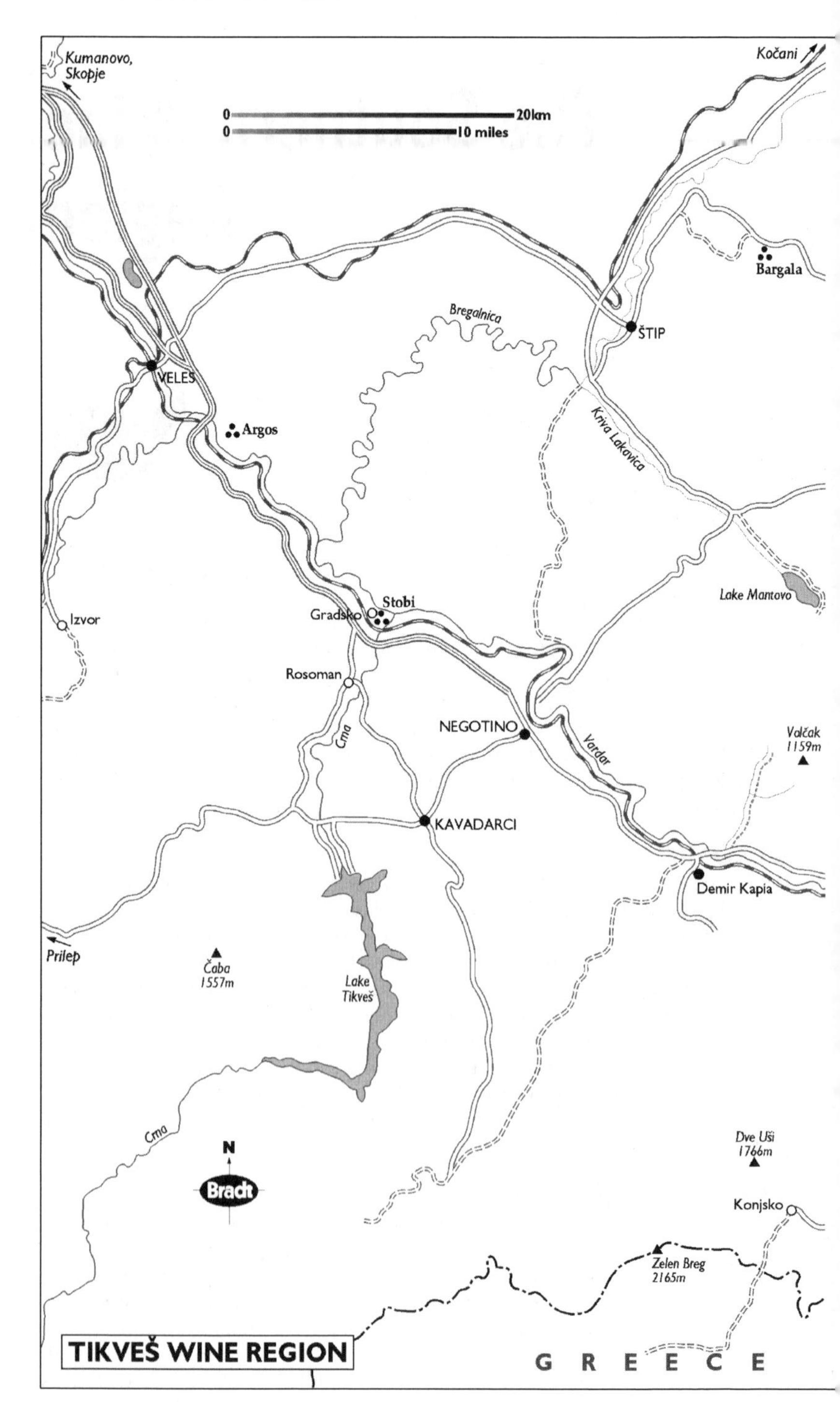
Kumanovo, Skopje
Kočani
0 20km
0 10 miles
Bargala
Bregalnica
ŠTIP
VELES
Argos
Kriva Lakavica
Lake Mantovo
Stobi
Gradsko
Izvor
Rosoman
Crna
NEGOTINO
Vardar
Volčak 1159m
KAVADARCI
Demir Kapia
Prilep
Čaba 1557m
Lake Tikveš
Crna
N
Bradt
Dve Uši 1766m
Konjsko
Zelen Breg 2165m
TIKVEŠ WINE REGION
GREECE

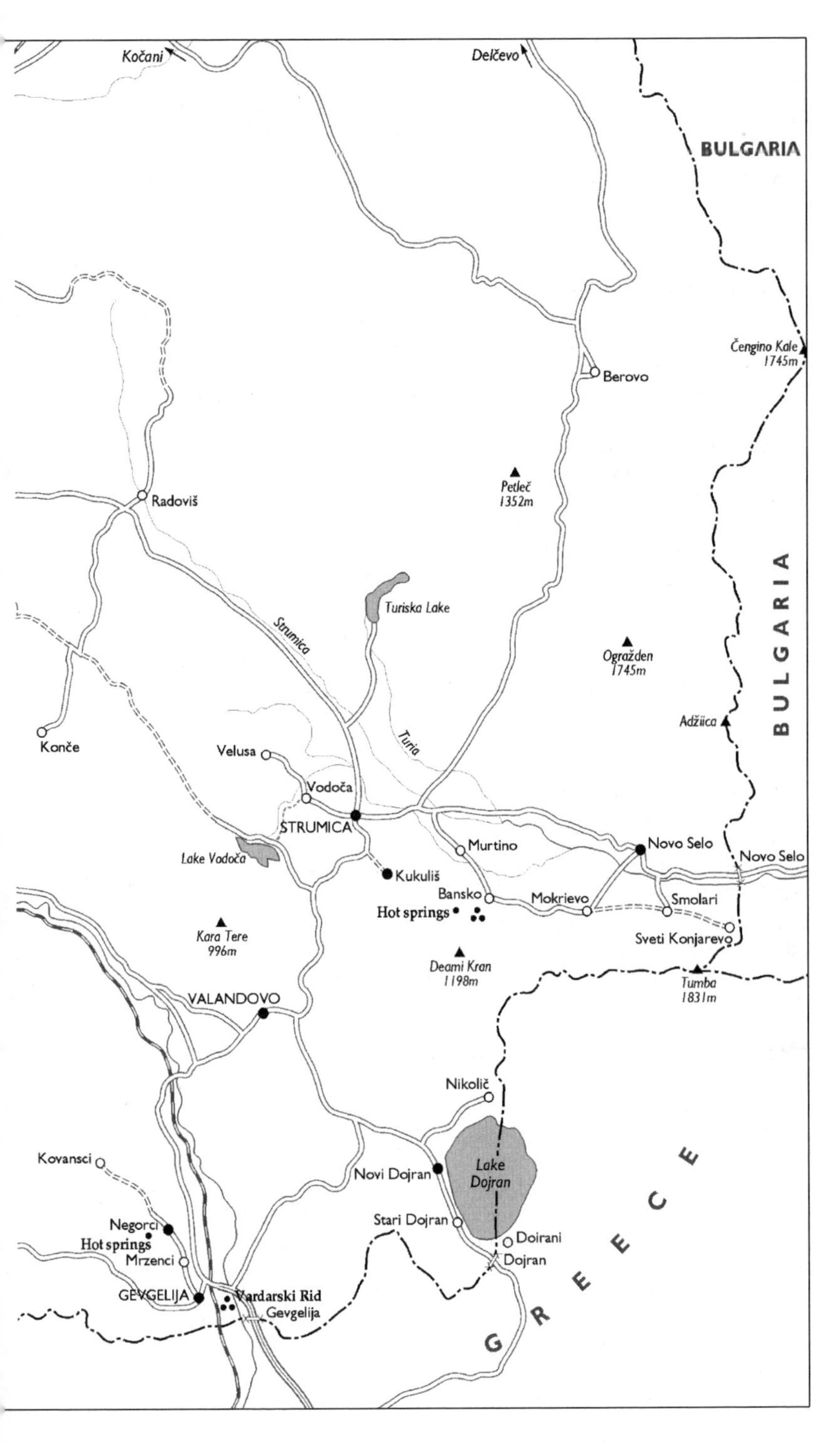

Kočani
Delčevo
BULGARIA
Berovo
Čengino Kale
1745m
Petleč
1352m
Radoviš
Turiska Lake
Strumica
Ogražden
1745m
BULGARIA
Adžiica
Turia
Konče
Velusa
Vodoča
STRUMICA
Lake Vodoča
Murtino
Novo Selo
Novo Selo
Kukuliš
Bansko
Mokrievo
Smolari
Hot springs
Sveti Konjarevo
Kara Tere
996m
Deami Kran
1198m
Tumba
1831m
VALANDOVO
Nikolič
Kovansci
Novi Dojran
Lake Dojran
Stari Dojran
Negorci
Hot springs
Mrzenci
Doirani
Dojran
GEVGELIJA
Vardarski Rid
Gevgelija
GREECE

offer tennis courts and a very clean outdoor swimming pool, as well as a restaurant. Nestled right against the Belasica foothills it is in a lovely setting, although a taxi ride away from Strumica nightlife. Prices including breakfast are 2,520MKD for a single, 3,640MKD for a twin, and 6,000MKD for an apartment with double bed.

Makedonska Kukja (16 beds) is a little further out than Hotel Sirius on the road to Valandovo. The hotel is in a well-groomed setting and rooms are clean and basic for 800MKD per person.

Even further away from Strumica, in the village of Bansko, is the Tsar **Samoil Hotel and Hot Springs** (165 beds; tel: 034 377 210). Lodging at the hotel gives free access to the indoor pool, which is naturally heated by thermal waters, but the hot springs can only be accessed with a doctor's prescription. This is a classic former-Yugoslav, dilapidated facility. Entry to the pool for non-lodgers is 50MKD. Full board single occupancy costs 1,100MKD, and double occupancy is 910MKD per person.

Far more authentic, but without heating in the winter, is the accommodation at the **Bansko Turkish Hot Springs** (10 rooms; tel: 034 377 210) next to the Tsar Samoil. The rooms and baths are arranged in a quadrangle around a 300-year-old tree in the central courtyard. Extremely basic but clean accommodation with starched white bed linen. The hot springs do not require a doctor's prescription and they are one of a few if not the only original working Turkish hot springs in Macedonia, including domed ceilings, a really hot pool and a bathkeeper of Turkish descent. There is only one pool, so the ladies' and gents' access to the pool alternates by the hour. If you go for full board here at 500MKD, you will actually eat at the Tsar Samoil. Just an overnight stay or use of a room is 300MKD per person including access to the hot springs. This price does not include breakfast and rooms are not en suite. Access only to the hot springs is 50MKD.

The main area to eat or go out for a drink in Strumica is the pedestrian street in the centre of town. Cafés and bars are found at the top end of the street on Josif Josifovski, and restaurants are found at the park end. **Café Zair**, midway towards the park, is always lively and plays good music, and the pizzerias **Arkada** and **Bonita** on the edge of the park are open long hours. The restaurant **Enigma** is set in the old workers' university which is currently undergoing renovation and offers more traditional Macedonian fare. The pedestrian street comes alive in the evenings with side-stalls selling food and knick-knacks and teenagers strutting their stuff on the way to the park.

What to see and do in and around Strumica

Despite Strumica town's claim to being one of the oldest in Macedonia, the town itself does not boast much to see. On the top of the hill overlooking the town are the **Carevi Kuli** (Tsar's Towers) of the **Strumica Fortress**, dating back to Tsar Samoil's time of the beginning of the 11th century. Between the two halves of the pedestrian area is a much larger-than-life **statue of Goce Delčev** for his part played in the Ilinden uprising in 1903 against the Ottomans. At the end of Stiv Naumov Street are the **Church of St Kiril and Metodi** and the **Museum of Strumica**. Aside from that you need to take a taxi, bus or drive to some of the area's treasures outside the town.

Out to the west of town through the Roma village of Banica is the very small settlement of **Vodoča**. This village is famous for the defeat of Tsar Samoil's army in 1014 by the army of Emperor Vasilie II (see box, page 9). The 15,000 troops left of Samoil's army after their defeat on Belasica Mountain

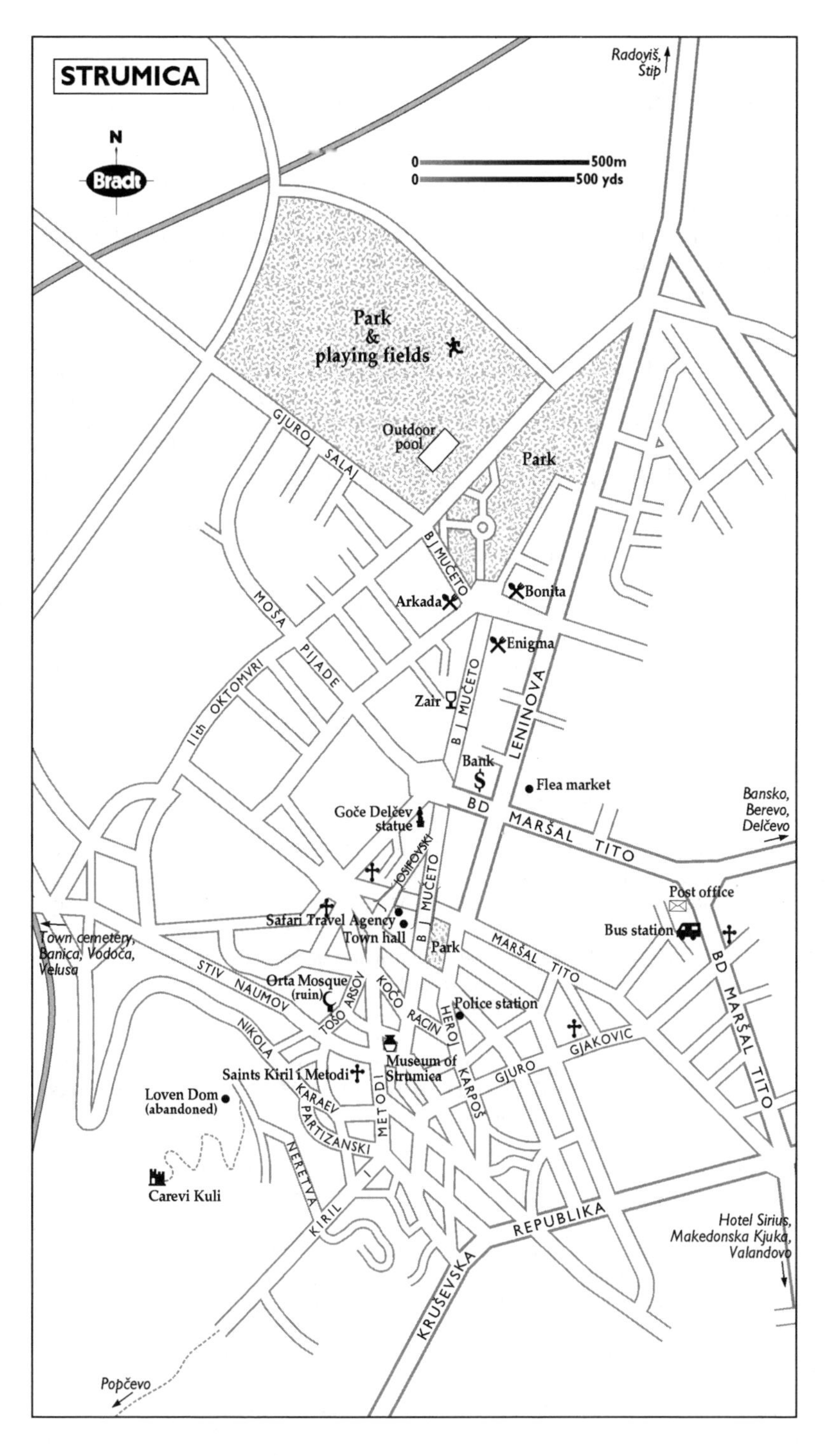
STRUMICA
N
Bradt
0 500m
0 500 yds
Radoyiš, Štip
Park & playing fields
Outdoor pool
Park
GJUROJ SALAJ
B J MUČETO
Arkada
Bonita
Enigma
MOŠA PIJADE
11th OKTOMVRI
Zair
B J MUČETO
LENINOVA
Bank
Flea market
Bansko, Berevo, Delčevo
Goče Delčev statue
BD MARŠAL TITO
JOSIFOVSKI
B J MUČETO
Post office
Safari Travel Agency
Town hall
Park
Bus station
Town cemetery, Banica, Vodoča, Velusa
MARŠAL TITO
BD MARŠAL TITO
STIV NAUMOV
Orta Mosque (ruin)
TOŠO ARSOV
KOČO RACIN
Police station
HEROJ KARPOŠ
NIKOLA KARAEV
Museum of Strumica
GJURO GJAKOVIC
Saints Kiril i Metodi
Loven Dom (abandoned)
PARTIZANSKI
METODI
NERETVA
Carevi Kuli
KIRIL I
REPUBLIKA
Hotel Sirius, Makedonska Kjuka, Valandovo
KRUŠEVSKA
Popčevo

were brought here where they had their eyes gouged out. Only one man in every 100 was left with one eye to lead the remaining blinded troops back to Tsar Samoil in Prilep. The place is now called 'gouged eyes' after the Macedonian *vadi oči*.

There is no monument here explaining this piece of Macedonian history, but a monastery was built here a few years after the defeat of Tsar Samoil's empire. The present **Monastery of St Leonthius** is a newer construction, but right next to the church dedicated to St Leonthius are the ruins of the original church, which was of an early basilica style including marble columns. The marble columns were later moved to another church, the church of the Holy Fifteen Martyrs of Tiberiopolis, in Strumica.

An earthquake in 1931 destroyed the vaults of the church but these were finally restored in 1995 with the restoration of monastery life throughout Macedonia. Lead flashing, which can be seen on the outside of the church walls, marks where the old church walls lie. After the church was completed, the monks, who had originally been living in the Monastery of Veljusa (see next) moved into the inns here. The inns used to be open to travellers wishing to stay the night, but at the time of writing these are closed again.

The reconstructed church is now a wonderfully simple, high-domed affair, showing the beautiful patterns of the original brickwork, with the remnants of a few frescos. It is very unfussy compared to a lot of Macedonian churches from later periods and is therefore very calm and peaceful. Some of the frescos, such as those of St Isavrij and St Pantelejmon, are now on display in the National Museum of Macedonia. Still remaining in the vaults of the church, however, are believed to be the relics of the wife and son of St Kiril. It is very unusual for a woman to have a burial place in a church, especially during those times. It is also just as unusual that Kiril's son should be buried with the mother rather than the father.

As for St Leonthius, to whom the church is dedicated, he was martyred in the year 320 for refusing to renounce Christianity. This imposition of the Roman emperors and their pagan gods earned him and 40 other martyrs the right to die by freezing in Lake Sebaste in eastern Turkey. By some unfathomable connection, the Day of the Newlyweds, March 22, is dedicated to the 40 martyrs and is also the festival day of the Church of St Leonthius.

A footpath along the River Vodočnica at the back of the monastery leads up to Lake Vodoča, sometimes called Lake Strumica. The 5km hike is shaded and cool and gives a good view of the valley from the lake.

Continuing along the same road from Vodoča, the next village is Veljusa. This is quite a large village which rises up into the hill and has two more churches as well as the church at the **Monastery of the Holy Mother of God – Eleusa**. The grounds of this monastery are extremely well kept and look out over the village and the plain of Strumica. The church was originally built in 1080 although the exonarthex was built later in the 14th century. It is a small church which suffered two fires in the last century, one in 1913 and the other in 1968. Soot marks can still be seen over some of the frescos, many of which have been destroyed over time, but some still remain, the most interesting of which is one of Jesus at the age of 12 in the ceiling of the eastern cupola. The floor of the church shows the original mosaic construction although some of it has been renovated over the years. Some of the original marblework of the church was taken to Bulgaria during World War I and is now kept in the Archaeological Museum of Bulgaria in Sofia. Copies in marble have been made since and are now in place in the church above the entrance to the nave.

Above Woman selling herbs at market (LM)

Left Old house in Ohrid (AT)

Above Looking down on Lake Ohrid (LM)
Below Fishing on Lake Ohrid (LM)

Since 1996, when the monks moved down to the Monastery of St Leonthius, this monastery has housed nuns.

Twelve kilometres southeast of Strumica is Bansko, the hot springs capital of Macedonia. It may not seem much when you first arrive, but the potential is there. Aside from the rehabilitation baths for the disabled, and the medicinal baths at the Tsar Samoil hotel, there are also the best-preserved original working Turkish baths and the **ruins of a Roman bathhouse**. As a museum of hot springs baths throughout the ages, from Roman to Turkish to communist, all that remains to be added is a swish first-class modern outdoor complex complete with sauna, massage rooms and a restaurant serving the latest health salads and smoothies à la Switzerland or Colorado. Whilst we wait for that to arrive, the Roman baths are being renovated and are probably the most complete refurbished Roman ruins to be found in Macedonia. A water outlet in the side of the excavation emits plenty of hot water direct from the ground, and will give you an idea of how hot the Turkish baths next door are – very soothing on a cold autumn day and well worth waiting for your other half for.

To get to Bansko there are several buses a day from Strumica bus station, or drive out towards the Bulgarian border and turn off to Murtino and Bansko. If you have 4WD it is possible to drive directly from the Hotel Sirius by turning right out of the hotel through the village of Kukliš.

The road from Bansko continues on through the pretty villages of Kolešino, which boasts of a beautiful **waterfall**, then on to Mokrievo and Mokrino, where the asphalt road ends. A dirt track continues directly to Smolari or the asphalt road can be taken from between Mokrievo and Mokrino back up to the highway at Novo Selo, after which there is a turning down to Smolari. This part of Macedonia clearly lies in an area influenced by the evangelical Methodist church. The main evangelical Methodist church is in Kolešino, but there are also lots of others around, some converted back to Orthodoxy, but they are given away by their church towers, which unlike Orthodox churches, are attached directly to the church or stand over the narthex.

In a corner of Macedonia equidistant from the borders of Bulgaria and Greece is the village of Smolari, above which is the 40m drop of the Smolari Waterfall. It is a small site but set in beautiful surroundings and the half-hour hike to get there is along well-maintained grounds. There are a couple of makeshift cafés on the way serving skara, beer and soft drinks, and many people go there with their own picnics.

To get there, there are several buses a day from Strumica bus station, or Atlantis Travel Agency can arrange a special bus if there is a big enough group. To drive there head toward the Bulgarian border and after Novo Selo turn off for Smolari. Take the first right turn at the edge of the village which is marked Vodopad (waterfall), then the next left after the village shop. This will take you to a car park. Follow the path at the side of the stream uphill for about half an hour to reach the waterfall.

The road south out of Strumica goes past the town of Valandovo and on to Lake Dojran and the border town of Gevgelija. Valandovo is renowned for its pomegranates and for a number of Roman ruins in the vicinity, such as the lost town of Idomena outside the village of Marvinci where Aleksandar III of Macedon is alleged to have his burial chambers, and the necropolis at Dedeli. Just to the west outside Valandovo is the 14th-century tower of King Marko, and to the north is the Monastery of St George in the hills above Valandovo. Valandovo is also the site of the fighting during World War I between the Irish 10th Regiment and the central powers of Germany and Turkey. A small graveyard to the fallen of the Irish 10th can be found on the outskirts of the town.

ST TRIFUN THE PROTECTOR OF VINEYARDS

St Trifun is considered in ancient Macedonian folklore to be the holy patron saint of wines and vineyards, even though his life has nothing to do with wine or grapes. It seems, therefore, that his patron day, disputedly somewhere between February 1 and 14, but usually celebrated in Macedonia on February 14, was used as the auspicious day to prune and tend the vines ready for the coming year, and after the work was done to open a bottle or two of the previous year's vintage.

Trifun was, however, known for his ability to ward off evil spirits and illnesses, hence perhaps his association by Macedonians to ward off vine blight. He was born in Kampsada, Phrygia, in present-day Syria in AD227, but like all the saints of this time period he ended his life early at the age of 21 on being tortured to death for his refusal to renounce his faith in Christ.

On his patron day, grape growers will ask for the holy water at the end of the church service in order to scatter it on their vines to bless them for a good and bounteous crop in the coming season. Later, back at the local tavern, the bar owner may declare an open house, and the person most drunk at the end of the evening is anointed the Tsar of the Drunks for the remainder of the year.

WINES FROM THE TIKVEŠ PLAINS

Wines from Macedonia are little known outside of Yugoslavia even though Macedonia is the fourth-largest supplier of bulk wine to Germany and supplies a fair portion of wine to the UK too. The wine, however, comes in as a blend with wines from other countries and is used for house wines or a supermarket's own label. The entire course of the Vardar Valley all the way down to Thessaloniki is fertile grape-growing country, and within Macedonia the Tikveš Plains between Titov Veles and Demir Kapija produce some of the best national wines. There are also vineyards further north around Skopje, and you'll find the local wines of smaller vineyards served in plastic bottles and cardboard cartons at any petrol station or local store.

Macedonian wines are unique amongst European wines for being made with very little, if any, additional sugar or sulphite preservatives. They are preserved, therefore, mostly by the grapes' own natural sugars and it is for this reason that almost all Macedonian wines are dry rather than sweet, and why you won't get such a big hangover the next day after drinking a bottle of *T'ga za Jug* (Longing for the South) or Alexandria.

A **visit to one of the famous vineyards** in September and October or around St Trifun's day in February (see box) is always well worth the time if you'd like to try out the season's newest, or the best of last year's stock. Scanagri, a Swedish-based organisation, is working with Macedonia's wine growing association, Vitis, to help Macedonia promote its wine industry. They occasionally organise tours to various vineyards, and hope to have these facilitated through travel agencies in the near future. In the meantime if you would like to get yourself on one of the tours, phone Vitis president, Aleksandar Ristovski, on 070 338 195 well in advance, and he will be able to put you on the next tour. A tour, including lunch, travel and drinks, costs in the region of €35–40.

In addition to Macedonia's biggest vineyard, Tikveš Wines, Kavadarci is also home to Čekorovi Wines and Kitvin Wines. Negotino is home to Macedonia's most prestigious wine label, Bovin Wines, and also to Fonko Wines and Povardarie. Other smaller labels include Ezimit, bottled in Bitola, and Vinea in Veles. Skovin Wines, grown and bottled near Skopje, are making an inroad into the prestigious niche of Bovin.

Near Demir Kapija is the old royal winery, Elenov, from the days of Royalist Yugoslavia. If you can get on a tour you will see all the old wooden wine barrels still in use as well as some of the old presses (no longer in use). The former queen's house is currently being renovated to become a restaurant, and eventually a hotel will also be built on the site.

TITOV VELES

The entrance to the Tikveš Plains from the north is at Veles. This unassuming town, despite its grand title using Tito's name, is barely more than an industrial transit town on the way to other places. Pollution from the lead works outside the town is said to be debilitating and local health groups are still investigating the effects on people born and raised in the heyday of the industry. Good news on the health side is that the industry is scaling down. This is bad news for the economy of the town, however.

Allegedly, the town is the site of the Paeonic fortress of Vilazora, but nothing remains to be seen of it, nor of any Roman ruins. The 14th-century **Church of St Nikola** in the old town rises imposingly over the town, and the recently refurbished **Monastery of St Dimitri** lies to the south of the town on the River Topolka, which empties into the Vardar. The old town also boasts a unique Black and White Mosque, as well as the **Clock Tower** from the Ottoman period, and it is the birthplace of the famous Macedonian revolutionary and poet Kočo Racin. Nine kilometres north of the town is Mladost reservoir, the poor man's Ohrid.

There is a very pretty **back road from Veles to Prilep** though the Babuna mountains. The mountain section is not paved, and a lot of the original cobbling from over a century ago can still be seen, as well as the original mile markers. Although it is the extension of the highway E27 coming from Štip, the road out of Veles is not signposted at all, and so can be a little hard to find. Taking the second exit into Veles from Skopje (or the third if you are approaching from the south) cross the bridge into the centre of town and take the second right off the double roundabout. Follow the road around through the north of the town, and take the next left after the sign for the hospital (*bolnica*) and the railway station (*železnička stanica*). Keep going straight until the T-junction and then turn right. This will take you through the one-way system to pop out at the end of the high street.

The road follows the railway line to Prilep until shortly before Izvor, when the road takes a sharp turn to the left over a picturesque old bridge into Izvor itself. **Izvor**, meaning 'water spring' does indeed have a large built-up spring right next to the main road. All the locals take their drinking water from here and you might want to fill up any spare water bottles too as the water is very good. After Izvor, the road rises sharply into the Babuna Mountains and at mile marker 144, just after the water fountain and the sheep pens, is the turn-off to the **monasteries of Sveti Stepanci** and **Sveti Dimitri**. Watch out for turtles crossing the road here as they are not used to cars. After this, hairpin bends snake all the way around the **Pig's Head** (*Svinska Glava*) and just before the pass at 1,134m above sea level is the dirt track turn-off to the local **mountaineering lodge**. A couple of kilometres later stop at the **Monastery of St Gjorgi** for a good view of the descent to Prilep.

KAVADARCI AND NEGOTINO

Both of these towns are singularly modern affairs with little left from ancient or Turkish times to give them much character beyond communist concrete and mid-rise flats. The town of Negotino dates back to the 3rd century BC when the town was called Antigona after its founder, the Macedonia King Antigon Gonat (277–240BC). Kavadarci was founded later in the Roman period, but most of the records of this period in its history are buried beneath **Tikveš Lake**, a manmade lake constructed in 1968 to provide irrigation and hydro-electricity to the surrounding area.

Two interesting churches in the area are **Marko's cave church** in Dradnija 4km west of the Tikveš Lake dam, and the 14th-century **Monastery of Polog** in the village of Poloski on the cliffs of Tikveš Lake. The church there, dedicated to St Gjorgi, is practically windowless, despite the number of window arches built into the walls, and the vaults of the church are claimed to hold the remains of Dragutin, the brother of the Serbian King Dušan. The monastery is accessible only by boat, or a 10km hike overland from the village of Pravednik.

STOBI

To the northwest of Negotino and just south of Gradsko, nestled into the crook of the Black River and the Vardar River, lies the ancient city of Stobi. Although many Macedonians would rate the ancient city of Heraclea (see page 153), near Bitola, higher than Stobi, in my opinion Stobi is nicer to wander around. Both cities were founded at the same time and both flourished under the Roman Empire, Heraclea becoming the capital of the region. Heraclea is a bit more of tourist trap, however, and you have to pay through the nose to take photos. Stobi on the other hand is not even signposted off the highway and in the low season it is free to get in. When it is manned at the entrance, it is 100MKD to enter. With views of the surrounding mountains and riverways, it is easy to stand on the site and imagine the hustle and bustle of the ancient city, with its numerous travelling traders plying their wares and telling their tales of far-off lands.

How to get there

It is easier to stumble across Stobi travelling south to north on highway one, than north to south, as you will see it in the hillside on your right as you approach the final turn into Gradsko. It is then just the next exit off the highway, which will take you straight to the parking lot. Travelling south take the first exit after Gradsko, 3km from the Gradsko exit, and go underneath the highway into the parking lot.

There is no public transport to the site, but you could take a bus to Gradsko or Rosoman and then a taxi for about €10, or walk from Gradsko along the river path for about 3km until you reach the ruins.

History

Stobi was first discovered in 1861, but excavation did not start until 1924, and even today only a fraction of the city has been uncovered. It is unclear when the area was first settled, but the earliest findings unearthed so far date back to the 4th century BC during the middle of the era of the ancient Kingdom of Macedonia. The town expanded under Roman rule and became the largest town in its province. The Goths destroyed the town when they invaded Macedonia in AD479, and although it was rebuilt shortly afterwards, the earthquake of 518 damaged the town further. Rebuilt again, further earthquakes took their toll on the town, and by the end of the 13th century the town was completely abandoned in favour of towns like Veles further north along the Vardar, and Negotino further south.

What to see, where to eat

The site is not very big and can easily be covered in an hour or two. Check out the 2nd-century **amphitheatre**, which was later turned into a gladiatorial ring. Some of the seats have the names of family holders engraved on them. Next to the episcopal **basilica** is a small **baptistry** with its mosaic floor almost intact. Further mosaics can be found surrounding **Theodosian's palace**. Three earthenware pithoses (vats) still stand in the large bath house, but most of the pottery, jewellery and sculptures are in the museums of Skopje and Veles. Two of the most famous pieces, a pair of bronze satyrs, are in the Belgrade city museum.

There is nowhere to eat in walking vicinity of the ruins, unless you walk back to Gradsko for basic fare. Seven kilometres from the ruins, however, is the town of **Rosoman**, where the **Kral Jo** (King Jo) restaurant offers traditional Macedonian grill, fish and salads. The restaurant is on the main street through town where all the buses stop on their way to Bitola. In the evening there is live music after 20.30 and sometimes performances of local dances.

DEMIR KAPIJA — THE IRON GATE

From Titov Veles via Stobi the southerly flow of the Vardar River takes it through the plains of the Tikveš region. The valley then narrows to a gap of barely 50m across where the surrounding mountains force the river through the Iron Gate Mountain gorge. The Turkish word for the gorge 'Demir Kapija' means 'iron gate' and is still the name used today for the small settlement at the foot of the rocks. Beyond the Iron Gate the valley sides remain steep for another 20km. This geographical formation has forced centuries upon centuries of invaders into upper Macedonia through this narrow corridor. They are effectively funnelled into a killing zone on exiting the Iron Door into the Tikveš Plain and hence the ominous name of the rock feature.

The **train ride** from the north through Demir Kapija to Gevgelija is spectacular, although the**drive** is probably more so, because of the stopping place on the road between two rock towers. This stopping place, barely big enough for half-a-dozen cars, gives the appearance of being in an open-topped cave. The towering rock faces are a favourite among **rock climbers**, and **hiking** in the surrounding hills is also popular.

A good hike directly from the stopping place between the two rock towers goes up the stream that created the rock feature and flows between them into the River Vardar. The path along the stream is easy to follow and leads up to the mountain villages of **Celevec** and **Iberlija**, but a lot of the hike requires fording the stream, so sandals such as Teva's which have a good grip in water are advisable. The early train from Skopje stops in Demir Kapija, but make sure you are back in plenty of time for the last train if Skopje is your return destination, as there is nowhere to stay in the quaint village of Demir Kapija.

A good place to eat near here, however, is **Vodenica** (tel: 043 366 111), serving good Macedonian food in a traditional setting. To get there take the first exit to Demir Kapija if you are coming from the north on the highway. Drive all the way through town and over the bridge. Turn right immediately at the end of the bridge and the restaurant is at the end of this lane.

GEVGELIJA

Gevgelija is probably Macedonia's busiest border crossing, especially since the arrival of KFOR troops in Kosovo in 1999. The train to Greece stops at the border train station (tel: 034 212 033), just outside town, and the bus station (tel: 034 212 315) on 7th Noemvri in the centre of town serves buses to the rest of Macedonia, but none to Greece. Taxis can cross the border, however.

The town has an interesting legend attached to its name but not much else to offer. Allegedly the name comes from the Turkish, *gel geri*, meaning 'come again' which was called to a *dervish* monk who had been banished by the locals. The monk had only stopped to rest overnight when he expressed his desire to stay because it was such a nice place. The locals of non-*dervish* religion took umbrage with the statement and made it very clear that neither he nor his religion were welcome to stay. As he left, the locals feared that the monk's god might take vengeance on them for banishing the monk and so they called after him, '*Gel geri, gel geri.*' No-one knows if he ever did return.

The small hill above the city, which displays a prominent communist monument to the National War of Liberation, ie: the partisan uprising, is also the site of **Vardarski Rid**, a Bronze Age settlement of some standing during the 2nd millenium BC. It was only discovered, however, as the foundations were being laid for the partisan monument. There is little to see there, but there is a nice café for coffee around the corner.

If you're driving to Thessaloniki from Skopje (or vice versa) for the weekend, a good place to stop to eat on the way is at **Restaurant Jabor** (tel: 034 212 920) in Mrzenci. Although really quite expensive by Macedonian standards, the cuisine is truly outstanding for traditional Macedonian fare. The restaurant is open throughout the day and receives a lot of Greek visitors who seem to be meeting their Macedonian cousins. Mouth-watering spit-roast lamb costs 700MKD, and a generous helping of *ordever* costs 500MKD.

To get there turn off the main highway into Gevgelija and take the second right heading north towards Negorci and Mrzenci. The restaurant stands out on the right before the small bridge 3km outside Gevegelija.

Another 1.5km along this road is the hot springs of **Negorski Banji**. These baths are well kept compared to some of the other baths in the country, as they are mostly used for medicinal purposes. Male and female baths are separate, and there are additional rooms for massage and therapies as prescribed by the resident doctor. Public entry into the hot springs alone is 50MKD. Full board at one of the three accommodation houses is 1,500MKD per person per day.

LAKE DOJRAN

Lake Dojran, once known for its beauty, is now turning into an ecological disaster zone. The lake is the third of its kind in Macedonia, after Ohrid and Prespa, having been formed from tectonic shifts in the earth's land plates four million years ago. It is the shallowest of all the lakes, being a mere 10m deep when the lake is at its fullest.

Unfortunately, recent years have seen the surrounding inhabitants drain the lake of its precious water in order to irrigate outlying crops and feed the demands of growing nations. The lake has lost a full 2m in depth, almost 30% of its water, and at some points the old shore road lies almost 1km away from the new shoreline. This has more or less killed recreation and tourism around the lake in an already depressed economic climate for Macedonia. The Macedonians blame the Greeks, as the water runs out of the lake on the Greek side. Sadly, the continued dispute between Greece and Macedonia over the official naming of

Macedonia, and Greek fears of a 'greater Macedonia' have prevented this ecological mess from being rectified, and who knows how soon is too late, if it is not already too late, to restore the biological and ecological diversity of the lake.

Some effort is being made on the Macedonian side to refill the lake, and at the Motel Istator turning towards the lake you can find the canal-way which funnels the water into the lake (and helps to prevent it being siphoned off). It is a small step, however, considering the number of outlets and inlets where water can be siphoned away from the lake.

The new shoreline is made up of a mixture of reeded banks and stretches of sharp splintered and bleached freshwater shells, making it difficult to simply sit around and lounge in the sun, never mind run around in bare feet. The shoreline, however, is still teaming with wildlife, and on a sunny spring day you can see more frogs than you can shake a stick at, water snakes eating tadpoles, a host of birds, butterflies and insects. If you are lucky, you'll also see some fish.

Getting there and away

Border crossing from Doirani

Entering Macedonia from Greece via the Greek village of Doirani is a simple affair. The small border control station is usually very quick compared to the main Gevgelija crossing in and out of Greece, and although the road to Doirani is not a highway, it has relatively light traffic, making the journey fast and easy. There is still the usual police presence on the roads around the border though.

Once through the Greek border control, there is a small Orthodox church in the border zone. Less than 50m from the Macedonian border control is the first hotel casino, **Hotel Mlaz**. The faded painted sign for 'Mlaz' on the sentry box opposite the entrance to the hotel is easy to miss, although the new signs for 'Hotel Casino' are very obvious. This hotel, like others in Stari Dojran, caters for Greeks who want to gamble with a little more freedom than is allowed in Greece (gambling is strictly regulated in Greece). The hotel was in its prime during the heyday of Yugoslavia, when there was water in the lake and those wanting a break from the overcrowded scene at Ohrid could while away a romantic weekend. The surroundings are still tranquil, and the hotel's 64 rooms are mostly empty, leaving you to wander the 1980s' décor in peace. For 2,170MKD/night for a double room en suite including breakfast, it's not too bad a place, but there will be the odd cockroach or two (usually dead) and views of the lake are only lacking water (which used to lap on to the terrace back in its heyday). No TV, no air conditioning and the mosquito screens are broken.

Stari Dojran

The old town of Dojran stretches for over 1km along the lake. From here you can access the innermost bank of the new shoreline by boat to fish for carp and trout. At the northern end of the town are the ruins of the St Iliya Church. Renovation of the church clearly stopped some time ago, and so there is still not really much to see there. The town offers a few more new hotel casinos and there are also a number of places to eat, including **Restoran Graniko** with a lovely terrace overlooking the lake, the **Pizzeria Renaissance,** and other smaller buffets and cafés.

The best place to eat in Stari Dojran, however, is **Fooktak** (tel: 034 255 320). Although this small restaurant can't boast views overlooking the drying lake, it is the oldest and most famous in the town (and well known across all Macedonia). The restaurant is over 120 years old, going back to the days of Macedonia's struggle to overthrow Ottoman rule. On the wall just inside the main entrance hang original photos of eight of the founders of VMRO (Revolutionary Organisation for an Independent Macedonia). Opened just after the new train line through (now Greek) Doirani, the restaurant is named after the sound that the train engine makes: 'fook-tak, fook-tak, fook-tak'. The menu offers the usual Macedonian fare: grilled meats, fish, salads, desserts and drinks. The food is good, and the freshly caught carp from the lake is exquisite, extremely tender with no trace of a muddy taste at all – undoubtedly, the best carp you'll find anywhere. After 20.30 at the weekends there is live musical accompaniment. A meal for two with wine will set you back 700MKD.

Novi Dojran

This area of new settlements has a long stretch of sandy beach and offers the more modern **Motel Istatov** (tel: 034 227 556), and Istatov physical training centre. Blagoj Istatov, the owner, was the Belgrade Partisani football team goalkeeper in 1973, and later became a coach in the Netherlands. More recently he was the Macedonian national coach, and even took the team to Dublin. There are football photographs in the bar and restaurant, which are a seventh heaven for any football enthusiast. There is also an outdoor pool, and the bedrooms have good views over the lake. Basic rooms go for 800MKD per person, including breakfast, and apartments for up to five people for 2,400MKD, excluding breakfast. The best place to eat here is at the **Hotel Kaldrma**, which also offers a few rooms. The hotel is owned by the Aice brothers – one is the cook and the other is the Mayor of Novi Dojran. It is at the southern end of town and even though the building is several years old, it still looks as if it's only just being finished! Excellent carp for 250MKD/person.

Humming-bird hawk-moth

Appendix 1

LANGUAGE

Macedonian language

Pronunciation and transliteration

Like most languages (English being the prime exception) Macedonian is pronounced (almost!) exactly as it is written, so once you have mastered the sounds of each letter it is fairly straightforward to pronounce. Verbs are conjugated, but gratefully, unlike Serbian, nouns are not declined. There is no indefinite article, so the word for 'one' is used instead, and the definite article is added at the end of the noun (or adjective if one precedes the noun). There is a formal and informal conjugation of 'you' singular, as in French or Old English, and in this appendix the informal conjugation follows the formal where applicable. For more information on the rules of the Macedonian language see Christina Kramer's excellent language book (full reference in Appendix 2).

Finally, a tip to sounding the correct stress on Macedonian words: with the exception of words of foreign origin, stress falls on the antepenultimate (third from last) syllable. The stress in words of less than three syllables falls on the first or only syllable. The stress in words of foreign origin tends to fall as they would in the native language.

As it is usually too difficult for short-term visitors to learn a new alphabet like Cyrillic, it is not used in this book, but the standard transliteration is. Cyrillic, transliteration and pronunciation are given in the table below.

А A as in father
Б B as in bed
В V as in very
Г G as in good
Д D as in door
Ѓ Gj as in Magyar
Е E as in bet
Ж Ž as in pleasure
З Z as in zoo
Ѕ Dz as in adds
И I as in feet
Ј J as in young
К K as in kit
Л L as in log
Љ Lj as in Anatolia, soft l pronounced at the back of the mouth
М M as in made
Н N as in not
Њ Nj as in canyon
О O as in lot
П P as in put
Р R as in mark

С	S	as in sit
Т	T	as in table
Ќ	Kj	as in cute
У	U	as in took
Ф	F	as in farm
Х	H	as in loch
Ц	C	as in cats
Ч	Č	as in church
Џ	Dž	as in edge
Ш	Š	as in shovel

Words and phrases

Courtesies

Hello	*Zdravo*
Goodbye	*Prijatno/čao*
Please	*Ve/te molam*
Thank you	*Blagodaram/fala*
Good morning	*Dobro utro*
Good afternoon	*Dobar den*
Good evening	*Dobra večer*
Good night	*Dobra nokj*
How are you?	*Kako ste/si?*
I'm fine	*Dobro/super*
Pleased to meet you	*Milo mi e što se zapoznavme*
My pleasure	*Milo mi e*
Excuse me	*Izvenete*
You're welcome/ help yourself	*Povelete*
Welcome!	*Dobredojde!*

Basics

yes/no	*da/ne*
OK	*može/važi*
maybe	*možebi*
large/small	*golemo/malo*
more/less	*povekje/pomalku*
good/bad	*dobro/lošo*
excellent/terrible	*odlično/lošo*
hot/cold	*toplo/ladno*
toilet	*toalet/WC* (pronounced ve-tse)
men/women	*maž/žena*

Basic questions

How?	*Kako?*
How do you say in Macedonian?	*Kako se vika na makadonski?*
What?	*Što?*
What is that?	*Što e toa?*
When?	*Koga?*
When does the shop open/close?	*Koga otvora/zatvora prodavnicata?*
Where?	*Kade?*
Where is there a telephone?	*Kade ima telefon?*
Who?	*Koj?*
Why?	*Zošto?*
Do you speak English?	*Zboruvate-li angliski?*
Do you understand French/German?	*Razbirate-li francuski/germanski?*
I do not understand Macedonian	*Ne razbiram makedonski*
How much does it cost?	*Kolku čini?*
What time is it?	*Kolku e saat?*

Getting around

Which way is the ...?	*Na kade e ...?*
mosque/church	*džamija/crkva*
fortress/museum	*zamok (kale)/museum*
archaeological site/hotel	*arxeologska naogjalište/xotel*
here/there	*tuka/tamu*
on the left/right	*na levo/na desno*

Where is …?	*Kade e …?*
taxi rank/train station	*taksi stanicata/železnička stanicata*
ferry/train	*brod/voz*
doctor/hospital	*doktor/bolnica*
police station/bank	*policiska stanica/banka*
restaurant/shop	*restoran/prodavnica*
town/village	*grad/selo*
house/flat	*kukja/stan*
cinema/theatre	*kino/teatar*
What is your telephone number?	*Koj e vašiot telefonski broj?*
What is your address?	*Koja e vašata adressa?*
My address in England/US is …	*Mojata adresa vo Anglija/US e …*
I want to change dollars to denar	*Sakam da smenam dolari vo denari*
How many denar will you give me for $1?	*Kolku denari kje mi dadete za eden dolar?*
When does the train arrive/leave?	*Koga stignuva/poagja vozot?*
I need a telephone	*Mi treba telefon*

Eating and drinking

What do you have to drink?	*Što imate za pienje?*
I would like to drink…	*Sakam da pijam…*
water/juice	*voda/sok*
tea/coffee	*čaj/kafe*
milkshake/milk	*frape/mljeko*
white coffee	*kafe so mleko*
wine/beer/rakija	*vino/pivo/rakija*
What do you have to eat?	*Što imate za jadenje?*
I want some bread, please	*Sakam malku leb, ve molam*
I want…	*Sakam…*
fish/meat	*riba/meso*
trout/eel	*pastrmka/jagula*
soup/salad	*supa/salata*
yellow cheese/white cheese	*kaškaval/sirenje*
vegetables/fruit	*zelenčuk/ovošje*
rice/potatoes	*oriz/kompir*
apples/oranges	*jabolko/portokal*
pears/grapes	*kruška/grozje*
figs/apricots	*smokva/kaijsija*
sugar/honey	*šeker/med*
nuts/eggs	*orevi/jajce*
I don't eat meat/fish	*Ne jadem meso/riba*

Numbers

0	*nula*	21	*dvaeset i eden*
1	*eden*	30	*trieset*
2	*dva*	40	*četirieset*
3	*tri*	50	*pedeset*
4	*četiri*	60	*šeeset*
5	*pet*	70	*sedumdeset*
6	*šest*	80	*osumdeset*
7	*sedum*	90	*devedeset*
8	*osum*	100	*sto*
9	*devet*	200	*dvesta*

10	*deset*	300	*trista*
11	*edinaeset*	400	*četiristo(tini)*
12	*dvanaest*	500	*petsto(tini)*
13	*trinaeset*	one thousand	*iljada*
14	*četirinaeset*	two thousand	*dve iljadi*
15	*petnaeset*	one million	*milion*
16	*šesnaeset*	two million	*dva milioni*
17	*sedumnaeset*	quarter	*četvrt*
18	*osumnaeset*	half	*pola/polovina*
19	*devetnaeset*	three-quarters	*tri četvrtini*
20	*dvaeset*		

Time

hour	*saat*	yesterday	*včera*
minute	*minuta*	morning	*utro*
week	*nedela*	afternoon	*popladne*
day	*den*	evening	*večer*
year	*godina*	night	*nokj*
month	*mesec*	this	*ovoj*
today	*denes*	next week	*slednata nedela*
tonight	*večerva*	now	*sega*
tomorrow	*utre*	soon	*naskoro*
Monday	*ponedelnik*	Friday	*petok*
Tuesday	*vtornik*	Saturday	*sabota*
Wednesday	*sreda*	Sunday	*nedela*
Thursday	*četvrtok*		
January	*Januari*	July	*Juli*
February	*Fevruari*	August	*Avgust*
March	*Mart*	September	*Septemvri*
April	*April*	October	*Oktomvri*
May	*Maj*	November	*Noemvri*
June	*Juni*	December	*Dekemvri*
spring	*prolet*	autumn	*esen*
summer	*leto*	winter	*zima*

Basic verbs

to be	*da se bide*		
I am	*jas sum*	we are	*nie sme*
you are	*ti si*	you are	*vie ste*
he/she/it is	*toj/taa/toa e*	they are	*tie se*
to have	*ima*		
I have	*imam*	we have	*imame*
you have	*imas*	you have	*imate*
he/she/it has	*ima*	they have	*imaat*
to want/like/love	*saka*		
I want	*sakam*	we want	*sakame*
you want	*sakaš*	you want	*sakate*
he/she/it wants	*saka*	they want	*sakaat*

Albanian language

Pronunciation

Albanian nouns are declined and they are either feminine or masculine. There is no neuter, except in certain set phrases. The indefinite and definite articles are used, the latter being added to the end of the noun, as in Macedonian. Verbs are conjugated, and there is a formal and informal conjugation of 'you' singular, as in French or Old English. Here the informal conjugation follows the formal where applicable, and 'they' is translated as in standard representation with the masculine version first, followed by the feminine version. Unlike English, Albanian spelling is completely phonetic, so once you have mastered the sounds, you shouldn't have too much trouble with pronunciation. Good luck!

A	as in father
B	as in bed
C	as in cats
Ç	as in church
D	as in door
Dh	as in the
E	as in bet
Ë	as in along, it is often not pronounced at all
F	as in farm
G	as in good
Gj	as in Magyar
H	as in hit
I	as in feet
J	as in young
K	as in kit
L	as in log
Ll	as in fall, pronounced at the back of the mouth
M	as in made
N	as in not
Nj	as in canyon
O	as in lot
P	as in put
Q	as in cute
R	as in mark
Rr	as in burrito, pronounced with a resonant roll
S	as in sit
Sh	as in shovel
T	as in table
Th	as in thin
U	as in took
V	as in very
X	as in adds
Xh	as in jam
Y	as in mural
Z	as in zoo
Zh	as in pleasure

Words and phrases

Courtesies

Hello	*Tungjatjeta*	Good evening	*Mirëmbrëma*
Goodbye	*Mirupafshim*	Good night	*Natën e mirë*

Please	*Ju lutem/të lutem*	How are you?	*Si jeni/si je*
Thank you	*Faleminderit*	I'm fine	*Jam mirë*
Good morning	*Mirëmëngjes*	Excuse me	*Më fal*
Good afternoon	*Mirëdita*		

Basics

yes/no	*po/jo*	good/bad	*mirë/keq*
OK	*mire/në regull*	hot/cold	*nxehtë/ftohtë*
maybe	*mundqë/mundet*	toilet	*nevojtore*
large/small	*madhe/vogël*	men/women	*mashkull/femër*
more/less	*më shumë/më pak*		

Basic questions

How?	*Si?*
How do you say in Albanian?	*Si thuhet në shqip?*
What?	*Çfarë?*
What is that?	*Çfarë është ajo?*
When?	*Kur?*
When does the shop open/close?	*Kur mbyullet /shitorja?*
Where?	*Ku?*
Where is a public telephone?	*Ku është telefoni publik?*
Who?	*Kush?*
Why?	*Pse?*
Do you speak English?	*A flisni anglisht?*
Do you understand French/German?	*A kuptoni frënglisht/gjermanisht?*
I do not understand Albanian.	*Unë nuk kuptoj shqip*
How much does it cost?	*Sa kushton?*
What time is it?	*Sa është ora?*

Getting around

Which way is the …?	*Nga është rruga për në …?*
mosque/church	*xhami/kishë*
castle/museum	*kala/museum*
archaeological site/hotel	*vend arkeologijike/hotel*
here/there	*këtu/atje*
on the left/right	*në të majtë/djathtë*
Where is …?	*Ku është …?*
taxi rank	*vendqëndrimi i taksive*
bus station	*stacioni i autobusave*
ferry/train	*target/tren*
doctor/hospital	*doktori/spitali*
police station/bank	*stacioni policior/banka*
restaurant/shop	*restorant/dyqan*
town/village	*qytet/fshat*
house/flat	*shtëpi/apartament*
cinema/theatre	*kinema/teatër*
What is your telephone number?	*Cili është numri i telefonit?*
What is your address?	*Cila është adressa juaj/tuaj?*
My address in England is …	*Adresa ime në Angli është …*
I want to change dollars to lek (the currency in Albania)	*Dua të këmbej dollarë me lek*
How many leks will you give me for $1?	*Me sa lek do më japish për një dollar?*

When does the train arrive/leave?	*Kur arin/niset treni?*
I need to make a telephone call	*Dua të marr në telefon*

Eating and drinking

What do you have to drink?	*Çfarë ka për të pirë?*
I would like to drink	*Do të doja të pi …*
water/juice	*ujë/lëng*
tea/coffee	*çaj/kafe*
hot chocolate/milk	*kakao/qumësht*
white coffee	*kafe me qumësht*
wine/beer/rakija	*verë/birrë/raki*
What do you have to eat?	*Çfarë ka për të ngrënë?*
I want some bread, please	*Dua pak bukë, ju lutem*
I want	*Dua*
fish/meat	*peshk/mish*
(Ohrid) trout/eel	*korab/ngjalë*
soup/salad	*supë/sallatë*
cheese	*djathë*
vegetables/fruit	*zarzavate/fruta*
rice/potatoes	*oriz/patate*
apples/oranges	*mollë/portokaj*
pears/grapes	*dardha/rrush*
figs/apricots	*fiq/kajsi*
sugar/honey	*sheqer/mjaltë*
hazelnuts/walnuts/eggs	*laithi/arra/vezë*
I don't eat meat/fish	*Unë nuk ha mish/peshk*

Numbers

0	*zero*
1	*një*
2	*dy*
3	*tre*
4	*katër*
5	*pesë*
6	*gjashtë*
7	*shtatë*
16	*gjashtëmbëdhjetë*
17	*shtatëmbëdhjetë*
18	*tetëmbëdhjetë*
19	*nëntëmbëdhjetë*
20	*njëzet*
21	*njëzet e një*
30	*tridhjet*
40	*dyzet*
50	*pesëdhjet*
60	*gjashtëdhjet*
70	*shtatëdhjet*
80	*tetëdhjet*
90	*nëntëdhjet*
8	*tetë*
9	*nëntë*
10	*dhjetë*
11	*njëmbëdhjetë*
12	*dymbëdhjetë*
13	*trembëdhjetë*
14	*katërmbëdhjetë*
15	*pesëmbëdhjetë*
100	*njëgind*
200	*dygind*
300	*tregind*
400	*katërgind*
500	*pesëgind*
one thousand	*një mijë*
two thousand	*dy mijë*
one million	*një miljon*
two million	*dy miljonë*
quarter	*çerek*
half	*gjysmë*
three quarters	*tre çerekë*

Time

hour	*orë*	yesterday	*dje*
minute	*minute*	morning	*mëngjes*
week	*javë*	afternoon	*pas dite*
day	*ditë*	evening	*mbrëmje*
year	*vit*	night	*natë*
month	*muaj*	this week	*këtë javë*
today	*sot*	next week	*javën e ardhshme*
tonight	*sonte*	now	*tani*
tomorrow	*nesër*	soon	*së shpejti*
Monday	*e nënë*	Friday	*e premte*
Tuesday	*e martë*	Saturday	*e shtunë*
Wednesday	*e mërkurë*	Sunday	*e dielë*
Thursday	*e ejte*		
January	*Janar*	July	*Korrik*
February	*Shkurt*	August	*Gusht*
March	*Mars*	September	*Shtator*
April	*Prill*	October	*Tetor*
May	*Maj*	November	*Nëntor*
June	*Qershor*	December	*Dhjetor*
spring	*pranverë*	autumn	*vjeshtë*
summer	*verë*	winter	*dimër*

Basic verbs

to be	*të jesh*		
I am	*unë jam*	we are	*ne jemi*
you are	*ti je*	you are	*ju jeni*
he/she/it is	*ai/ajo është*	they are	*ata/ato janë*
to have	*të kesh*		
I have	*unë kam*	we have	*ne kemi*
you have	*ti ke*	you have	*ju keni*
he/she/it has	*ai/ajo ka*	they have	*ato/ata kanë*
to want	*të duash*		
I want	*unë dua*	we want	*ne duam*
you want	*ti do*	you want	*ju doni*
he/she/it wants	*ai/ajo do*	they want	*ato/ata duan*

Appendix 2

GLOSSARY OF ARCHITECTURAL TERMS

acropolis	a fortified hill
amam	Turkish baths, usually using water from a natural hot springs
amphitheatre	a Roman theatre, circular or semi-circular in shape with tiered seats, used for animal or gladiatorial fights
an	an inn for travellers, usually four-sided around a well in an open courtyard, where travellers would sleep upstairs and animals and produce would be stored downstairs
apse	a semi-circular recess in a wall
atrium	the inner courtyard of a Roman villa
basilica	a roofed Roman public hall which by the 5th century BC had become a place of early Christian worship or formalised church
cardac	a large niche in the wall on the second floor of a Turkish house
chancel	the altar end of a church. In the Orthodox church this area is usually prohibited to women
čardak	first-floor balcony
cupola	domed roof
dolap	wardrobe or drawers for clothes
exonarthex	an open hall or lean-to built on to the side of a church
forum	a Roman marketplace or public square
fresco	a wall painting
icon	portrait or likeness of a saint, often inlaid with silver and gold, and having holy and healing powers
iconostasis	the screen dividing the chancel from the nave of a church
konak	formerly describing a large Turkish house, now used for the inns of a monastery
madrese	a school teaching the Koran
methoses	land or estate owned by the church
mihrab	the niche in the eastern wall of a Mosque indicating the direction of Mecca
mimbar	the pulpit of a mosque, from where the sermon is preached
minaret	a thin circular or many-sided tower attached to an outside wall of a mosque
minder	cushion
minderlik	narrow fitted wooden benches with fitted cushions built into a room
mosaic	pictures usually depicting flora and fauna, people or buildings, made of small coloured tiles, usually laid as a flooring, but occasionally on a wall or ceiling
musandra	a built-in wardrobe for linen and bedding
narthex	the front lobby, porch or entrance hall of a church
nave	the main room of worship in a church

necropolis	a Roman graveyard
pithos	a large clay jar or jug used for storing foodstuffs
plinth	a square block of stone or marble at the bottom of a column
portico	a row of columns holding up the exonarthex roof of a church or mosque
sergen	a glass cupboard or shop window
teke	the *Bekteši* equivalent of a monastery
turbe	a tomb usually found outside a mosque but within its grounds
zograph	title of a skilled fresco painter

Appendix 3

FURTHER INFORMATION

Books

There are a whole host of books written on Macedonia by Macedonians, some of which have been translated into English but are generally only available in Macedonia. These are listed separately below the more internationally available books (which can be ordered through most bookshops or amazon.com, or can be borrowed from a good university library). All the Macedonian books listed are available from Ikona, Tabernakul, Kultura or Matica bookshops in Skopje.

History/politics

Brown, Keith *The Past in Question: Modern Macedonia and the Uncertainties of Nation* Princeton University Press, 2003. Looks at Macedonia's work on historiography of the Krusevo Republic of 1903 and how this has been an effort to create an identity for a nation uncertain of itself. Engaging reading in parts.

Celebi, Evlija *Book of Travels, The Seyahataname, Volumes 1–9* Brill Academic Publishers, 1999. This is the best and often only source of what went on during the 17th century in the Ottoman Empire. Massively informative, if sometimes a bit dense.

Chiclet, Christophe and Lory, Bernard (eds) *La République de Macédoine* Editions L'Harmattan, Paris, 1998. This is a useful update (in French) on a lot of Hugh Poulton's book (see below).

Clark, Victoria *Why Angels Fall, A Journey through Orthodox Europe from Byzantium to Kosovo* Picador, London, 2001. The 44 pages covering Macedonia also include Aegean Macedonia. They give an insight into the relationship between these two sides of geographical Macedonia and the role that the Church still plays.

Daskalis, C *The Hellenism of the ancient Macedonians* Thessaloniki, 1981. This book presents a mainly Greek view of the history of Macedonia.

Glenny, Misha *The Fall of Yugoslavia* Penguin Books (3rd edition), London, 1996; and *The Balkans: Nationalism, War and the Great Powers, 1804–1999* Penguin, USA, 2001. Both books by this journalist are an excellent read, although depending on where you are in your knowledge of the Balkans, the books can either be too broad or too detailed! With the advantage of hindsight, the latter book has a weak ending.

Hammond, N G A *History of Macedonia*, Cambridge, 1979–88. For the time covered, ancient up until the early 20th century, this is the standard reference in three volumes.

Maclean, Fitzroy *Eastern Approaches* Penguin Books, London, 1991. An excellent account of Fitzroy's missions through the Balkans during World War I.

Pettifer, James (ed) *The New Macedonian Question* Palgrave, Basingstoke, 2001. This is a collection of essays and articles covering a wide variety of topics concerning Macedonia. Extremely informative.

Pouqueville, F C H L edited by James Pettifer, 1998 *Travels in Epirus, Albania, Macedonia, and Thessaly*, Loizou Publications, 1820. Early 18th-century travels through Ottoman-held territories with only a few pages on Vardar Macedonia.

Poulton, Hugh *Who are the Macedonians?* Indiana University Press, Indiana, 1995. A somewhat dry book that goes into great depth regarding the origins of the peoples who now occupy the present-day Republic of Macedonia and what that may mean in terms of their identity.

Silber, Laura et al *The Death of Yugoslavia* (revised edition) Penguin Books, London, 1996. An indepth account of the ins and outs and minutiae that led up to the death of Yugoslavia. The BBC TV series is much easier to watch.

Sokalski, Henryk J *An Ounce of Prevention: Macedonia and the UN Experience in Preventive Diplomacy*, United States Institute of Peace, 2003. Analysis by the head of UNPROFOR/UNPREDEP of the UN's first military mission in preventative diplomacy. Could the conflict of 2001 have been avoided if UNPROFOR was not pulled out of the country?

Thucydides *History of the Peloponnesian War*, Penguin Books, London, 1972. This is *the* account of the wars over the Greek city states and islands, a foundation work in political science, and describes the beginning of the end of the Greek Empire. Paeonia and the royal house of Macedon are referred to in Book Two.

West, Rebecca *Black Lamb and Grey Falcon* Canongate Books, Edinburgh, 1993. Lots of 'Balkan experts' in the international community rave about this book. On the one hand it is one of the few accounts available of the Balkans in the early 20th century; on the other hand it is the account of a privileged upper-class lady with undisguised ethnocentric tendencies.

Macedonian authors

Kumanovski, Risto *Ohrid and its Treasures* Mikena Publishing, Bitola, 2002. Gives a good introduction to some of Ohrid's best sites, including 25 of its churches and monasteries.

Pavlovski, Jovan and Mishel *Macedonia Yesterday and Today* (3rd edition) Mi-an Publishing, Skopje, 2001. A very readable account of Macedonia's history up until the first session of the Anti-fascist Assembly of the National Liberation of Macedonia (ASNOM) in October 1943.

Šeldarov, Nikola and Lilčikj, Viktor *Kralevite na antička Makedonija i nivnite moneti vo Republika Makedonija* (The Kings of Ancient Macedonia and their Coinage) National and University Library of Kliment Ohridski, Skopje, 1994. The invaluable reference book on the ancient kingdom of the Macedons including maps of the kingdom, its tribes and towns, as well as drawings of many of their minted coins. Macedonian only.

Stojčev, Vanče *Military History of Macedonia*, Military Academy General Mihailo Apostolski, Skopje, 2004. Just what it says it is, covering the period from 7BC through World War II. A beautiful compendium of maps accompanies the main 777-page volume. Hard copy.

Natural history

Mitchell-Jones, A J *et al The Atlas of European Mammals* Academic Press 1999. A weighty tome with lots packed in.

Polunin, Oleg *Flowers of Greece and the Balkans, a Field Guide* Oxford University Press, Oxford, 1987. Invaluable.

Hoffman, Helga and Marktanner, Thomas *Butterflies and Moths of Britain and Europe* Harper Collins. London, 1995. Small with a plastic cover, very handy for expeditions.

Svensson, Lars *Collins Bird Guide* (new edition) Harper Collins, London, 2001.

Karadelev, Mitko *Fungi Makadonci, Gabite na Makedonija* PGUP Sofija Bogdanci, Skopje, 2001. Available only in Macedonian, this is an excellent book with page by page descriptions and colour photos of all the mushrooms to be found in Macedonia.

Macedonian literature

Cho, Carol *A Hitchhiker's Guide to Macedonia … and My Soul* Forum Publishing, 2002. Written by an Amer-asian woman who spent three years living in the Macedonian community over the period of the most recent conflict. Although the book mentions little of the conflict itself, it offers excellent insights into the trials and tribulations of a young woman coming to terms with her own self and with Macedonia. Written as a refreshingly honest diary and reflection.

Pavlovski, Bozin *The Red Hypocrite* AEA Publishers Pty Ltd (Australia), 2001. One of the most famous modern authors to emerge from Macedonia, who now lives in Australia. Other books by Pavlovski available in English include: *Duva and the Flea; Eagle Coat of Arms; Egyptian Dreamer; Home is Where the Heart is; Journey with my Beloved; Miladin from China; Neighbours of the Owl; Return to Fairy Tales.*

Miscellaneous

Kramer, Christina E *Macedonian, a Course for Beginning and Intermediate Students* The University of Winsconsin Press, Madison, 1999. An extremely well-presented and comprehensive language learning book with exercises. Explanations are in English and a separate CD-Rom can be purchased to accompany the book in order to listen to native spoken Macedonian.

Kusevska, Maria and Mitovska, Liljana *Do you speak Macedonian?* MEDIS-informatics, Skopje, 1995. This course book, accompanied by a work book and cassette tape, is written entirely in Macedonian, so it is impossible to use as a beginner without the cassette tape, and you'd better have your Cyrillic in pretty good order before you read page 1! Vocubulary at the back is listed with English translations.

Murgoski, Zoze *Dictionary, English-Macedonian, Macedonian-English* National and University Library of Kliment Ohridski, Skopje, 1995. A handy little paperback dictionary for carrying in your back pocket or bag. The definitive *English–Macedonian Dictionary, The Unabridged Edition* also by Murgoski, is all you will ever need for finding those awkward words like 'sovereignty' and 'fennel'. Unfortunately, Murgoski has not yet brought out čthe Macedonian–English version.

Web resources

There is probably more information on Macedonia online than there is in print. Unfortunately, many of the sites are hosted free with advertising, and so they stay up forever even though they might not have been updated for a few years. Check when the site was last updated before acting upon any of the information. If the phone numbers given on the site are out of date then convert it with the phone reference on page 24.

General

news.bbc.co.uk/2/hi/europe/country_profiles/1067125.stm For a good overview of the recent history of Macedonia.

www.macedonia.co.uk The Macedonian Cultural and Information Centre for lots of useful info to help you get to know the country before you go.

www.gomacedonia.com.mk An excellent site with up-to-date, accurate information on places worth visiting in Macedonia.

www.f1.net.au/users/igortoni The site of Cyber Macedonia – extremely good on towns, the history of famous Macedonians and all sorts of other facts.

www.popovashapka.com/macedoniainfo/cities Useful for information on Macedonian towns and history.

faq.macedonia.org Another very informative site on all aspects of Macedonian life.

www.mymacedonia.net Macedonian history from a nationstate perspective, including articles from leading Macedonian historians Risto Stefov and Alexander Donski.

www.macedon.org/anmacs/frame.htm An extensive site debunking the Greek argument that Macedonians are Greek.
www.culture.org.mk A good site on places of cultural interest in Macedonia.
www.ohrid.com.mk The official site for Ohrid.
www.manaki.com.mk Official site dedicated to the Manaki brothers, pioneers of film and photography in Macedonia.
www.mazedonien.org A good site on Macedonia in German, French and English.
www.kniga.com.mk Where you can find most Macedonian books, maps and software. Only available in Macedonian at time of writing.
www.vardar.co.uk/index.htm And after you've fallen in love with Macedonia and returned back home, this is where you can buy all your favourite Macedonian things.

Travel and accommodation

www.airports.com.mk Flight information for Skopje and Ohrid.
www.magiclakes.com/indexEn.asp A useful site for private accommodation in Macedonia, Albania and Greece. Not all the options work, but keep persevering and it will come up with some telephone numbers.
www.lakes-travel.com Another good site for private accommodation and hotels.
www.savana.com.mk/index.htm A popular travel agent website.
www.unet.com.mk/oldmacedonianmaps For all you map freaks.
www.exploringmacedonia.com The official tourist site for Macedonia.

Sports clubs and associations

www.mmsf.com.mk Homepage of the Macedonian Mountaineering and Speleology Association, sadly only available in Macedonian.
www.korab.org.mk/some_english/some_english.html Korab Mountaineering Club homepage in English.
www.ohridonline.com.mk/bigblue Homepage of Ohrid's local hang-gliding and paragliding club, with contact details of other clubs in Skopje, Prilep and Bitola.
scsofka.tripod.com A very new site for Sport Club Sofka in Skopje who organise regular road-cycling competitions.
www.yoga.org.mk/index_e.htm Macedonian yoga association.
www.amfora.com.mk Diving centre in Ohrid.

Government, media, communications, etc

www.culture.in.mk A very good site by the Ministry of Culture giving all the latest news on events and shows.
www.mt.net.mk/e English homepage of Makedonski Telekomunikacija with all the latest news in Macedonia and useful links to other sites.
directory.macedonia.org/organizations An excellent site run by the Soros Open Society Institute listing links to all the major organisations, international and non-governmental, who operate in Macedonia, plus some other cool sites. Links also to many Macedonian diasporas, societies, events and loads of other useful pages.
www.yellowpages.com.mk Macedonia's online business phone directory, with an optional English interface, although you still need to be able to read the answers in Cyrillic. Go to the 'help' page to see how to input Cyrillic names using a non-Cyrillic keyboard. Useful links to other Yellow Pages around the world.
988.mt.com.mk Macedonia's online phone directory for private addresses. The English interface works with the same quirks as the site above.
www.president.gov.mk To see what the president is up to.
www.vlada.mk/english/index-en.htm For the latest from the government.
www.sobranie.mk Website of the Macedonian parliament.

KEY TO STANDARD SYMBOLS

Bradt

International boundary
District boundary
National park boundary
Airport (international)
Airport (other)
Airstrip
Helicopter service
Railway
Footpath
Car ferry
Passenger ferry
Petrol station or garage
Car park
Bus station etc
One way arrow
Underground station
Hotel, inn etc
Campsite
Hut
Wine bar
Restaurant, café etc
Post office
Telephone
Internet café
Hospital, clinic etc
Museum
Zoo
Tourist information
Bank
Statue or monument
Archaeological or historic site

Historic building
Castle/fortress
Church or cathedral
Buddhist temple
Buddhist monastery
Hindu temple
Mosque
Golf course
Stadium
Summit
Boundary beacon
Outpost
Border post
Rock shelter
Cable car, funicular
Mountain pass
Waterhole
Scenic viewpoint
Botanical site
Specific woodland feature
Lighthouse
Marsh
Mangrove
Bird nesting site
Turtle nesting site
Coral reef
Beach
Scuba diving
Fishing sites

Other map symbols are sometimes shown in separate key boxes with individual explanations for their meanings.

Bradt Travel Guides

www.bradtguides.com

Africa

Africa Overland	£15.99
Benin	£14.99
Botswana: Okavango, Chobe, Northern Kalahari	£14.95
Cape Verde Islands	£13.99
Canary Islands	£13.95
Burkina Faso	£14.99
Cameroon	£13.95
Eritrea	£12.95
Ethiopia	£15.99
Gabon, São Tome, Principe	£13.95
Gambia, The	£12.95
Georgia	£13.95
Ghana	£13.95
Kenya	£14.95
Madagascar	£14.95
Malawi	£12.95
Mali	£13.95
Mauritius, Rodrigues & Réunion	£12.95
Mozambique	£12.95
Namibia	£14.95
Niger	£14.99
Nigeria	£15.99
Rwanda	£13.95
Seychelles	£14.99
Sudan	£13.95
Tanzania, Northern	£13.99
Tanzania	£14.95
Uganda	£13.95
Zambia	£15.95
Zanzibar	£12.95

Britain and Europe

Armenia, Nagorno Karabagh	£13.95
Azores	£12.95
Cork	£6.95
Eccentric Britain	£13.99
Eccentric Edinburgh	£5.95
Eccentric France	£12.95
Eccentric London	£12.95
Eccentric Oxford	£5.95
Faroe Islands	£13.95
Lille	£6.99
Paris, Lille & Brussels	£11.95
River Thames, In the Footsteps of the Famous	£10.95
Switzerland: Rail, Road, Lake	£13.99
Albania	£13.99
Baltic Capitals: Tallinn, Riga, Vilnius, Kaliningrad	£12.99
Belgrade	£6.99
Bosnia & Herzegovina	£13.95
Bratislava	£6.99
Budapest	£7.95
Croatia	£12.95
Cyprus see North Cyprus	
Czech Republic	£13.99
Dubrovnik	£6.95
Estonia	£12.95
Hungary	£14.99
Kiev	£7.95
Latvia	£13.99
Lithuania	£13.99
Ljubljana	£6.99
Macedonia	£13.95
Montenegro	£13.99
North Cyprus	£12.95
Serbia	£13.99
Slovenia	£12.99
Spitsbergen	£14.99
Riga	£6.95
Tallinn	£6.95
Ukraine	£13.95
Vilnius	£12.95

Middle East, Asia and Australasia

Great Wall of China	£13.99
Iran	£14.99
Iraq	£14.95
Kabul	£9.95
Maldives	£13.99
Mongolia	£14.95
North Korea	£13.95
Palestine, Jerusalem	£12.95
Sri Lanka	£13.99
Tasmania	£12.95
Tibet	£12.95
Turkmenistan	£14.99

The Americas and the Caribbean

Amazon, The	£14.95
Cayman Islands	£12.95
Costa Rica	£13.99
Chile	£16.95
Chile & Argentina: Trekking	£12.95
Eccentric America	£13.95
Eccentric California	£13.99
Ecuador: Climbing & Hiking	£13.95
Falkland Islands	£13.95
Peru & Bolivia: Backpacking and Trekking	£12.95
Panama	£13.95
St Helena, Ascension, Tristan da Cunha	£14.95
USA by Rail	£13.99
Venezuela	£14.95

Wildlife

Antarctica: Guide to the Wildlife	£14.95
Arctic: Guide to the Wildlife	£14.95
British Isles: Wildlife of Coastal Waters	£14.95
Galápagos Wildlife	£15.99
Madagascar Wildlife	£14.95
South African Wildlife	£18.95

Health

Your Child Abroad	£10.95

CLAIM YOUR HALF-PRICE BRADT GUIDE!

Order Form

To order your half-price copy of a Bradt guide, and to enter our prize draw to win £100 (see overleaf), please fill in the order form below, complete the questionnaire overleaf, and send it to Bradt Travel Guides by post, fax or email. Post and packing is free to UK addresses.

Please send me one copy of the following guide at half the UK retail price

Title	*Retail price*	*Half price*

Please send the following additional guides at full UK retail price

No	*Title*	*Retail price*	*Total*
...	....	....	....
...	....	....	....
...	....	....	....

Sub total ....

Post & packing outside UK ....

(£2 per book Europe; £3 per book rest of world)

Total ....

Name ....

Address..

Tel .... Email ....

☐ I enclose a cheque for £ .... made payable to Bradt Travel Guides Ltd

☐ I would like to pay by VISA or MasterCard

Number .... Expiry date ....

☐ Please add my name to your catalogue mailing list.

Send your order on this form, with the completed questionnaire, to:

Bradt Travel Guides/MAC
23 High Street, Chalfont St Peter, Bucks SL9 9QE
Tel: +44 1753 893444 Fax: +44 1753 892333
Email: info@bradtguides.com
www.bradtguides.com

WIN £100 CASH!

READER QUESTIONNAIRE

Win a cash prize of £100 for the first completed questionnaire drawn twice yearly.

All respondents may order a Bradt guide at half the UK retail price – please complete the order form overleaf.

(Entries may be posted or faxed to us, or scanned and emailed.)

We are interested in getting feedback from our readers to help us plan future Bradt guides. Please complete this quick questionnaire and return it to us to enter into our draw.

Have you used any other Bradt guides? If so, which titles?..................

....

What other publishers' travel guides do you use regularly? ....

....

Where did you buy this guidebook? ....

What was the main purpose of your trip to Macedonia (or for what other reason did you read our guide)? eg: holiday/business/charity etc. ....

....

What other destinations would you like to see covered by a Bradt guide?

....

Would you like to receive our catalogue/newsletters?

YES / NO (If yes, please complete details on reverse)

If yes – by post or email? ....

Age (circle relevant category) 16–25 26–45 46–60 60+

Male/Female (delete as appropriate)

Home country ....

Please send us any comments about our guide to Macedonia or other Bradt Travel Guides. ....

....

....

....

Bradt Travel Guides

23 High Street, Chalfont St Peter, Bucks SL9 9QE, UK

Telephone: +44 1753 893444 Fax: +44 1753 892333

Email: info@bradtguides.com

www.bradtguides.com

Index

Page numbers in bold refer to major entries; those in italics indicate maps